MW01030910

PATHS MADE
BY WALKING

PATHS MADE BY WALKING

The Work of Howzevi Women in Iran

—◠◠◠—

AMINA TAWASIL

INDIANA UNIVERSITY PRESS

This book is a publication of

Indiana University Press
Office of Scholarly Publishing
Herman B Wells Library 350
1320 East 10th Street
Bloomington, Indiana 47405 USA

iupress.org

© 2024 by Amina Tawasil

All rights reserved
No part of this book may be reproduced or utilized in any form or by any means, electronic or mechanical, including photocopying and recording, or by any information storage and retrieval system, without permission in writing from the publisher.

First printing 2024

Cataloging information is available from the Library of Congress.
978-0-253-07085-2 (hdbk)
978-0-253-07086-9 (pbk)
978-0-253-07087-6 (web PDF)

For my children

CONTENTS

LIST OF ILLUSTRATIONS

PREFACE

QUITE OFTEN I AM ASKED why I chose to do this study. I usually provide a template response highlighting that women's Islamic education is varied depending on local histories and contexts. In part, this answer stems from my need to fit into the model of academia, to curate a professional presentation of self. Doing so allows me to dodge how my research question has been inextricably tied to my subjectivity in its fullest sense. But subjectivity, as it stands in the academy, is too often a routinized display of subject merely internalizing and then reproducing ideology. It has become something that does not take into account the complicated histories that lead us into certain trajectories of learning—of scholarship. My own experiences as a Muslim in a world that continues to depict the Muslim person as a dangerous object shape my research interest in Iranian women's Islamic education and the 1979 revolution. Yet there are unwritten, invisible standards about complex positionalities in academia and how these shape research questions. My concern is not knowing how much someone like me is allowed to write about my subjectivity in a way that is palatable to academics. And so, rather than curating my work just for academics, I am writing for people, scholars and practitioners alike, who are interested in these complexities.

I am a Muslim Tausug from the Sulu Archipelago. The Tausug, a word that means *people of the ocean currents*, established an Islamic sultanate and launched piratical raids against Spanish colonial settlements for five hundred years, well up until the United States' creation of the Philippine Commonwealth in 1935. For generations, Filipinos read from history books that described us—the Moros, Muslims from the Southern Philippines—as savages with tails like monkeys. My father was from a generation of children who were schooled by the Roman Catholic oblates of Notre Dame into "civilization," in essence to become colonial agents of change. They were beaten and humiliated for speaking Tausug, among other practices. In 1972, civil war broke out between the Muslim South and the Philippine government, commonly referred to as the Catholic North. I grew up on the violence of that war's death and military raids until we migrated to California in 1979.

We eventually became part of a California Muslim community whose members came from all over the world. There I learned about the different stories of colonialism. The stories that were shared from Palestine, Egypt, Pakistan, Afghanistan, Chechnya, Bosnia, Algeria, Tunisia, Somalia, and Sudan were not too different from the stories of my childhood. The state of the imagined Muslim ummah, the larger community of Muslims outside of my rapidly growing Muslim community, was the dominant concern. In 1987, the first intifada in Palestine erupted, followed by the widespread armed insurgency in Jammu and Kashmir in 1989. In 1991, a civil war in Somalia and the Persian Gulf War broke out. A year later, the war in Bosnia-Herzegovina shocked the world and left traces in our local Muslim community as we began to accommodate the influx of refugees. In 1994, before the end of the Bosnian war, Chechnya entered its first war for independence. We were privy to these events because they deeply affected many of our friends and their families.

During my first semester as a doctoral student, the Iranian president at the time, Mahmoud Ahmadinejad, gave a speech at Columbia University. The university's president, Lee C. Bollinger, publicly rebuked him in his introductory speech. In response, Ahmadinejad invited the audience of students, researchers, and academics to visit his country in order to test the accuracy of media reports about Iran. I recalled then that when my family and I had arrived in San Francisco from the Philippines in 1979, my father had asked me to sit next to him as he watched news footage of the Iranian revolution with Ayatollah Khomeini walking down an airplane's staircase on his arrival in Tehran. "I want you to see this," he said. "This is what Muslims can do against oppression." The television screen was full of women covered in black cloth marching in support of Ayatollah Khomeini and the revolutionaries. It captured my father's imagination and the imaginations of millions of Muslims like him around the world as a story of a rare triumph. It was David against Goliath, and David had won. If my father and his friends could not defeat imperialism where they were from, it was enough to know that someone else did. It gave my father something. But, I also realized that women were absent in my father's imagination of this triumph.

With Ahmadinejad's invitation, I decided I would go to Iran to do my dissertation research. My hope was to be able to develop questions around women's Islamic education and their participation in the revolution by living with women like those I had seen on that television screen. In the spring of 2008, I learned that the Dehkhoda Persian Language Institute, an extension of the University of Tehran then, processed student visas. That summer, without a specific field site, persons in mind, or language skills, I left for Tehran asking myself, *What does an attempt to build an Islamic state look like in the lives of women and girls who are enabled by it?*

I stayed in Tehran for about three months in the summer of 2008 in the neighborhood of Elahiyeh, near the language institute. Before traveling to Iran, I had been told that a university previously called Sepahselar had been converted into a seminary after the revolution. I made my way there first, and three days after my first visit, I was introduced to Dr. Sajjadpour, a professor of what eventually became Madraseh Ali. I explain the details in the introduction and elsewhere beyond this book. He introduced me to five women; two of them were Maryam and Sara, both in their early thirties at the time, who eventually introduced me to their friends. I interviewed a total of thirteen women in 2008. I attended Persian language classes in the morning and met with women in the afternoons and on weekends.

Initially, I tried avoiding the possibility of gateways like Dr. Sajjadpour who would handpick women for my research. I worried about establishing validity and making sure I collected accurate information. But given the unpredictability of my interactions, the absence of previous relationships to draw on, and that I would most likely be under surveillance, I was open to all possibilities. Even if they introduced me to women who best represented the howzevi population, which was not ideal for anthropological work, at least I would have some information to analyze. I also knew that this initial access would increase the likelihood of my being introduced to other groups of women. I took my chances.

Dr. Sajjadpour and the women he introduced me to set the wheels in motion by inviting me into their spaces and to be publicly visible with them when I first traveled to Iran in 2008. Although I remained in contact with Maryam and Sara after returning to New York City in the summer of 2008, I could not return to Iran after the violence that erupted around the 2009 presidential election. I was eventually able to return to Iran in the fall of 2010 for a total of fifteen months of participant observation. This trip was a different experience, however. Dr. Sajjadpour was not as accessible because he was exceptionally busy working on several projects. Like many Iranians who were not part of my research, he was perhaps hesitant to be associated with a foreigner like me just one year after the 2009 protests. Further, the howzevi were aware of the risks when deciding whether to participate in my research. The women recognized that descriptions, no matter how benign they may be, often carry with them some unintended impact on individuals. They were quite concerned.

Between the fall of 2010 and the winter of 2011, I spent weekday mornings at Dehkhoda Institute and continued to develop fieldwork relationships in the afternoons and on weekends. However, it took about five months for some of the women to interact with me. Early in my fieldwork, I spent most of my days with Maryam, as her neighbor in Pirouzi, South Tehran, where I lived for nine months. My eldest daughter traveled to Iran and stayed with me briefly in 2010. She took Persian language courses and art classes from Yaghoub Amamepich, a well-known artist in Tehran. In hindsight, my daughter's presence gave the women I interacted with an opportunity to observe my parenting style and to ask us questions about my family life, which was important for them. I eventually began meeting with Sara. The longer I stayed, the more other women became familiar with my presence. I depended heavily on the long-established credibility of the people around me as well as their descriptions of me to others, since credibility and reputation often determined access to resources and information among the howzevi. Maryam began introducing me to other women similar to how Dr. Sajjadpour had done in 2008. From then on, women began allowing me to have brief exchanges with them.

Often, I would be introduced with adjectives in the following order: a doctoral student from Columbia University, and a Sunni Muslim Filipino who happened to be raised in America. The women were enthused to talk to me about the Sunni and Shi'i divide. Because of what I knew about Islam and Islamic text, perhaps there was an assumption that I was gauging them by way of Islamic text, albeit from a Sunni worldview. The histories, differences, and commonalities in practices interested them the most. Further, my religious upbringing as part of the Shafi'i, an Islamic jurisprudent school of thought, was interesting for many of them because it recognized Shi'i practices as valid. The chance I took in 2008 worked in my favor by February 2011, when I began spending time with howzevi from other seminaries who did not know each other.

One concern I had throughout my fieldwork was my ability to comprehend the Persian language. From October 2010 to January 2011, I did not have everyday interactions with howzevi women except for Maryam. This gave me time to improve my level of Persian language comprehension. During the few interviews I conducted at this time, Maryam and Sara, on separate occasions, helped me with conversational translations in real time. By May 2011 I had completed the Persian language study program from Dehkhoda Institute, and could fully communicate in Persian. However, as I write elsewhere and in the introduction, most of the women spent time with me in order to practice conversing in English. Therefore, we communicated in English and Persian with each other throughout my fieldwork. To make sure I was documenting accurately, however, Drs. Najmeh Bathaee and Alireza Bazargan, who were both doctoral students in engineering at the time, helped me translate audio recordings while I was in Iran. One of the howzevi helped with Islamic jurisprudent language, and her sister helped translate audio of public speeches.

I end the preface of this work with this final note. It has taken me a decade to write for an audience beyond members of my dissertation committee. I am uncomfortable sharing this book for many reasons. First, the challenge of staying true to anthropology's work of humanizing has been overwhelming since having completed my fieldwork, especially in the context of the protests against the Iranian government that resulted in protestors' deaths. Second, the very same system responsible for colonialism in the Philippines—specifically against my people, the Tausug in the Sulu Archipelago—birthed an institution, Columbia University, that gave me the privilege to travel to Iran that is, in my view, couched in this very process of dominance. It is a kind of reckoning I needed to put into words here.

Being a doctoral student from Columbia University's Teachers College at the time was an affiliation I needed in order to justify my presence in Iran. While conducting research was allowed, it was impermissible for me as a foreigner to participate in what authorities would consider social or political activism. Having my university's Institutional Review Board approval certificate that detailed the participants' rights largely facilitated feelings of safety and ease between the women and myself. I made sure to point out the telephone number they could call in the event that I violated any of those written rights.

On a different register, outside of my research and in my daily public interactions, I was sometimes mistaken for an Afghan refugee because of my physical features. Sometimes I was mistaken for a domestic servant since there were Filipino servants in north Tehran. Both groups endured a certain amount of discrimination, more so the Afghan refugees who suffered public humiliation in north Tehran. This is the sort of social pathology the 1979 revolution sought to eradicate. But at the same time, had I not come from the very system that the revolution saw as the enemy, I would have had to endure more discrimination than I already had. That is, I was able to pass through this maltreatment because I could interact as a Columbia University student with an American English accent, IRB certificate in hand. This privilege remains unsettled for me for the reasons I have previously noted, but I was able to learn how a group of women in Iran navigate their way through systems of power in ways that both limit and facilitate their movements, in ways that eventually include and exclude others, and in ways that leave traces. This book is one of those traces.

Amina Tawasil
August 25, 2023
Brooklyn, NY

ACKNOWLEDGMENTS

THIS PROJECT WOULD NOT HAVE been possible without the generous support from Columbia University's Earth Institute Advanced Consortium on Cooperation, Conflict, and Complexity, Middle East Institute, and the late Lambros Comitas, who helped fund my travel to Iran. The American Association of University Women's 2012–2013 Dissertation Fellowship made completing the first write-up from this research possible. I would also like to thank Indiana University Press's Bethany Mowry, Sophia Hebert, and Faculty Board for considering the potential of this manuscript. I would especially like to thank all the reviewers for their insight that helped strengthen sections of the book. I am extremely grateful for my mentors, colleagues, students, and friends who have supported me as an individual in the many years of research and in writing this book. Their support is neither a reflection of their beliefs nor of their politics. Many, if not all, have and will continue to disagree with me on aspects of this book.

I am enormously grateful to Lila Abu-Lughod, who guided me throughout my research, writing, and publication process, and for the guidance I received from the previous faculty of one of the few remaining programs of anthropology and education: Hervé Varenne, Charles Harrington, the late Lambros Comitas, and George Bond, and members of my dissertation committee Lesley Bartlett and Fida Adely.

Thanks to the Andrew W. Mellon Postdoctoral Fellowship 2013–2015 at Northwestern University's Middle East and North African Studies Program (MENA), I was able to write, present parts of this research, and teach courses on women and gender. I am grateful for the mentorship I received there from Jessica Winegar, Brian Edwards, Robert Launay, and Amanda Logan. My time at MENA taught me the value of forming writing groups, a practice that led to a publication. Thus,

I would like to thank Mona Oraby, Nurhaizatul Jamil, and Lorena Alvarado. I thank Shabana Mir for her feedback, and Shenila Khoja-Moolji for her comments on my first publication from this research. Finally, I would like to thank the Columbia Center for the Study of Social Difference and Women Creating Change for hosting "The Power of Women in Islamic Education," which I co-organized with Lila Abu-Lughod in 2013.

I learned the value of writing slowly and deliberately during my two years at the University of New Mexico's International Studies Institute, where I was given the opportunity to present on the practice of wearing the black chador for the first time in 2017. I thank Christine Sauer, the late Eleni Bastea, Loyola Chastain, Farah Nousheen, Les Field, Mozafar Banihashemi, Theodore Jojola, and the late Dely Alcantara. I am equally grateful to have had the pleasure of writing with Amanda Hamp and Lara Gunderson. Cheshmak Shahsiah, Sara Siavoshi, Amir Reisi, and I created a special kinship there, which allowed me to transform parts of my writing style in ways they were not aware of. I thank them immensely. While in New Mexico, I met two giants of philosophy and anthropology, Edward Casey and Renato Rosaldo. They were generous beyond measure with their time in reading one of my chapters, pointing me to relevant sources, and giving me advice on how to approach the introduction. Finally, I want to thank Rose Wellman for all the feedback and insight on my writing, and for inviting me to take part in the Ethnography of Iran at Princeton University in 2015.

I am fortunate to have received encouragement to keep writing from my colleagues Hervé Varenne, Nicholas Limerick, and Grey Gundaker at Columbia University's Teachers College Programs in Anthropology as I completed this manuscript from 2017 to 2022. Hervé Varenne gave me space to develop my scholarship through teaching and writing. I am grateful for that. I also especially want to thank Grey Gundaker for her patience in reading through the first iteration of the manuscript. In addition, I thank Dianne Marcucci-Sadnytzky, Bridget Bartollini, and Rachael Simon for their moral support. I also thank Dahlia El Zein for organizing the Middle East Studies Association panel in 2019, as well as Soheila Shahshahani and Mary Hegland for inviting me to my first IUAES Middle East Congress conference in Krakov, Poland in 2019. I am very grateful for all the library resources support I received from my former students Paola Muñoz, Dalila Mendez, and Jazz Digao, and for Reid Pierce with the index. My virtual writing group, Daniel Burgos-Rudas, Jonthon Coulson, Cassie Smith, Elena Peeples, Sara Ahmed, Omavi Shukur, and Krystal Wang, helped me stay focused during the pandemic. I thank them. I also thank all the graduate students who have been writing with me every Friday in the different cafés in New York City since September 2021.

I am thankful for the generosity of the trustees at Salam Center and M. Yaqub Mirza, who helped me when I had no funding as I formulated my pilot fieldwork plans during my first semester at Teachers College. I thank Nisrin Elamin, Marcelle Mentor, Rika Prodhan, and Aladdin Diaz for making themselves available to my family in New York City while I was away. I thank Ruqia and Saeeda Islam, Nabill Idrisi, Ahlia Kattan, Fatima Hassan Ali, Maham Mela, Nada Ramadan, Zaid Adhami, and Marjan Soleimanieh for taking the time to respond to my emails from Iran. Many thanks to Houman Harouni for introducing me to the beauty of the Persian language over a decade ago and to Lou Cristillo, Hassan Hossein, Michael Scroggins, Jennifer Van Tiem, Gillian Andrews, Kamil Yilmaz, and Brian O'Hare for providing valuable insight during the early stages of my writing in 2012. I am also extremely grateful for all the support I have received from Mehdi Javanmard, Hoora Manzoori and family, Shadi Sajjad and family, the Bazargan family, Tooran Valimurad, Lida Kavousi, Najmeh Bathaee, Ali Batouli, Barin Kayaoglu, Gizem Kasoturacak, Zahra Roghaniha, Hamideh Alimoghadam, and my Persian language instructors at the University of Tehran's Dehkhoda Institute.

My highest appreciation goes to my children for their faith in me, and the rest of my family for their moral support. Last but not least, I owe an immense debt of gratitude to all the men and women in Iran who were a part of this research, who opened their lives to me and taught me more than I can capture in words.

NOTE ON TRANSLATION
AND TRANSLITERATION

MY TRANSCRIPTIONS FOLLOW THE IRANIAN Studies scheme. Persian and/
or Arabic words are in italics for the first usage. Arabic words are Persianized:
Ramadan is Ramazan, rawda is rowzeh, and hawzah is howzeh. Hence, when a
speaker expressed the words in either Persian or Arabic, I wrote them according
to the scheme that closely resembles the way they are pronounced. Because in
Persian the sound between the 'ayn and alef is almost nonexistent, I have not
used diacritical marks unless it is necessary because of the speaker's emphasis in
pronouncing the words. In that case, I use ' at the end of the letter. I distinguish
between the aleph long and short vowels by using *aa* in my transliteration. The
words spoken in Persian are translated into English. I wrote words that were said
in English as word-for-word direct quotes. I do not add -s to Persian words like
hijab, chador, maktab, or howzeh to make them plural. Each of these have plural
forms in Persian, such as hijabha or howzat, but these plural forms do not reflect
the spoken form. Therefore, in English, I use *a howzeh* to refer to one howzeh,
and I use *the howzeh, or the howzeh elmiyeh* to refer to the system composed of
many howzeh.

PATHS MADE
BY WALKING

INTRODUCTION

IT IS EASY FOR IMAGES to be misunderstood, for an event or an encounter to go unnoticed, and for stories to be forgotten. If not retold, shared, or mass produced, they will disappear, especially in the muddle of politics between nation-states. Time and again, women have been written out of historical events. Certain women are especially prone to being erased from the record at any given moment of history, depending on which ideologies of personhood are en vogue. I wrote this ethnography in the hopes of inserting a group of women into the historical record: the *howzevi*, or the seminarian women—specifically, women among them who have been placed at the forefront of strengthening the Islamic Republic of Iran.

Women's Islamic education in Iran has taken on various forms since before the 1979 revolution, as evidenced by both the well-documented historical presence of women in Islamic scholarship and the existence of autonomous howzeh systems in the cities of Esfahan, Shiraz, Tabriz, and Mashhad. But in 1984, one institution, Jami'at Al-Zahra in the city of Qom, emerged as the largest women's howzeh, which has accommodated an annual enrollment of twelve thousand in the last four decades. This initiative was born out of the Islamic Republic's need to produce a specific type of woman—the militant (*mubariz*) Iranian Shi'i Muslim (*musalman*) mother (*maadar*) who would work on turning revolutionary ideals into practice.[1] To do so, Ayatollah Ruhollah Khomeini and his allies institutionalized Jami'at Al-Zahra, an initiative that led to centralizing the women's *howzeh elmiyeh*, or seminaries (*howzeh* from here on). By 2010, the Management Center of the Women's Seminaries in Qom was overseeing approximately three hundred women's howzeh nationwide. Since 1979, Islamic education in support of maintaining a society founded on Shi'i Islam has become an ongoing nationwide

1

project through women's work. Unexpected outcomes were inevitable. As the government provided expansive educative access for religiously conservative women, it also bestowed new opportunities on them.

I traveled to Iran in the summer of 2008 and from the fall of 2010 to the end of 2011 to learn from these women what their lives have been like since the revolution. This was a special time worth recounting for the lessons we might learn about women and the project of creating an Islamic Republic—a kind of retelling that would make this ethnography from over ten years ago a historical document about these women. Their work is the inspiration for the title of this book. It is taken from an artwork entitled *A Line Made by Walking*, in which the artist walked up and down a field of grass to create a line.[2] This line, marked by the bent grass, was visible only with close examination. I liken this to the work the women in this book have been doing—work that continues to be unseen. Yet because of this, there is no going back to a time in Iran when religiously conservative women's participation in religious and sociopolitical discourse was inconceivable.

The women deemed their work of strengthening the Islamic Republic as a noble undertaking. A wholesale demonizing of their project was not enough of a reason to convince them otherwise when, as one howzevi student explained, women in other countries were continuously applauded for working to support governments that sought to have power over other countries like Iran. It is difficult to write about these women without tension and negative traction. As a group they are thought of, as Susan Harding referred to in her work on Christian fundamentalists, as "the repugnant others . . . treated as a category of unreasoned people . . . produced by modern discursive practices."[3] In the case of howzevi women, however, their interpretation of Islam that led to a revolution makes them suspect. They are also part of a system of governance we have come to associate with fear. I, like many outside Iran, was familiar with this popular image before arriving in Iran: the image of women being ruled by an unwanted few in turbans and robes who were predisposed to silencing all forms of opposition, and who had failed to progress with the rest of the world.[4] Edward Said draws a correlation between the negative response to Iran's 1979 revolution and what he had written in *Orientalism* (1978) about a long-established disposition regarding Islam and the Orient, with Islam as a "threat of a return to the Middle Ages."[5] Iran was the perfect example of what could go wrong if Islamic fundamentalists were to occupy positions of power and of what could go wrong in the lives of women who rally behind the project of an Islamic Republic.

I arrived in Tehran for the first time with this preconceived image of an exhausted Iran held captive by Ayatollah Khomeini's irrational followers. I was a doctoral student imposing myself onto one of many social landscapes that I had very little exposure to except through books, articles, radio, television, and the internet. I learned quickly that its sociopolitical context is much too diverse and contentious to be mapped out simply as bad Iranians holding good Iranians captive.[6] Iran's social and political atmosphere has always been, and continues to be, replete with tension.[7] Two of the more popular examples of this are Ayatollahs Mohammad Mousavi Khoeiniha and Hossein Ali Montazeri. Ayatollah Khomeini appointed Khoeiniha as state prosecutor general after the 1979 revolution. He was the leader of the students who took over the US embassy in November 1979, decades later referred to as Akhound-e Sorkh, the red "leftist" cleric, and identified as the force behind the reformists. He accused the administration of corruption and rigging the 2009 elections in favor of Mahmoud Ahmadinejad. Ayatollah Montazeri, once the successor to Ayatollah Khomeini, had a clash with Khomeini in 1989 over government policies.[8] Montazeri, as a proponent of an Islamic state, argued that Iran was not being governed the way an Islamic state should be. He remained one of the main critics of the Islamic Republic's domestic and foreign policies and an advocate of minorities' and women's rights until his death in 2009. There are many more examples of these tensions.

This image of Iran held captive by ayatollahs persists today in the wake of Mahsa Amini's death while in the custody of Iran's morality police for improper veiling. While protests against compulsory veiling are common in Iran, Amini's tragic death has led to the largest widespread protests inside and outside Iran since 2009. A great number of protestors who were arrested and charged with espionage—more specifically, conspiring with Israel and the United States—were sentenced to death. The sentencing and executions have led to further waves of nationwide protests. These events together birthed the global Women, Life, Freedom movement, the signatories of which include prime ministers, diplomats, executives, lawyers, and artists. The movement seeks to remove Iran from the United Nations' Commission for the Status of Women. Since Amini's death in September 2022, many from the Iranian diasporic community have flocked to social media in support of economic sanctions against Iran and of US military intervention to bring the Pahlavi regime back into power. A bomb threat and smear campaigns have surfaced against Iranian American academics accused of having connections with the Iranian government in their attempt to provide a more comprehensive analysis of the protests.[9]

The context in which I attempt to publish this book today is reminiscent of the disturbing circumstances during my return to Iran in 2010; just one year previous, the paramilitary forces, or the *Basij*, had killed Neda Agha Sultan while protesting against the 2009 presidential election results. In December 2022, Iran's religious morality police was disbanded, only to be reinstated in July 2023.[10]

In these critical moments, it becomes easy to dehumanize opposing sides of the conflict. As a result, the women I write about in this book and their varied

experiences are swallowed up in all of it. Prior to recent events, they were carica-
tured as puppets of the Islamic Republic. There are those who write about them
as mouthpieces of male relatives, "generally illiterate, simple-minded supersti-
tious" women who were moved by "their own sense of adventure."[11] Thus, from a
distance, we are limited to speculation about their work, purposes, and identities
based on what we think we know about those around them—men we associate
with fear. The work of understanding the women is layered and complex. I don't
doubt that many of those I spent time with could live up to the stereotypes and
assumptions we make. I experienced great difficulties, and I witnessed violence
during my fieldwork. But these did not change the fact that behind the terror
or the condescension we might feel based on these associations, the women I
became neighbors and friends with for a year and a half were people with very
impactful and meaningful lives that we can learn from about how womanhood,
Islamic education, and revolution intersect in this context.

This book's ethnographic labor is grounded in a commitment to understanding the human condition in all its forms. It is an invitation to reconsider our
imagination of women who are part of the workings of the Islamic Republic of
Iran. I argue for the necessity to make space for understanding their process as
women who, as a population, have been historically dismissed as both incapable
and suspect by their Iranian male counterparts and, as I explain later, Iranian
secularists and feminists.[12] From afar, our understanding of these women risks a
similar outcome. But their stories of their education, personal interactions, and
relationships are very much connected to the political future of the Middle East.
Because although these women work without visibility, they, as a group, have an
impact on policy.

They remain always at work in unseen motion. Thus the interactions among
them in educational settings open a window to understanding a phenomenon
that is commonly considered only in global politics: the ways Iranian theocracy
continues to exist and to plague US foreign policy in the Middle East. They are
women from small towns who at times research controversial edicts, who experience difficulty managing their personal interests and familial obligations, or who
are trying to make sense of and address a new generation of Iranians who did not
witness the socioeconomic and political conditions before the revolution. By
bringing to light the centrality of the women's histories, practices, and personal
connections, we can understand how they come to support the establishment of
an Islamic Republic. Their story begins at the ground level—an analytical point
that resonates with the idea that history begins locally, on the ground, where,
according to Lila Abu-Lughod, human beings are in their particulars with their
own set of terms.[13] This particular for the howzevi was personal, gendered, and
political, and its boundaries were drawn in terms of religiosity and revolution.

A GATHERING IN BEHESHT-E MAADARAN

It was my first time riding a bus owned by Madraseh Ali. With its overextended curved hood, faded dark gray exterior, and wide seats supported by uncomfortable, worn-out spring coils, the bus appeared as if it had been pieced together in the 1970s. The driver, whom the women thanked upon our arrival at the park, was in his late sixties. Being with us this morning meant he would be spending part of his day off driving us to and from Behesht-e Maadaran, the Mothers' Paradise, also called Park-e Banuvan or Women's Park. All eleven women with us were in their twenties and were master's students of *Huquq*, or Islamic rights, and *Fiqh*, or Islamic jurisprudence. Two women who were students of *Falsafeh-ye Islami*, Islamic philosophy, would later join us. Some of the women were Maryam's students. Maryam, in her thirties, gave birth to her daughter, Fereshteh, now eighteen months old, while writing a comparative analysis between Shi'i Islamic jurisprudence and the United Nations charter on international trade for her dissertation. Maryam came from a small town outside Esfahan, half a day by bus from Tehran. She had just become a student at the highest level of study in the howzeh, the *Dars-e Kharij* level, under Ayatollah Ali Khamenei in 2008. On this day, Maryam was given the responsibility of chaperoning her students for a picnic at the park.

We walked along a path toward the park's back entrance and found a gazebo to settle in. There, a green metal wall separated us from the rest of Tehran. The women took off their *chador*, or black open cloaks, and hung them on the gazebo pillars. Some removed their *hijab*, or headscarves, brushed their hair, and put on jewelry, while others took turns playing ball with Fereshteh. We chatted as we ate breakfast together on a cement platform a few feet away. Each of us had a story to tell, but of all the women I had met previously, Zahra's Persian sounded noticeably different to me. Maryam later told me that Zahra was from the southernmost part of Iran. At some point, Nahid quietly excused herself. She returned wearing a purple *manto*, a knee-length coat, and a purple motif scarf. A gray purse hung on her shoulder. She sat down, opened the purse, and one by one took out a lipstick, eyeliner, eye shadow, and face powder. The women smiled, then laughed, as if they were watching a scene from a play. Nahid then began to pretend to know how to apply makeup on her face. She chuckled and then tried to appear serious only to laugh again. The women teased her, saying how she actually did not know what makeup was to be applied to what part of her face. She laughed in agreement, but everyone somehow knew she wanted to put on makeup, which she would otherwise not do beyond this moment. One of them touched her cheeks and began helping her.

Since men were not allowed inside the park, the gardeners, vendors, and guards were all women. The guard near us blew a whistle every time she saw women taking out their cameras. Many young girls and women passing by wore tank tops and sweatpants. Some wore the manto and scarves while walking in pairs or in groups. Young girls played music and danced. *Daf*, or handheld drums, as well as *zaghred*, a high-pitched sound, could be heard in the background from other areas of the park. Ma'ede eventually came running toward me with a ball and, while laughing, said she wanted to practice her English with me. Ma'ede was twenty-five years old, and though she had been born in Tehran, her family was originally from Kashan. Her brother had completed his master's degree in electrical engineering and was living in Calgary. Her husband was from a village near Qom and was finishing his PhD in aerospace engineering at Sharif University, known throughout Iran as the primary feeder institution for engineering programs at Stanford University. She had been in the same engineering program for the first two and a half years, but she decided to transfer to Madraseh Ali, where she felt happier. She made this decision because she initially wanted to know more about the different kinds of laws.

Explaining her interest in philosophy and international law, Ma'ede remarked, "America speaks about human rights, but they don't live it. They create wars in the world and oppress people. They want to rule the world." She proceeded to tell me that Morteza Motahhari's teachings had inspired her, especially his teachings about women's rights and international human rights. "Shahid Motahhari's opinion of the universal declaration of human rights is that it is wrong, because it only took people into consideration. It does not speak about the relationship of God to the people, even though God was the one who gave these rights. It cannot be universal," she explained. She admired Ayatollah Abdollah Javadi Amoli's work on the philosophy of human rights, especially his critique of humanism. Ma'ede eventually wanted to study Dars-e Kharij with Ayatollah Ali Khamenei, the supreme leader. She had recently heard Ayatollah Khamenei's speech urging people to make books more Islamic. "Right now, everything in the science textbooks comes from Western theories. Even if the writer is Iranian, the theories they use are still from the West," she added. She hoped to change this with her education. Ma'ede was studying Islamic jurisprudence and Islamic rights for her master's degree because she wanted to work toward making the laws in Iran closer to Islamic laws.

We eventually went downstairs to join the rest of the women to play *vasati*, a game that resembles dodgeball. We played until the point of exhaustion and then sat on the cemented edge of the grass area. Alimeh was the only one in her immediate family that was studying at Madraseh Ali. Her cousin was a student of Islamic sciences, but he had recently died while patrolling the Afghanistan-Iran border. With a smile, she said she was not interested in marriage. Alimeh was twenty-seven years old and was writing her master's thesis on the laws of investment shares while teaching undergraduate courses that semester. During lunch, one of the women asked Maryam about the types of stipulations a woman could include in a marriage contract. In response, Maryam asked who among them were married already, so that perhaps they could share some ideas. Rayhane jokingly inserted in English, "If I were married, I would not be here!" She put her finger up in the air as if lecturing someone and jokingly said, "*Gheyrat!*" She was referring to her would-be husband's protective feeling of responsibility for her. Everyone laughed. Elham then began reciting poetry about love and longing for the beloved. In the midst of the laughter, someone began teasing Elham.

Like nuanced signposts, our gathering at Behesht-e Maadaran sampled the interplay of human touch, voice, and affection in the telling of self, others, and futures that constituted the social world of students of the howzeh. It provides an estimate for how they moved in and with their surroundings as well as their concerns, on which I build my analysis about women and a particular kind of women's Islamic education in Iran that develops and maintains a society that ideally supports the work of spiritually bringing oneself closer to God. It reveals the various research they committed themselves to. They addressed research concerns with their Islamic education from the howzeh, using Islamic knowledge grounded in over one thousand years of Islamic scholarship including philosophy, jurisprudence, and the language of Islamic rights. This was an education supported by an entire collective: religiously conservative women and men like the bus driver; the women's fathers, brothers, and husbands; and, most importantly, the Islamic Republic.

Many women like Maryam were raising children and managing their households or caring for their parents and siblings while completing programs in the howzeh. Like Zahra from southern Iran, they came from different regions and from varied backgrounds. Their family members were engineers or stationed at the Afghan-Iran border. Unfettered by their fathers' authority, howzevi women traveled from all over Iran to study any one of the Islamic sciences. Yet, like Nahid and others, they had to be specific kinds of women who observed Shi'i Islamic practices. In other words, they had to be women who could distinguish the proper time and place for behaviors like wearing makeup, playing ball, laughing out loud, maintaining gender separation, or wearing the black chador. As Elham signaled, they needed to be women who married men with gheyrat, or men who had a sense of protective emotional responsibility for them and their children.

This gathering tells us that these women were not merely surviving their limitations and waiting for the right moment to undermine them. The 1979 revolution Islamized public space as never before, which made it safe for them to take advantage of having access to Islamic education and possible for them to work on strengthening a system that positions them at the center rather than on the

periphery. They held contemporary Islamic scholars like Ayatollah Morteza Motahhari, who was assassinated in May 1979 right after the revolution, in high
regard. They, like most religiously conservative Iranians, use the honorific title
shahid for men like him to remind others that they died for an Islamic cause. It's
also used to describe someone who died fighting in the Iran-Iraq War from 1980
to 1988. As we can see from Ma'ede's educative vision, the howzevi's work often
involves seeking ways to maintain a system that is committed to supporting the
personal work of *khod shenasi*, an individual's effort toward self-awareness in
order to create a spiritual nearness to the divine.

Ma'ede, like the others, made sense of her immediate concerns like secular
laws and universalized human rights as always in relation to God. That is, any
kind of work that involves solving human problems cannot be divorced from a
conversation about God—more specifically, the purpose of life itself. The women
I spent time with shared this assertion and added that the laws that govern most
of the countries originated from some religious text and conceptualization of
human life and world. Political factors like US imperialism were important parts
of this constellation. Through her Islamic education, Ma'ede saw herself as acting on her plans to do something about her concerns. She hoped to eventually
partake in Ayatollah Khamenei's class so that she could replace secular laws in
Iran with Islamic laws and replace Western thought in Iranian books with Islamic
thought. As a result, it was a kind of work that continued to push back against
American and European domination in Iran and the greater Middle East, a way
to end, in their words, "oppressive conditions," including those that women continued to experience.

One outcome of this access to the women's howzeh elmiyeh has been the
system-wide transformation. As a result of women's efforts to develop the system, the women's howzeh has eventually become a degree-granting institution
wherefrom graduates become qualified to work in institutions that affect policies in Iran. They continue to be a crucial component of the Islamic Republic
as they work behind the scenes on domestic policies and the educational and
social programming that affects public life in Iran. The creation of Behesht-e
Maadaran along with gyms, sports complexes, and parks exclusively for women
provides clues to the extent the howzevi have been engaged with the transformation of public space since the revolution, an engagement that was not always
possible for religiously conservative women. As a result of all this, access to a
howzeh education has opened up the potential for an increase in the number of
mujtahideh, or women who make legal decisions for themselves and other women
through independent interpretation of the Qur'an, the sacred book of Muslims,
and the Sunnah, the documented lifeways and the manners of the Prophet Mohammad. Equally important, there has been a shift in the curricular direction of

the women's howzeh, away from producing Islamic scholars and toward producing supporters and developers of the Islamic Republic.

PARTICIPATION AS RESISTANCE

My challenge is to effectively present narratives that reflect both methodological integrity and a commitment to anthropology's humanizing endeavor. To do this, it is important to find ways to make sense of the howzevi's logic and ways that allow for a shift in perspective about the possibilities of womanhood. Theoretical frameworks play a crucial role in this effort. They can open up ways to understand human phenomena. But the theories we use can also obscure parts of the human experience. What one theory can help explain, another theory may not. Thus, it's important to choose theoretical approaches, or a combination of them, that will best explain lessons learned from the field. In the following, I first explain which frameworks would be counterproductive to the humanizing work of this book. I then explain those that are more aligned with the book's objective: theory of agency, situated learning, the anthropology of becoming, play and humor, and indigenous theories from Islamic philosophy—essential motion and self-knowing.

As I demonstrate in the following, the dominant analytical framework used to explain Iranian women's participation in contemporary sociopolitical discourse is politicized resistance. This refers to actions interpreted as a subversion of an existing sociopolitical order patterned after the rule of men, more specifically, where the conception of the household, by implication—law, is assumed to function naturally through the authority of men. Participation, therefore, is largely equated with transgression against the government, which is both Islamic and offering up patriarchy. This framework is useful for reiterating a scholar's prior commitment to emphasizing resistance against male authority. More specifically, it is useful for explaining women's subversive work, especially work that mirrors our contemporary desires for recognition, autonomy, leadership, and authority.

This prior commitment is linked in part to another supposition—that there is a universal good life, in this case for all women. This good life is to be acquired by women aspiring to become and becoming autonomous. In a Kantian sense, a good life consists of "a way out," the freedom from a mindset that accepts the authority of others over our own reasoning, a marker of which is the obligation "to dare to know," *sapere aude*, as evidence of maturity.[14] In this context, inside every woman is a desire to dissent in order to be free from constraints; as Azadeh Kian-Thiébaut writes, Iranian women desire "to form an identity which is no longer founded on traditions."[15] Through this frame of autonomy, the self is the source of moral order, and individuals, families, social networks, churches, and governments eventually become obstacles to this way out because these entities are carriers of ideology.[16]

What this desired life of freedom for all women looks like is quite vague, other than the register of nontradition. The problem is that any human action, when practiced repetitively through time, eventually becomes tradition. So what exactly could non-tradition be? Freedom from that remains unclear. Based on what women who call for a regime change in Iran describe, this life most likely resembles what we imagine to be middle class sensibilities in Europe and North America.[17] Its very basic markers are women who have individuated goals for a future that involves schooling as a means to these goals, women who have unhindered choices in dress and spouse, acquiring enough mobility to have a career and, if so desired, to be publicly visible in her political, social, economic, and educational aspirations. In this call for freedom, it seems that outside Iran is where this freedom exists. Out there is where women's lives are conceived of as already full with liberating possibilities.

A universal kind of womanhood undergirded by a desire for autonomy is the unspoken premise, and is assumed simply as common sense. It is an expectation placed on women.[18] The coupling of a universal good life and aspirations for autonomy is part of everyday common sense through this lens. To interrogate this, Clifford Geertz writes, "The opposite of someone who is able to come to sensible conclusions on the basis of them is a fool. . . . It is in short, a cultural system. . . . It rests on the same basis that any other such system rests; the conviction by those whose possession it is of its value and validity."[19] This expectation placed on women as common sense is what makes feminism both an analytical and a prescriptive project.[20] If women do not have this common sense, they must learn how to possess it. This framing of womanhood hinders our understanding of the women in this book.

An example of this is how feminist research on Iranian women attempts to establish causality in order to develop a prescription to overcome patriarchal dominance in Iran. Haideh Moghissi argues that despite women's refusal to properly observe mandatory veiling, their efforts lack gender consciousness and do not do much against the injunction.[21] Maryam Poya proposes that the oppression of working-class women is ingrained in the workings of an Islamic state since Islam propagates unequal access to resources, legal rights, and public space. Conformity is considered a nascent resistance since women bargain with patriarchy.[22] Both conclude that the women's movement in Iran continues to be defeated because women are too immersed in their subjugation. The solution, then, is to do away with Islam, and for Iranian women to refuse to yield to the government.

Another example is Islamist women's participation as politicized resistance. As a response to the charge that Iranian women are passive, this approach has focused on the role of Islamist women in interpreting Islamic text.[23] The focus is often on "elite" Islamist women who are working on changing the laws and social conditions for Iranian women by engaging in acts of resistance against outdated clerics.[24] Yet while this approach successfully makes visible some women's accomplishments, it does not escape the liberal expectation on women to move toward an imagined autonomy.

This expectation also informs the decision to categorize some women as either Islamists or Islamic feminists. Though these two groups have similarities, they are not the same. Islamist women and Islamic feminists both work toward bringing back the egalitarian conditions that are believed to have been created by the Prophet Mohammad and his companions over one thousand years ago, traces of which may be found in Islamic text and scholarly debates of the past. Yet while Islamist women are said to work to establish and support a state governed by Islamic law with the aim of preserving the Islamic Republic, Islamic feminists work within different systems of state power and prioritize reinterpreting Islamic knowledge from a gendered perspective. Islamic feminists locate their feminism in Islam.[25] Thus, reinterpretations of Islamic knowledge for them would be a viable alternative to move toward women's emancipation.[26]

The framework of Islamic feminism, in particular, is often used to explore women's Islamic education in Iran. It holds that women must, in the end, work to emancipate themselves and occupy publicly visible positions of power or authority.[27] Roja Fazaeli, one of the few pioneer scholars on Islamic feminisms across different generations in Iran, makes this move. She classifies Ayatollah Khomeini's supporters as Islamic state feminists and describes how religiously conservative women who support the supreme leader have come to realize that Iranian laws did not reflect the promises of the revolution, and by the late 1990s "a new wave of more powerful state feminists was appointed to top governmental positions."[28]

A problem with the classification of Islamic feminist is that it disregards the possibility that some women who do the work of bettering women's status may not think of themselves as Islamic feminists, or may even see it as an affront to be called one.[29] The women in this book fall under this category. Although they did not identify themselves as Islamists, most if not all of them refused to be called feminists and found the label offensive to their project. They see feminism as a form of Western invasion and a symptom of immorality. Elizabeth Buccar, who conducts research on religious women's moral agency, writes of a similar experience when she referred to Shahla Habibi, the special advisor on women's affairs under former president Hashimi Rafsanjani, as an Islamic feminist. In response, Habibi became upset and said, "I am not a feminist. Do not call me a feminist. I do not believe in your feminism."[30] Buccar, in reflection, writes, "A scholar assuming an autonomous model of the moral life would most likely focus on Habibi's arguments that seem to resist her local conditions. This was essentially what caused my faux pas with her."[31]

Confining the concept of participation to politicized resistance produces at least two kinds of analyses. First, an Islamist woman can be seen as deficient in womanhood because she does not meet what is expected of her: to naturally desire to be free from her limitations. As Janet Afary writes, "Women like them are classic examples of what Fromm and the Frankfurt School called authoritarian personalities . . . individuals, who, fearing the insecurities that the freedoms of modernity bring, seek to escape from their anxiety by joining authoritarian movements."[32] Because dissent against authority is believed to be innate in all women, all Iranian women are expected to have predictably similar desires when male authority is absent; that is, inside every Islamist woman in Iran is a potential awakening to become a non-Islamist. Had the 1979 revolution not happened in Iran, they would naturally choose not to be Islamists as they are today. They would choose to keep their Islam in the privacy of their homes. Until then, the Islamist woman can be thought of only as complacent because she is, in essence, a carrier of male authority over women. She is an instrument of her own oppression and the oppression of other women.

This framework positions an Islamist woman in a double bind. She is either deficient or ill-fated for not wanting to be in positions of publicly visible authority or held suspect if she so desires for her association with those we have come to know as the enemy of the free world. Through this lens, Ma'ede and her friends would be considered failures, wrong sorts of people, insufficiently self-governing and individuated. They fail to reject the invisible male-centered ideology that has taken hold of their entire being, which they themselves could not see, but I, as a researcher, could. In the context of but not unique to Iran, the Islamist woman then continues to remain blind until and unless she enters a "new self-consciousness."[33]

Signs of this new self-consciousness may come in the form of bargaining with patriarchy or participating in purposeful subversive work, which brings me to my second point. Another kind of analysis produced out of this framework is to look for these signs of new self-consciousness out of the ethnographic experience, a deductive top-down approach. Nahid's attempt to put on makeup at the gathering in the park; women beautifying themselves by wearing dresses and shorter coats; women debating their teacher about marriage, learning English, or laughing at jokes about men can all be read as signs of a hidden desire to be autonomous. This analytical take assumes desires are fixed states and are not part of whole spectrum of desires that compete with one another. Thus, in the context of the howzevi, this analysis disregards other complicated aspects of their lives, which I illustrate in the following chapters.

The framework of politicized resistance underlines contemporary Iranian feminist discourse, and rightly so because countless Iranians have had to live in exile and women's rights have been transformed drastically since 1979. It helps us understand those who seek to break away from any status quo. However, it prevents us from understanding the women of this book.

FROM THE GROUND UP

The usefulness of a theoretical explanation depends on how it is deployed, either inductively or deductively or both, in order to produce different kinds of analyses. Prioritizing the interlocutors' experience and staying true to the totality of ethnographic accounts on the ground will produce an explanation that is different from looking for specific instances to support an already existing theory. That is, receiving information is a different experience from looking for or expecting specific information. A prior commitment to feminism produces the latter. My ethnographic work, however, focused on inviting the howzevi to teach me about themselves and their education.

There are scholars who choose similar theoretical approaches to women in Iran—those who develop propositions from the ground up, whose approaches are more in line with the purpose of this book. They shift the focus to providing context to the varied conditions of women, prioritizing the women's perceptions of their work and bringing these into conversation around the overall discourse on Iranian women, women in the Middle East, and women in Islam. Of these, there are studies that complicate the compliance-resistance paradigm by way of historical analysis and localizing the objectives of transformations. In a study of written work at the turn of the century, Afsaneh Najmabadi traces the development of the "educated housewife" and argues for a more profound understanding of transformations as not just emancipatory but also regulatory or disciplinary. In a later work, Najmabadi argues for a reconfiguration of the ways in which Iranianness is thought of. For as much as secular feminists have worked to undermine the government with great strides, Najmabadi puts forth the contribution of Islamist women. She asserts that the "muddled" hybridization of both groups of women working on common ground issues is advantageous for women. In this complex relationship, both groups are able to work together.[34]

The political discourse on the status of women in twentieth-century Iran is Parvin Paidar's focus. Specific to this research, Paidar shows that the state plays a significant role in establishing a link between notions of gender and nation through policies affecting women and families. By recognizing women's participation in both formal and informal social networks, she demonstrates that women have power in various spheres and networks. She points out that when research focuses solely on formal power structures, other types of participation are bound to be overlooked. Roksana Bahramitash looks at way the Iranian government mobilized the majority of women as volunteers, which paved the way for future changes. She shows that nationwide literacy campaigns mobilized women in great numbers, and as a result women who had no access to education under the previous secular regime became literate.[35]

Grounded analysis is a marker of many prerevolution ethnographies of Iran from the 1970s. In particular, these seek to develop an understanding of women's experiences with Islamized spaces. Mary Hegland and Erika Friedl, who did ethnographic fieldwork in the rural areas of Iran in the late 1970s, problematize public-private roles when analyzing the status of women. They blur the difference. Hegland conducted ethnographic research among women in Aliabad and demonstrates the significant role of women in the political process, where women traders were expected to be politically active and wives of political figures made their presence known in social networks. "By maintaining social interaction with enemy factions, women could facilitate reproachment later," Hegland writes.[36] Friedl provides several examples of women's political orchestration within and outside the domestic space, from a fight over the operation of a flour mill, to a teacher's refusal to comply with a new order, to bride price negotiations. "A woman's political acuity and power are partly a function of her husband's (father's, sons') political standing.... In turn, however, a politically astute ... woman will use her network of relatives ... to empower her husbands or sons, thereby broadening her own power base," she writes.[37] Anne Betteridge, who conducted fieldwork in Shiraz in the late 1970s, shows that women dominate local pilgrimage shrines.[38] For this reason, the practice of visiting them is held suspect. But it is also valued and necessary since shrines are sites where both men and women seek help from saints.

In the 1990s, Zahra Kamalkhani and Azam Torab looked closely at women's participation in the *jaleseh*, the neighborhood religious meeting group. It became a transformative space for women after the revolution. Kamalkhani's ethnography on women's religious participation in ritual performance and Islamic revivalism in the city of Shiraz shows that women's participation provides opportunities for forming new religious identities.[39] Torab, who spent time with predominantly lower middle-class women who participated in Islamic rituals in south Tehran argues that persons are not bound by gender constructs.[40] Through an analysis of over seventy rituals and religious gatherings, Torab demonstrates that gender construction is inherently in flux and vague.

Arzoo Osanloo writes that Iranian women have been talking about human rights as locally conceptualized since the mid-1990s.[41] She contextualizes women's conceptions of rights as influenced by other factors that they experience around them, as these rights are intertwined with local practices and regulations.

She shows that although these rights hint at liberal values, they are localized in application and definition. For the Iranian women she conducted research with, Islam, not liberal values, authenticates equal footing with men.

THE ETHNOGRAPHIC OBJECTIVE

My contribution to this body of work comes from what my work does not do as much as what it offers. As an anthropologist, I do not make a case for what takes place cognitively or what individual intentions are. I avoid writing on motivations like selfishness, vanity, or the intent to manipulate or deceive others because I simply do not know what goes on in someone else's thoughts at any given moment. Instead, I assume all of these and all sorts of other motivations to be part of social interactions that are always in motion. In other words, the women, with all kinds of motivations, are participants in activities couched in a set of continuous social relations between themselves and the world around them. The closest thing to describing motivations here is that I explain the role of Islamic teachings in terms of what constitutes their common sense or logic.

Further, this book does not aim to verify and evaluate models of analysis. For instance, I neither predict nor interpret how the Iranian government makes decisions or responds, or how it has conceived of its citizenry. Shirin Saeidi's work is of great import here. Saeidi investigates everyday encounters to make a case for the way the Iranian government is pushed "toward a balancing act to pacify its female population." Her focus is on how the government produces different kinds of citizenship—"citizens who cross, abide, and [at times] manipulate the state's formal boundaries."[42] Additional important research concerned with women and governance is Nazanin Shahrokni's distinct work on state policies after the Iran-Iraq War and gender-segregated spaces. She develops her own theory on how the state's mode of regulation on gender segregation, from prohibition to provision, has also resulted in a discursive shift—from protecting women according to Islamic morality to protecting women's rights and safety along the lines of secular liberal citizenship.[43]

Neither of these is what I have set out to do. This book is an ethnography about people and possibilities—that is, what howzevi women do with themselves and each other in the context of their Islamic education. The work to describe these involved what Renato Rosaldo referred to as "deep hanging out," or research work that required the spatial practices meant for interpersonal relationships.[44] More importantly, it is not a study *of* the howzevi. Rather, I learned *from* them by way of repeated visits, collaboration, observation, conversation, apprenticeship, and friendship.

My writing is descriptive and interpretive; thus it details processes, relationships, situations, systems, and people. Processes point at what is of value.

Relationships tell us what people do for and with each other. Situations provide
context that is specific to a setting and interpretation of histories. Systems inform
us of logics in operation, and a description of people teaches us how they constitute and reconstitute these logics. As I explain further, this work develops newly
learned concepts from those I spent time with and elaborates on existing ones
from previous research.

Critique, therefore, is a necessary component of detailing processes, relationships, situations, systems, and people in these chapters. It is embedded in the
context of the women's Islamic philosophies and teachings. One such example
of critique is the exclusionary nature of the social interactions in the seminaries, which contradicts the work of khod shenasi. In order for this critique to be
recognized, it must be located in the phenomenon that made it possible. Without
positioning critique in its particular, we are left with only one kind of learning
from research: how others are wrong.

Good ethnographic writing, which includes critique as an essential component, is dependent on showing possibilities that are an invitation to return the
gaze onto the audience in contemplation of their conditions. These possibilities
include the positive, the negative, and those in-between. This is part of anthropology's tradition. Therefore, rather than being concerned with representation,
deduction, or motivation, my ethnographic work is grounded in the telling of
possibilities. It shows that possibilities in one place can help us think about different possibilities elsewhere in a deep and meaningful way.

Finally, what I write in the following chapters is not a representation of all howzevi or a prediction of what might happen to them. It applies only to the women
I spent time with in Iran as examples of what was and continues to be possible
among them. My ethnographic examples and analyses are only for the moments I
share. As I noted earlier, I witnessed violence and experienced extremely difficult
situations during my fieldwork, not from the women themselves but from pro-
government and government actors. Time and again these moments reminded
me of the precarity of my situation. But I made a conscious decision to write
about this elsewhere so I can center the narrative around the howzevi, away from
centering it on myself. Therefore, what I write here is not meant to represent all
of what I experienced during my fieldwork.

THE USE OF CATEGORIES AND INDIGENOUS
AND ANTHROPOLOGICAL THEORIES

I approach this writing as if I were introducing one group of friends to another—
the howzevi women I lived with in Iran and those who are interested in meeting
them. To do this successfully, I needed to know what to call the women. Like the

scholars I have mentioned, I cannot escape this problem of classification. I use the word *howzevi*, the phrase *religiously conservative women*, or what they called themselves and those around them: *mazhabi*. The latter comes with a negative connotation, especially when used interchangeably with *hezbollahi* by antigovernment Iranians. These categories and labels have become a foil to Iranians who consider themselves modern and create strong reactions among them.[45]

Loosely defined, a mazhabi or hezbollahi is someone who is religiously conservative and often supports the government—more specifically, the institution of Vilayet-e Faqih, the Guardianship of the Islamic jurist. Though the women referred to themselves as mazhabi in this sense, those who are antigovernment labeled them as such to communicate to others that the women are antifreedom, whatever this may mean. As my friends in north Tehran have said, "Mazhabi people have ruined our country." Iranians in the diaspora share a similar sentiment about them.

The howzevi I spent time with did not see themselves as people who have destroyed Iran, however. They saw themselves as liberating Iran from Western imperialism and trying to create a society that will cultivate piety, goodness, and justice. Therefore, I use *mazhabi* in this way, not in the way we have come to tie religious conservatism to blind following. I also use *mazhabi* in the context of their history of exclusion as the previous ruling class deemed their way of life a burden to modernization.

In what follows, I use congruent theories to help explain what I have learned from my time with howzevi women. Saba Mahmood's work on cultivating self-piety is useful for explaining the howzevi's religious practices. Mahmood argues that agency is not only about resistance to some hegemonic power. Agency is also about committing oneself to practices that appear to be constraining in order to achieve a larger but less apparent objective. These practices and objectives sometimes appear unrelated to each other. As it stands, however, Mahmood's ethnographic account implies that bodily practices are or can be completely internalized. She writes, "Bodily form ... serves as the developable means ... through which certain kinds of ethical and moral capacities are attained."[46] I contribute to Mahmood's framing of agency in two important ways. First, I illustrate how Islamic bodily practices among the howzevi are not internalized in their totality. I do so by connecting ordinary everyday encounters, sensations, and experiences in my analysis, and I consider other aspects of human interaction such as the role of timing, play, and humor in cultivating the Muslim self, which Mahmood does not account for.

Second, I prioritize the women's indigenous philosophies as my attempt to decolonize expectations on what theorizing human interaction must look like because, in order for me to effectively make this contribution, I first have to situate what howzevi women do in what they speak of. One is the concept of *nafs* or *khod*, or the self, in *haraka jawhariyya*, or essential motion, toward becoming the *ensan-e kamel*, or the Ideal Person. The other, tied to the first, is the concept of khod she-nasi, or self-knowing. I provide an explanation of each later on.

Additionally, I draw on other anthropological theories that are relational and processual. The howzeh elmiyeh is composed of women whose levels of expertise range from novice to expert. The howzeh education, therefore, is an apprentice-ship, a movement from the periphery to the center, both of which are constantly shifting. The incoming students gain the knowledge and skill required to move toward full participation in the howzeh's everyday practices from the more senior howzevi. Jean Lave's and Etienne Wanger's *situated learning* is a useful framework to help explain the women's mobility within the howzeh elmiyeh, as "commu-nities of practice . . . engaged in the generative process of producing their own future."[47] In following Lave's position on cognition, learning is not limited to what takes place inside someone's head. Thus, as I've noted, I don't make a case for what takes place cognitively among the howzevi. On the point of cognition, Lave writes, "'Cognition' observed in everyday practice is distributed—stretched over, not divided among—mind, body, activity and culturally organized settings (which include other actors)."[48] Through situated learning, learning is seen as a long-term relationship between individuals, their position, and participation.

My use of indigenous and anthropological theories overlap. Actions are inevi-tably picked up as markers for others to decipher in unexpected ways. This lack of predictability makes belongingness an unending process. I position the instabil-ity of belonging in Martin Heidegger's work on *dwelling*; in particular its relation-ship to mortality.[49] Working off of Gilles Deleuze and Felix Guattari, João Biehl and Peter Locke argue that human beings are not fixed in place. Our work with others and ourselves is always unfinished. They refer to this as the *anthropology of becoming*. The unfinishedness of the human subject as always under construction, or "in the midst of social life within asymmetries and constraints,"[50] is a useful paradigm to think about transformations when bodily practices are not com-pletely internalized. The concept of unfinishedness resonates with the women's philosophical outtakes influenced by Mulla Sadra, a seventeenth-century Islamic philosopher. Mulla Sadra argued that *haraka jawhariyya*, or essential motion, consisted of "an ongoing project of the self"[51] and that "all existent, except God, are in the process of becoming."[52] Haraka jawhariyya, like Biehl's and Locke's becoming, is open-ended and incomplete and takes place in the middle. The howzevi are, in essence, always unfinished.

To do this introduction successfully, it is also important that I lay the ground-work of clarifying assumptions that might be made about commonalities. The notion of self is an important common ground. But we differ in our ideas of what constitutes the self, or "the architecture of the self."[53] I situate this difference with what the women taught me about Twelver Shi'i Islamic teachings and the philosophy of the Muslim self, a framework I consider to be the logic behind much of what they do, logic that guides them on how to view their surroundings, their position in the world, and their Islamic education. Though it did not determine their decisions, it certainly influenced them. Having this background shows us that the paradigm of autonomy, which, as I've explained, sees the self as the source of moral order, cannot account for the howzevi's educative experiences. Setting the introduction in this manner is critical in our attempt to understand how they belabor creating and re-creating an Islamic society, one that is guided by the laws derived from the Qur'an and by the morals of the Prophet Mohammad and his household.

THE WORK OF KHOD SHENASI

The howzevi frequently used the term khod shenasi when explaining the reasons for why they decided to become part of the women's howzeh elmiyeh. Khod she-nasi is one's personal endeavor toward self-awareness or self-knowing in order to create a spiritual nearness to the divine, a kind of "seeing" of God that takes place when a person attempts to answer existential questions about themselves. This overall attempt is called *ma'rifat en-nafs*. To journey within the self, to scrutinize the self ultimately leads to the knowledge of the divine.[54] The work of khod she-nasi, which I use interchangeably with self-knowing moving forward, is a science all on its own. It is based on the Qur'an and the traditions of the Prophet Moham-mad, both of which translate to the study of Islamic ethics and Jurisprudence.[55]

The foundation of Islamic teachings for the howzevi is embedded in the rec-ognition of the oneness of God, or *tawhid*. God is singled out as the creator of all creations, the only one worthy of worship. There is no consideration of self without situating it in its relationship to God. Since the source of self is God, the idea of self begins with God and ends with God. The purpose of life, then, is to worship God. This life, therefore, is a means to an end. This is expressed in the saying "he who knows himself knows his Lord." As to why God created human beings to worship is an aspect of self-knowing that cannot be explained with words because it is assumed that human beings cannot explain everything. These types of knowledge were relegated as part of the Hidden knowledge or the Secret, and were perhaps more experiential than represented by words.

The Nafs, Ruh, and Qalb

The work of khod shenasi is, first and foremost, an acknowledgement that the women conceptualize themselves and others as constituted by many layers of selves. The English word *self* cannot capture the complexity of what this entails.[56] The concept of many selves or a layered self is not unique to the howzevi or to Muslims in general. For instance, the fact we speak of self-control implies that we recognize many degrees of awareness, or the presence of a self that controls another self.[57] In Islamic thought, human beings are constituted by a *ruh, qalb,* and *nafs.*

Of the three, the ruh, translated as the spirit or soul, remains elusive or difficult to explain. What is known from Qur'anic text is that the nature of the soul is an *'amr,* a will of power or command from God, and by default it recognizes God as the source of all creation. Meaning the soul has no other disposition except to worship.

When speaking about working to improve themselves, their ways of being in the world, or problems in Iranian society, the howzevi used *khod* when speaking in Persian, and they used the word *nafs* when speaking about Islamic ethics and Islamic text in Arabic. These terms were used interchangeably to mean self, but I will use the word *khod,* constituted by a greater and lesser self, to stay as close as possible to the women's usage.

What remains a divine mystery is where the soul, ruh, ends and where the self, khod, begins. Whether they are separate entities or if the latter is a product of the former and the body remains unresolved. Thus, it is part of the hidden or secret knowledge. Like the ruh, the original disposition of the khod, or *fitrah,* is to worship God. This disposition can be described as a passive state; God is nearer to the human being than their body's physiological lifeline, the jugular vein.[58] This knowing of and recognition of God is considered the baseline existence of the khod. In other words, human beings, and all creations for that matter, worship, consciously or not. This self with the disposition to worship God, which I now refer to as the Original Self, is called *khod-e asil.* This is the Muslim self. To freely allow the khod in its original form to worship without any deterrence or distraction is considered *freedom.* Preventing the Original Self from doing so is antifreedom, a form of bondage or slavery, as I explain later.

Aside from being godly, however, and unlike the soul, the khod is also inherently forgetful.[59] It is easily distracted from the worship of God by what I call *lesser tendencies.* Two of the more pronounced lesser tendencies are indulgence in experiencing pleasure and in seeing oneself as the best of all creations. These lesser tendencies have the potential to eventually overcome a person to the point that they become disconnected from God. The Umayyad ruler Yazid and his men would be an example of figures in Islamic history that allowed their lesser tendencies to overcome their being. Yazid killed members of the Prophet Mohammad's family and ordered the decapitation of the Prophet Mohammad's grandson Husayn, because he had seen Husayn as a threat to his power. The "wickedness" of those who crucified Jesus Christ would be another example of people who nurtured these lesser tendencies in Christian scripture. The knights and soldiers playing dice under the crucifix for the robe of Jesus Christ is one of the many scenes of the crucifixion that depicts what happens to people when they are engulfed by these lesser tendencies. Taking Jesus's life was not enough. There was callousness toward the suffering of death in exchange for material gain.

The concept of qalb, the heart or the spiritual seat of emotions, is easier to grasp. It is the seat of deep spiritual knowledge that nourishes the whole person. Thus, the spiritual heart mediates between the spirit and the self. The qalb can control the khod and direct the whole person to nourish the ruh.

In Two Realms

With the soul and the self in one physical body, human beings simultaneously exist in the divine realm, *alam-e bala tar*, with the presence of the everlasting divine soul, as well as in the material world, *alam-e tabiat o madeh*, through the senses of the physical body. It is in this existence in both realms that the struggle of the self to return to and preserve the Original Self, its original divine-like form, in remembrance of God, begins at birth and ends at death. It is what Islamic philosophers like Mulla Sadra refer to as the effort to become the Ideal Person, *ensan-e kamel*.

The occultation of the Twelfth Imam is an important part of this constellation because the work of self-knowing ends at death but is also about preparing for his reappearance.[60] Briefly, God prolonged the life of the Twelfth Imam and concealed him "from the eyes of men" to protect him from his enemies.[61] Someday, God will make him appear, or bring him back as the Mahdi, who will fight alongside Jesus Christ against the Antichrist in an apocalyptic battle. The Twelfth Imam, also known as the Hidden Imam, Imam Mahdi, or Al-Imam al Muntazar (the Awaited Imam), will then establish a new order the same way the Prophet Mohammad had done. Biblical texts refer to this event as the Rapture or the Second Coming of Christ.

The Twelfth Imam's arrival is always positioned in the future, inevitable but unknown. Muslims are to prepare for his arrival so they can choose the correct side in this final battle against the Antichrist. To increase the possibility of success in that future moment, Muslims are to work on bringing themselves closer to God. That is, *to continue doing* in the spirit of being mindful of God's graces and presence. Developing Shi'i Islamic sensibilities will eventually lead one to choose the right side of the battle when the time comes. I avoid using the term *waiting*, as is commonly used in the context of Al-Imam al Muntazar (The Awaited Imam), which implies that he has waiting subjects. Without further examination, the concept of waiting implies a passive state for the one waiting. But, as I've explained, an active yet imperfect form of labor actually marks this waiting.

The idea of difference between all creations plays a significant role in this struggle. Khanum-e Yasseri, a senior howzevi, explained:

> We believe that the worth of people will depend on their spirit not their body, not their sex. . . . Our spirit doesn't know any sex. It is [already] equal for both men and women. The value belongs to the spirit, not the body. . . . We can make a way to Allah and can be near to Allah. . . . On the other hand, we believe that there is a necessity to have some difference in the material world as you can see this difference between animals and [between] plants. . . . You can see these differences between human beings, too. It is the necessity of the material world.[62]

Difference, in this context, is a sign of God's omnipotence, a necessity so that creations can identify and recognize each other.[63] The senses serve as a channel between the body and the material world, but it is also through the senses that the khod slowly becomes cloaked from remembering God. These layers must be peeled away through the work of self-knowing in order to return to the Original Self.[64] What one does with the difference that exists between God's creations in the material world is what makes returning to the khod-e asil the greatest challenge in life.

Freedom

The material world is important only to the extent of fulfilling basic needs to survive, to recognize other souls, and to establish justice. But a human being's movement through the world must not be based solely on the desire to experience pleasure through the senses. This, the women said, can lead a person to become addicted to what their senses experience in the material world. Without the purposeful effort to remember God in every action, a person slowly forfeits their Original Self's freedom to worship. The lesser tendencies will then overpower their purpose in the world. The pleasured senses eventually become the chains of antifreedom. An attachment to the material world takes place, and then an addiction to this attachment develops. The person will eventually desire more of this attachment. At this state, the self becomes *na khod*, the self of not oneself. Na khod is the self that feels like the Original Self but is actually blind to the Original Self's remembrance of.

It is at this point that human beings are thought to become slaves to their senses, and the attachments developed out of these attachments become a form of worship. This state of being, marked by stagnation and a feeling of emptiness, is considered the opposite of freedom. Motahhari, a contemporary Islamic scholar whom the howzevi frequently cited, considered the accumulation of wealth as the beginning of moral deterioration, often described as the dichotomy between slavery and freedom.[65] Greed is framed as a form of slavery because a greedy person loses his sense of self with the accumulation of wealth. This version of the self is then caught in the neediness of money and therefore loses its freedom to worship God. This self misrecognizes the means, the material world, as an end. God is eventually forgotten in all experiences, and the material world in due time becomes God.

Freedom, as I've explained, is framed as an unhindered return to the divine-like Original Self in the surrender or losing oneself within God, the source of its being. This return is marked by a freedom from material attachments, a state of being referred to as *zuhd*. Doing the work of self-knowing strengthens the power of reason, or *'aql*, and diminishes the lesser tendencies. The labor of how to return to the Original Self is the fundamental question in Islamic ethics. The concern for this struggle is the essence of the Qur'an, which serves as a guide on how to strengthen the disposition to worship God. The goal is to co-opt the tendency to forget to an advantage—that is, to forget the lesser tendencies and remember only God. In this state, a person is considered to have returned to the Original Self.

This ideal trajectory of simultaneously existing in both the material and divine realms is, of course, different from the actual experience. It is a lifelong struggle that involves, again, recuperating and protecting the Original Self. The work of self-knowing is not specific to the howzevi. Ethnographic work has been done on the cultivation of piety among family members in Shi'i families in Iran. In Rose Wellman's ethnography, family members emphasize the importance of learning about the origin of the self in both spiritual and reproductive terms. She writes, "In Iran, the person is composed of a pure, moral inside (bāten) and a corruptible, appetite driven outside (zāher)."[66] Her interlocutors put forth that in order to understand Islam, questions such as "Where were you? Where are you? and Where are you going?" must be asked. In a society that is rife with problems, kinship is to be protected. Wellman demonstrates that family members engage in pious acts such as praying and visiting kin as a way to do so. She writes, "Individuals seek to create not only virtuous selves but also virtuous families through pious and relational acts of prayer and food sharing." The family is the location of pious cultivation, and food plays a significant role. She writes, "It is an agent of transformation and a vehicle for channeling divine blessings, whether directed inward to the pure family core."[67]

Islamic education plays an important role in finding out how to properly do khod shenasi. One way to learn is to become students in the howzeh elmiyeh to learn the various Islamic sciences, as the women of this book have done, and the more challenging path toward this self-work is to become a mujtahideh because of the heavy burden of responsibility the position requires. I return to this point in chapters 3 and 4. Regardless of how and where the knowledge is gained, the objective is to develop this kind of self-awareness. More importantly, it is in that chosen context of learning that the howzevi's personal effort will manifest itself and will naturally be challenged and tested. In the case of the howzevi, this context includes the backdrop of developing education programs that aim to support socioreligious norms conducive to self-knowing, striving toward the ideals of Shi'i womanhood, confronting different forms of exclusion, and protecting a social, religious, and political project against the United States and its allies.

This concept of self is threaded throughout the chapters discursively, because Maryam and the many others conceptualized the self and their work in this manner, and their being in the world is, more than not, marked with struggle. I weave this throughout the analytical turning points of the chapters to remind us that there is a local indigenous logic of operation that places Islamic teachings and practices at the center.

FIELDWORK

This work is based on fifteen months of participant observation in the Islamic Republic of Iran with over twenty-one women from 2010 to 2011, and from my experiences during our initial contact in the summer of 2008. I have written elsewhere in more detail about my experience doing ethnographic fieldwork with the howzevi. For the sake of brevity, here I provide only an inventory of how I conducted this research. Of twenty-one women, five were students of Ayatollah Ali Khamenei, the supreme leader of Iran, and Ayatollah Sadegh Larijani, the chief justice of Iran, at the Dars-e Kharij level. The twenty-one women were from three groups of howzevi; the women of Madraseh Ali, students of Ayatollah Khamenei, and the women of Howzeh-ye Kowsar. Of all the women I interacted with, over twenty identified themselves as reservists or active duty members of one of the branches of the Basij-e Mostaz'afin, or Mobilization of the Oppressed, the volunteer paramilitary organization overseen by the Islamic Revolutionary Guards Corps (IRGC). I lived in the neighborhood of Pirouzi, in south Tehran, for nine months as a neighbor to five howzevi. The rest of the women lived in neighboring districts of central and south Tehran. For the remaining months, I lived in north Tehran below the home of Tooran Valimourad, a woman who worked closely with Maryam Behrouzi and served as a signatory to Etelaf-e Islami Zanan, the Coalition of Muslim Women.[68] Although she was not part of my research group, she provided valuable insight on my research.

During my fieldwork, the women and I visited family and took care of children together. We traveled, observed local pilgrimages, and attended prayers, religious ceremonies, English classes, doctor appointments, social gatherings, and other everyday activities. In the course of spending time with the women, I collected about 140 questionnaires, which were used only to gauge my direction while in Iran. I interviewed key figures from both conservative and reformist camps, including Ayatollah Mousavi Bojnurdi, the head of the Research Institute of Imam Khomeini and the Islamic revolution. In the city of Esfahan, I visited Ayatollah Morteza Mastejabi, who, in his younger years, had been close to Mohammad Mosaddegh.

Five months into the fieldwork, I was given permission to do participant observation in Madraseh Ali and Howzeh-ye Kowsar. I participated in the classroom at Howzeh-ye Kowsar as well as in the social interactions among howzevi, staff, and teachers at both Madraseh Ali and Howzeh-ye Kowsar. From this, I observed and recorded about thirty-five *mobaheseh*, or disputation sessions. Many of our interactions were audio recorded with permission, especially the rituals and ceremonies we attended together. Additionally, I devoted one night a week to distributing food to the homeless around Maydan-e Shoush with an NGO for five months, an activity that allowed me to draw some relationships among the activities of howzevi women and other groups in Tehran. Spending time in different parts of the city in this manner allowed me to ask those who were not a part of my research about my research, the howzevi, and the institution of the howzeh.

As I noted in the preface, even though I had completed the advanced-level Persian language program at the Dehkhoda Institute, I was concerned about the limitation of language throughout my time in Iran. To make sure I was documenting as accurately as possible, I made it a practice to ask the women I spent time with for clarification when needed. I also asked Persian language speakers for help in translating parts of audio and written work. Unexpectedly, the frustrations of not having the slightest knowledge of Persian at first facilitated my physical movement among and across gendered spaces where women would normally not be allowed to move about freely. My time would eventually be sought by the howzevi on the basis of speaking English with me.

Sara and Maryam introduced me to other howzevi: their colleagues, former classmates, and heads of institutes and offices. I met women at the Kharij level, women doing their master's degrees, and those finishing their doctoral studies. I requested their time and space to teach me about themselves and whatever else they wanted to share, including matters that were difficult for me to understand, or difficult for me to accept. On this, I am cognizant of protecting the women's identities and their private lives. As a foreigner, I was a burden on many in a way that risked their standing in their community. For this reason, I have given each howzevi here a different name, and I have written vignettes in a way that do not make them easily recognizable. I have made three exceptions: Khanum-e

Alosvand, Khanum-e Safiri, and Khanum-e Rasti, who all held public positions of leadership at the time. I use the actual institutional names of Jami'at Al-Zahra, Madraseh Ali, and prerevolution religious institutions because these are iconic spaces in the Islamic Republic. However, I have used the assumed name Howzeh-ye Kowsar because it was at the time a smaller institution like the hundreds of localized howzeh in Iran. In the passing of a decade, and with the contentious social and political shifts in Iran, these details actually matter more than they ever did.

OUTLINE OF THE CHAPTERS

This book is divided into three sections, with a prelude before each one. Each prelude is a continuation of the previous one about one event: an English class in Tehran. The theme of each one descriptively sets the tone for each section of the book. Part I contains chapters that describe how howzevi women have experienced the establishment of the women's howzeh elmiyeh after the 1979 revolution, as well as its organizational transformations. In the first chapter, I provide accounts from women who would be considered the first generation of howzeh students after the revolution. Positioned in the Islamic concept of self, the work of khod shenasi, and sociopolitical experience of exclusion, we begin to understand the logic of their continued efforts to use their Islamic education to strengthen the Islamic Republic. The second chapter focuses on what happens when the objective of Islamically educating women moves beyond solely educating oneself on spirituality and into producing graduates who will do the work of preserving a society that fosters that work. For instance, a woman's Islamic education could no longer be exclusive to becoming a mujtahideh. It needed to be an education with practical use. Using ethnographic lessons from senior howzevi, the third chapter examines probable explanations for why there were very few mujtahideh at the time, after three decades of having unprecedented access to the women's howzeh. In doing so, I look at other forms of success, those that are informed by the work of khod shenasi, in their Islamic education, most important of which is the opportunity to create and develop social circles.

Part II of this book contains the basic philosophical underpinnings of the women's practices that tell us what is of value for them. It is a continued discussion on their rubric for success. By implication, we begin to make sense of why, out of the thousands of howzevi graduates annually since the 1980s, very few have taken up visible positions of leadership. The women I spent time with expressed disinterest in this.

A close look at what the howzevi did with others to do the work of self-knowing is the focus of the fourth chapter. This includes practices that I refer to as *anonymity* in order to cultivate virtues like sincerity and humility. I analyze the consequential totalities to explore what the black chador accomplished for them in this context. Though the attempt was expectedly imperfect, it was the kind of work that could render them as credible sources of Islamic knowledge. The practice of disputation, which was often marked by play, is the focal point of chapter 5. Here, mobaheseh, a standard practice and pedagogical approach in the howzeh, was the antithesis of the practice of wearing the black chador and other behaviors associated with it. In this chapter, we get a glimpse of the women's educative training and the personal connectedness that is developed in this space.

The final section of this book, Part III, contains the ethnographic chapters of howzevi women's individual experiences that make up the social life of the women's howzeh elmiyeh. In chapter 6, I tell the story of two unmarried women, Farideh and Zaynab, who were at the early stages of their education. Both spoke greatly of politics and religion, motivational teachers, discovering their interests, and how they wanted to use their Islamic education to create an understanding between Iranians who found themselves on opposite sides of the sociopolitical spectrum. They experienced different levels of rejection, and they responded to these in different ways. By examining the way they addressed their challenges, we learn about the social norms around them—in other words, the expectations women have of each other. But we also learn that their responses to these challenges are relatable. These interactions finally inform us that these social norms become malleable within the bounds of Islamic teachings and practices.

In chapter 7, I look at the story of Maryam and what khod shenasi looked like in her life as a young woman, as she became a wife and mother while trying to do her best in her studies. Being meticulous in her practices was part of her work of remembering God, but it also inevitably became a marker of the kind of woman she was, one that was working hard to become more knowledgeable in her Islamic practices. Situated in her family's practices and interest in studying the Islamic sciences, her story highlights her labor to overcome the difficulties of taking up the study of Islamic jurisprudence at Madraseh Ali both as a newcomer and, later, as a new mother. It shows that her mobility was attached to other kinds of constraints. One focus of attention is her family's consequential role in supporting her decision.

The final chapter is about the work of howzevi women against what they called the Soft War, Jang-e Narm, against the Islamic Republic by the United States and its allies. I provide an ethnographic account of what deliberations between howzevi women look like in their attempt to work on strategies in this context. I describe what for them constituted the Soft War in relation to khod shenasi, especially upon discovering that it was being reframed by forces they believed to be doing the work of destabilizing Iranian society. I explore the way the women saw

themselves and their education in this context and detail the content and logic of
their response. I finally conclude the book with a coda of future considerations.

NOTES

1. For these categories, see Sakurai, "Women's Empowerment," 32–58.
2. Ingold, *Lines*, 44, citing Fuchs 1986. Ingold takes note of an artwork made by Richard Long in 1967 entitled *A Line Made by Walking*.
3. Harding, "Representing Fundamentalism," 374.
4. Human Rights Watch, "Iran: Authorities Defiant," 2012.
5. Said, *Covering Islam*, 51.
6. Fayyaz and Shirazi, "Good Iranian," 53–72.
7. Bakhshayishi, *Ten Decades*, 31–33; Zaman, *The Ulama*. 105.
8. Fischer, "The Rhythmic Beat," 497–543.
9. Sener, "NES Chair Ghamari-Tabirizi"; Jaiswal and Janssen, "IOP Staff Sent Home"; NIAC Action, "Bomb Threat."
10. Motamedi, "Iran's 'Morality Police."
11. Nafisi, "Tales of Subversion," 264; Sanasarian, *The Women's Rights*, 143.
12. Betteridge, "Muslim Women," 288.
13. Abu-Lughod, "Writing against Culture," 466–79.
14. Foucault, "What Is Enlightenment?" 34. In a Kantian sense of possibilities as "a way out," an *ausgang*. Foucault states that Kant defines the "way out" as that which typifies what we know as the Enlightenment. It is a process that liberates human beings from "immaturity."
15. Kian-Thiébaut, "From Islamization," 141.
16. Okin, *Justice, Gender*, 6–40, 134–169; Okin, "Is Multiculturalism Bad," 9–24.
17. Rajavi, "Women, Voice of the Oppressed."
18. Bignall, *Postcolonial Agency*, 3, 155-190. Bignall addresses the way agency toward difference is influenced by the Western understanding of desire, subjectivity, and history-making, and this produces implicit imperialism.; Cronin-Furman et al., "Emissaries of Empowerment."
19. Geertz, "Common Sense," 8.
20. Mahmood, *Politics of Piety*, 10.
21. Moghissi, *Populism and Feminism*, 37–53, 57–71.
22. Poya, *Women, Work*, 160.
23. Afshar, *Islam and Feminisms*, 16–17; Kian-Thiébaut, "From Islamization," 127–42; Sedghi, *Women and Politics*, 189; Tohidi, "Beyond Islamic Feminism," 18–22.
24. Afshar, *Islam and Feminisms*, 16–17.
25. Ahmed, *Women and Gender*, 66.
26. Mir-Hosseini, *Islam and Gender*, 7; Majid, "The Politics of Feminism," 322.
27. Sakurai, "Women's Empowerment," 53; Sakurai, "Shi'ite Women's Seminaries," 744; Künkler and Fazaeli, "The Life of Two," 129.
28. Fazaeli, *Islamic Feminisms*, 64, 70.
29. Afary, "Portraits of Two," 52.
30. Buccar, "Dianomy," 664.
31. Ibid, 668.
32. Afary, "Portraits of Two," 77.
33. Kian-Thiébaut, "From Islamization," 127–42; Moghissi, *Populism and Feminism*, 117.

34. Najmabadi, "Crafting an Educated," 91–125; Najmabadi, "(Un)veiling Feminism," 39.
35. Paidar, *Women and the Political*; Bahramitash, "Saving Iranian," 102, 104, 108.
36. Hegland, "Political Roles," 222.
37. Friedl, "The Dynamics," 209.
38. Betteridge, "Muslim Women," 276–89.
39. Kamalkhani, *Women's Islam*, 113-132, 179-183.
40. Torab, *Performing Islam*, 1-67.
41. Osanloo, *The Politics of Women's*, xii.
42. Saeidi, *Women and the Islamic*, 1.
43. Shahrokni, *Women in Place*, 5.
44. Clifford, "Spatial Practices," 189, citing Renato Rosaldo, 219, fn 2.
45. Wellman, *Feeding Iran*, 17, 170.
46. Mahmood, *Politics of Piety*, 148–49.
47. Lave and Wenger, *Situated Learning*, 58.
48. Lave, *Cognition in Practice*, 1.
49. Heidegger, "Being-in-the-world," 149–68.
50. Biehl and Locke, *Unfinished*, 4, 42.
51. Jambet, *The Act of Being*, 198–99, citing Mulla Sadra.
52. Ibid, 191.
53. Mahmood, "Feminist Theory," 217.
54. Shomali, *Self-Knowledge*, 18.
55. Nasr, "Part I: Religious," 21–39.
56. Qur'an Chapters 7:205 and 79:40–41. For the conceptual complexity of the nafs.
57. Nasr, "Self-Awareness," 319–20.
58. Qur'an, Chapter 50:16; this original disposition to worship God is evidenced by a momentous event called the Covenant, *al-Mithaq*, when all the souls were gathered to bear witness to God's Lordship. This verse of the Covenant is found in chapter 7:172. By experiencing al-Mithaq, the Original Self is divinelike and is influenced by reason, or *'aql*.
59. The Arabic word for humankind, *insan*, is based on the trilateral *na-sa-ya* and is shared by the verb *nisyah*, to forget.
60. In Shi'i Islam, *imam* is the honorific used for leaders of the community who have been divinely chosen to be perfect examples and lead all humanity in all aspects of life. This figure is central to Twelver and Ismaili Shi'i belief.
61. Momen, *Introduction to Shi'i Islam*, 165.
62. Khanum-e Yasseri, Qom, July 24, 2008, referenced in a conversation in 2011.
63. For more on difference, see Qur'an Chapters 30:22 and 49:13.
64. Nasr, "Self-Awareness," 320.
65. Shimamoto, "The Question of 'Self Knowledge,'" 36.
66. Wellman, *Feeding Iran*, 63.
67. Ibid., 46, 35, 61.
68. They are a group of women from both the religiously conservative and feminist groups in Iran who joined forces to change two laws in Iran around 2006 to 2007.

PART I

THE SYSTEM

—҂—

PRELUDE

Dr. Hassanpour was a professor of comparative literature at a university in Tehran who finished his doctoral studies in England. Dr. Hassanpour held a women-only English class, which took place once a week in a conference room in an institute in Arjantin Square affiliated with one of the universities in Tehran. Students were first chosen through referrals from various organizations and offices and then were invited to attend. Sara and I had just walked into the conference room. Maryam, sitting at the head of the table, was close to finishing reading from her paper. "Radical feminism is an attack on the foundation of the family and society in the end," she read in English. Some of the women in the room smiled at us as we sat across the room from the sound booth. There were thirteen women including Sara and Maryam. Two of the women held positions that directly impacted the workings of the government, while the rest worked in offices related to education and research. Khanum-e Asadollahi worked directly under President Ahmadinejad's council on women and family, and Khanum-e Molaei, a medical doctor, had just been voted in to the Islamic Consultative Assembly, the legislative body of Iran. Khanum-e Tabesh was the head of one of the institutes of Qur'anic studies and memorization in Tehran at the time. Khanum-e Moallem was a university professor of Islamic mysticism. Khanum-e Refaei was an administrator for a howzeh in Tehran, and Khanum-e Rafi was a head counselor for women university students. Khanum-e Mousavi was a civics education and Islamic philosophy teacher, and Khanum-e Amjad was a student and teacher at a howzeh. Najmeh Khanum, whose father was a cleric, was about to defend her dissertation in Islamic mysticism, Khanum-e Marashi was a doctoral student in Islamic philosophy, and Khanum-e Shojaei was a master's student conducting comparative research on the role of women in revolutions.

33

ONE

—∿—

THE REVOLUTION AND THE WOMEN'S HOWZEH ELMIYEH

ISLAMIC SCHOLARSHIP IS MEANT TO support an individual's effort in khod shenasi, the work of self-knowing through the Islamic sciences. Thus, women's participation in Islamic scholarship predates the 1979 revolution. This participation, however, did not always involve a howzeh education. While the howzeh organized by reputable Islamic scholars had been accessible to Iranian men since the 1500s, these institutions were not easily accessible to women who did not belong to a family of Islamic scholars until the 1979 revolution. In this chapter, I briefly suspend engaging the precise workings of khod shenasi in order to look closely at what gaining access to the women's howzeh elmiyeh looked like for the more senior howzevi. I explain the way a handful of them who had witnessed the revolution made sense of this access. Theirs is a narrative about exclusion. This matters on two fronts. To be excluded from easily accessing Islamic knowledge also means exclusion from gaining the necessary knowledge on the way to properly observe khod shenasi. While men had this access, women did not. Addressing their history of exclusion is also important because the howzevi, as religiously conservative Iranian women, are depicted in literature as sheltered women who, out of their boredom, were motivated to become mere accessories to their fathers and brothers who were seeking power at the time of the revolution.[1] How they were excluded from the public sphere and sociopolitical discourse in the first place is overlooked.

The following is an account of women in constant motion, of women contributing to the revolution's vision of reworking social conditions that ideally normalized and supported the work of khod shenasi, with laws derived from Islamic law and Islamic teachings. The result of this participation created paths that were previously nonexistent for many. The situation was new for them, and it was not

34

until the revolution that a daughter of a taxi driver or a fruit stand seller could embark on a fully funded path toward Islamic scholarly aspirations. This access enabled them, at the very least, to engage in discussions about Islamic law and its applicability in Iranian society.

I traveled to the city of Qom several times to speak with women about their experiences with Islamic education before the revolution. Khanum-e Alosvand was one of them. I boarded a bus for the city of Qom from Terminal-e Junoob at 9:45 a.m. The bus driver spent about forty-five minutes collecting people to get on board. Leaving Tehran, and after passing Behesht-e Zahra and Ayatollah Khomeini's tomb, a scene all too familiar slowly unfolded. The heat rose from the asphalt as the big boulders on the side of the freeway turned from gray to brown to maroon. The desert itself spoke as if I were about to enter a realm with a different set of rules all together, ones I might be completely unaware of without first trespassing them unintentionally. The last time I had gone to Qom, I had made the mistake of sitting in the front, behind the short staircase to the door, as I had been doing on my trips to other cities. The elderly men sitting behind this seat had been quick to signal me away to the back with frowns and strong hand waves. I was told later that this was unusual in 2011 in Tehran, but it continued to be commonplace in Qom. After several bus trips to the city, I became more aware that women sat with women and men with men unless they were traveling as a family. Some women on the bus wore chador; some wore the plain manto, a knee-length overcoat; and some, including myself, wore what has been termed *bad hijab*—a wraparound colored scarf that would frequently slip off. An hour into the trip the bus broke down. It was intolerably hot and dry outside the bus, so we waited inside for twenty minutes until another bus arrived to pick us up. Right before arriving at the Haftod-o Do Tan Square in Qom, I, like the other women on the bus, fixed my bad hijab and wore the black chador I had kept in my bag.

This would be my third of many meetings with Khanum-e Alosvand, the head of the largest women's research center in Qom, which conducted research for various ministries, universities, howzeh, government agencies, and Marja'e Taqlid. Her assistant picked up the phone to let her know I had arrived. He instructed me to wait downstairs in the small basement library. Its doorway was lined with shoes and draped with a heavy black tarp to prevent people on the outside from seeing the women inside. Surrounded by shelves of books, women sat and worked behind cubicles and at a long desk. One of the books caught my eye: a translation of Michel Foucault's *Archaeology of Knowledge*. Journals on feminism were propped up next to it. Khanum-e Alosvand's assistant finally called the librarian to let me know she was ready for me upstairs.

The large conference table in the room where we met was still in the same place it had been the last time I'd visited. The whiteboard with a list of research topics such as domestic violence, women in the workplace, the effects of a welfare state on women, and a larger heading on responses to CEDAW (Committee on the Elimination of Discrimination against Women) had been removed since the last time I'd been in this room. Like Agha-ye Samani, who brought us tea and cookies, every person who worked on this floor was a man. Khanum-e Alosvand always wore a black chador draped to her waist or shoulders. Whenever someone knocked to enter, she pulled her chador over her head. This had not been the case previously, when we'd been downstairs in her windowless office in the basement, the size of a walk-in closet with just enough room to fit a desk, an extra chair in front of it, a potted plant near the door, and a bookshelf behind her.

I wanted to learn about the way howzevi women made sense of gaining access to Islamic education in Iran. During this visit, Khanum-e Alosvand explained that although the revolution had facilitated women's access to Islamic education, women in Iran had already had access to Islamic scholarship, evidence of which had begun to appear about a hundred years earlier. The contradiction in this statement is obvious, but we must put the explanation on hold for the moment. There are historical accounts of women's participation in decision-making councils that indicate their expertise is at the caliber of a mujtahideh, a woman who is trained to make legal decisions through independent interpretations of the Qur'an and the Sunnah. Khanum-e Alosvand also considered the possibility that some of the published work with nameless authors might have been written by women—that there were women who were considered prolific scholars but were known not to have written their names as the authors of these books. Finally, she echoed what the other howzevi and historical literature have noted: that brothers, fathers, husbands, or private tutors who were reputable in their fields of study commonly schooled girls and women in the privacy of their homes.

The question becomes, why do howzevi women hold very strong sentiments about the revolution creating this access for them if Islamic scholarship has long been made available to women? To make sense of this, I look closely at two historical manifestations of women's access: belonging to a scholarly family and the presence of the *maktab*. I start with Khadija, the Prophet Mohammad's first wife. Her effort to comfort and seek clarification for Mohammad when he received his first revelation from God through the angel Gabriel is quite telling. The task of clarifying and relaying divinely ordained text has been of interest for women throughout Islamic history for this reason. Examples following Khadija's are Fatimah, the daughter of the Prophet and wife of Ali, and her daughter Zaynab, sister of Imam Hussain. And since the seventh century, Muslim women have historically had access to advanced training in Islamic scholarship. Their presence is especially evident in the study of transmission of Hadith, a collection of sayings and daily practices of the Prophet Mohammad that serves as the main source of guidance aside from the Qur'an.

The presence of women has been considerable in Shi'i texts such as *Zanan-e Daneshmand va Raviye Hadith, Rayahayn Alshariah, Al-Dhariah, A'lam al-Nisa al-Mu'minat, Mustadrak a'yan al-Shia, Riyad al-Ulamah,* and *Al-ijazah al-Kabirah.* Mir Sayyed Hojjat Mohaved Abtahi provides a lengthy list of women scholars from the city of Esfahan in *Risheho va Jeloho-ye Teshia va Howzeh Elmiyeh-e Esfahan.*[2] These sources have a number of shared descriptive characteristics. First, the Iraqi cities of Karbala, Baghdad, and Najaf became famous as centers of Islamic scholarship with the participation of women whose expertise and accomplishments varied. Second, many women in these books were simply identified as daughters or mothers because they either did not publish or did not place their names on their written work. Finally, the majority of the women belonged to well-known families of scholars and were also somehow related to each other by marriage.

For instance, Mulla Azizullah Majlesi's daughter, whose name was not specified, wrote multiple textbooks on jurisprudent issues, especially on marginal issues. Sheikh Bahai's wife, also known as bint Sheikh Ali Minshar, the daughter of Sheikh Ali Minshar, was a prolific scholar who taught jurisprudence, Hadith, and the sciences to women.[3] Nahla Gharavi Naeeni compiled and translated 210 brief biographies in English of Shi'i women who were Hadith transmitters.[4] The compilation also makes mention of these kinship ties by marriage. Mulla Sadra's two daughters, Zubaydah and Ma'sume Qawwami Shirazi, were two of the women she included. They were both Hadith transmitters, or *Muhadith,* and memorizers of Qur'an, or *hafiz.* They also delivered Qur'anic explanations as *Mufassir,* having both studied with their father. Zubaydah eventually married Mohammad Fasawi and wrote *Sharh al Shafiyah.*[5] They had a son, Mohammad Taqi Majlesi, whose daughters also became accomplished scholars. Amina Begum was one of Mohammad Taqi Majlesi's daughters. She was married to her father's student, the scholar Mulla Saleh Mazandarani. She became a renowned scholar, having learned from first her father and then her husband. Her work includes a book of notes from her husband's *Sharh Usul Kafi.* They had a daughter who also became a well-known scholar and a granddaughter, Zaynab Begum, who also became a scholar.[6]

The biographies in these texts include women from well-known families of scholars, like women from the Majlesi, Mazandarini, Qazvini, Al-Tusi, Baha'i, Shirazi, and Ravidashti families.[7] Their fathers, uncles, brothers, or husbands would teach them at home, accompany them in scholarly circles, or invite scholars to their homes. This enabled these women to advance their levels of expertise, publish books, and subsequently have their own students. In these examples, we can see that accessibility of education applied mostly to specific Muslim women who had the means, including those who belonged to families of Islamic scholars.

The second manifestation of women's access to Islamic education was the presence of the prerevolution maktab, a school-like space where basic Islamic instruction took place in many parts of Iran. While the howzeh or higher institutions of Islamic learning, were accessible to men as early as the 1830s, the maktab for women were subjoined to many of these.[8] Four of them were well-known, two of them I highlight here.[9] Translated in English as an Islamic high school for girls in the city of Esfahan, the Maktab-e Fatimah, founded by Banu Amin, Nusrat Begum Amin al-Tujjar Esfahani (d. 1983), reached 600 students at one point.[10] Ayatollah Kazem Shariatmadari (d. 1986), who was known for his broad views, also opened a section for women in the mid-1970s in his Dar Al-Tabligh howzeh for men, where teachers taught from behind a curtain. In two years' time, it had 150 women in attendance.[11] With these two examples in mind, the existence of the maktab long before the revolution may debunk the claim that the newly formed government provided women access to the howzeh elmiyeh. To understand the howzevi's sentiments necessitates a closer look at the maktab before 1979.

First, the maktab as an entity was not held at the same esteemed level as a howzeh.[12] The locals, laypeople, or religious people with minimal Islamic training generally built or supervised the maktab. The term *maktab* for women was used in the context of preliminary attempts at organizing a group for the purpose of giving and receiving lessons.[13] A maktab did not have an established program of study or supervision, and classes were held in a temporary location with very little administrative structure. In the villages, the local clergy managed the maktab for men as a school-like setting where students, children and adults, learned to read Arabic and to read and discuss interpretations of the Qur'an.[14] Therefore, the maktab was an institution that struggled to define its significance when the shah's nationwide literacy programs privileged science and mathematics.

Second, assuming that the maktab had been accessible to women since the 1830s, the maktab must be imagined in the pre-1979 social context where religiously conservative families conceived of the public space as unsafe for their women,[15] especially in the aftermath of Reza Shah's unveiling program in 1936.[16] Third, this deterrence must be combined with the scarcity of the maktab in the different regions. There were only about 340 kilometers of paved roads and railways combined in early twentieth-century Iran, where donkeys and mules were the common mode of transportation. Highway robbers and tribal bandits concerned travelers.[17] Thus, access to the maktab, even those existing in a nearby larger town, may have been limited for many.

Fourth, the more prominent maktab, like the one mentioned in Esfahan, must be examined in a way that accounts for the possible challenging realities of women from non-scholarly families. Most girls and women, especially in the rural areas, did not know how to read and came from families whose labor, such as carpet weaving and harvesting crops in the vicinity of the home, was a necessity. In some cases, girls were taught to read, but they were not taught to write, so as to limit their access to communication.[18] These were possible obstacles to girls and women who were kept at home before the revolution.

By looking closely at these forms of access, we begin to understand the howzevi women's logic for giving credit to the revolution for their access to Islamic education. A young Iranian girl from a village, small town, or impoverished neighborhood of Tehran did not have this privilege. These historical accounts do not negate the possibility that women of less privileged backgrounds have had access to some form of Islamic schooling. However, their general absence in these accounts further reinforces Khanum-e Alosvand's explanation that the 1979 revolution paved the way for women's access to advanced levels of Islamic education nationwide.

FROM BANU AMIN TO REVOLUTIONARY WOMEN

While Khanum-e Alosvand recognized that there were other maktab for girls in Iran before the revolution, she set apart Banu Amin's Maktab-e Fatimah as having had the most impact throughout Iran. Khanum-e Alosvand proposed that this maktab set off a dramatic shift in women's Islamic education from taking place in private scholarly circles to a formally recognized space of religious learning for girls. Banu Amin's authorship was well received in the men's howzeh beyond the cities of Esfahan and Qom. Khanum-e Alosvand hypothesized that perhaps this shift was made possible because her books were well-known in the men's howzeh and, more importantly, renowned scholarly men traveled from distant places to learn from Banu Amin.

Banu Amin's work with women in Esfahan influenced Maktab-e Towhid, which was established in the early 1970s for women in Qom. Although it was not a complete howzeh, its organizational structure and systematic operations, including its classes and pedagogical approaches to teaching and learning, were like those of the men's howzeh. The various maktab in Qom were developed based on Maktab-e Towhid's example.

Agha-ye Yusufian, the international students' liaison officer at Jami'at Al-Zahra, whom I met in 2008, explained that these maktab played an important role in the revolution. In the 1970s, many women participated in the religious meetings taking place in these. In 1978, they organized protests that would soon lead to the revolution of 1979. Because of their presence in organizing the protests, ideas for a Jami'at Al-Zahra began forming. But women, I also learned, were thought to have a critical role in raising men who would eventually occupy positions of authority—the institutionalization of the women's seminaries with Jami'at Al-Zahra leading the way.

For Women Who Will Raise Men

If revolution had been part of the maktab ethos since the mid-1970s, as I learned in 2008, then it is equally possible that women had already been asking for the formalization of a women's howzeh before 1979. If so, it seems the request may not have been acted upon by the clerics during the time of the shah, perhaps not until the nation was on the brink of the revolution, because women were thought of as doing the work of mothering future revolutionaries. For women like Khanum-e Alosvand, this made sense for reasons that will be revealed in the following chapters. She explained that after the revolution, a group of women asked Ayatollah Khomeini to combine the efforts of the already existing maktab in Qom in order to institutionalize a women's howzeh.

At the same time, Ayatollah Khomeini's advisers who traveled to different cities informed him that nationwide-accessible centers of Islamic learning for women needed to be secured even if the classes were held inside small rented buildings. Ayatollah Khomeini supported the idea and drafted a plan along with other revolutionary clerics including Ayatollah Ali Qoddosi (d. 1981), who directed the men's Haqqani howzeh and managed Maktab-e Towhid. Khanum-e Alosvand added, "Imam told the group of organizers not to worry because an endowment would support it." Ayatollah Khomeini and Ayatollah Qoddosi secured financial support from guilds and allotted resources for the centers' financial backing. This project came to fruition in 1984 and would be known as Jami'at Al-Zahra.

According to Khanum-e Alosvand, Ayatollah Khomeini was aware that there would be women who would not feel safe about studying outside the home, and for this reason, either the women would bypass this opportunity or their families would not allow them to attend classes. Ayatollah Khomeini and his allies facilitated women students by providing a transportation service "from every corner of Qom" to the Jami'at Al-Zahra campus. They also created a childcare center. In 2008, I was given special permission to visit the childcare center which at the time was at full capacity—one thousand children under the age of five. Staffed with its own teachers and caretakers for newborns, it was fully equipped with cribs, classrooms, and play areas. The center occupied the basement of one of the buildings and was easily accessible from the courtyard.

Working through Logistical Challenges

Khanum-e Alosvand explained, "There were a lot of important obstacles to this [project] because this had not existed before. If you count the number of teachers,

Figure 1.1. One classroom in Jami'at Al-Zahra. Qom, 2008. ©Amina Tawasil.

there was not enough. . . . They [women] would only want to learn from women (not men)." For this reason, there was a need for women teachers as well as materials and curriculum. When the project's proponents and organizers realized they could not immediately accommodate the number of women nationwide who wanted to study, they needed to work from the bottom up to find the means to accommodate the numbers. There was financial support for the howzeh elmiyeh outside of Qom. The larger problem was logistical: location and infrastructure. The women in Tehran, as we will see, were faced with the same logistical challenges.

This point brought me back to a previous conversation with Khanum-e Alosvand when she provided a general description of the way different women's howzeh were maintained. She emphasized that the kind of organizational support Jami'at Al-Zahra received was different from the way other seminaries were maintained. The resources, tools, and services for each howzeh depended on the kinds of activities and students it had in that local population. A template policy for funding services for students did not exist. A howzeh typically depended on local sources, such as a *vaqf* or endowment, private donors, trade guilds, and businesses. Special cooperatives commonly provided aid to the howzeh, such as food for students and building libraries. Charity groups funded the howzeh in distant frontier areas or the howzeh that did not have enough private donors. These sources of funding came from religiously conservative constituents. I return to why this is important later. Khanum-e Alosvand pointed out that at the time of our conversation, this assistance paved the way for almost three hundred women's howzeh aside from those in Qom and Mashhad. Jami'at Al-Zahra alone had about three hundred teachers. The nationwide structure for the women's system at the time was divided into five *mantaqe,* or regions, with the exception of Esfahan, Mashhad, and Qom since these cities already had their own administrative systems. An administrative office to provide local support such as teacher preparation, student support, or construction of buildings supervised each mantaqe.

Since the howzeh was a project for women developed in large part by women, directives were not top-down from men or the government, as we will see in the following chapters. Through the participation of women like Khanum-e Alosvand as well as Khanum-e Safiri and Refaei, whom we will meet in the following accounts, access to the women's howzeh elmiyeh opened doors for thousands of women throughout Iran.[19]

Khanum-e Alosvand spoke of her experience as a howzevi in Khuzestan, in the city of Masjed Soleiman. She said it was the first city where permission for oil exploration in the Middle East had been granted. For this reason, she said, "the culture of the English was very visible there, and one could see evidence of it through language." For instance, one would write in English, rarely in Persian. "People began to take notice and wanted to change the situation," she said. "Between 1978 and 1979, those who wanted access to an Islamic education decided to establish a howzeh elmiyeh in that area." She witnessed the changes that took place in her city: "They set up the howzeh. . . . In general, after ten years the city changed. . . . Students of religion spread religious teachings themselves. They would teach children the classes in the schools. . . . Many howzeh in the areas of Khuzestan were established and developed, and the place changed."

Based on Khanum-e Alosvand's estimation, a yearly average of sixty-five thousand women attend the women's howzeh all over Iran. This includes the twelve thousand annual average enrollments at Jami'at Al-Zahra and the estimated fifty-three thousand in seminaries nationwide. The capacity of the howzeh infrastructure does not accommodate the demand. According to Keiko Sakurai, who has conducted research on women's seminaries in Iran and Pakistan, 10 percent of the total annual applicants were being turned away in the mid-2000s.[20]

More obvious signs of the transformation of religious spaces emerged right before the revolution. For instance, Tehran's Hosseiniyeh Ershad became a space for bringing together supporters of the revolution, and the women's maktab in

Qom facilitated women's participation in protests. This spirit was carried over well after the revolution; religious spaces such as the jaleseh, or religious study group for women, and the *hay'at*, or religious gathering for men, were transformed into spaces where people were expected to engage with each other and their organizers or study leaders rather than merely receiving lectures.[21]

The way the literature interchangeably uses *howzeh, madraseh,* and *maktab* also indexes the fluidity of religious education.[22] Thus, when an Iranian howzeh was spoken of during my fieldwork, there was an implication that the institution had changed significantly since the 1830s into what I had seen. But for many of the howzevi, this form of howzeh education that is recognized and systematized nationwide became widely accessible only after the revolution. With the establishment of the women's howzeh elmiyeh, the purposes of an Islamic education were no longer limited to women becoming future jurists or scholars like those from scholarly families. The focus began to shift to producing graduates that would properly educate the masses on Islam.[23] Part of this move from purely scholarly work to praxis came from the logistical problems of not having the infrastructure and the workforce to maintain the women's howzeh. The howzeh's transformation attests to the fact that it is dynamic—continuously renewed and transfigured. This development has arguably been one of the most salient pillars of the powerful Islamic Republic that Iran is today.

To propose that the women's movements in Iran today is only about resistance and subverting the Islamic government becomes inaccurate when you take stories, narratives, and accounts like Khanum-e Alosvand's into consideration. Being largely absent from the discourse, in fact, even after more than forty years of calibrations and increased participation, puts the howzevi collectively in a position of power. That is, being absent in the literature allows the howzevi to continue their work without the challenges that may arise from being front and center the way the male-dominated clerical establishment has been since the revolution.

As the center of Shi'i Islamic scholarship in the world, the city of Qom drew people, often religiously conservative, from different countries to study in its institutions. Thus, the social experience in Qom was different from that of other cities in Iran. Because I spent most of my time in Tehran, I provide a description of such a social experience in Tehran's Pirouzi and Baharestan with howzevi women like Khanum-e Safiri and the women of Madraseh Ali. Khanum-e Safiri and Khanum-e Alosvand were of the opinion that the women's howzeh must make space for developing curriculum that will prepare women to work for the maintenance of a Shi'i Islamic society, inclusive of pursuing the women's Islamic rights. In what follows, I provide Khanum-e Safiri's account as a pioneer among the howzevi in Tehran.

THE HOWZEVI AND REVOLUTIONARY
TRACES LEFT BEHIND

Spring 2011. Maryam was putting on her chador as I held her baby, Fereshteh, and opened the front door. Maryam did not own a car and walked long distances to take a shared taxi to her classes early in the morning, at which time her husband, Mohammad, looked after Fereshteh. This day was an exception. We were going to take a private taxi to Madraseh Ali, the largest howzeh in Tehran that accommodates both women and men separately. Though the largest, it has a significantly smaller number of howzevi women compared to Jami'at Al-Zahra. We were on our way to visit Khanum-e Safiri, professor and head of the women's section. Maryam is both a PhD student and an instructor there. This visit was one of the few attempts Maryam made to go to the library since giving birth to Fereshteh at the end of 2009.

Madraseh Ali was located on the same grounds as the Islamic Consultative Assembly. Construction was taking place on the right-hand side of the women's building when Maryam and I arrived. A red brick building, about three stories high at that time, was being built. The way it stood in this alley was the new conversing with the old Baharestan buildings of the 1930s. The gate to the women's section, which was covered by a hanging heavy black tarp, was propped open on both sides. Straight ahead, two old cars and a dented white van were parked outside the main door. The thick, heavy tarp from the driveway entrance kept the women in this yard from plain sight at certain times of the day. After school, however, hired taxis were allowed inside to pick up students.

The building resembled neither the other five seminaries I had visited nor the architecture of renowned universities in Tehran. Inside, at the end of the hallway, there was a door to the right that led to the teachers' room, a door that led to the cemented courtyard, and a door to the library. The light feeling of the doors, the wall trimmings, and the fluorescent lights at the center of the hallway ceiling indicated the building was not new. At the time, the hallways were painted baby yellow, with two bulletin boards near Khanum-e Safiri's office door. As part of a three-week-long commemoration of the martyrdom of Fatimah, Prophet Mohammad's daughter and Imam Ali's wife, there were long black felt banners on the walls with the writing *Ya Fatimah Zahra*.

There was a small kitchen across from Khanum-e Safiri's door where Khanum-e Maleki, the building's caretaker, prepared tea and cookies. Next to it was the copy machine room where Khanum-e Moin sat behind her desk. A large tree stood in the cemented courtyard outside the office window, and behind it were dried wheat straw–covered benches where students could sit without their chador. Maryam explained that sometimes while classes were in session,

Figure 1.2. A hallway at Madraseh Ali's women's section. Tehran, 2011. ©Amina Tawasil.

a student's husband would stand under this tree text messaging his wife to look outside the window for a wave or a glance. Maryam laughed and said, "As newlyweds. They are young, you know?" As we conversed, Fereshteh walked to and from the door to Khanum-e Safiri's desk. The squeaky sound from Fereshteh's shoes and the sound of women's voices and laughter from the yard became the soundtrack for most of our conversation.

The First School for Girls

Khanum-e Safiri explained what it was like for her and her friends at the time of the revolution:

> It's true after the revolution restrictions were placed on women who did not wear hijab, the universities were closed down for some time and so on, but before the revolution the *mahdudiyat* [restrictions] were on women who were mazhabi. The time came when we did not want that we were without hijab, we did not want that we were without religion. . . . We were up front and center, we ourselves were straightening up the situation. Motahhari was among us and was our leader. This is what we had in our hands. In society,

this [Madraseh Ali] did not exist. This kind of talk [about advancing women's religious education], this study, was not on the radio or television. On television was the shah speaking.[24]

Khanum-e Safiri was referring to the limited position mazhabi women saw themselves in before the revolution. I look at what scholars of Iran have written about the history of schooling for girls in Iran to examine Khanum-e Safiri's point. The issue of schooling for girls became a point of contention between pro- and anti-constitutionalist politics in the 1900s. In response to conservative clerics who opposed girls' schooling on the grounds of girls' families losing reputation, elite women argued that modern schools must replace the already accessible but "worthless" maktab.[25] Women close to the royal family and women whose families supported the Constitutionalist revolution provided the means for girls' schooling through anjumans, semisecret societies of women. For instance, they held garden parties to fundraise and accommodated schools for girls in the private homes of distinguished women.[26]

Reza Shah's 1934 visit to Kamel Ataturk's Turkey and its expansion of schooling for girls is said to have had an impact on his conception of state-sanctioned girls' schooling in Iran, which resulted in his push for social advancement in Iran.[27] This overall civilizing effort, which began before his visit, was placed on both men and women. From 1925 to 1941, the only people who were allowed to wear religious robes were the clergy because Reza Shah found it "backward and repugnant."[28] He and his circle of elites regarded the chador as an impediment to the modernization of Iranian women. Minoo Derayeh writes that they proposed legalizing unveiling after "the shah instructed his minister of education, Ali Asghar Hikmat, to 'provide facilities in girl's schools in order to free these innocent kids from the captivity of the black chador.'"[29] Despite opposition and proposals toward a gradual approach, Reza Shah banned the headscarf from 1936–1941 "as a step toward modernity, progress, and women's emancipation."[30] With the support of women from his circle of elites, he founded the Ladies' Centre to prepare women for kashf hejab, or the decree of unveiling. The center held lectures on unveiling as well as debates on the status of women. Women were encouraged to wear hats instead.[31]

Many women supported the decree. Firoozeh Kashani-Sabet writes, "Writing in 1953, more than a decade after the deposition of Reza Shah, Najmeh Najafi remarked, 'Some new rich who have taken on Western ways very rapidly allow their women to meet in public places and to drink tea and other things, to play cards, to shop in the Westernized stores.'" However, the jolt of banning the veil in public spaces vexed thousands of families. Kashani-Sabet goes on to write, "But in the old conservative families, men will not allow their wives and daughters such liberties."[32] There were exceptions, but overall girls from families who disagreed with the decree were kept at home with some form of religious education.[33]

It is necessary to clarify the notion that the decree of unveiling caused families to confine women at home because it is misleading. First, women staying at home had already been part of the norm among Iranian families, where women were initially thought of as "the house to manager of the house."[34] It was not until the turn of the twentieth century that educating women became part of the national discourse. This was especially common among the well-to-do and the Islamic intellectual class, as I previously explained. Case in point, in the early 1900s Zia Ashraf Nasr, Sheikh Fazl Allah Nuri's granddaughter, was taught to read at home but not to write because writing implied the possibility of communicating with those outside the home.[35] The 1936 royal decree of unveiling merely intensified the already existing practice for many families and removed the possibility of their women ever having access to the public space.

Second, forced unveiling signaled something greater, more systemic, at work—the effort to remake the modern Iranian, where the Pahlavi regime decided what was modern and what was not. Kashani-Sabet writes that Reza Shah and his architects "forged the modern Iranian through 'renewal' . . . that required cosmetic changes, as well as intellectual indoctrination. . . . The modern Iranian literally had to embody this message of renewal." The expectation was for the ordinary citizen to completely break away from ways of life they had come to know, which veiling and domesticity symbolized. Regardless of religiosity, many opposed this coercive push for a transformed personhood. Kashani-Sabet, citing Najmeh Najafi, writes, "Many women felt alienated by such reforms and opted not to participate in the renewal movement."[36] This point becomes clearer in the following explanation regarding the process of marginalization after the decree of unveiling.

There were two consequences relevant to this decree. First, thousands of people who were once part of the social landscape were marginalized, evidence of which lay in the fact that a decree was even necessary in order to force a change in human behavior, and that forcing women to unveil eventually became difficult. The practice of veiling was very much part of the established ways of using public space in the early 1900s. Women commonly veiled when stepping outside the home regardless of religiosity. Although the practice differed among families, cities, and regions, veiling was part of the many socially acceptable ways of being a woman in what was geographically known as Persia.[37] On forced unveiling, Nikki Keddie writes, "Some women saw this as the equivalent of going out naked and refused to leave their homes, as gendarmes sometimes tore chadors from women on the streets."[38] Ziba Mir-Hosseini writes, "This not only outraged clerics but some ordinary women to whom appearing in public without their cover was tantamount to nakedness."[39] Derayeh provides several accounts of women from various backgrounds who refused to leave their homes because of the disdain for and aggression against the practice of wearing the chador.[40]

Although education and employment rates for women increased, Reza Shah's police resorted to enforcing more coercive prohibitions such as harassing veiled women in public, arresting them, closing streets to them, barring them from attending *Ashura* rituals, and instructing the service industry to refuse them service.[41] Keddie, citing Houchang Chehabi, writes, "Police and gendarmerie used physical force to enforce the ban, thus violating the innermost private sphere of close to half the population.... The practice of limited coeducation for prepubescent children in traditional maktabs was discontinued after girls were forced to go to school unveiled.... While educational opportunities improved for women ... many girls in observant families were deprived of education, as their parents took them out of school."[42] This was what Khanum-e Safiri referred to as mahdudiyat.

The response to this marginalization was continued protest in different cities.[43] As a result, even women who were not inclined to wear the chador stayed at home of their own accord, or their families kept them at home. The decree of unveiling, therefore, increased the number of families who began keeping women at home and the number of women who chose to stay at home, because even those who wore the veil as part of the social norm were gravely affected. Girls' schools, which at the time had been developing into a common space for girls and women of different backgrounds, became socially and politically fragmented, disabling one group of women while enabling another.[44] By the mid-1930s, there were at least four thousand women in Tehran from the Western-educated middle to upper class without veils and chador.[45]

The imaginations of those who could afford to travel to Europe in the late 1800s and early 1900s very much informed this modernizing effort. In 1936, women's bodies served as sites for modernization. Here, the chador did not mirror the elite's desired European-like construct of womanhood, which brings forth the second consequence of the unveiling decree. Those who refused to reform continued to be marked as obstacles to modernization. That is, the decree had succeeded in marginalizing those from whom the ruling circle disavowed themselves in the first place. Lines were drawn: the people who supported unveiling and wanted to be modern versus people who were a burden to modernization by insisting on veiling, especially wearing the chador.

In this drawing of lines, as I have just noted, Iran's sociality was not always polarized between the veiled and the unveiled.[46] But the decree made it possible for future generations to continue to marginalize those who refused to unveil based on their assumed religiosity from the rest of the Iranian social landscape. This was evident in the aftermath. Mir-Hosseini writes, "Between 1941 and 1979 wearing hejab was no longer an offence, but it was a real hindrance to climbing the social ladder, a badge of backwardness and a marker of class. A headscarf, let alone the chador... prejudiced the chances of advancement in work and society.... Schools and universities actively discouraged the chador, although the headscarf was tolerated. It was common to see girls from traditional families who had to leave home with the chador arriving at school without it and then putting it on again on the way home."[47] This badge of backwardness seeped into perceptions of students of the howzeh "as an embarrassment that should be helped to wither away as quickly as possible."[48]

For thousands of families, the public space became equated with the belittlement of the chador. Many women deemed the space outside the home no longer physically and morally safe. It was especially seen as an inappropriate space for girls and women whose families conceived of short skirts, tight-fitting clothes, and gender-mixed social spaces as out of the norm, as affronts to personhood. On the other end of the social spectrum, and more implicitly, by way of the chador, Iranians' way of life in the villages or small towns where the chador was designated as a mark of backwardness were seen still "drowning in the sea of superstition."[49] In other words, they were in need of reform out of the conventions they had previously been part of.

As I have noted, the labels *mazhabi* and *hezbollahi*, among many others, both carry a negative connotation today, the former as blind followers of religion and the latter as public controllers of women.[50] However, the people referred to as either of these today have in turn co-opted this vocabulary to demarcate their politics from those they perceive as adhering to the ideologies behind the 1936 decree of unveiling, like Westernization or modernization. As we see, Khanum-e Safiri used *mazhabi* to describe those who experienced the mahdudiyat, as she had before the revolution. As I explained in the introduction, I use the category *religiously conservative* or *mazhabi* because it was the way the women of this study described themselves. In a way, they saw themselves as part of the "downtrodden of the world." In Ayatollah Khomeini's terms, "Pure Islam is the Islam of the weak, the barefoot people of the earth, defiant mystics, and those who have suffered throughout history, and its pioneers are poor, oppressed, and downtrodden people of the world."[51]

Iranian women's experiences with education and education policies have historically been closely tied to their socioeconomic class, as I have demonstrated.[52] At this juncture, we can infer that the access to girls' schools in the early 1900s benefitted girls from the urban upper and middle socioeconomic classes who did not see the space outside as unsafe. It did not benefit girls who were kept at home.[53] In certain circumstances, women, especially those who did not come from families of Islamic scholars, used Islamic edicts to create ways to learn from the clergy. They would arrange an unconsummated temporary marriage of a few minutes with a clergyman and one of their daughters, so that the former could became a son-in-law. This would then make the clergyman non-marriageable kin whom they could learn from.[54]

Khanum-e Alosvand's narrative about Khuzestan and the following from how-zevi women in Tehran informs us that this situation changed immediately after the revolution. While specific laws such as mandatory veiling placed a population of Iranian women at a disadvantage, the same laws accommodated the participation of the previously marginalized women like Khanum-e Safiri.[55] Working to establish an ideal Islamic Republic also meant creating a social order that would normalize gender separation and veiling again, two shifts that would make the space outside the home a safe space for those who were previously marginalized by the ban on veiling.

Perhaps of greater value, it also meant that the family's patriarch would have little reason to prevent the family's women and girls from leaving the home to attend school. Thus, it was not until after the revolution when an overhaul of Iran's school system took place, privileging Islamic education with a strong Shi'ite identity, that girls and women like Khanum-e Alosvand and Safiri increasingly began taking hold of their access to schools.[56] Around 1984, this included the howzeh elmiyeh for women, previously accorded widely to men.

Slowly Transforming the Mazhabi Opinion

Aside from the given reasons of providing financial resources for the women's howzeh elmiyeh, as Khanum-e Alosvand described, and creating a safe public space for howzevi women, as Khanum-e Safiri explained, these words of gratitude toward Ayatollah Khomeini are prompts to look more closely at the relationship before the revolution between the howzeh and the religiously conservative population for whom decisions on Islamic laws mattered the most. Michael Fischer and Muhammad Zaman describe the longstanding relationship between the howzeh and the religiously conservative population, in particular the power of the latter over the former.[57] In order to remain independent of the governing bodies, the howzeh depended on financial contributions from the people, often from the religiously conservative. They were, and still are, its financial stronghold. Thus, what was socially acceptable among the religiously conservative impacted the workings of the howzeh.

According to Zaman, citing Motahhari, the howzeh could not advance its programs at a faster rate before the revolution because the *mujtahid* of a howzeh avoided taking risks in their edicts or research for fear of offending their religiously conservative supporters, who at any given moment could switch allegiances to other mujtahid.[58] What might be acceptable practices within scholarly families were not necessarily acceptable among the very people who provided financial support for the howzeh, especially when normative assumptions about the nature of women were called into question.

In her work on women's local pilgrimage practices in Shirazi shrines, Betteridge illustrates some of these assumptions about women. While men's religious practices were associated with reason and intellectual discourse, women's practices were considered shallow. She writes, "Women in Muslim Iran are regarded as frivolous, emotional, irrational, and at times dangerous; the things with which they are associated are consequently dismissed as . . . inconsequential. . . . Even women's dreams are described in Persian as *chap* (unreliable, off the mark)."[59] In this context, it makes sense that promoting the acceptance of women becoming interpreters of Qur'an for the masses might cause allegiances to change.

When Ayatollah Khomeini gained enormous popularity and formed allegiances within the clerical establishment, he publicly encouraged women toward an Islamic education. I noted in the introduction that one of the more challenging but rewarding paths that informs the personal work of khod shenasi is for a woman to attempt to become a mujtahideh because the position carries with it enormous reward but also heavy responsibility. As I explain in chapter 3, it is one of the most highly esteemed educative paths because, besides the divine reward that comes from becoming one, it removes the necessity to rely on another authority figure to interpret Islamic edicts. A mujtahideh makes a legal decision through independent interpretation of Islamic sources for herself.

Khanum-e Yasseri, whom I introduce in the following chapter, explained that Khomeini encouraged women to study to become mujtahideh. By doing so, he also transformed the public perception of religiously conservative women. The success of that attempt, at least for the women in this book, was evident. This encouragement simultaneously legitimized alternative forms of religious authority for women. If a woman could be a mujtahideh, then it could only follow that she could publish books, teach, and counsel about Islam. Men could no longer prevent howzevi women in general from earning this authority on Islamic text.

Madraseh Ali's Opening

Khanum-e Safiri proceeded to explain that just as Ayatollah Qoddosi played a key role in opening the women's howzeh in Qom, he had convinced Ayatollah Mohammad Emami-Kashani, appointed as the head of Madraseh Ali, that an institutionalized and fully funded howzeh education for women in Tehran was possible. Khanum-e Safiri detailed that Ayatollah Emami-Kashani, known to his students as a strong supporter of women's education, planned for the inclusion of women at Madraseh Ali and consequently its inclusion in the endowment.

On a previous visit with Khanum-e Safiri, Khanum-e Moqadesi, who at first taught and managed the program for women, was mentioned. I learned that when Madraseh Ali first opened in 1983, Khanum-e Moqadesi convinced Ayatollah Emami-Kashani to accept about sixty girls for the incoming class. In the beginning, the women's section employed teachers from the howzeh and the university. Teachers would be brought in from Qom. It also began with a howzeh curriculum with only one field of study. Khanum-e Safiri was in that first incoming class of about sixty girls, and along with the first group of students, she helped developed its curriculum. She and the women from the first incoming class were serving as howzeh administrators by the time we met. Madraseh Ali high schools for girls were established all across Iran, and their reach had already expanded to a total of forty howzeh in Tehran and surrounding areas under the supervision of Mantaqe Yek Howzeho-ye Elmiyeh Khoharan, or Region One Women's Howzeh Elmiyeh.

COLLECTIVE MEMORY

The task of expanding research requires looking at narratives about what took place at the intersection of women, Islamic education, and the role of the government. The women's accounts were very much grounded in a historical event, and my work as an ethnographer involved drawing from their accounts as pioneers of a state project. I understood their accounts as oral histories I could learn from regarding what from the past was a compelling aspect of their present-day life. In a similar vein to the ways in which exilic Iranians recall the violent circumstances of the moment they fled Iran, the howzevi, too, adhered to a specific recollection about the revolution. I do not seek to diminish either one, but I wish to make a simple point about collective memory. That which continues to impact both the individual and the collective in the present becomes worthy of recollection and is sometimes memorialized.

Maryam expressed very little knowledge of the detailed history of the howzeh in Iran and of Madraseh Ali. She brought up names that she had heard were involved in the making of the institution, and Khanum-e Safiri corrected her statements. The discussion about historical details between the two women was not simply a lapse in memory. Specific names such as Banu Amin and Ayatollah Khomeini, Qoddossi, Kashani, and Motahhari and others were repeated, but overall, the women appeared not to care much for the historical details of the who-did-what of an institution they were a part of. The names and events worth remembering, often those that maintain a system that allows for a particular logic of recollection to continue, were repeated. For the howzevi, the names and events worth remembering were those that had a direct impact on the resources they gained access to after 1979.

Figure 1.3. Banu Amin's tomb. Esfahan, 2008. ©Amina Tawasil.

Evidence of this emerged in the way the women consistently credited Banu Amin. Although Khanum-e Alosvand acknowledged that women from Islamic scholarly families had already been contributing to Shi'i Islamic scholarship in Iraq and Iran decades before the revolution, she, like the other women of this study, consistently mentioned Banu Amin's influence. They did not concern themselves much with the other names of the scholarly women I have noted in this chapter. The fact that one of Banu Amin's books, *Kanz al-Irfan*, was being taught in the men's howzeh in Qom between 1975 and 1977, in a class on rules of conduct and law, strengthens Khanum-e Alosvand's hypothesis about Banu Amin's important influence in Iran.[60] However, their lack of interest in other accomplished women scholars while consistently giving credit to Banu Amin indexed a reverence not just for individuals but for a logic that says they should not have been excluded, restricted, or limited from participation.

Khanum-e Tabesh, a senior howzevi, explained, "Before the revolution we had no access to the howzeh, only in Qom. We did not even have access to a normal education, only a few. After the revolution, we started going to one howzeh in Tehran. Now we have more howzeh." Banu Amin's effort to provide and push for access to rigorous Islamic education for women signals that logic. Her impact on the howzevi's access to institutionalized forms of Islamic education came to fruition after 1979. In 2008, the women took me to the city of Esfahan to visit Banu Amin's tomb, which was shaped as a woman's head under a chador. The lack of interest in taking me to other sites was part of their narrative, a collective memory about the revolution and their Islamic education.

Rather than laboring to disprove them on specifics, I use their accounts as a starting point for looking at what their interpretation of events has produced. Khanum-e Safiri said, "And in time we have (for example) in one neighborhood someone, who would otherwise sit at home and not work, is now a graduate of Shahid Motahhari [Madraseh Ali]." The women here could not foresee the kinds of projects or work they would eventually be involved in, and neither of them had fixed goals, only the general objective to work toward building an Islamic Republic in accordance with Islamic law.

From leaving the constraints of the home, women like Khanum-e Alosvand, Safiri, and others entered other sets of constraints associated with being a howzevi. I cannot discount the limitations they experienced being perceived as supporters of state repression, or as women who were oppressed, or as women who oppressed other women. Other mechanisms of power were also at work, largely influenced by the context of the prerevolution era, with the national discourse about foreign and domestic threats.

Their accounts were not about women being manipulated by men or about women emancipating themselves from the constraints of religious practice. The notion that they would undermine the very system in which they continued to reify would be an incomplete analysis. The women's accounts tell us that their memory of exclusion was crucial. The only way to prevent that was to produce and maintain a society that is conducive to the work of khod shenasi—in other words, a society that will continue to value their work toward the ideal Muslim personhood.

Administrators and students alike perceived the utility of a howzeh education beyond producing religious authority. For the howzevi, acquiring a strong Islamic education also meant producing Islamic researchers, propagators, teachers, counselors, law makers, and so on that together would potentially strengthen the Islamic Republic; in other words it would, at the same time, diminish the possibility of returning to a time when they, as a religiously observant collective, were thought of as unworthy of full consideration. This is political work through various means: education, religious, bodily, and sometimes gendered. Thus, the republic's attempt to produce revolutionary women who will raise revolutionary men was, for them, more than a rational objective, and their participation in that work was a noble endeavor. It comes as no surprise that some of the howzevi, like those I mention in this chapter, were responsible for influencing the direction of the howzeh that necessarily involved designing processes that made the howzeh inaccessible to many Iranian women who were not of them.

This chapter acquaints us with the kind of work the howzevi have participated in that has made it possible to push forward and develop debates about which direction the howzeh elmiyeh as an institution should be headed, and debates about the place of women in positions of religious and political leadership—specifically, becoming a mujtahideh for all and, consequently, a Marja'e Taqlid. The debate continues today. Khanum-e Safiri spoke at length about having to mitigate the enduring issues they faced; clerics in Qom continued to exclude women from their Dars-e Kharij classes, and their access to resources they had not had before also needed to be safeguarded.

NOTES

1. Nafisi, "Tales of Subversion," 264; Sanasarian, *The Women's Rights*, 143.
2. Abtahi, *Risheho va Jeloho-ye Teshia*, 490–91, 643–72.
3. Abtahi, *Risheho va Jeloho-ye Teshia*, 643–44.
4. Naeeni, *Shi'ah Women Transmitters*, 13-312.
5. Naeeni, *Shi'ah Women Transmitters*, 199–200, citing Mustadrak A'yan al-Shia vol. 3, 83.
6. Abtahi, *Risheho va Jeloho-ye Teshia*, 491.
7. Abtahi, *Risheho va Jeloho-ye Teshia*, 490–91, 643–72.
8. Künkler and Fazaeli, "The Life of Two," 129.
9. Sakurai, "Women's Empowerment," 32-58.
10. Künkler and Fazaeli, 135.

11. Sullivan,"Eluding the Feminist," 215–42.

12. Sakurai, "Women's Empowerment," 32.

13. Fischer, *Iran*, 42.

14. Street, *Literacy in Theory*, 132.

15. Afary, "On the Origins," 71-72.

16. Derayeh, *Gender Equality*, 130-133; Fischer, *Iran*, 98, 114; Kashani-Sabet, *Conceiving Citizens*, 162-163; Keddie, *Modern Iran*, 100; Sullivan, "Eluding the Feminist," 223-28.

17. Abrahamian, *A History of Modern*, 3.

18. Sullivan, "Eluding the Feminist," 221.

19. Adelkhah, *Being Modern*, 121.

20. Sakurai, "Women's Empowerment," 35.

21. Adelkhah, *Being Modern*, 110–12.

22. *Howzeh* is the Persianized word for the Arabic hawza and *madraseh* for the Arabic madrasa; both are places where learning and teaching is done. A maktab is an informal school.

23. Sakurai, "Women's Empowerment," 34.

24. Khanum-e Safiri in Tehran on April 24, 2011.

25. Afary, "On the Origins," 72, footnote10 in chapter 1. Afary writes that a woman during the constitutional revolution, in protest against the religious conservative clergy, described the maktab as "worthless."

26. Afary, "On the Origins," 71–73. Derayeh, *Gender Equality*, 119.

27. Kashani-Sabet, *Conceiving Citizens*, 154–56.

28. Fischer, *Iran*, viii.

29. Derayeh, *Gender Equality*, 130.

30. Ibid.; Keddie, *Modern Iran*, 100; Najmabadi, "(Un)veiling Feminism," 47; Abrahamian, *A History of Modern*, 95; Sedghi, *Women and Politics*, 38; Paidar, *Women and the Political*, 105–07.

31. Paidar, *Women and the Political*, 106–07; Derayeh, *Gender Equality*, 130; Kashani-Sabet, *Conceiving Citizens*, 153–60; Mir-Hosseini, *Islam and Gender*, 73.

32. Kashani-Sabet, *Conceiving Citizens*, 163.

33. Derayeh, *Gender Equality*, 130; Torab, *Performing Islam*, 39.

34. Najmabadi, "Crafting an Educated," 91; Kashani-Sabet, *Conceiving Citizens*, 131.

35. Sullivan "Eluding the Feminist," 221.

36. Kashani-Sabet, *Conceiving Citizens*, 150–51, 163.

37. Abrahamian, *A History of Modern*, 86.

38. Keddie, *Modern Iran*, 100.

39. Mir-Hosseini, "Women and Politics in Post-Khomeini," 155.

40. Derayeh, *Gender Equality*, 131–33.

41. Ashura marks the day Imam Hossein was killed in the Battle of Karbala; Keddie, *Modern Iran*, 100; Mir-Hosseini, "Women and Politics in Post-Khomeini," 155; Kashani-Sabet, *Conceiving Citizens*, 158. In 1936, veiled women were barred from attending Ashura rituals in Esfahan.

42. Keddie, *Modern Iran*, 100.

43. Derayeh, *Gender Equality*, 131–32; Kashani-Sabet, *Conceiving Citizens*, 159.

44. See Najmabadi, "(Un)veiling Feminism," 62.

45. Abrahamian, *A History of Modern*, 84.

46. Najmabadi, "(Un)veiling Feminism," 62.

47. Mir-Hosseini, "Women and Politics in Post-Khomeini," 156. "Fashionable hotels and restaurants refused to admit women with chador" and men "were increasingly expected to appear with their wives at social functions"; Bahramitash, "Saving Iranian," 101–10.

48. Fischer, *Iran*, 38.

49. Kashani-Sabet, *Conceiving Citizens*, 159.

50. Kamalkhani, *Women's Islam*, 136.

51. Mehran, "Iran: A Shi'ite," 59, citing "Binesh-e Islami," 12th Grade Textbook, quoting Ayatollah Khomeini.

52. Bahramitash, "The War on Terror," 232.

53. Keddie, *Modern Iran*, 100; Adelkhah, *Being Modern*, 175; Afary, *Sexual Politics*, 30.

54. Afary, *Sexual Politics*, 259; Torab, *Performing Islam*, 40. This was the case with Marzieh Dabbagh and other such women like the Khanum-e jaleseh, or women's study group leaders, in Torab's work.

55. Afary, "Steering between Scylla," 43–46; Mir-Hosseini, *Islam and Gender*, 53; Bahramitash, "Saving Iranian," 108; Mir-Hosseini, *Islam and Gender*, 53, 57–58; Poya, *Women, Work*, 11–12; Sedghi, *Women and Politics*, 261–62; Sullivan, "Eluding the Feminist," 223–28.

56. Menashri, *Education and Modern Iran*, 308; Mehran, "Iran: A Shi'ite," 53.

57. Fischer, *Iran*, 10, 85–88, 91–95; Zaman, "Competing Conceptions," 243–247.

58. A mujtahid is a man who makes legal decisions through independent interpretation of the Qur'an and Sunnah. Momen, *Introduction to Shi'i Islam*, 200; Zaman, "Competing Conceptions," 246.

59. Betteridge, "Muslim Women and Shrines," 288.

60. Fischer, *Iran*, 250.

TWO

—∞—

KHOMEINI'S PROJECT, A DEBATE

MUCH OF WHAT WE KNOW ethnographically about Islamic education in Iran comes from work about men. When I traveled to Iran in 2008, over thirty years after Michael Fischer's fieldwork, I did not find the predominance of the free university that he described in his work about men in the howzeh. As I explored in the previous chapter, perhaps it was because the establishment and development of the women's howzeh in relation to the 1979 revolution differed from that of the men's howzeh. Based on what Fischer observed, I had imagined that students sat on the floor or in the courtyard in a circle around the teacher, freely moving around choosing teachers. The howzevi I shared this description with joked that I was lacking in imagination. This setting, where students sat in circles around one teacher, may have existed for women a hundred years ago, they said. They suspected this was still true for the men's howzeh because study circles in courtyards had been the typical atmosphere for the men's howzeh for hundreds of years. Perhaps it continued in the experience of sitting in a Dars-e Kharij–level class with a mujtahid or Marja'e Taqlid. But they, the women, had buildings, classrooms with tables, chairs, blackboards, and, in the case of Jami'at Al-Zahra, auditorium-size classrooms. They spoke proudly of these amenities as I continued to probe into what might have been lost in exchange.

As I have stated, one of the many possibilities born out of the 1979 revolution and the remaking of Iranian social life into one that was ideally conducive to the work of khod shenasi was for a woman to become a mujtahideh. But keeping this possibility open requires maintaining the very system that makes it possible. Thus, a woman's Islamic education could no longer be solely committed to the work of becoming a mujtahideh. It also needed to serve practical purposes, to inform the work of protecting and strengthening their project of an Islamic society so they and others could ideally continue to do the work of khod shenasi.

In this chapter, I look at the transformation of the women's howzeh elmiyeh. I look at the markers of "women's work" in the context of strengthening the Islamic Republic and what women have been doing to transform the women's howzeh elmiyeh into an institution that can potentially produce graduates who will do this work. Their participation calls into question an image of them as unthinking and incapable subjects controlled by the men around them. With their personal and individual work of khod shenasi as the backdrop, the women work behind the scenes and organically collaborate with each other. They design and implement solutions to institutional challenges that often require a balancing act and trade-offs. Centralizing the system and changing the howzeh curriculum to accommodate a certification system have facilitated graduate employment and transfers to university graduate programs. These have led to the transformation of male-dominated spaces like government offices or Dars-e Kharij–level study circles.

These transformations are not unique to the women's howzeh. Fischer, for instance, describes in detail the innovations that were taking place in four of the men's howzeh in Qom.[1] The transformations I describe in this chapter, however, have also simultaneously diminished the long-standing value of a student-centered education, a pinnacle of Islamic education, and the well-known reputation of the Iranian howzeh of having independence from governmental resources. Finally, just as religiously conservative women were excluded from participation before the revolution, their continued work to strengthen the Islamic Republic has enabled them to exclude those who are not in line with their vision of a future Iran. I end the chapter with a description of a newly formed howzeh in Tehran, Howzeh-ye Kowsar, and the way its founder, Agha-ye Sharifi, and its students navigate their challenges. I do so to illustrate the different ways the howzeh elmiyeh system is transformed in unexpected ways and to demonstrate that men, like those mentioned in the previous chapter, facilitate the women's educative mobility.

THE SIGNIFICANCE OF ISLAMIC EDUCATION

In both Sunni and Shi'i Islamic scholarship, it is understood that God is the Creator, and only God has the right to create laws for what God created. The purpose for sending prophets and messengers is to proclaim these divine laws, not to create them. Islam and its laws are derived from the Qur'an and the Sunnah. The Qur'an is a direct source from God, and understanding its verses often involves *tafsir*, or the work of interpretation by Qur'anic scholars. The Sunnah, on the other hand, is accessed by way of hadith, a large body of text that contains narrations, or *rivayat*, of the way the Prophet Mohammad and his family lived their lives. The science of hadith involves studying the authenticity of the narrations. All of these serve as a guide for the way to do the work of khod shenasi and, thus, live ethically.

The teachings of Shi'i Islam are distinct from Sunni Islam on the role of the imam, referring to leaders of the community. The concept of imam is central to belief in Shi'i Islam. The imam is the successor of the Prophet Mohammad, and he acts as the preserver and interpreter of Islam and its laws. For Twelver and Ismaili Shi'i Muslims in particular, God has chosen imams as perfect examples of khod shenasi for humanity because they are free from committing any sin.

For Shi'i Muslims, the work of khod shenasi requires receiving guidance. This is done in one of two ways. The first is by way of *taqlid*, or imitation.[2] Once a person has come to understand and accept Islamic beliefs, it follows that that person adheres to the *Shari'a*, Islamic law, by imitating a mujtahid, someone who can make independent juristic interpretations. The *Marja'e Taqlid*, which means the source of emulation, plays an important role. A Marja'e is the highest-ranking jurist who has been designated by other high-ranking jurists as the most qualified to lead when it comes to matters of religious practice and law because of his training in the Islamic sciences.[3]

The other option would be for a person to become a mujtahid. As a mujtahid, they could do *ijtihad*, make independent juristic interpretations of the Qur'an and the Sunnah for themselves. This educative process initially requires the labor of imitation, resembling an apprenticeship. The end goal is that they would no longer have to imitate a mujtahid. The process of ijtihad, therefore, is the opposite of imitation, since ijtihad involves self-interpretation.[4]

There are two kinds of mujtahid: one who specializes in a single topic and one who is an overall expert. There are also two kinds of recognized authority: a mujtahid who can do ijtihad for themselves only and a complete mujtahid who can do ijtihad for all. The latter, which I explore in the following chapter, has not yet been allotted to women in Iran. Howzevi women who are recognized as knowing how to do ijtihad, called mujtahideh, can do it only for themselves and, depending on the extent of their expertise, for other women.

All this learning begins with studying with a scholar, or at the howzeh elmiyeh. The word *howzeh* in Arabic means "to hold or grasp something firmly," and in Persian it means "a side of, a part of, or middle of a kingdom."[5] The word *elmiyeh* refers to knowledge in both languages. Therefore, a howzeh elmiyeh is a place of knowledge or a circle of knowledge. The Shi'i madrasas of Iran and Iraq as a system are referred to as howzeh elmiyeh.[6] More specifically, they are Islamic theological institutions of higher religious learning where a personal teacher-student transmission of knowledge, oral and written, of ancillary Islamic sciences and Islamic jurisprudence take place. This place of knowledge has taken on various forms throughout its history, from a fixed location to one that was more mobile or impermanent. These resembled meetings or study groups under a specific teacher in varying locations.[7]

In the mid 1970s, Fischer examined the Iranian howzeh elmiyeh for men as an Islamic form of educational system, comparable to the Jewish yeshiva and the Catholic studium, by which the *ijaza*, a certificate or verbal permission to teach from a more senior religious authority, takes place.[8] At the heart of Fischer's analysis is the role of the howzeh's transformation in terms of expanding its networks, thereby influencing individuals in creating a support base for the 1979 Iranian Revolution. Fischer also takes notice of the pedagogical strategies in the howzeh setting; the way students were taught in the analysis of materials, and the methods of debate used in arriving at conclusions. Fischer provides firsthand accounts of *bahes*, the dialectic practice of disputation between students and teachers. He describes the howzeh of the early 1970s as a "free university" because of the absence of grade levels or the notion of failure. Students, referred to as *talabeh azad*, were free to move from one instructor to another or between several howzeh at any given time. Students learned for learning's sake, according to Fischer.

The culmination of all this learning to become a mujtahid in Iran takes place at the Dars-e Kharij level under the direct tutelage of a grand scholar, or higher authority of knowledge. The program of study at the Kharij level continues to be a challenge for both men and women, as it may take at least fifteen years for a student at this level to master the skill of interpreting canonical texts. Historically, finishing substages of the Kharij level involved the process of the student acquiring a number of ijaza. In recent decades, however, the process of acquiring an ijaza has slowly been losing its value, as I explain in this chapter.

UNEXPECTED OUTCOMES

At this intersection of women, unexpected outcomes have been inevitable. The movement of religiously conservative women from under the patriarch's watchful eye into public participation, as I have explained, was one of these outcomes. Another was related to maintaining the access to the howzeh by way of supporting the government that provided this access. Therefore, maintaining this access also meant producing constraints on other women, especially those who were against the government. Another reordering has to do with the transformation of the women's howzeh, which is unique neither to the ethnographic present nor to Iran.

As a result of the work of women like Khanum-e Alosvand and others who have secured a future for the women's howzeh, two key questions were being debated about the women's howzeh elmiyeh among its administrators and developers. The first was whether a woman could eventually occupy the position of a complete mujtahid, which would later on give a woman the option to become Marja'e Taqlid. I address this in the following chapter. The second question was whether the curriculum for the howzeh elmiyeh for women should be directed toward producing women who would do the work of building and developing an Islamic society favorable to the work of khod shenasi, or toward producing mujtahideh, women who could derive rulings for themselves about Islamic edicts. I look at the work howzevi women have been doing around this question, and I explore what supporting this work looks like in practice.

Considerations on Women's Work

Khanum-e Alosvand and many women in this book took the position that a howzeh education should not limit women to just becoming a mujtahideh. Pushing this idea further, the curriculum in the women's howzeh should also not limit women to just becoming religious teachers and/or mothers who will vaguely educate future generations of Shi'i revolutionaries. The institution's objective could instead be steered to that of preparing women for work. By work, Khanum-e Alosvand meant preparing women for positions that would strengthen the Islamic Republic through Islamic knowledge and action. The nature of such positions include research, teaching in schools and universities, counseling, writing, and drafting policies and laws. Overhauling and redirecting the entire howzeh system could accomplish this.

Khanum-e Alosvand's take on the matter was based on two demands coming together. First, the revolutionaries had placed the howzevi on the front lines of confronting the challenges common people had been facing long before 1979, issues pertaining to education, economics, crime, war, human rights, and women's rights.[9] In short, Islamically educated women were expected to do the social and educational programming in Iran, and there were simply not enough of them to do this work. Second, howzevi women began to demand that they be issued formal certification to become members of the bureaucratic workforce.

Women's work meant a variety of things for the howzevi. For the sake of brevity, I separate it into two broad categories. The first is participation in developing programs and curriculum for the women's howzeh elmiyeh so it could prepare women to build and maintain the presence of Islamic teachings in society. The second is participation in supporting the Islamic Republic's revolutionary ideals outside the howzeh—that is, women who do research; draft laws and policies; develop social, education, and mass media programs; and teach in schools and universities.

In Support of the Islamic Republic

Howzevi women have been doing many kinds of work in support of the Islamic Republic. I describe some of them here. This entanglement of the categories of women, Islamic education, and the state, however, is not unique to Iran. In

Figure 2.1. Howzevi women attending the Women's 9th International Congress of Qur'anic Research. Tehran, 2011. ©Amina Tawasil.

contemporary Morocco, women train in a one-year program and are deployed as *Murshidat* and the *Alimat* in order to dampen the influence of political Islamic groups.[10] Though less visible than men, about one-third of state-sponsored Islamic preachers in Turkey are now women because educational programs are made available to them.[11]

While the work of women in Morocco and Turkey was limited to mosques and study circles, the role of women who participated in the 1979 revolution was not. The revolutionary figure Marzieh Dabbagh as an example of women's work comes to mind. At least two of the senior howzevi I met worked under Marzieh Dabbagh, who was still alive while I was in Iran. She married at the age of thirteen and had eight children. She found a way to learn the Islamic sciences privately from a cleric and joined a small circle around Ayatollah Khomeini before the revolution. She was arrested and tortured by the SAVAK in 1972. She then became Khomeini's bodyguard in Paris in 1978 and became involved in mobilizing Shi'i fighters in Lebanon and Syria and anti-shah forces in Iran. She served as a military commander in the eight-year Iran-Iraq War. While in the Islamic Revolutionary Guard Corps, she participated in dismantling groups like the Kurdish Komeleh and secret cells in opposition to the Republic like Fedayin. She served four terms in the parliament.[12]

Inspired by notions of Islamic social justice, the newly established government in 1979 depended on the work of women to deliver social services nationwide, from literacy campaigns to health care and education. Bahramitash writes, "The nationwide literacy campaign in particular mobilized women in great numbers, bringing masses of illiterate women to the mosques for education. As a result of such mass programs, women who had no access to education under the previous secular regime became literate."[13] Ayatollah Khomeini and his allies also positioned women like Massoumeh Ebtekar, Marzieh Vahid Dastjerdi, and the late Maryam Behrouzi at the forefront of their project to develop social programs.[14]

Behind the forefront, there were other kinds of work like teaching and research. I met four women in Qom who had been part of the handful of women's maktab in Qom before the revolution and who participated in the street protests in the late 1970s. They were also part of the group that rallied behind the creation of Jami'at Al-Zahra. Three of the four women continued to attend Dars-e Kharij classes in Qom, but one of them, Khanum-e Yasseri, opted to become an Islamic philosophy professor rather than pursuing an education toward Islamic jurisprudence. She was conducting research and publishing books on the works of Mulla Sadra.

Another example are the educative choices Khanum-e Alosvand and her staff, which includes men, have made. They decided to do research for the women's center while attending classes and study circles in Qom. The trustees of the women's research center recruited Khanum-e Alosvand to lead a project while she was a student at Jami'at Al-Zahra. She has since been putting her research experience to use while tapping into her network of howzevi women to do more research. As a result of their work, "The research center provides a link between Islamic studies about women and its practical application in society to the howzeh or universities." The credibility of the research center, which includes men, depended highly on its members' and researchers' credibility. The minimum qualification to be a researcher at the center was a master's degree, or a Sat'h 3 level from the howzeh.

The center has carried out research for governmental agencies and educational institutions. For instance, if an educational institution, which includes the howzeh, was asked to address practical challenges regarding women, this center would conduct the research, provide findings, and prescribe solutions to the institution. At the time of my visits to Khanum-e Alosvand, Iranian women were finding it more difficult to balance work and home life based on previously collected data. The researchers at the center were finding ways to help them face challenges in the workplace, such as finding a proper place to pray or having to work fixed hours. Their objective was to provide practical solutions for women to maintain employment and further their careers while still observing Islamic rules and maintaining their familial obligations. Khanum-e Alosvand added that one of the goals for this research was to provide a "comparison between the situations today from the past while providing foreseeable trends in the future."

They also carried out research on women's issues internationally, but did so from an Islamic point of view, as Khanum-e Alosvand said, "because we recognize that most of the women's studies research is done from the point of view of feminism." Their research at the time included the impact of other forms of governance on women's lives. For instance, they looked at welfare states from 1920 onward. They compared longitudinal outcomes for women living in welfare states. They have also been doing research on ways to curtail domestic violence against women. Previous to that, they were designing educational materials for Islamic countries on the way to prevent violence in the Muslim home.

Khanum-e Alosvand and her team of researchers, like others in a later chapter, were constantly researching strategies to ward off what they referred to as the influence of Western feminism. The study picked up speed in the early 2000s when they focused on a response to the 1995 U.N. Fourth World Conference in Beijing. They concentrated their efforts on gender equality and discrimination against women. Khanum-e Alosvand noted, "We investigated their claims. And we wanted to know the relationship between their claims and Islamic rulings about the family."

Reinventing Madraseh Ali

To produce more women like Khanum-e Alosvand, women had to do what falls under the first category of women's work, re-creating the women's howzeh el-miyeh.[15] The howzeh administrators and developers reformulated its objective, operation, and curriculum design. They did so in a way that reflects their vision of producing Islamically educated women that can both become mujtahideh and contribute to the project of creating a society that is, again, beneficial to doing the work of khod shenasi. In the case of Madraseh Ali, women's participation in overhauling and repurposing the entire women's howzeh system was crucial.

Serving as administrators, Khanum-e Safiri and the first incoming class of Madraseh Ali were steering Islamic education away from producing only scholars into producing both women scholars and practitioners who would do the work of developing such a society. The women, at the time, were well into considering the benefits of incorporating aspects of the university system into Madraseh Ali to accommodate students' needs to work. They developed parts of the curriculum to resemble courses taught in the university system. Khanum-e Safiri further explained, "The aim of this system is to bring together the positive points of the howzeh with the positive points of the university in order to improve and develop it [the howzeh]."

The transformations within the women's side of Madraseh Ali and the other women's howzeh in Tehran illustrate this shift. By 2010, significant operational changes at Madraseh Ali and the surrounding howzeh were already set in motion. Administrators were actively adding classes to the howzeh, replacing thousand-page books with abridged versions or new books, setting an age limit for admissions, quantifying student assessment, and replacing the ijaza with the *madrak*, or certificate of program completion. I will return to this later. The only exception to this reconstruction was the Dars-e Kharij level, which, as it is translated as "A Lesson of the Outside" [to tradition], remained in its core design at the discretion of the mujtahid or Marja'e Taqlid.

In addition to applicants taking the general concour exam to apply for Iranian universities, undergraduate applicants to Madraseh Ali were required to take a Madraseh Ali entrance exam and do well in an oral interview. At the time, an average of twenty students were accepted annually into the Madraseh Ali undergraduate, or *lisans/karshenasi arshad*, program; between twenty and thirty overall, including incoming students, enrolled in Islamic jurisprudence and the study of rights, and about fifty enrolled in philosophy. The student to instructor ratio per class was twenty to one. Students who applied for master's degrees were required to go through the same process. The master's degree application was said to be more difficult, with ten to twelve new students enrolling and sometimes just one or two. Application to its doctoral-level program was more competitive and had become more stringent since 2003. While admitted students were not charged a fee to enroll in the smaller populated howzeh, Madraseh Ali began to charge fees for its graduate-level students.

One of the many consequences of these changes was the creation of a hierarchy based on the privilege of having time—that is, committing one's time to focus solely on completing programs without attending to other familial obligations. This, by implication, means filtering for age. A more formal and rigorous admissions policy was put into place at all levels, and an age limit cutoff was implemented for this reason. Undergraduate applicants needed to be under twenty-one years old. Sixteen year old applicants, the youngest age group they admitted, must have finished high school. Master's degree and PhD applicants in 2008 did not have an age limit. Under normal circumstances, a student had four years to finish the undergraduate program, three years for the master's degree, and more than four years to finish a PhD.

In addition to offering courses on Islamic jurisprudence; the study of rights, philosophy, and *kalam*; and the study of fundamental theological discourse, they also offered classes on Islamic economy, Islamic psychology, and civil law, which the other howzeh in Tehran did not yet offer. The students at Madraseh Ali took comparative courses on law as well as Islamic jurisprudence. Students also studied Sunni Islamic jurisprudence during the last semester of their undergraduate degree for two credits, and more in depth at the master's degree level. Finally, students were required to take comparative Sunni and Shi'i Islamic jurisprudence for research purposes at the master's degree level.

In 2011, the men's section, which was under separate management from the women's, offered Islamic jurisprudence and Islamic law degrees for the undergraduate level but not Islamic philosophy. Madraseh Ali for women, however, offered degrees in the field of Islamic jurisprudence, the study of rights, and Islamic philosophy starting at the undergraduate level. Khanum-e Safiri did not know the exact reasoning behind this since the men's section was under a different administration. She entertained the possibility that "maybe ... girls or ladies are more successful in philosophy than boys" and proposed that perhaps Ayatollah Emami-Kashani wanted to better develop the foundation for women's education in his original curriculum plan. This kind of support is also evident in Madraseh Ali's spatial arrangements. While women were allowed to take graduate-level classes in the men's section, men were not allowed to go near the women's section. The administration turned a blind eye, however, to the howzevi husbands who would every so often stand under the one tree outside the women's building to catch a wave or hello from their wives inside the classroom.

There were between twenty and thirty faculty members comprising both men and women in the Islamic jurisprudence and Islamic law departments. In philosophy, there were four or five faculty members; two or three were women at any given time. Madraseh Ali also had twenty-six feeder high schools all over Iran—thirteen for boys and thirteen for girls, inclusive of the girls' high school in Tehran. Khanum-e Safiri added, "We plan to expand the fields of Islamic jurisprudence, the study of rights, Jaza' (criminal law), and private law at the undergraduate level in the next few years."[16]

As briefly mentioned, Madraseh Ali had extensive reach throughout the howzeh system in Tehran, which means that transformations within Madraseh Ali also meant necessary shifts within the other howzeh. Khanum-e Safiri worked on programming and curricular development with Khanum-e Rasti, the director of the Region One Women's Howzeh Elmiyeh, who oversaw the workings of the women's howzeh in Tehran and surrounding cities. Khanum-e Safiri received project development requests from the Region One office, and once the design was complete, the Region One office would then develop it further to fit their needs. The proposal would have gone through several rounds of review by the time it reached the specific howzeh.

Transformations within the Region One howzeh system in turn became one of the causes for change within Madraseh Ali. That is, Region One howzeh needed more staff and teachers.

Iran's university system did not have the same challenges after the revolution, since the new government merely took over the already existing system the Pahlavi regime had developed and recalibrated its programs "to advance their goals."[17] This was not the case for the women's howzeh. Khanum-e Alosvand explained that they had to develop the women's howzeh from the ground up. As Khanum-e Safiri explained, "All this development was from the revolution, after thirty years." She added, "The work that Madraseh Ali women have in their hands increased starting about seven or eight years ago. Every region of the howzeh elmiyeh for women has increased its workload for staff and teachers. The work has increased because the number of students and programs being developed has multiplied." Therefore, this demand for change in Madraseh Ali comes from the logistical challenge of not having enough Islamically educated women to maintain and develop the women's howzeh.

Because Madraseh Ali produced instructors for the Region One howzeh, Madraseh Ali administrators needed to consider changes in its course design in order to respond to this demand. Madraseh Ali administrators shortened the amount of time for students to master course materials. One of Khanum-e Safiri's innovations at Madraseh Ali at the time involved dividing the larger books into different sections.[18] She then divided these among different instructors. As an instructor, Maryam welcomed this change. Maryam had been struggling with the way to teach certain materials without losing students' interest. The materials that needed to be covered in Islamic jurisprudence had been too much to cover in one term. Students were previously required to read about a thousand pages from Arabic text and then translate them into Persian. Both the teachers and students had begun to lose focus and interest in the topics.

Another one of Khanum-e Safiri's innovations in Madraseh Ali had "its roots in the (old) howzeh." She decreased the class time from two hours, 8:00 to 10:00 a.m., to fifty minutes, with a ten-minute break before going to the next class or to the second half of the class. Maryam was quick to interject that the men's section had rejected these reinventions, but it had been beneficial for the women's section. "This was one change with the best result. This was her idea. It didn't happen in the men's department. . . . They didn't like the approach. They have a different idea. But, the result was much better for the women, even for the teachers," Maryam detailed.

Another change was in part out of Maryam's input, an idea she took from her brothers' student-teaching experience in the howzeh in Qom. In exchange for fees, Maryam proposed to teach undergraduate and master's students as well as classes in the howzeh in Tehran. Maryam showed that student teaching through repetitive delivery of course content allowed doctoral students to master the material in a shorter amount of time. "Teaching is the best way to learn," she explained. Madraseh Ali agreed to the arrangement and offered the same option to all doctoral students. Khanum-e Safiri downsized her classes from thirty to fifteen or up to twenty students per class, increased the number of courses offered, and produced students who could begin to teach the basics of Islamic jurisprudence in the Region One women's howzeh in Tehran.

The purposes of an Islamic education were no longer limited to women becoming future jurists or scholars like those from scholarly families. Howzevi women began to focus on spaces beyond scholarly circles, advocating to properly educate the masses on Islam and their divinely ordained rights. This development has arguably been one of the most important pillars of the powerful Islamic Republic that Iran is today. Also, since the howzeh was a project for women developed in large part by women, directives were not entirely top-down from men or the government. The women at the administrative, teaching, and student levels were making key decisions on ways to change the howzeh's focus.

Repurposing the Women's Howzeh Elmiyeh

The Region One howzeh shared a similar process of transformation. Student demands and administrative responses were making shifts in the system, as we shall see from the work of Khanum-e Refaei. I met Khanum-e Refaei for the first time in 2008 through Dr. Hassanpour's English class in Arjantin. She had already been studying at the Dars-e Kharij level with Ayatollah Khamenei for two years at the time. Khanum-e Refaei, in her late thirties, was married and had one daughter. Both her husband and younger brother were engineers. Her youngest sister was a student in a howzeh in Tehran who had just finished memorizing the Qur'an and had been accepted to Madraseh Ali.

Khanum-e Refaei described the way she had a passion for learning about Islam beyond the basics but also loved the hard sciences and mathematics. She had just graduated from a mathematics-focused high school when she began thinking about where to continue her studies. She had never been to a howzeh, so she consulted with her sister-in-law, who at the time was a student at a howzeh in Tehran. She was conflicted for some time, until her husband traveled to Syria to pay homage to Hazrat Zaynab, sister of Imam Husayn, who was buried in Damascus. She told her husband to ask Hazrat Zaynab to pray to God for her to make the right decision with her education. Two weeks after her husband's return, her sister-in-law again suggested that she visit the howzeh to see whether she would fit into that environment. When Khanum-e Refaei asked for the name of the howzeh, she was told Howzeh-ye Zaynab.

Telling me this story with a smile on her face, Khanum-e Refaei described the way she felt at that moment, after hearing the name Zaynab. She said she knew that was a sign from God. She felt she had a calling but did not yet know what about, except that she belonged in that howzeh. She finished her *Sat'h* 2, equivalent to an undergraduate degree, and proceeded to complete her master's degree at Madraseh Ali. She then became an instructor of topics in Islamic jurisprudence at Madraseh Ali and in the Region One howzeh for women.

I had a conversation with her and Maryam about the transformations that have taken place in the Region One Women's Howzeh Elmiyeh since 2003. Khanum-e Refaei explained that at some point, the students from the Region One howzeh began requesting opportunities to teach Islam in schools and to groups involved in religious propagation. But to do so required a madrak, a certificate of completion that showed they had in fact reached a certain level of education and qualified training. So, the students also began requesting certificates from the howzeh. Governed locally at the time, the Region One Women's Howzeh Elmiyeh was not completely prepared for the task of overseeing the process for student certification since they had been occupied with securing infrastructure and finding qualified teachers. They began issuing the certificates of completion to students around 1997 to meet the students' demands. When the howzeh's decision became public knowledge, there was a sudden increase in applications.

The administrators also wanted to provide more options for students in terms of qualifying for graduate programs at higher education institutions like the University of Tehran. To accomplish this, the women's howzeh needed to establish common ground with higher educational institutions and get these institutions to recognize the howzeh certificate of completion. The entire howzeh system needed to overhaul its approach to education. Khanum-e Refaei explained that their objective was simply to change it from "nonsystematic" to "systematic"—meaning they would have to work with the universities in Tehran to synchronize the curriculum, methods of assessment, and program completion requirements and would have to attach numerical value to student progress.

ACCOMMODATING THE MADRAK

Still remaining a separate entity from the ministry of education, the women's howzeh in Tehran and the universities drafted a plan for changes to be made so that other institutions of higher education could recognize the howzeh certificate. Before 2003, the women's howzeh consisted of the maktab (high school), Sat'h 1 (associate's level), Sat'h 2 (undergraduate level), and Sat'h 3 (master's level). Thereafter, a student would be qualified to be part of a Dars-e Kharij class anywhere in Iran. The system had changed significantly by the time Khanum-e Refaei and I met.[19] For example, they had begun working on adding Sat'h 4, which would be an equivalent to a doctoral level. The Dars-e Kharij level would then be considered a postdoctoral level.

The adjustments made to accommodate for a madrak created system-wide changes, including the administrative structure. Previous to the changes in 2003, one or two people could manage one howzeh. Khanum-e Refaei explained that after the change, "the howzeh has financial officers, education research, a culture of research, and more." From being managed locally, it became part of a centralized system under the Management Center of the Women's Seminaries located in Qom. As I've noted, the Kharij level is the only level that has not changed. Its management and program continued to be at the discretion of the mujtahid or Marja'e Taqlid leading the circle of students, to the extent that some have not allowed women from attending.

The approach to the curriculum has had the most notable change, according to Khanum-e Refaei. Courses were assigned credits. A student needed to have completed a certain number of required credits to be given a madrak. Electives were also added. While students were still not required to pay tuition, the howzeh began to offer English, history, and computer courses. Some howzeh offered other foreign languages like German. There were also courses like home economics and parenting. Sat'h 2, equivalent to a bachelor's degree, was added to all of the howzeh. Sat'h 3, equivalent to a master's or *fogeh lisans*, was already being incorporated in six Tehran howzeh in 2011.

Based on her experience of providing curricular and instructional support, Khanum-e Safiri explained that the Region One women's howzeh elmiyeh were more developed than Madraseh Ali. To give an example, they published their own magazine with content that contributed to developing topics in different fields of Islamic sciences. It also had a much more in-depth and disciplined approach to the course materials than Madraseh Ali. However, the amount of time to finish studying books had completely changed. Previously, it would take an average of three years to finish studying a book, since the book, its author, the transmitters of its narrations, and sometimes its grammatical structure were studied in detail. After the curricular changes, students in the howzeh were expected to complete the book in one semester.

Like Madraseh Ali, the women's howzeh elmiyeh in Tehran also filtered for age for applicants who wanted to receive a madrak. Previously, women could join the howzeh regardless of age, with the exception of Madraseh Ali in Tehran and Jami'at Al-Zahra in Qom, since both institutions were developed from the idea of combining the howzeh and the university system from the start. This had to change. Khanum-e Refaei explained, "They must be free to study here to take part in class. So, for example, the howzeh needed to slowly lower the enrollment rates of ladies who are old, because they would not be able to keep up." For them, a woman's age determined her chances of keeping up with her cohort.

The assumption was that a woman with familial obligations would not keep up with the demands of the howzeh. In another conversation with Khanum-e Safiri and her friend Khanum-e Ray, an administrator in one howzeh, they explained that enforcing age limitations ensured that students in a class would be at a similar level of effort. "A forty-year-old woman could no longer be in the same class as the fourteen-year-old girl," one of them added. They determined that single women between the ages of fourteen and twenty-five could apply to be admitted into the howzeh. In this category, potential applicants came from two kinds of educational backgrounds. The first were students who completed the guidance cycle (equivalent to middle school). If admitted, these students needed to study in the howzeh for seven years to finish Sat'h 1 and 2. Those who graduated from high school were another type of applicant. It would take them five years to complete Sat'h 2.

In the other age category, women between the ages of twenty-five and thirty-one, there were three kinds of potential applicants. If married without an undergraduate degree, a woman could apply before the age of twenty-seven. Married or single, if she had an undergraduate degree elsewhere, she could apply before her twenty-ninth birthday. If a student had a master's degree, she would have to join the howzeh before the age of thirty-one. If the applicant was a talabeh azad, a freely roaming student, before joining the howzeh, they would have to take exams considered equivalent to the courses offered at the howzeh. Then, depending on the exams they passed, they could complete the program in fewer than five years. There were freely roaming students, however, who did not receive a madrak, as Khanum-e Refaei explained: "For example, if you are a formal student and your mother wants to take classes with you just for learning, she will not receive credit for the madrak. She can sit with you and take the classes. These students are called talabeh azad, and there is no age limit."

In all cases, students were required to finish Sat'h 2 before choosing a topic of research. They were required to write their findings and defend them to their mentor or advisor. They then qualified for Sat'h 3, equivalent to a master's degree, which would take approximately three years to complete. The Management Center of the Women's Seminaries had hoped to complete designing the program for Sat'h 4 by 2011. Sat'h 4, equivalent to a doctoral degree, would take three to four years to finish in the new system.

Interviewing potential students had always been a part of the admissions process before these changes were made. But because of the increased number of applicants, administrators became concerned about the types of students applying

Figure 2.2. Howzevi women participate in organizing annual events like the *Shir Kharegan* in Mosalla that are attended by thousands of women. Tehran, 2011. ©Amina Tawasil.

to the howzeh. She explained that some of the students entering the howzeh "did not wear hijab or were not good in hijab; they just wanted to go to the howzeh for the madrak." They needed to differentiate between applicants who were entering the howzeh for either purely gaining Islamic knowledge or acquiring this to work toward the ideological objectives of the Islamic Republic versus those who simply needed a job. To address this, Khanum-e Refaei and those who came before her had to create a more formal admissions process. They turned to using both examinations and interviews. They added a "private concur," as she called it, which was a standardized entrance exam for all the howzeh that issued a madrak. This was separate and different from the exam taken for academic-focused universities such as University of Tehran or Shahid Beheshti University. The exam was designed in the city of Qom and distributed to all the howzeh that issued the madrak. If the student passed the exam, she would then have to pass an interview in front of a panel. Despite the changes in admissions policies, Khanum-e Refaei asserted that acceptance rates continued to increase.

The Barter: Howzeh, Talabeh Azad, and Ijaza

With all the reworkings of the women's howzeh taking place, three major concepts and practices changed. The first was what constituted a howzeh. For the purpose of analysis, and in consultation with the women of this study, I categorize Madraseh Ali as a howzeh. One reason was that it was conceptualized as one, since it was to be a place to learn Islamic sciences from renowned scholars. To the people outside its walls, it was known as a howzeh, often a government howzeh. Another reason was that after finishing a master's degree at Madraseh Ali, a student might qualify for the Dars-e Kharij level, the highest level of education in the howzeh system. In Tehran, students from Madraseh Ali qualified to apply for Ayatollah Khamenei's and Larijani's classes. The last reason, and I think most compelling, was that Madraseh Ali provided curricular and programming support and teachers for the Region One Women's Howzeh Elmiyeh, which was made up of the howzeh in Tehran and surrounding areas.

Khanum-e Safiri and other administrators then developed its programs "to bring together the positive points of the howzeh with the positive points of the university" as a response to other sociopolitical forces. For this reason, its students and staff did not refer to the institution as a howzeh nor a university. Though its official name is Shahid Motahhari University, students and staff commonly called it Madraseh Ali. The decades-long transformations changed the way its students thought of themselves. From being a student of Islamic knowledge in the seminary, howzevi, they shifted to being a tolab or talabeh, a student of Islamic knowledge and/or its sciences. While both terminologies refer to a student of Islam, a talabeh learned directly from individual scholars, without the seminary. Thus, a howzevi was a talabeh, but a talabeh was not necessarily a howzevi. The ambiguity of what to call themselves and their institution points to the systematic transformation that has been taking place through the work of women like Khanum-e Safiri.

The second major change was the figure of the talabeh azad, a freely roaming student. This was once the representative figure of the seminarian all over Iran because students in the howzeh "roamed" from one scholarly circle to another, or from one howzeh to another. This kind of mobility was prevalent because, as Fischer wrote, the system was student-centered.[20] Classes were accessible to students of any age so long as they were accepted into the howzeh or a scholar's study circle. Perhaps with the exception of Madraseh Ali that opened its doors with a more formalized curriculum, this student-centered approach had been the norm in the women's howzeh up until the institutional move to create a certification system that began in the early 2000s. Because of this institutional move to coincide with the university system, the student-centered approach was no longer possible for many women who wanted only to gain expertise in specific fields.

In 2011, the figure of the freely roaming student was made up of neighborhood women such as housewives and the elderly who attended howzeh classes on the basics of Islam whenever their schedules allowed them to. Many of the Region One howzeh still offered such classes without providing a madrak. What constituted a freely roaming student had been reformulated as an outcome of these institutional changes.

The third element of Islamic education impacted by the transformation of the women's howzeh was the practice of issuing an ijaza by the teacher to the student. As I've previously explained, the ijaza is a written certificate or a verbal permission to teach from a more senior religious authority. It comes in the form of either a personal written letter or a verbal approval stating the permission. Overall, the ijaza is one of the testaments to the ways in which the personal connectedness of human beings, *ittisaliyah*, serves as the basis of Islamic educative practices.[21] This connectedness is characteristic of the relationship between the howzevi and her teachers, marked by a personal knowledge of each other and by assessments that were student-centered.

A student earned an ijaza after having been evaluated by their teacher on how they teach either a section of a book or an entire book. For Qur'anic memorization and recitation, the evaluation is focused on the recitation. Students used to travel from one Islamic scholar to the next to study and eventually collect ijazas. Historically, some forms of ijaza absorbed the practice of *isnad*, whereby the transmitters of knowledge from teacher to student were also documented on the ijaza itself. Meaning, when the student acquired a written ijaza, a genealogy of names that included their teacher and their teacher's teacher were written on the ijaza. This was especially true for an ijaza in Qur'anic recitation and transmission of Hadith, the narrations from the Prophet Mohammad.

The value of an ijaza in Islamic scholarship has somewhat diminished in part because of the ease of acquiring one, and because of the abundance of information on Islamic text and edicts available on the internet. Though it may not have been as drastically transformed among Shi'i scholars in the other cities of Iran, the word *ijaza* was rarely used among the howzevi I spent time with. They did not use it to describe their teaching and assessment activities during my fieldwork. A handful of student teachers explained that it was no longer necessary; the contemporary certificate of completion had replaced the ijaza.

Though having an ijaza was no longer necessary to teach in the women's howzeh and not recognized for employment outside the howzeh system, Ayatollah Bojnurdi continued to evaluate his students on a section of a book or an entire book in 2011. Khanum-e Tabesh explained that he could issue them his ijaza, which qualified them to teach the materials he or she was tested on. However, an ijaza from Ayatollah Bojnurdi in Tehran may or may not be recognized as a document of teaching certification in other howzeh unless it was certified in Qom. It could be political. That ijaza almost certainly would have teeth within his circles but not for a teaching position in an elementary school. In other words, though it is highly regarded within clerical circles, an ijaza may not be considered proof of qualification in the workplace.

As bureaucracy continued to increase within the howzeh elmiyeh, the process of acquiring a madrak continued to become a priority. The madrak required a student to have spent a quantifiable number of hours learning in a classroom, accumulating a standard number of classes and passing standardized exams created in Qom with a passing score of at least twelve out of twenty. The most noticeable trade-off for the madrak thus has been the personal connection between a student and the teacher when it came to assessments. It used to be that the teacher would personalize the assessment geared towards the unique strengths and weaknesses of a student. Assessments became more standardized through time. A personalized student-centered assessment of progress was no longer a predominant attribute of the women's howzeh educative experience as part of Tehran's Region One Women's Howzeh Elmiyeh. To experience student-centered assessments, students must reach the Dars-e Kharij level or not become part of madrak-granting howzeh program.

AGHA-YE SHARIFI, HOWZEH-YE KOWSAR, AND THE JAHADI BASIJ

This final section samples the further diversification of the howzeh. I introduce Howzeh-ye Kowsar, whose howzevi population were active members of both Jahad Sazandegi, also called Jahadi Basij, the Reconstruction Corps, and the Basij-e Daneshjooyi, the University Basij. Jahadi Basij is one of the many Basij subgroups developed out of the paramilitary volunteer organization Ayatollah Khomeini established during the Iran-Iraq War. Jahadi Basij is dedicated to literacy, vocational training, construction of schools or clinics, medical missions, distribution of staple foods, and Islamic propagation in remote areas of Iran. This section sheds light on the relationship between the howzevi and Jahadi Basij. This was one kind of work that women did with their howzeh education. Here, the experience of a man, with his network of unnamed men and howzevi women, shows that political difference cuts across gender lines. I use Howzeh-ye Kowsar to capture this and the importance of recognizing the howzeh's ever-changing landscape.

Howzeh-ye Kowsar was different from the Region One howzeh and Madraseh Ali in many ways. First, most of its students had finished their undergraduate and master's degrees at a university. The students decided to enroll in this specific howzeh to learn from its founder, Agha-ye Sharifi, and through the students' involvement with the University Basij. One of its students, Mehdiyeh, described the students at Howzeh-ye Kowsar as going from "beta to alpha," from the university to the howzeh. She learned about Howzeh-ye Kowsar from the students who traveled with her over the summer to south Khorasan for a Jahadi Basij mission. Mehdiyeh and others explained they did not feel they were well versed whenever anyone would ask them questions about Islam, especially during the Jahadi missions. They hoped that spending a few years studying at Kowsar would allow them to respond better. Hoorieh was specific about feeling inept whenever someone would ask her about rituals. She wanted to know how to respond to questions without having to always resort to quotations. Like others, she wanted to provide answers that were based on Islamic philosophy and from interpretations of different scholars.

Howzeh-ye Kowsar became the meeting point for those who were involved in the different Jahadi Basij groups and the various University Basij groups, such as Elmo Sanat Jahadi Basij and Amir Kabir University in Tehran. Agha-ye Sharifi was an active participant in Jahadi Basij, among other youth-related engagements in the city. Fatimah, Hoda, and those in their Jahadi Basij groups became familiar with Agha-ye Sharifi's work through his university lectures, which were often arranged by the University Basij groups. Agha-ye Sharifi was in his late thirties, and his family was originally from Esfahan. About a decade previously, he was an engineering student at Amir Kabir University but left his program to study in one of the howzeh for men in Qom. He completed a certain level in the howzeh that gave him enough aptitude to become a howzeh teacher in Tehran. He returned to Tehran and enrolled in Sharif University to finish his engineering degree. At the time I was introduced to him, he was finishing this degree while managing and teaching classes at the howzeh for men and women in two different parts of Tehran. He and his wife had a nine-year-old daughter, and his wife was then teaching Islamic philosophy at Howzeh-ye Kowsar. At the time, the supporting network behind his project was the supreme leader's committee for universities.

In addition to the howzevi at Kowsar having completed a university education, another aspect of Howzeh-ye Kowsar that made it different from the Region One Women's Howzeh Elmiyeh was that it was going through a transition as Agha-ye Sharifi had been working on its accreditation. This would not be approved until the following fall semester. The other difference was Kowsar's curricular focus. It did not revolve around Islamic jurisprudence. They were not concerned with producing students that could draft policies. Having observed that most of the howzeh in Tehran were focused on teaching Islamic jurisprudence, Agha-ye Sharifi and his friends decided to create an educative space for other Islamic sciences like Qur'anic and Hadith studies.

Although Islamic jurisprudence was necessary to educate students and future teachers on religious obligations such as praying, fasting, giving alms, and engaging in business transactions, other subfields of Islamic sciences such as the knowledge of the Qur'an and the life of the Prophet Mohammad were as essential in the work of khod shenasi. Agha-ye Sharifi and his friends created Howzeh-ye Kowsar to fill this void. He spoke of these necessities or Islamic obligations in layers. The study of Islamic jurisprudence was the external layer. The other Islamic sciences served to inform Islamic jurisprudent discourse. These disciplines reinforced and enriched the other. For Agha-ye Sharifi and his friends, it was also crucial that students know how to find a balance between the diversity of religious interpretations, practices, and philosophies.

He likened the Islamic disciplines to a metal ball, similar in form, different in content: "Religion has a core, haqiqat, a truth, inside it that shows this core, this core expresses itself or emerges to the surface." He and his friends wanted to provide an avenue for students to engage this core: "If a howzeh wants to do something new to change what they did before, it should look at religion from different angles, from different sides, and these sides are linked with each other."[22] Students flocked to Howzeh-ye Kowsar to find out what that was.

Howzeh-ye Kowsar and Accreditation

Since 2003, the howzevi have seen a significant turn in the centralization process. This process alienated local initiatives to establish howzeh that were not intended to become part of the centralization process. Agha-ye Sharifi, however, had every intention to join the centralization process. He had been working on getting Howzeh-ye Kowsar for women and its men's section accredited in Qom for the past five years, since it had first opened. He remarked that if Kowsar was the only one of its kind in Tehran, he hoped others would follow suit.

Howzeh-ye Kowsar created a space for students to focus on teaching Arabic, Tafsir, or the work of Qur'anic interpretation, Qur'anic memorization, Islamic history, philosophy, the study of theological discourse, morals, the principles of Islamic jurisprudence and Islamic jurisprudence. Like the other howzeh, there was a focus on reading Nahjol Balaghe, or The Path of Eloquence, a famous collection of sermons, letters, explication of verses of the Qur'an, and narrations attributed to Imam Ali. On Saturdays, Howzeh-ye Kowsar held discussions about the afterlife according to the Qur'an. Students were being trained to remember sections of the Qur'an where specific topics may be found. This would then enable them to answer questions with verses of the Qur'an.

Despite the absence of accreditation, Agha-ye Sharifi took what he experienced in Qom as a student and readjusted it for his students in Tehran. The classes, books, schedule, and internal networking of teachers who were also students in other howzeh were put together to form Howzeh-ye Kowsar. Students were taught to engage in the dialectic practice in class, bahes, and required to form disputation circles, mobaheseh, after classes. During this period of pre-accreditation, Howze-ye Kowsar's approach to assessments was student-centered. Different groups of students rotated in designing and creating weekly exams for students for two classes. Though students were aware that they would not be receiving a certificate of completion, they continued to participate in the assessment processes, composed of pass or no pass outcomes, to see what subjects or topics they needed improvements in. To complete the program, students were required to write a final thesis. New students continued to take the entrance exam and interview for admission, and enrollment increased every year. Although tuition was free because Howzeh-ye Kowsar received an endowment, it was customary among students to donate about 10 toman (less than $1) every month.

In the spring of 2011, Howzeh-ye Kowsar could not yet issue a madrak to their students. Agha-ye Sharifi and his volunteers, teachers, and students were attempting to develop their curriculum to become accredited without losing much of the howzeh practices he inherited from Qom such as student-created assessments. This was in contrast to the way the other howzeh had been co-opted into the process of centralization and bureaucratization. When I first began visiting Howzeh-ye Kowsar in the spring, there were fifty to sixty women, mostly in their twenties and thirties, with all ages ranging from eighteen to possibly fifty years old. There were eight to ten teachers, including Agha-ye Sharifi and his wife, who were physically present only to teach. One of the students was a student teacher. She taught Arabic. The only administrative mainstay in the howzeh was Khanum-e Ahmadi, who kept records of absences and managed the logistical aspects of the daily schedule; her secretary, Khanum-e Hassani, made copies and oversaw kitchen duties among the students.

On a few occasions, the students mentioned that Agha-ye Sharifi had difficulty ensuring accreditation for the howzeh. In one of the class lectures I attended, he talked about the relationship between having knowledge and having humility, saying that having knowledge fostered humility rather than arrogance. These are concepts I explain in chapters 4 and 5. But, in the same lecture, he mentioned that an administrator in Qom once told him, "You have a difficult and challenging task ahead of you because you are dealing with students who think they are better than others." The administrator was referring to what was unique about Howzeh-ye Kowsar—the student population was composed mostly of women who had earned their undergraduate or graduate degrees at the universities. The administrator's opinion indexes one of many stereotypes among clerics about university-educated women: that they have a condescending disposition toward Islamic education.

Agha-ye Sharifi was forced to work through these stereotypes about his students within his networks in Qom and in Tehran in order to get accreditation for the howzeh. Despite the adverse perceptions and obstacles Agha-ye Sharifi had to overcome, he frequented meetings in Qom in an attempt to convince the governing body of the howzeh to recognize their program so that Howzeh-ye Kowsar could begin issuing certificates for its students. For that reason, the howzeh was initially defined and referred to as "a howzeh" to all the students but was not recognized by Qom formally as an institution that could issue certificates of program completion.

Pieces of Agha-ye Sharifi's explanations all point to the fact that there were other men and women behind this project, as well as other men who continued to help facilitate its accreditation despite enormous odds. In both locations, he secured a room in one of the floors with computers and internet access. Other Islamic-related institutes that occupied different floors of the buildings used the same room at different times of the week. Many women would use this room during break time and after the mobaheseh, or disputation sessions, in the afternoon to do work on their online Hadith courses taken through the College of Hadith. The students maintained that Agha-ye Sharifi funded them if they expressed an interest in pursuing the study of Hadith in more depth.

In the fall of 2011, Howzeh-ye Kowsar received accreditation and moved to an entirely new location in central Tehran, to a building that was being renovated on the first floor, a location they shared with an after-university program for women students to take howzeh courses. The previous summer, students, old and new, had to take an entrance exam to be admitted into the new Kowsar. Old students were told they had to begin their programs again if they were to receive certificates at the end of the program.

Agha-ye Sharifi divided his students into two groups. There were twelve students from the "old Kowsar" who took the entrance exam and passed. Agha-ye Sharifi prearranged for the students of the old Kowsar to finish their program for the remainder of that school year in the floor above where he would also teach. These twelve students would have to start the program from the beginning, disregarding the units earned in previous years. There were fifty students enrolled in the certificate program, which eliminated memorization of the Qur'an. Students could continue their memorization in other Qur'an institutes in Tehran, however. The new Kowsar had new amenities such as lockers, new desks, newly carpeted floors, a white screen, and a screen projector. The students were also provided with free lunch. Additionally, each student had an option to borrow a laptop for the year.

SHIFTING PRIORITIES

There is something relatable in the women's work with educational bureaucracy—the work of providing solutions creates other problems. This is not unique to the howzeh and its administrators, who are attempting to develop and maintain a society that nurtures the work of khod shenasi. Trade-offs come with the process of transformation. As I have shown, however, the women actively made decisions and implemented solutions to their challenges in ways that made the most sense for them at the moment and in ways that were not easily visible to the untrained eye. Undoubtedly, the Islamic Republic bestowed opportunities for them.[23]

Maryam explained that as their level of education increases, the more work they see around them that they must do. That is, as more students graduated to become teachers, the more programs were developed. Today, graduates of the howzeh become qualified for positions in institutions that affect various policies in Iran. A shift in focus has taken place. It seems the women's howzeh is slowly moving away from producing Islamic scholars and into producing developers of a revolutionary Shi'i society as envisioned by its founders.

Without close examination, this claim almost sounds like empty rhetorical propaganda for inclusivity. However, as I've shown, this phenomenon was at the expense of traditional educative practices and the long-standing reputation of the Iranian howzeh as wholly independent of the government and its resources. In addition, this access came with meeting demands, thus, exclusions based on an applicant's age, reputation, and educative objectives, which emerged during the process of re-creating the women's howzeh. An applicant's reputation and bodily practices like wearing hijab indexed their political leanings. The admissions process, thus, was a way to make sure that secularists and/or known reformists were excluded from having control of the government's programs. Like Khanum-e Refaei and Safiri, many of the more senior howzevi saw this process of exclusion as a logical strategy to protect their project, which essentially included protecting access to an Islamic education from anything or anyone who seemed to dilute either its content or the quality and diligence of those who would receive such education.

Whether the women's howzeh elmiyeh, dynamic as it was, did in fact produce the graduates they hoped to produce was not a given, since human beings never fully accept the conditions of their surroundings. Educational anthropologist Hervé Varenne writes, "Human beings . . . are always at work constructing something somewhat different from that which they experience."[24] But we do know that the women's howzeh had become a degree-granting institution so that women like Maryam and Ma'ede could qualify for employment in offices managed by the dictates of men. With their presence, men can no longer dominate these spaces. This phenomenon of including howzevi women in the project of developing a Shi'i society transformed institutions, common practices, and characteristics of Islamic education in Iran.

The project of howzevi inclusion continues to change what constitutes the howzeh and a howzevi woman. As I have written elsewhere, the fervor in learning the English language to export the revolution to the rest of the world and to up the value of their research has certainly been one indirect outcome of becoming a howzevi. The women inevitably read topics in English literature that would challenge their assumptions about different ways of life.[25]

Another indirect outcome of women's access to a howzeh education that focused on Islamic jurisprudence has been the possible increase in the number of mujtahideh. Here, I am not referring to an increase of this possibility over time, since possibilities are constantly in flux. Instead, I am referring to a change of demographics: what used to be hundreds of women studying behind curtains with men has grown to over sixty-five thousand women annually in the entire country. In 2008, there were twelve women in Ayatollah Khamenei's Dars-e Kharij class. By 2011, there were about sixty. Even if one were to argue that the curriculum for training women for the practice of ijtihad was grossly incomplete, the possibility of a woman becoming a mujtahideh remains. It has become an unavoidable and ongoing conversation.

Although the debates between curriculum developers in Qom continue about which direction the institution should take, the concern does not dictate what women will decide to do with their education. There are seemingly contradictory but important considerations worth exploring. For instance, providing access to education, regardless of objective, does not guarantee that women will want to become public authority figures. Out of the thousands of howzevi graduates since the 1980s, there are not many women who have taken up publicly visible positions of power and authority like becoming a mujtahideh or a member of the parliament, the various state offices, and state-run media organizations. At the same time, there were women open to all possibilities who consistently took advantage of all access. Both can be true at once. We need to understand the way these howzevi women come to decide what is of value for them and the way they are valued by those around them. I consider all these in the following chapters.

NOTES

1. Fischer, *Iran*, 83.
2. Taqlid (imitation) is observed in the details of religion, of the "how to" worship, but not in the fundamentals of the faith, the "what to" believe in.
3. Momen, *Introduction to Shi'i Islam*, 143. The historical development of the doctrine and the rise of the Marja'e Taqlid.

4. Motahhari, "Principles of Ijtihad in Islam."

5. For Arabic, see https://www.almaany.com/en/dict/ar-en/%D8%AD%D9%88%D8%B2%D8%A9/; for Persian, see https://archive.org/details/AComprehensivePersian-English Dictionary-FrancisJosephSteingass/page/n438/mode/1up.

6. Zaman, "Competing Conceptions," 241.

7. Berkey, *Formation of Islam*, 186.

8. Fischer, *Iran*, 1980.

9. Najmabadi, "(Un)veiling Feminism," 52–53.

10. El Haitami, "Restructuring Female Religious," 229.

11. Hassan, "Women at the Intersection," 111.

12. Afary, *Sexual Politics*, 257–62.

13. Bahramitash, "Saving Iranian," 108.

14. Massoumeh Ebtekar was part of the revolutionary student movement that took over the US embassy in 1979. She became the publisher of the women's magazine *Farzaneh* in 1996 and vice president and head of the Department of Environment in 2000 under the Khatami administration. Marzieh Vahid Dastjerdi was the first woman to have occupied a ministry position, as the minister of health; Maryam Behrouzi (d. 2012) was the head of Jami'at Zaynab, a conservative women's group. She was a howzevi and served in the first four post-revolutionary parliaments. She actively worked on removing barriers for women in occupying political positions.

15. For a visual representation, refer to appendix B.

16. Khanum-e Safiri, Madraseh Ali, April 24, 2011.

17. Menashari, *Education and the Making*, 301–02.

18. The titles of some of these books are in appendix A.

19. See appendix B.

20. Fischer, *Iran*, 61-63.

21. Graham, "Traditionalism in Islam," 501.

22. Agha-ye Sharifi, Howzeh-ye Kowsar, April 19, 2011.

23. Afary, *Sexual Politics*, 292–322; Najmabadi, "(Un)veiling Feminism," 52; Sakurai, "Shi'ite Women's Seminaries," 743; Sedghi refers to them as "proponent women." Sedghi, *Women and Politics*, 261–62.

24. Varenne, "The Social Facting," 373–89.

25. Tawasil, "Reading as Practice," 66–83.

THREE

—ᚨᚨ—

THE HOWZEVI AND IJTIHAD

SITTING WITH MARYAM, SARA, and Mahgol in the front office waiting for Khanum-e Yasseri in Qom, I noticed two pictures hung above our heads side by side, one of Ayatollah Khomeini and one of Ayatollah Khamenei. The entire side of the room to my right was made of glass. We could see directly into the courtyard with a lone tree planted right in the middle of it, its branches serving as a shade for the 102-degree desert heat in Qom. The wind often blew into the yard just outside the glass window, but its warmth did little to alleviate the heat inside the room. As we fanned each other with magazines placed on the coffee table in front of us, Khanum-e Yasseri entered the room. We stood up to greet her, and as we sat down, she was the first one to remove her chador with her *rusari*, a dark-colored head scarf closed from the chin downward, still intact. I followed suit, removing the top of my chador to drape over my shoulder. The women I traveled with did not. She sat near the window, and we proceeded to introduce ourselves.

I learned later on that Khanum-e Yasseri was a research assistant for one of the very few publicly acknowledged mujtahideh in Iran. Khanum-e Yasseri became interested in studying the Islamic sciences while she was a biology premedical student at the University of Tehran in the early to mid-1970s. Philosophical questions about existence, the purpose of life, and why Islam represented the truth became a focal point in her life as a young woman in Tehran. After getting married to Agha-ye Janebzadeh, who at the time was a student in one of the howzeh for men in Qom, she moved to Qom and joined a women's study group that later became a maktab for women. That maktab was key in mobilizing women to take part in the revolution. She then enrolled and focused on Islamic theology and Islamic philosophy at Jami'at Al-Zahra when it opened. Khanum-e Yasseri did not opt to become a mujtahideh herself; she opted for another kind of participation, the kind that works behind the scenes with a public figure.

This chapter is situated in the highly contested subject regarding women's Islamic education: the objective. In this chapter, I complicate two claims made about howzevi women that, when examined closely together, are contradictory. First, I challenge the expectation that, in order for howzevi women to be considered successful, they must use their education to liberate themselves and others by occupying publicly visible positions of authority. Other possibilities of success are overlooked and need to be accounted for. I argue that since what constitutes success for the howzevi is taking actions that will strengthen the work of khod shenasi, this work must be included in the rubric of educative success.

Second, I take issue with the charge that when and if howzevi women remotely take on positions of leadership, they must be, like their male counterparts, hungry for power. Much of what we know ethnographically about Islamic education in Iran comes from research about the men's howzeh, which is marked by an ethos of competition. I look closely at what this ethos among men implies about teacher-student relationships, and I demonstrate that women experience these relationships differently. They guide, support, and model skills for other women without necessarily becoming an authority over others.

In the following, I first analyze probable explanations for why very few howzevi were publicly visible as mujtahideh after three decades of having access to the women's howzeh. I then describe the educative pathways of three howzevi women to explore other forms of success such as teaching, conducting research, and publishing in the context of strengthening the work of khod shenasi.

WOMEN'S ACCESS, KHOD SHENASI, AND IJTIHAD

In theory, women become part of the howzeh to learn what the work of khod shenasi requires through the Islamic sciences. With years of hard work and persistence, the women will ideally learn to some degree the way mujtahid do ijtihad, the process of making independent juristic interpretation. Ijtihad is a necessity because time and place are constantly changing. That is, new Islamic rulings are always needed, and jurisprudent scholars need to consider making revisions to rulings that are informed by the current conditions of the time and place. The position comes with enormous responsibilities and difficulties, thus it strengthens the work of khod shenasi at the individual level but also at the collective level by way of leading others toward goodness, the necessary humility and sincerity in the remembrance of God. For both reasons, taking up the position of a mujtahid brings with it divine merit.

A woman becoming a mujtahid was considered an anomaly all the way through the 1970s.[1] However, in Iran today, doing ijtihad for themselves but also potentially for others is possible for any woman who becomes a student of the howzeh. Ayatollah Khomeini "opened the door of ijtihad" for both men and women, according to Khanum-e Yasseri. As I've explained, it was because of Ayatollah Khomeini that it became widely accepted in Iranian society for women to do ijtihad at all. Khanum-e Yasseri explained further, "Imam Khomeini prepared a situation for women to make this progress quicker. Imam Khomeini encouraged them [women] to participate, to go and study these religious matters in order to become mujtahid."

What is often overlooked about this access is the existing limitation on women. In 2011, men could eventually do ijtihad for other people. Women, on the other hand, were confined to doing ijtihad only for themselves, and at most for other women. This meant a woman would not qualify to occupy the position of a Marja'e Taqlid, the highest-ranking position in the clerical establishment, because she would first need to be recognized as someone who makes independent juristic interpretations for other people. As men continue to pursue their howzeh education, the possibility of becoming Marja'e Taqlid in the future was open to them. This is not the case for women.

THE DEBATE ABOUT WOMEN AND IJTIHAD

Despite that limitation, there should already be thousands of women who are publicly known as mujtahideh for women, now forty years after the revolution. However, with the exception of the late Banu Amin and Zohreh Sefati, that number is low, if not nonexistent. In fact, none of the women I spent time with had ever reported having taken ijtihad-related assessments in 2011.

One side of the debate regarding the objective of women's Islamic education held that women could do ijtihad for other people and thus potentially become a Marja'e Taqlid. This would give her the authority to collect and distribute the *khums* tax, one-fifth of a person's yearly income, and make legal decisions for followers and less-credentialed clerics in the future. The other side of the debate held that women could make juristic interpretations only for themselves and women concerning only women's issues. Women could also assist the Marja'e Taqlid in doing research. This was a practice already in motion when I was in Iran.

The life of Fatimah, the Prophet Mohammad's daughter and wife of Imam Ali, was often cited as an example that someday women could become Marja'e Taqlid as a necessity, because women understand women's issues better than men. This necessity was inherent in the process of ijtihad. Khanum-e Yasseri stated, "Women can become Marja'e Taqlid when the time comes. . . . Fatimah

Zahra, the Holy Lady, isn't just the role model for women; she is the role model for both men and women. If she can be a role model for both all over the world all the time, the women who imitate her, who follow her way, can be the same . . . if we find a suitable situation. Women can gain their degree in their knowledge and science and become Marja'e Taqlid. This is in ijtihad." However, that time had not yet come.

The more senior howzevi urged women to prepare themselves so that by the time the edict changed, there would be thousands of women ready for the role, if not in this lifetime then in the generations of howzevi to come. They recognized and hoped for that possibility for the reasons I have stated. Here, God is not lost in the conversation in that God created women to be better than men in certain responsibilities. The howzevi had experienced for themselves that women could relate better to the work of khod shenasi in the family, in the educational system, and in any other such institutions and practices that involve women in any way. This included raising, marrying, and supporting men, fighting against their enemies (also men), and raising women who would have to do the same.

I continued to ask women what their thoughts were regarding the debate about a woman becoming a mujtahideh for all people or a women's mujtahideh. It was difficult to discuss the topic openly. In one conversation, two women agreed that a woman could eventually become a Marja'e Taqlid. It was for the same reason Khanum-e Yasseri had explained to me—that it would someday become a necessity. In another conversation, they retracted their opinions. Sometimes women responded by shrugging their shoulders, changing the topic, or remaining silent on the issue. Agreement or disagreement could just as well have been based on a detailed examination of Islamic text and the various arguments around the issue, but the absence of articulating where one stood on the issue was indicative of something more.

It was possible that my attempt to ask the question was read as a feminist concern. It was possible that the women I asked were still working through the Islamic texts that could inform their position on the issue. Another possibility was that the debate itself revealed existing ideological boundaries, and choosing a side might inadvertently reveal a sociopolitical alliance they may or may not want to be associated with. Mujtahid, like Ayatollah Bojnurdi and Sanaei, who were proponents of women becoming mujtahideh, were known reformist clerics. Being identified as a reformist in 2011 was a problem since reformists fell out of power in the 2009 election. For instance, classes offered by Ayatollah Bojnurdi were shut down. Efforts at sifting individuals at the structural level continued to take place, in addition to the politics of groups contending for their own interpretations of Islam. Finally, it was possible that some women were apathetic toward the subject matter. Becoming a Marja'e Taqlid was not a primary concern. Maybe they were simply more interested in other forms of participation like teaching and conduct-ing research in their Islamic education.

Expectations about Participation

I return to the concept of participation. In the literature on Iran, participation is largely equated with going against the government as both Islamic and pa-triarchal. This is sampled in the work of Sakurai and Mirjam Künkler and Roja Fazaeli on women's Islamic scholarship in Iran. Künkler and Fazaeli argue that while women have self-initiated their entry into a government-supported how-zeh education in Iran, the government itself prevents women from aspiring to become mujtahideh for all. This is because of the curricular redirection. Women would still not have access to occupying the position of Marja'e Taqlid in the long run despite having gained access to the howzeh. Women, therefore, are not interested.[2] Along the same lines, Sakurai argues that although women's access to the howzeh has opened up new possibilities for women, this access has not actually "weakened" the position of men in the clerical establishment.[3] Again, this is because the institution's curriculum is consistently being redirected away from women becoming Islamic scholars.

The measurement of success in both analyses is that a woman's objective should be to become a mujtahideh for all people and eventually become a Marja'e Taqlid, a publicly visible form of leadership. Without this, women will remain unmotivated. It is an understanding limited to women's participation as acts of subversion against an existing order, in opposition to a male-dominated Islamic Republic, and is framed on the assumption that publicly visible forms of leader-ship will also result in weakening the authority of men. This form of leadership serves as the only viable standard for legitimate participation by women in Is-lamic higher education.

I call this framework into question in order to consider further possibilities of success. First, there is an underlying assumption about outcomes when women occupy positions of power. In this instance, women who become mujtahideh for all people would result in more women rallying behind interpretations of Islamic laws in favor of women. Although many howzevi recognize that women relate bet-ter to women and family-related issues, a woman occupying a position of power and authority does not guarantee transformations in favor of women. Women being anti-woman are not unique to Iran or the howzevi. In the case of Iran, some of the laws thought of as benefitting women have been and are often blocked by women members of the Islamic Consultative Assembly of Iran.

In 2006, a bill was submitted to the parliament related to the protection of families. During the review process, the Executive Branch added Article 23 on *Ta'adod-e Zawjat,* or the number of wives, to the bill, which made it easier for men to take on up to four wives. Etelaf-e Islami Zanan, the Coalition of Islamic Women, composed of women from feminist groups, reformists, and ultra-conservative women, campaigned against it—the first time in twenty-eight years where a nongovernmental organization demanded to ratify a bill, in this case the removal of Article 23. The battle went on for about five years. In July 2011, a commission removed Article 23 before the bill reached the General Assembly. Women members of the 8th Parliament were against its removal, accusing Etelaf-e Islami Zanan of being secularized and Westernized.

There are factions. This situation is also quite probable in the case of women becoming a women's mujtahideh. What holds true is that a conversation based on Islamically grounded arguments about the extent of a woman's influence as a mujtahideh is well on its way today, always informed by the increased participation of women in the howzeh elmiyeh in the past three decades. But a woman becoming a mujtahideh does not guarantee the transformation of laws and social conditions to favor women.

Second, challenging this paradigm of the universal desire for leadership and authority warrants a return to examination of the practices around khod shenasi. Certain aspects of the howzevi social practices I observed while living in Pirouzi, like those I describe here and in the following section of the book, complicate the attempt to establish the exact cause for the low number of women's mujtahideh in Iran. To make sense of the role of these practices, I first describe the basic requirements for the Dars-e Kharij level and the way assessments at this level are generally experienced.

Dars-e Kharij: A Lesson of the Outside

The Dars-e Kharij level, translated as "A Lesson of the Outside" [of tradition], is the only part of the howzeh system that the centralizing process of the women's howzeh has not affected. This level is taught, managed, and financially supported directly by a senior mujtahid or a Marja'e Taqlid. A howzevi must reach this level in order to begin a more focused training to do ijtihad. A student must have completed Sat'h 3 (master's degree) to be at this level. She will have mastered, at the very minimum, the scholarly histories, genealogies, and associations of specific books like Ayatollah Wahid Khorasani's work on the roots of Islamic jurisprudence Al-Kifaya fi'l Usul, Sheikh Morteza Ansari's work on Islamic jurisprudence Al-Makasib, and Allameh Mohammad Hossein Tabatabaie's Islamic philosophy books Bidayat Al-Hikmah and Nahayat Al-Hikmah. Students at this level attend each meeting with only notebooks in hand and are expected to engage in the lessons with the materials they had mastered in the previous years. Recollection of histories and contexts of proper sources is key. Expertise in disputation, mobaheseh, is of utmost importance at this stage.

Although the women used the word *emtehan*, exam, to talk about the way they and their teachers determine their progress at this level, I move away from translating it as "examination" here. I do so because the possibility of failure, the inability to perform to the minimum of a standardized and universalized rubric, is embedded in the concept of examination. More appropriate phrases are *to make an assessment* or *to gauge* in order to make adjustments. When either a student or a teacher requests to assess student progress, the teacher is merely gauging the way the student processes the topics being discussed in the meetings. This approach implies a kind of calibration or adjustment of what more the student needs to do to reach a goal without being bound to time limits. Students at this level technically have the rest of their lives to meet these goals. They cannot fail, unless they quit.

There are two kinds of assessment at this level, one for content on Dars-e Kharij level materials and another to determine a student's progress to do an ijtihad. The scholars that participate in the ijtihad-related assessment are high-ranking clerics who are mujtahid and/or Marja'e Taqlid. Likewise, the breadth covered in the ijtihad-related assessments is significantly greater—about thirty years' worth of work. These assessments come in phases. There are many formats to assessments, but generally they are held in discussion and debate formats. Khanum-e Tabesh described one basic approach, which commonly involved a teacher asking questions about topics from Islamic jurisprudence and its principles, or all of the sciences like *Ahkam*, the study of arbitration, about praying, fasting, and all rituals of worship. The teacher can also bring together two to four more teachers to do the assessment. If the teachers determine that the student is ready to share this knowledge with others, the student will then select a topic and publish a book. But this is not enough. The final determination of whether a student is a mujtahid or mujtahideh is socially designated, as I explain in the following chapter.

Doing well in a Dars-e Kharij assessment, which is also in discussion and debate format and more topical in focus, may accumulate toward being considered for an ijtihad-related assessment. But this does not guarantee one's success in being recognized as someone who could do ijtihad later on. After three years at the Kharij level, a student may request her first assessment directly from her teacher. For instance, Ayatollah Khamenei made an assessment on Khanum-e Tabesh's progress on one Islamic jurisprudence topic, and Ayatollah Larijani made another one on a topic from the principles of Islamic jurisprudence. Doing both did not guarantee that Khanum-e Tabesh could become qualified to do ijtihad, though these were steps that needed to be taken in order to know what she needed to focus on to meet her goals. Overall, students at this level can opt out of assessments all together.

Women's Ambivalence

One reason scholars cite for why a woman could not become a mujtahideh for all people and eventually a Marja'e Taqlid was based on a woman's obligation to ask her husband for permission to leave the home and, more generally, to move about. Theoretically, in the context of being a Marja'e, a woman would then have to consistently ask her husband for permission to fulfill her public obligations. The logic of this reasoning is outside the scope of this chapter but is found in a later chapter about a howzevi marriage. For now, I bring attention to the several conversations I've had with howzevi women of different generations about their thoughts on why at the time, in the thirty years after the revolution, there were visibly fewer women who were women's mujtahideh compared to men.

Only two women cited as a reason the marital obligation I explained because most of the women I spent time with knew there were many ways to curtail this limitation. One would be for a woman not to marry, which in and of itself would be reason to disqualify her for the position. Whether this form of disqualification was based on a social norm or Islamic practice was up for debate. We catch a glimpse of such awareness in Zaynab's story later, as well as with the women of Howzeh-ye Kowsar who were debating on delaying marriage, which I also describe in a vignette in a following section of the book. The howzevi I spent time with challenged these idealizations of marriage either through debate or in the social space.

Another way to overcome this obstacle was for a woman to marry a man who would agree to give her lifetime permission to carry out her duties as a Marja'e—that is, permission to follow in the footsteps of the many women of the Islamic past like Fatimah, the daughter of Prophet Mohammad and wife of Imam Ali, and her daughter, Zaynab. Despite being married, both women mediated conflict, accompanied armies to battle, made critical decisions that impacted generations of Muslims, and fought against tyrants. Knowing the way to bypass this limitation is not the point, however. Both the limitations of a howzevi marriage and the way to curtail these limitations only mattered if, in fact, the women I was with were interested in becoming religious authorities in the first place.

There were women who were simply not interested in devoting their entire lives to studying. For many howzevi, the sacrifice of time and energy required to become a mujtahideh was already uninviting before these institutional transformations. Khanum-e Alizadeh explained, "The system is very hard and [the process is] very long for them, with the baby and the house ... and women don't want to become mujtahideh for this. So, women want to teach, which will take four years to learn how to do. They will learn a lot about the *deen* [religious way of life], *mazhab* [practice], and address the public with these. Whereas to become a mujtahideh is very long, and is very hard for a woman." Khanum-e Alizadeh, who had been studying in the howzeh for a total of about twenty-two years in 2011, explained that she and her friends had already spent "too many years studying."

Arezu was studying Islamic law at Madraseh Ali because she considered it to be good work for society, but she felt that the amount of time to complete her program was competing with her long-term plans to have children. Arezu and her husband, who was working as an engineer, had decided to wait for three years or until she finished her master's degree before having children. She was eager to finish her program for this reason. I spent most of my morning commute to Howzeh-ye Kowsar with Fatimah and Hoda, watching and listening to them prepare for their lessons on the metro or in a taxi or bus. With this in mind, I can understand that imagining themselves in a position of religious authority was unappealing altogether.

As we've learned, the system changed because the women demanded it be changed to accommodate a certification process. Many women felt relieved that the new system would shorten the duration of program completion by ten years. Although the program of study would be more intensive, it would at least accommodate women's familial obligations. The women could fit time for teaching, counseling, or researching into their schedules without compromising much of their obligations at home, whereas confining themselves to decades of learning countless books could not. Some of the howzevi, as I mention in an upcoming chapter, did not want to pursue any education after high school. They wanted to be married and have a family. But their families pressured them into becoming part of Madraseh Ali.

On this note, the desire to be a wife, and eventually a mother, must be factored in when expecting women to occupy positions of religious authority. Wifehood and motherhood compete with the labor to become a mujtahideh, and many women prioritized the former. The satisfaction they gained from seeing themselves as having achieved wifehood and motherhood allowed them to continue their path to a howzeh education, but in the direction that accommodated for those roles.

Lack of Visibility

As I noted in chapter 1, Khanum-e Alosvand pointed out the practices, which I refer to as anonymity, of not revealing their successes to others and remaining socially unseen. Khanum-e Alosvand described the relationship some howzevi have had with assessments: "They don't want to go there [the stage of emtehan]. Just this. And if they do pass the exam, they don't usually tell people." Briefly, anonymity involves the purposeful attempt not to inform many people, if any, about what they have accomplished or what they know about Islamic text while simultaneously contributing to the workings of the Islamic Republic. I explain this in detail in the following chapter. Part of the work of khod shenasi was to create a balance between doing what one needed to do while remaining unattached to the outcome of that labor. Keeping their achievements a secret facilitated not becoming too attached to the pleasures of the material world. Many if not all of the women I spent time with practiced anonymity to avoid being praised and recognized for their accomplishments.

Though Künkler and Fazaeli have argued that there are not enough mujtahideh in Iran, there are howzevi women like Monireh Gorgi, a member of the Assembly of Experts, or Maryam Behrouzi, the head of Jami'at Zaynab, who do take on very public roles. From an analytical approach that prioritizes representative sampling, this fact appears to contradict the practices of anonymity. But the existence of women in public roles does not actually negate the existence of howzevi women who were not interested in public roles. Both phenomena can be true at the same time.

Shifting the analytical approach away from representative sampling opens up ways to look closely at other possibilities. First, the practices of anonymity encompass a range of actions and decisions that lead to downplaying their positionalities, unless these have to be made public out of obligation. The practice is not just about visibility in the public eye. Second, the fact that religiously conservative women occupy public roles does not lessen the importance of anonymity in their practices. It is possible for seminarian women who hold public office or leadership positions to fulfill their public obligations while still attempting to abide by practices of anonymity. It just makes doing both even more challenging. There are other possibilities that can emerge; what is crucial in this process is to move away from expectations and generalizations and to commit to paying attention to local logics, categories, and explanations. I look closely at what their practices entail in the following chapter.

Because their practice of anonymity was both a measure of and a definition of success among the howzevi, it was difficult to establish a howzevi's accomplishments, which includes attempts to meet their educative goals. It was possible that women were reaching the level of ijtihad within their own circles of mujtahid teachers and their peers but were reluctant to say so. For Khanum-e Alosvand, this phenomenon of refraining from talking about passing exams might be related to manifesting one's humility, which is itself a result of gaining knowledge. She said, "[It] is not for people to know; your intention is to know your religion better." Khanum-e Alosvand and the other howzevi saw this effort to not tell others as virtuous.

EDUCATIVE POSSIBILITIES

Being unseen did not necessarily mean women were not taking advantage of access to opportunities. Some of the senior howzevi addressed the notion of ijtihad-related examinations, which I coined earlier as a process of gauging student progress, as unnecessary. Khanum-e Alosvand proposed, "Women don't go there; they educate themselves for many years and in the end, when they can go there and pass the exam, they don't go there." Khanum-e Alosvand remarked that based on her debates with women about specific issues, she knew many of them could speak only from the position of already doing ijtihad, yet they did not acknowledge themselves as doing so. She added that many of these women were at a "higher level of knowledge" than many of the men she had held the same discussions with about Islamic law. These women continued to pursue Islamic education for the sake of gaining knowledge itself. Ijtihad-related examinations did not weigh in on their success.

Furthermore, it is possible that those who did take the assessments were uninterested in becoming mujtahideh for other people, not because they lack consciousness of their conditions but because they were content with doing it for themselves. The fact that a woman was enabled through her education to do ijtihad for herself meant that she no longer had to imitate others in religious edicts in her work of khod shenasi. Making independent juristic interpretations only for herself also meant being free from responsibility for others. Hence, for many women, doing ijtihad for themselves was their primary goal, nothing more.

For Khanum-e Yasseri, it was advantageous to have more mujtahideh in order to prepare for the time when women could eventually become Marja'e Taqlid out of necessity. If readers knew the author of a book was a known mujtahideh, they might be more inclined to read the book. Khanum-e Alosvand was also of the opinion that it would be better if women became women's mujtahideh. But many of the same women who were in agreement did not want the heavy responsibility of making decisions for hundreds if not thousands of people regarding Islamic practices. They also did not want the public pressure on themselves and their families.

On this point, Khanum-e Alosvand articulated that it was not necessary that all women become a mujtahideh "to solve problems of society." Students had other options for their education, and there were women who were simply interested in other fields of study. As Khanum-e Alosvand explained, "She can teach, do religious propagation, do research, and attend international conferences and seminars. All these." Khanum-e Yasseri's quest for more answers to deeper philosophical questions about the self and existence led her to continue on the path of Islamic philosophy rather than Islamic jurisprudence. From there, she began conducting research on the potentials of women as full participants of building an Islamic society.

Howzevi women occupied positions of influence within polities that were largely dominated by men at their leadership core, such as Nahad-e Rahbari, the

Organization of the supreme leader, the Basij, research institutes, faculty in co-educational universities, university counseling offices, and media outlets. These were positions that, among many engagements, affected laws about women and families in Iran, education about these laws, and their implementation. These positions were continually being accorded to the howzevi as long as they continued to pursue what the howzeh offered. This was so despite the difficult task and the years it would take for a howzevi to gain enough credibility to enter scholarly debates, which also included interpretation of Islamic text. What I am emphasizing here is that they gained access to these positions as a result of their continued work. That in itself could be considered success. Again, gaining access to very public positions of authority and leadership was neither an expectation nor a benchmark of their success by their own standards.

This is not to say that these women did not tackle the problem of misogyny. But the way they confronted misogyny was grounded in the work of khod shenasi. As I've explained and will further elaborate on in chapter 4, the source of moral order here is not the self, and life's purpose is not to achieve autonomy. Both are assumed in the feminist paradigm. Some women were researching a better approach to inform women of their rights during the courtship period, marriage, and divorce, like Khanum-e Tabesh. Some were finding ways to exert pressure on some clerics in Qom to allow women to partake in their Dars-e Kharij classes. Some women conducted Islamic jurisprudent research with men on topics that would eventually impact Iranian families such as laws on *diyeh* (blood money), inheritance, and the custody of children.

Khanum-e Yasseri explained that at that time, the custody of children automatically went to the father, even if the father was a drug user. Howzevi women were conducting research on conditions of exception and were attempting to push for changes in this ruling so the custody of the children would go to the mother in this context. There was also research being done about the validity of a woman's request to ask for *talaq*, or divorce. Many considered working on these challenges as a form of success in itself.

Misogyny was only one out of many challenges they faced. Some women did not know what they wanted to do next: get married, get a PhD in engineering, or work. They were bound only to a momentary obligation "to do anything with it." By changing the benchmark of success from leadership roles to strengthening the work of khod shenasi and gaining divine merit, we can see that this uncertainty by itself can also be a form of success.

Women attended the howzeh for other reasons that I will not explore here. For instance, there were women who started taking classes at the howzeh in order to leave their homes to socialize without violating their families' observation of the proper public space for women. There were many who wanted to receive training in religious teaching, as I've written elsewhere. These wide-ranging objectives and varied perceptions of success cannot be accounted for if the only measure of success is linear toward a position of higher religious authority.

THE THREE TALABEH AZAD

There were women who accepted the edict that women could not become a mujtahideh for all but continued to do the work to become a mujtahideh. They attended different Dars-e Kharij classes open to them and took Kharij-level assessments from their teachers. They also moved alongside the system-wide transition by taking exams to convert their educational experiences into quantifiable units for a madrak. They saw exams as a resource, not an obstacle. Khanum-e Alizadeh, Khanum-e Tabesh, and Khanum-e Shahriari were such women.

Though quite advanced in their studies, Khanum-e Tabesh, Alizadeh, and Shahriari belonged in the category of talabeh azad—the freely roaming student, once the dominant figure in the Iranian howzeh, which had clearly changed in Tehran, as I've explained. Despite these changes, students in the howzeh could still become eligible to become mujtahideh if they continued to pursue their education. In theory, a student with or without a madrak, like the freely roaming student, today composed of housewives and the elderly who attend afternoon classes, could technically qualify for an assessment to partake in the Dars-e Kharij level study circle.

Khanum-e Tabesh, Alizadeh, and Shahriari were from the old system of the howzeh of the 1980s and through the 1990s. Most of their education experiences consisted of moving from one teacher to another in one howzeh, or between different howzeh. None of them had ever had to take an entrance exam nor go through a rigid interviewing process to become part of a howzeh. While many of the women they started out with had stopped taking classes, the three of them persisted and encouraged each other to move onward. They had been students of various high ranking clerics at the Kharij level for over a decade when we met and at the time were attending Ayatollah Khamenei's and Ayatollah Larijani's Dars-e Kharij class together.

Influenced by Ayatollah Khomeini, Khanum-e Shahriari started attending the howzeh in Khorasan after getting married. She wanted to know the relationship between the Qur'an and its relevance to forming Islamic law. Later on, she wanted to understand the way rulings were derived from the narrations of the Prophet Mohammad and his family. She also wanted to know Arabic and "the deeper meanings of prayers." She studied for about seventeen years in the Khorasan howzeh system. After twenty years, she began attending Dars-e Kharij level classes. Of the three women, she was the eldest and had been a howzevi the longest. Unlike Khanum-e Tabesh and Alizadeh, whose families invested their time in Islamic education, she was the only member of her family studying in the howzeh. Her husband, an engineer, had been an important figure in her education as he continued to encourage her interests in the Islamic sciences.

Khanum-e Alizadeh was in her late forties when we first met in 2008. Like Khanum-e Tabesh, she had been a student at the Dars-e Kharij level for almost eleven years, having spent ten years in preparation. Her family originally came from Naraq, but she was raised in and attended high school in Tehran. Her husband and son were both civil engineers who ran the family business. Her daughter was a housewife but had been studying in the howzeh for five years. Her mother likewise studied in the howzeh for three years. She began attending classes in a local howzeh because she wanted to strengthen her "commitment to obeying the orders of God, and then teach about these." Already with three children, she began taking classes when she was about twenty-eight years old. In the late 1990s, she also began taking classes at Elahiat University, where she received her undergraduate and master's degrees.

Khanum-e Tabesh was in her mid-forties and had been studying at the Dars-e Kharij level for about ten years when we first met in 2008, taking classes from Ayatollah Bojnurdi, Ayatollah Hashemi Shahrudi, and Ayatollah Khamenei. At the time, she was a codirector of an institute of Qur'anic studies and memorization for women in Tehran. She came from a wealthy family, and her marriage to a wealthy merchant was something she had expected. On numerous occasions she would encourage women to marry men who could provide for the same lifestyle they, the women, were raised in. Her daughter was a student at the Madraseh Ali High School in Tehran, and her sister was a teacher in a Tehran howzeh.

Before taking howzeh classes, Khanum-e Tabesh was a student of the hard sciences in preparation to eventually become a medical doctor. But the revolution "against their enemies" created the need to strengthen her knowledge about Islam. "It was not enough to hear something from your parents, your grandparents. You should study this religion yourself, and from there, study original sources to get the main idea of it," she said. Her sister, a teacher in the howzeh who had written several books on Islamic mysticism, convinced her to take classes at a local howzeh. Khanum-e Tabesh read a narration by Imam Ali where he said, "If a person knows himself, as a human, then he or she can know God." This made an impact on her, and she wanted to find answers to her questions about life and about who she was, her purpose, where she came from, and where she was headed.

Khanum-e Tabesh started attending a nearby howzeh in the late 1980s. She wanted to attend Jami'at Al-Zahra but could not because she would have to travel to Qom from Tehran. "And it was not a good situation," she added. Traveling that distance was unsafe, so she had to make do with what was available in Tehran.

She first attended an old howzeh in Imam Husayn Square. She took classes there for ten years. She also took classes in different parts of the city, one where Ayatollah Bojnurdi taught and another at Dar Al-Tahvis on Iran Street, where she would eventually meet Khanum-e Alizadeh and Shahriari, studying under Ostad Dashti. It would be here that the three of them would continue together, though not quite sure where they were headed.

Moving through the Transition

Hundreds of middle-aged women like them were inevitably caught in the transition between the old and the new systems. These women experienced being a talabeh azad between the mid-1970s and the late 1990s. They studied topics of interest and developed some kind of expertise as they advanced their readings. By the early 2000s, they were informed that they would soon need a madrak to be recognized as having done the work. Teaching referrals I describe later were pivotal for them for this reason.

At some point, women like Khanum-e Tabesh, Alizadeh, and Shahriari needed to make a decision on what to prioritize—to convert their learning experiences to a madrak or to become mujtahideh. If they chose to become mujtahideh, they could continue to move their way through different study circles, Dars-e Kharij level classes, and any howzeh open to them as they had been doing for decades. But if they chose to receive a madrak, they would have to take exams to convert their learning experiences into prerequisites in order to have a seat in a classroom. Women who began as freely roaming students and passed a number of exams to be categorized as having reached the beginning of Sat'h 3 (level 3, equivalent to a master's program) may qualify to receive a madrak after fulfilling requisites for Sat'h 3. At the end of Sat'h 3, a written exam would be taken and a *payan-e nameh*, or research paper, on a specific topic would be written and then defended. Though the center in Qom had not yet fully developed and implemented a Sat'h 4 program (equivalent to a doctoral program) in 2011, they had already created eight exams that could qualify in-transition examiners into this level.

Several theoretical reasons may be provided for why standardized exams were created and forced upon students—a situation not unique to the howzevi. In an increasingly changing environment where certificates were needed as proof of a person's skills and accomplishments, standardized assessments have been one of the many ways to certify. The focus here is not *the why* of standardized assessments but what these exams may tell us about the howzevi: what they were doing with these situations and the way they perceived these exams.

During the transformation of the system, Khanum-e Shahriari decided to continue moving freely between scholarly circles like that of Ayatollahs Khamenei and Larijani. Khanum-e Alosvand explained that women who chose that path were well respected: "women want to be powerful in this science. They want to be knowledgeable. They don't want to have the degree or certificate. It is not necessary." Khanum-e Tabesh and Alizadeh, on the other hand, decided to do both—move between scholarly circles while also taking exams to convert their learning experiences into qualifications for a madrak.

CREATING AND EXPANDING SOCIAL CIRCLES

Khanum-e Tabesh and Alizadeh had already taken four of the eight required exams to be considered for the Sat'h 4 level in 2011. Khanum-e Alizadeh briefly accounted for her experience in doing so: "The exams are very long . . . on the books Makaseb and Kefaye and Bedaye. For every book there is an exam. The written exam is in Tehran. The oral exam is in Qom. The exams in Qom are on Islamic jurisprudence, the study of rights, the principles of Islamic jurisprudence, Hadith, the study of theological discourse, history of Islam, Qur'anic interpretation, and philosophy. You choose your subject, pass an exam, and then write the thesis."

Preparing for these exams by itself took an enormous amount of time. Khanum-e Tabesh and Alizadeh could not find time to study as much as they would have liked. They described, "Women like Banu Amin are rare in history because there are many obstacles for women to continue. We already have many duties in the house. And . . . we are busy addressing every issue in society because there are many problems for our young people at the university. . . . For this reason, we do not study. . . . We want to be able to do ijtihad, but we do not."

Without further analysis, it may seem like obstacles are purposely put in front of women like them so they may never become mujtahideh, even if only for themselves. But they had the option to switch tracks at any time and follow Khanum-e Shahriari in choosing to remain a talabeh azad studying at the Kharij level. They did not. Hence, the choices they made continued to create more work for them in addition to preparing for Dars-e Kharij or ijtihad-related assessments.

There are important but unstated realities about Khanum-e Tabesh and Alizadeh's education. They did not need to put themselves through preparing and taking these conversion-credit exams. The exams might or might not help them qualify for ijtihad-related assessments in the future. Neither of them needed a madrak to maintain their teaching and research positions. Also, it was highly probable that Khanum-e Tabesh and Alizadeh were already overqualified for the Sat'h 4 level, having been at the Kharij level for over a decade with different high-ranking clerics. Yet they embraced what I had seen as obstacles to becoming a women's mujtahideh.

Both tracks come with opportunities to expand their social circles. These are inherent in the howzeh social life. As women move through each level, which includes navigating strenuous but valued pedagogical practices like disputation with teachers and peers, they develop support systems to help them learn. The challenges of creating these circles will become more apparent in the following sections of the book, but why women would do so in the first place is worth a pause. An obvious explanation would be that there is divine reward in strengthening the work of khod shenasi by sharing and teaching Islamic knowledge. But one could also posit that women like Khanum-e Tabesh and Alizadeh create more work for themselves because they are competing for followers like their male counterparts, in order to strengthen their hold on power over others.

The problem with the latter is that it lacks ethnographic evidence, not only from my experience with the women but also from the absence of women-centric work about howzevi women in Iran. Though the work is not about the howzevi, one closely related ethnographic work would be Torab's research on women's neighborhood Islamic study circles, whose participants express negative sentiments towards "theologically trained women." To counter previous scholarship on women's passivity in these circles, Torab shows how women who lead these circles also compete for followers.[4] Besides this, the source of what we know about howzeh education in Iran comes from research that has been done on the men's howzeh. A "knowledge economy and knowledge market"[5] is characteristic of the men's howzeh in Qom. The number of attendees of any given lecture delivered by a cleric was the measure of success for men. Fischer and Zaman have written similar descriptions, in which student teachers and clerics alike competed for followers.[6] Fariba Adelkhah referred to this men's network of followers and allies as *posht*, "often used to describe solidarity among a group of individuals, and to indicate the interdependence of roles and interests within it."[7] What happens between women in the women's howzeh is then subsumed in this scholarship.

To highlight the nuances of the women's experiences, I refer to their social groupings as *social circles*. Personal connectedness between women as well as students and teachers constitute these circles. I detail this in chapter 5. For now, I return to Lave's and Wenger's situated learning in communities of practice to preface the significance of these circles and the function of teaching within them.[8] Through this paradigm, Khanum-e Tabesh and Alizadeh are participants within a set of continuous social relations between people and the world around them. Their motivations, or "the arrangements of knowledge in the head," are already assumed in the way they participate, not separate from it.[9] Being power hungry for followers, for instance, is a possibility for some or many women, among other possibilities, since interactions, processes, and surroundings are all "coming into being" in relation to each other.[10] All possibilities, therefore, are temporary. However, taking in situated learning allows us to consider women's experiences in creating and developing social circles as distinct from the experiences of men.

Like the networks in the men's howzeh, social circles in the women's howzeh consist of both mentors and mentees as well as peers and allies. The practice of disputation is also often the doorway to developing these relationships. But what constitutes these circles may differ from what has been written about the men's circles. For instance, the howzevi women here created and actively participated in more than one social circle. Moreover, rather than considering achieving excellence as a way to compete for more followers, women considered doing assessments with their teacher as personal labor and part of the work of creating a spiritual closeness to God. Khanum-e Alosvand considered that women perceived their place within the howzeh differently from men in terms of what characterizes their social interactions. She explained that "men have already made it a habit to want to become a mujtahid for hundreds of years, where men valued being assessed by their teachers as a way to earn credibility among teachers and other students." This was not in alignment with the way howzevi women perceived their education as both a private affair and worth the many years of their lives.

Inasmuch as the work of khod shenasi is thought to be a personal endeavor, it is tried and tested in social relationships. Incoming howzevi gain the knowledge and skills required to move toward full participation in scholarship and the howzeh social world by learning from the more senior howzevi. The more senior howzevi eventually give way to up-and-coming newcomers. There is tension in this process, where different personalities, preferences, and tendencies to compete as well as social expectations come together. It is also political in that sense, where practitioners encounter forms of exclusion based on disagreements within one social circle. Consider belonging to and participating in several circles. Ideological divisions emerge based on the way women stand on interpretations of Islamic practices, as I show in the last section of the book.

Through all this, women seek advice and consult with each other about all sorts of decisions. The sense of accountability that organically emerges out of these relationships benefits those who have difficulty maintaining certain Islamic practices like fasting or memorizing the Qur'an. Women keep each other in check about their daily practices but also about their understanding of Islamic teachings. These circles strengthen their effort to do the work of khod shenasi from the moral and emotional support they receive from each other. As I show later, through time women in these circles form kinship connections like that of Khanum-e Tabesh, Alizadeh, and Shahriari. Howzevi women also gain credibility from these circles in order to take up responsibilities like teaching and research.

TEACHING AND PUBLISHING

As teachers, both Khanum-e Alizadeh and Tabesh received very little monetary compensation for the amount of time they put into their work. On average, a howzeh teacher is paid 1,000 touman per hour (a little less than a dollar in 2011). Madraseh Ali student teachers did not get paid, however, since their work hours were put toward their tuition fees. They received financial compensation only for the commute. Women who were teaching for some time would, on average, make 2,000 touman per hour (a little less than $2 in 2011). Khanum-e Alizadeh and Tabesh were making 4,000 touman (a little more than $3.50 per hour) if they were teaching Sat'h 3. Khanum-e Alizadeh added, while laughing, "It is for the sake of God. The payment for this work is nothing. It is only the cost for getting the job done." It seemed that for them there was something more to teaching, beyond financial gain. Teaching was a way to expand and improve the quality of their circles.

Teaching played a very important role in the women's educative experience, which began when they were student apprentices and proceeded as they became novice teachers. In other words, a movement from being a newcomer to an old-timer took place. As students, Khanum-e Alizadeh, Tabesh, and Shahriari emulated good teachers and the way they created spaces for students to engage with the material better. Mobaheseh, disputation, which I devote a chapter to explaining, plays an important role in this. Each of the women shadowed teachers who then modeled the way they could be effective in their disputation. Listening is a full-body experience, and their teachers modeled for them what it meant to become worthy of being listened to. Their teachers would in turn sit with them during their mobaheseh with other students. Mobaheseh was the space where their teachers and the managers of the howzeh looked for students who were *khob bashe* (good), *zerang* (clever) with Islamic text, and *qavi* (powerful) in retaining information, characteristics I explain in the last section of this book. Through this one-on-one approach, each of the women earned feedback and, eventually, social credibility among their peers. This process eventually led to student-teaching opportunities outside the howzeh.

This form of apprenticeship between teachers and students opened doors for countless other women to teach in organizations, universities, and the howzeh in and outside Tehran. Teachers who were impressed by a student's progress made phone calls to the other howzeh for referrals. Howzeh managers would also ask for student recommendations. The names of students who had earned high rankings in their class circulated between the various howzeh for teaching opportunities.

The three women developed their teaching practices through time by accepting teaching opportunities they hadn't considered before. The first time Khanum-e Alizadeh was asked to teach came about in a similar way. She was first asked to teach Arabic at Jami'at Zaynab. After, she was asked to teach in Sazman Tableghat-e Eslami, or the Organization of Islamic Propagation, and in the howzeh. The task of teaching and gaining access to teaching positions played a critical role in howzevi's mobility within and outside the howzeh, and through teaching they would continue to make their way through each level of study in the howzeh. In 2003, examination scores became a part of these referrals. But as we shall see in a later chapter, it does not always work out for some students even if they produce high examination scores.

The extent to which their teachers influenced their work allows us to consider an important characteristic of the connection between howzeh teachers and students—that is, students were expected to live up to their teachers' good name while developing their own reputations. When a teacher recommended a student to teach at an organization, the implication was that it came from someone who was a credible judge of character. The understanding was that the teacher had already earned her stripes and was fully aware of who would be a good fit where, who was trustworthy, and so on. In essence, she would put her reputation on the line for every recommendation she made. The howzevi were then expected to work hard in maintaining, advancing, and making use of these opportunities in order to carry that recommendation forward on their teachers' good name. But the teachers' involvement ended there.

As novice teachers, Khanum-e Tabesh, Alizadeh, and Shahriari were expected to develop their individual reputations from the very start of their teaching careers. Part of honoring their teachers was to create a good name for themselves, both socially and intellectually. Ensuring they did not depend solely on their teachers' good reputation was key. Creating something out of the teachers' knowledge was honorable, but allowing the teachers' scholarly opinion to dominate the students' opinion was not.

This point is crucial in challenging the idea that howzevi women compete for followers when expanding their social circles. *Competing for followers* assumes that howzevi women endeavor to perfectly reproduce their ideas through their students, in the same way their teachers' ideas have supposedly been produced through them. It is worth noting that this assumption about ideological reproduction exists among those in the government who have sporadically banned clerics like Ayatollah Bojnurdi from conducting their study circles. It assumes that ideologies are in fact perfectly reproduced through human bodies—in this case, followers. Thus, there exists the desire for more followers to reproduce these ideologies. However, this was not the way the women of this study experienced their social circles, as I have illustrated in previous work, because howzevi women identify not only with different social circles but also with competing ideologies.[11]

Khanum-e Alizadeh described the role of her teachers in the context of transforming policies. She became part of a group called Jami'at Zaynab. They were credited for having changed a portion of inheritance laws for widows. "If you have a knowledgeable teacher, it has a very deep effect on your situation in society, but normally the students do not ask me 'who is your teacher?' And even when I present and give my program, they do not ask me who was my teacher. My program or my way is very important, they do not just accept my work because of my teacher," she explained. When it came to drafting bills that could potentially change laws for women, she said, "What is important is how you use the reason, how good you explain this reason. They will not ask you who was your teacher in approving that matter. They will ask how she came to this conclusion, how she did her research, and how strong she did her work. . . . The way we make the design and argument is important."

Teaching enabled a howzevi to expand her circle to include family, friends of family, and others and was also a path to earn credibility as an 'adil, a just individual, as I explain later. The referrals from teachers and managers eventually reached important heads of organizations and offices outside of the howzeh system. Neither of the women imagined they would be in the positions they occupied in 2008 or 2011 when they met at Dar Al-Tahviz. The three of them earned enough credibility through teaching to become students at the Dars-e Kharij level with Ayatollah Khamenei and Larijani. Khanum-e Shahriari became a teacher of Qur'anic recitation and lectured university audiences about Qur'anic interpretation. As teachers, Khanum-e Alizadeh, Tabesh, and Shahriari were in turn expected to open up doors of opportunity to their students as their teachers had done for them in the past.

Through teaching referrals, Khanum-e Alizadeh became an advisor for howzevi writing their research papers. She published on Islamic topics and made guest appearances on domestic and international television shows and radio programs. She had been working with the office of the president and the supreme leader. Khanum-e Alizadeh was offered teaching positions in organizations, universities, and the howzeh in cities like Mashhad, Ferdowsi, and Ahvaz. Other women described her as "very active" with her work. In 2011, she had already been teaching for fifteen years and became one of the few women in Tehran to begin teaching at the Sat'h 3 level in three of the six howzeh in Tehran that offered Sat'h 3. She also taught Sat'h 2 in one howzeh every Monday, which meant she spent every day of the week at the howzeh.

The labor the women put into their teaching practices became a path to gaining access to other spaces, including new scholarly circles. In 2011, Khanum-e Tabesh was giving lectures at universities in Tehran about women's rights during the courtship period and in marriage. I attended one lecture with at least one hundred university women, many of whom approached her asking to continue working with her afterward. She came to be in charge of taking groups of students on pilgrimage trips, held classes on various topics in her office for small groups of university women, and delivered lectures on marriage and the marriage contract in the universities in Tehran. Khanum-e Tabesh and Alizadeh also established an organization for the sole purpose of researching and teaching on women's rights in Islam under the supervision of Nahad-e Rahbari, the women referred to as *Nahad*. Nahad creates and develops education programs for religious propagation and, expectedly, has an office in every university that operates directly under the supreme leader. In this context, it functions as the eye of the government. Among other kinds of work, the office chooses faculty and monitors the university socio-political atmosphere.

Besides teaching, the more senior howzevi published their research. The more publications are read, the greater the possibility of being challenged but also, again, of growing their circles. Howzevi like Khanum-e Alizadeh could publish to share research with other interested students and scholars. In addition, publications did not have to make arguments. They could be descriptions of different rulings about rituals and practices. A howzevi could also write papers providing an overview of current and ongoing research, or as a research assistant she could write entries in a larger body of work. Khanum-e Tabesh and Alizadeh took assessments as a way to reinforce their writing for publication and to gauge whether they had enough experience in answering challenging questions from their students. The end goal would be to publish a book on the topic of the exam.

A good example of a howzevi publishing scholarly work and developing a network of allies is Khanum-e Ghorbani, whose annual *rowzeh-khani*, or reading of an elegy for the Shahadat-e (martyrdom of) Fatimah, I detail in the fourth chapter. She published an article with valid evidence from Islamic exegesis and proposed that for the protection of the family unit, only unmarried men could engage in temporary marriages. Although she was not making a ruling for other people, she was at the level of knowledge that those around her could begin to understand that she had earned an expertise in a special subject. She was not a Muslim feminist and did not espouse the idea of Islamic feminism. But she raised eyebrows among a handful of clerics for her proposition—perhaps all the more reason for other scholars and her teachers to assess her progress toward ijtihad. About two hundred, mostly her students from the different howzeh in Tehran, attend her annual rowzeh-khani. All this is to say that even though a woman may be uninterested in becoming a mujtahideh, there are other forms of success. Changing the benchmark of success from leadership roles to strengthening the work of khod shenasi allows us to recognize these.

The Husband

Women's mobility to expand their circles simultaneously requires that the women impose on themselves religious practices that appear to limit their mobility in

Figure 3.1. Khanum-e Tabesh, whose back is turned from my camera, is responding to university students after her lecture. Tehran, 2011. ©Amina Tawasil.

other spaces, as I illustrate in the following section. Furthermore, not many women shared the same enthusiasm as Khanum-e Alizadeh and Tabesh about taking any kind of exam. Because some of the women made mention of the near impossibility of traveling alone to other cities in Iran, I assumed that for many howzevi women, traveling to Qom by themselves was an obstacle in and of itself. It required not only permission from men in their families but financial resources and arrangements for traveling companions and accommodations. None of these would allow for anonymity or easing the pressure to do these exams with time and resources at stake. But Khanum-e Tabesh, Alizadeh, and Shahriari continuously took exams in Qom and Tehran and attended different classes in and outside Tehran. Unlike other women, their privilege of mobility came from having supportive husbands.

As I've explained, while Nahad paid Khanum-e Tabesh and Alizadeh for their time, the compensation was barely enough to cover their out-of-pocket expenses. At times it would take months to receive reimbursements. But their husbands supported them so they could do their work without having to worry about financial compensation, unlike many of the young women I met who did not have much

Figure 3.2. Khanum-e Alizadeh's Qur'an with English translation while she and Khanum-e Tabesh were doing mobaheseh. Tehran, 2011. ©Amina Tawasil.

family support. Their husbands paid for all the necessary expenses of attending the howzeh from the time they began taking classes. They hired housekeepers and drove their wives to venues or hired car services to do so when needed.

Khanum-e Tabesh's husband often came up in our conversations. He wanted his daughter and son-in-law to become scholars of Islam, and he wanted Khanum-e Tabesh to become a mujtahideh. "My husband told me when you arrive to ijtihad I will be satisfied with life," Khanum-e Tabesh told me. She continued, "One day I told my husband, 'I apologize if I don't do my duties at home and I am not at home all the time.' He told me, 'When you become a mujtahideh [arrive to ijtihad] I am satisfied from you.'" Khanum-e Tabesh's husband was a *bazari*, a man who belonged to a powerful and most religiously conservative network of bazaar merchants historically known to have financially supported the 1979 revolution. He helped start Khanum-e Tabesh's and Alizadeh's nonprofit organization that worked to educate women on their rights in Islam. He covered all the overhead and operating expenses like rent for office space and staff and instructor salaries. He funded their projects like renting event spaces to hold small conferences or project meetings. "If our husbands didn't support us, we wouldn't have made it to this level of work or situation," Khanum-e Tabesh explained in appreciation of her husband. This speaks to Hamideh Sedghi's rendition of Winston Churchill's words "behind every successful man there is a powerful woman." She writes, "The reverse is true in today's Iran: behind every successful woman, there may be a powerful man."[12]

Perhaps it is this kind of support, the personal connection between teacher and student, and the accumulation of teaching efforts taken up by thousands of women like Khanum-e Tabesh, Alizadeh, and Shahriari that continue to contribute to strengthening the Islamic Republic and the importance of women within the republic.

IN THE THOUSANDS

From what I have explained here, becoming a religious authority was only one of many possibilities produced out of the women's education. Other forms of success would be glossed over if occupying positions of religious authority is the only marker of success. It is important to situate the notion of success in the work of khod shenasi. I also have demonstrated that howzevi women experience their social circles differently from men in that women deem their accomplishments and teacher-student relationships as part of the work of creating a spiritual closeness to God rather than a way to compete for followers.

Much of what I have shown in this chapter is about continuous movement behind the scenes. The women's continued effort is not visible, in part because they are not easily accessible as a group. But they are hard at work of their own volition. Whether or not women were interested in taking up positions of religious authority, they were pursuing what was made available to them until the coming of future transformations, which will necessitate their greater participation but not always in publicly visible positions.

The women in this chapter frowned at unnamed Islamic scholars who were notorious in preventing women from sitting in their classes or opposed the notion that women could learn to do ijtihad. They wished to challenge such practices. They continued to participate in the howzeh in ways that would improve the presence of Islamic teachings in and outside the howzeh. The senior howzevi women recognized and hoped for the possibility that women could someday become mujtahideh for all, not just for women. They believed women were better at the work of khod shenasi in aspects of life that men were not privy to.

The fact that they could entertain the possibility shows that, metaphorically, a line was made merely by walking. The point between almost having access to something and what was available "right before that moment" was a potent one for the women in this chapter like Khanum-e Tabesh and Alizadeh. Their story as freely roaming students provided insight to what women like them did with their imaginations of the future. Not having the desire for power was not something I could be certain about. But I do know that even though the women agreed with the logic of their exclusion from becoming mujtahideh for all people, they could no longer be excluded from continued participation in the howzeh by the thousands.

In 2011, it was becoming common for groups of howzevi women to answer women's questions when contacting a Marja'e Taqlid's office. Many of the senior howzevi wanted to push this further. They proposed replicating Ayatollah Khamenei's approach of putting howzevi women to work on researching women's issues in the offices of other Marja'e Taqlid. This initiative meant that women would be informing the Marja'e Taqlid's religious edict for women. If necessary later on, they would propose to have howzevi women in every single Marja'e Taqlid office to inform any religious edict the Marja'e Taqlid would release to the public. This proposition had not yet been considered in 2011.

Many of the women in Ayatollah Khamenei's and Larijani's Dars-e Kharij level class remain indispensable to and determine the workings of the Organization of the supreme leader. The number of participants did not include the howzevi women sitting in Dars-e Kharij classes in Mashhad, Qom, and Esfahan. Speaking about women's ijithad assessments, Khanum-e Alosvand explained, "I think if they participate in the exams right now, one of them will succeed. I can't say more than this, and it is my guess, and it is possible that the number in Tehran or Esfahan can be higher than this. You may come ten years later and see women who become a mujtahid and it will not be a strange thing." I now detail what this possibility entails, with Islamic practices of developing the Muslim self in mind.

NOTES

1. Fischer, *Iran*, 163.
2. Künkler and Fazaeli, "The Life of Two Mujtahidahs," 154–57.
3. Sakurai, "Shi'ite Women's Seminaries," 727.
4. Torab, *Performing Islam*, 40.
5. Personal communication with Mohsen Kadivar, a mujtahid who was at the time a research professor at Duke University, February 10, 2011.
6. Fischer, *Iran*, 65–66, 76-97; Zaman, "Competing Conceptions," 246.
7. Adelkhah, *Being Modern*, 42.
8. Lave and Wenger, *Situated Learning*, 58.
9. Lave, *Cognition in Practice Mind*, 1.
10. Ingold, *Perception*, 227. Ingold uses the term *region*, which is "the world as it is experienced by an inhabitant journeying from place to place along a way of life"; Locke and Biehl, *Unfinished*, 44.
11. Tawasil, "Reading as Practice," 13.
12. Sedghi, *Women and Politics*, 262.

PART II

CONSTITUTING PRACTICES

—⚡—

PRELUDE

A CLASS IN ARJANTIN SQUARE: A
DIFFERENT VEIL, STILL A VEIL

All the women in the class at Arjantin Square, including myself, wore the black chador. At first, the chador made them appear to be a homogenous group. Looking around the room, it became more apparent that not only did the women differ in age, but also underneath each chador was a different color headscarf worn in several ways. Some wore the *maghna'e*, a slip-on headscarf sewn below the chin area; some wore the *shawl*, a rectangular cloth wrapped around the head; and some wore the *rusari*, a square cloth folded into a triangle and pinned at the chin. Some of the women were constantly fixing their chador to make sure they would stay on their heads. Some had one hand holding both sides of the chador more on one side of the face, some held the chador by biting the two sides, and some found a technique to keep it on without making necessary adjustments every few minutes.

FOUR

—ɯ—

THE BLACK CHADOR

BY THE TIME WE ARRIVED at Khanum-e Ghorbani's gate, sweat was dripping from my ears, which were tucked under my headscarf. Khanum-e Ghorbani was hosting an elegy, a rowzeh-khani, for the death of Fatimah, the daughter of the Prophet and the wife of Imam Ali. She had just published an Islamic jurisprudent article in which she argued for limiting the permissibility of temporary marriages to unmarried men on the basis of protecting the integrity of the Iranian family. She was met with opposition within the clerical establishment. But this afternoon, there was a line outside her home. A blue tarp had been spread out on the covered driveway to accommodate seating for late attendees. Sitting in the driveway would not be an ideal situation for them as the air quality index in this one hundred–degree heat had been moving between orange and red the past three days. But at least there was space. Countless number of shoes were piled and scattered on the left-hand side before the doorway to the house.

We squeezed ourselves into the tiny floor space underneath the living room window. There must have been almost two hundred women attending that afternoon, including those who made their way to the second floor. The guests were mostly Khanum-e Ghorbani's students from the howzeh. Laleh and Sana, two of her students from a howzeh in south Tehran, asked her for permission to bring me along with them. Laleh was in her early thirties and was completing her research paper on inheritance law at the time. Sana was in her late twenties, from Shahr-e Ray, and had one more year to complete her program. Like everyone in the room, we wore our black chador, a large tentlike cloth, over our headscarves, manto, and pants. When the lights flickered to signal the start, we all slouched our shoulders and draped the chador over our faces. We were there to bring our memory of Fatimah to the present. Fatimah's moment of death was political in this gathering,

114

like those elsewhere in the world who continued to suffer the way Fatimah had suffered under the rule of the first three caliphs. This mournful storytelling was a call to action to be mindful of the injustice and tyranny in this world.

Yasmine, Laleh's seven-year-old daughter, looked at me, pouted, and motioned with her finger moving downward like teardrops from her eye. "*Geriyeh kon,*" she whispered in Persian. *Make yourself cry.* I could not be certain what each of us would eventually cry for, but I knew it was time to grieve and to wish we could be with Fatimah over hundreds of years ago to help alleviate her suffering. We wept on cue, in sync with the *rowzeh-khan,* the woman reciting the elegy, with high and low vocals until the end. The outbursts of cries were slightly louder when she said, "They took her garden!" Crying in this particular way taught me that this was more than just the experience of weeping on cue.

Marcel Mauss's *Techniques of the Body* comes to mind. What scientists diminish and consider "miscellaneous" according to Mauss is "where there are truths to be discovered."[1] These are the moments that must be closely examined for what they teach us about the way we use our bodies, about what is going on with the forces around us, and what we do with these forces. In this gathering, the women and I created comforting composure out of the sauna-like discomfort for over an hour. Crying mournfully and staying put required a kind of physical and emotional labor to push through the tough moments like keeping overly active toddlers close by, suppressing the need to urinate, or putting off thirst and hunger. But for many of us in the room, this moment of coming together was worth the effort. This worthiness speaks to the work howzevi women put into creating a spiritual nearness to God so they may return to the Original Self. The effort is cumulative and essentially becomes a marker of belonging—in this instance, enough to be invited to cry with Khanum-e Ghorbani in her home with other howzevi. Women who were invited needed to be particular kinds of women who conceptualized Islamic knowledge as the ultimate ethical and moral guidance above all other forms of knowledge. Yet their sense of belonging was neither bounded nor completely hegemonic. I would not have been invited otherwise. I had been fortunate enough to gain Laleh's and Sana's trust weeks before, and both, with permission, invited me to come. Whoever gave them permission to invite me somehow trusted that these two students knew what sense of belonging to look for in a stranger like me.

In this chapter, I show the way the practices of wearing the black chador reflect the complexities I am attempting to demonstrate. Wearing the black chador deems both the practitioner and their activities hidden. The notion of being unseen has been understood as a position of disadvantage and, worse, a marker of being exploited. On Karl Marx's theory of the first who are exploited, Claude Meillassoux states, "Women, despite their crucial role in reproduction, never appear as vectors of the social organization. They are hidden behind men, behind fathers, brothers and/or husbands. And as we have seen, this is not a natural given condition but one which results from changing historical circumstances, and always linked to the exploitation of women's reproductive functions."[2] I complicate this.

The practice of wearing the black chador is flexible in its purpose. But, for the howzevi, it must be contextually situated in the work of khod shenasi: again, doing the work of self-awareness in an effort to return to and preserve the Original Self, the self that is, of its nature, drawn to God. In this framework, the black chador is a tool, the path toward freedom, to freely allow the khod in its original form to be in its inclination to worship God without any deterrence or distraction. For a constructive exploration of possibilities, the practice must not be located in the Kantian notion of self as the sole source of moral order and of autonomy as the freedom from life scripts and the authority of others. Rather, framing the analysis through khod shenasi opens up ways to make the women's practices more relatable or less strange. It also paves the way for another consideration: that being unseen can be a position of power.

I offer a phenomenological focus on what the howzevi did with others to live up to the ideals of khod shenasi. Though these attempts were expectedly imperfect, they were kinds of work that could render women like Khanum-e Ghorbani unseen but simultaneously credible sources of religious insight within the clerical establishment and among religiously conservative Iranians. I examine the practice of wearing the black chador as one of the many complex markers of this labor. I discuss the way the howzevi created comfort out of their self-imposed discomfort through the practice and show that it was possible for self-control to be agentive. I analyze the consequential totalities of the women's practice of wearing the black chador as students of the howzeh elmiyeh, and I ask, what does the black chador accomplish for them?

THE CONTENT AND FORM OF VEILING

There are generally two forms of veiling in Iran, both of which include wearing clothes that cover the entirety of the arms down to the wrists and legs down to the ankles. The way women observe these forms vary. The first form involves wearing the headscarf or hijab completely over the head, and the second form involves wearing the black chador, a large tent-like cloth that women wear on top of, or in addition to, the hijab. When worn, the chador covers the entire length of a woman's body all the way to her feet. The light polyester material is commonly nontransparent. Inside their homes, many women wear the *rangi* chador, made of cotton and printed with colorful dainty flowers, to pray. Novices, like children or newly practicing women, start off wearing the chador with sleeves

Figure 4.1. Howzevi women just finished their midday prayer behind a line of clerics in front of the room. Tehran, 2011. ©Amina Tawasil.

while old-timers wear those without sleeves. Some chadors are tailored with a garter or two strings underneath both sides of the forehead. This, with the help of the mouth and teeth, hands, and elbows, helps to keep the chador from slipping off a woman's head. The use and symbolism of both forms of veiling fluctuate depending on the practitioner, the audience, and the local history of the practice.

In general, the practice of veiling in Iran and elsewhere is as complex as the different interpretations of it. The role of men or the state in coercing women to veil is a common focus of criticism in which women are seen as having fewer rights than men in Iran or women in predominantly non-Muslim countries.[3] Brenda Anderson and Franz Volker Greifenhagen, who have researched perceptions of Muslim identity in Canada, take note of the prevalence of presenting the veil as a practice forced on women.[4] The cloth itself is sometimes likened to oppressive forces that "have denied women's access to their true selves."[5] A specific type of veiling, the face veil or *niqab*, is described as an antidemocratic symbol.[6]

Yet many women continue to observe forms of veiling. Hanna Papanek argues that rapid urbanization affects the way women make decisions on wearing the *purdah* in South Asia.[7] In her work on the practice of wearing the purdah, a head cover and face veil, among Indian women, Patricia Jeffrey makes a case for the way the practice is part of an economic system tied to the transfer of property. The women's marital futures were of great concern because they belonged to the wealthy strata of society and, thus, were socially segregated.[8]

Regarding the face veil, none of the women Anna Piela interviewed in the United Kingdom were forced to wear it or saw it as an obligatory act of worship. They considered wearing it a recommended practice. Some husbands were opposed to their wives' wearing the niqab; some families disowned women for wearing it. While some women reported wearing it because of scholarly interpretations, some were indifferent to these.[9] For some, wearing the niqab was a way to explore a different religious experience from just wearing the headscarf. Women also reported covering their faces as a way of maintaining their relationship with God, a spiritual expression of higher devotion, or as a gift to God that required an "inner strength" in the face of social challenges. They were willing to endure the challenges in order to fulfill a spiritual need.[10]

The practice of veiling, however, is not always about religious practice in Iran.[11] I've seen the black chador gifted to women who returned from pilgrimage to Mecca and used as a sheet to sleep under or over, to haul items from one side of the room to the other, to cradle babies to sleep, to cover satellite antennas, and so on. It concealed identities and signaled respect toward saints when entering a shrine. When worn inside out at Imam Reza's shrine, it could signal a woman's availability for temporary marriage, a concept I address in a later chapter. I met many women who wore the headscarf but not the black chador. They saw the practice as outdated or a commitment they could not live up to. Some of them wore the black chador only when going to their villages or hometowns.

Veiling can be a marker of socioeconomic class in Iran. For instance, the black chador can be a marker of class depending on the situation and the observer. Wearing it produces an interesting effect on the body since it inadvertently puts a spotlight on what is worn on a woman's hands and feet. A piece of jewelry or the shoe itself becomes a clue to a woman's socioeconomic standing. The texture and flow of the black chador is also telling of the cost of the cloth and sometimes which store it was purchased from. Additionally, the effort to cover the body using the black chador could also be about differentiating oneself from women whose lifestyles one sees as immoral. Although I did not meet women who expressed this to me, Torab makes note of this in her work among the women in Mrs. Omid's study group. The women explained that the forced veiling policy in Iran deprived them of visible ways to differentiate themselves from sex workers who, like them, were forced to veil.[12]

Beyond these reasons, the practice of veiling can signal political leanings.[13] How a woman wears the veil can sometimes tell us about ideological differences between veiled women, like the Islamist versus Muslim feminist associations. For some, the practice is an act of political resistance, as Fadwa El Guindi writes about Algerian women during the Algerian Revolution.[14] More recently, Pia Minganti writes about the way the burqini, a women's full bodysuit beach garment, serves as a protest against sexism.[15] It's equally possible for veiling to be thought of as a response to traumatic events such as the demonizing of Muslims after September 11. In that case, veiling becomes a symbol of solidarity and political awareness.[16]

The Shi'i women of south Beirut in Lara Deeb's work saw veiling and volunteerism as ways to authenticate their Islamic knowledge. Both practices resulted in uplifting the Shi'i community second-class status and were considered proofs of modern-ness.[17] In her work on religious bodily practices among Cairene women, Mahmood shows that veiling was one of the many ways women of the mosque movement responded to the pervasiveness of secularism. Veiling was part of the women's effort to develop pious selves who were in constant remembrance of God. Mahmood points out that although the practice was not necessarily political, the increased presence of veiled women was changing Cairo's visual landscape.[18]

On this, unveiling can equally be a tool of protest. In 2018, a number of Iranian women with access to Instagram began posting photos and videos of each other every Wednesday either wearing white headscarves or unveiling in public spaces as protest to four decades of forced veiling. These events came to be known as White Wednesday.[19] But just as unveiling could become an act of protest against the Islamic government, veiling for the howzevi was also an act of resistance against their "enemies"—the United States, Israel, its European allies, and those within Iran who were in support of the United States. Situated in the language of Western imperialism, veiling can be considered a source of power for religiously conservative Iranian women against secular women.[20] The howzevi not only wore the state-mandated headscarf, but they also wore the black chador over their headscarves as a double emphasis on this resistance.

One of the many reasons eighteen-year-old Somayeh wore the black chador was to show her support of the Islamic government. Although Somayeh was too young to witness the revolution, she had access to an Islamic education because of it. That education trained her to read Arabic text and, in her words, "debate anyone in a logical way about almost anything." Her black chador was a symbol of strength against Islam's enemies, especially against the Islamic Republic's enemies. In her summation, a strong *chadori*, a woman who wears the black chador, was an example for everyone to be successful in her education, in their career, and in learning English and, in her words, "to be strong in being logical in their communication with others." Similarly, the black chador for Khanum-e Tabesh symbolized the collective resistance against tyranny, a resistance that led to the

1979 revolution. She traveled with her family for the first time to Malaysia and Singapore, where she and her daughter decided to wear the black chador because they wanted to bring the 1979 revolution outside Iran.

MUJTAHIDEH IS A SOCIALLY DESIGNATED POSITION

For the women in this book, there was more to their practice beyond what political symbolism and resistance could capture. I return to the way the practice of wearing the black chador is connected to the work of khod shenasi as a framework of self-transformation. The howzeh in Iran for both men and women served to instruct students on the Islamic sciences so that they may benefit themselves and then properly convey, in the broadest sense, Islamic knowledge to others. Each howzeh varied slightly in program focus, and depending on the howzeh's focus, students were generally instructed, at the very least, in the basics of how to do ijtihad for themselves. For instance, although the women of Howzeh-ye Kowsar focused primarily on studying the Islamic sciences that would forward their religious propagation work, they also benefitted from the basic instruction on the methods of ijtihad. Howzeh-ye Kowsar were training students to excel in *bahes*, the dialectic between a teacher and students, and *mobaheseh*, the practice of disputation between members of a study circle.

Most of the women I spent time with belonged to a howzeh that focused on training women to do ijtihad. Regardless of the howzeh's curricular focus, training for ijtihad carried with it social demands from a student that, when met, signaled their trustworthiness and credibility to speak of divine knowledge. That is, the act of doing ijtihad itself was tied to codes of conduct based on Islamic teachings. This meant a howzevi was, by default, expected to observe those codes of conduct required of a future mujtahideh, even if she did not intend to become one.

In its finality, the label *mujtahideh* for women or *mujtahid* for men was socially designated. Her audience must interpret her participation in the community of Islamic scholars as legitimate. Moojan Momen writes, "The status of mujtahid can only be achieved by public recognition . . . until he gathers among the public a following who are prepared to acknowledge him a such."[21] Therefore, social relationships and interactions without a doubt shaped mobility. I learned from the women that it was not enough for a student to do well on assessments or to become an expert in Islamic jurisprudence to be identified as a mujtahideh. Her scholarly circle must identify her speech, written work, and actions as grounded in Islamic knowledge.

All of these add up to develop her reputation within and outside her circles. Members of this circle must "read" the mujtahideh as a person capable of interpreting or translating Islamic knowledge to others. Occupying the position did not automatically command respect from others. This rubric for social designation applied to both men and women. In 1972, Brian Street described a clergyman's (mullah) experience with this social designation in a small Iranian village. Some clergymen were scorned: "they are seen to be 'hypocritical', too 'serious' or simply 'lazy'. . . . The status and credibility of a mullah, then, is contingent on how they are judged as individuals in . . . both religious and mundane practices and they do not receive automatic respect due to an office holder."[22]

To be given respect was not inherent in this elevated position. On the contrary, gaining the trust of others must be constantly renewed. This labor is not static. Economic and sociopolitical conditions have an impact on these terms, as I noted in a previous chapter about clergymen and their constituents. Once a student has been acknowledged as a mujtahideh, her upward mobility depends on her "public acclaim of . . . piety and learning." I frame what these social expectations might look like for the howzevi within five requisites to be identified as a mujtahideh.[23] A mujtahideh must be a free person of legitimate birth, past the age of puberty, sane, a Muslim, and an 'adil.[24]

An 'Adil, the Body and Practices

Of these, the requisite of being an 'adil was the most ambiguous. An 'adil is a person whom those around him would consider to be ethical and just. What all this looked like or what these referenced in different moments was complicated. But, to first make sense of the way being an 'adil might be both achievable and legible, I revisit the concept of khod shenasi, an effort toward self-knowing in order to create a spiritual nearness to the Divine, the end goal of which is a return to the Original Self. One example of this work is to answer the question "Who am I?" or "Who are we?"—the answers to which are embedded in a person's remembrance of God. The idea is that by working hard to heighten knowledge of oneself and life's purpose, a person also strengthens the power of reason in their lifelong struggle against their lesser tendencies.

Mulla Sadra, whom the women I worked with most often quoted, philosophizes on the experience of drawing oneself closer to God by describing the relationship between the human being and this singular opportunity for its transformation. Christian Jambet best summarizes Mulla Sadra's philosophy on this experience.[25] In this struggle, the perception of the human body is sacred, not as an object of worship but as the one and only flesh that the soul, or *ruh*, will ever be a part of. The outcome of this fusion is a self that is, among many possibilities, forgetful, pliant, and at the same time resistant, as I explained in the introduction.

For Mulla Sadra, the human being can be worked on to become other than what it was before. As a result, the human being is an ongoing project always moving between two points, becoming a tyrant on one end and becoming *ensan-e kamel*, the Ideal Person, on the other. This opportunity to become the Ideal Person is facilitated by the work of imitation and intelligence. Here, *intelligence* refers to many aspects of life, but in this context it refers to learning what is required of imitating the Prophet but also the effort to become self-aware, as I have already explained, in order to bring oneself closer to God.

Equally important here is that this transformative struggle takes place only in one lifetime, which begins at birth and ends at death. Because of this one and only opportunity, the human body must be guarded and on guard. It must do the transformation and be transformed. The human body, thus, is both the instrument and object. To bring it back around, this is, again, reminiscent of Mauss when he writes, "The body is man's first and most natural instrument. Or more accurately, not to speak of instruments, man's first and most natural technical object, and at the same time technical means, is his body."[26]

Freedom for Mulla Sadra is the transformative goal to free oneself from all matters that get in the way of always remembering God. More specifically, the goal is not to hinder the Original Self from its natural disposition to worship God. Liberation is couched in becoming "angelic" or "reflecting the light of God" since angels are thought to be spontaneous and made of light. The attempt to move *closer to God* is in direct opposition to tyranny. Thus, being ethical and just, which is the opposite of being a tyrant, is directly related to becoming the Ideal Person, who moves the self continually closer to God. The idea here is that becoming an ethical and just person is an indirect but inevitable outcome of an attempt to bring oneself closer to God.

The Legibility of Being an 'Adil

Imitating the life ways and practices of the Prophet Mohammad and his family is supposed to help accomplish this. Verses from the Qur'an and Hadith narrations about these inform this labor. Again, taqlid, or following a mujtahid and/or Marja'e Taqlid's legal interpretation, helps to navigate ambiguous aspects of religion. These imitations are part of the process of developing specific dispositions, or particular ways of behaving, interacting, and thinking about others and one's surroundings. As obligatory practices, the howzevi observed the five daily required prayers, fasted during the month of Ramazan, performed *Hajj*, or pilgrimage to Mecca, and gave alms. They also tried to observe optional practices such as saying "bismillah," or "in the name of God," before every action; saying supplications before eating and leaving or entering the home; reciting Ayat

Al-Qursi before and during a journey; looking after a neighbor's property; or fasting on specific days during the week.[27]

Imitating the Prophet and his family was not a clear-cut process, however. These sources of guidance amounted to 1,300 years of Islamic scholarship. Together, text as guideline to imitate amounted either to no specific set of instructions because of the texts' complexity or to several sets of instructions to be used in different settings for various practices. For instance, Maryam and Sara described scholars they followed and learned from as "fair," "interpreted with justice," "respectful," or "concerned about people," but they did not have explicit and direct instructions on the way to navigate what being an 'adil meant in different situations.

The idea that imitation was not a well-defined process is worth contemplating. Imitation is social in nature.[28] The howzevi women, even as children, were not unsocialized human beings before they began to imitate the lifeways of the Prophet Mohammad and his family, thus bringing with them different experiences and assumptions about the way the world works. Torab writes, "Learning through doing does not mean that the actors cannot reflect on what they do."[29] In this reflection, the women would have competing priorities at any given moment, especially when conditions and situations are always shifting, always unfinished. They are then perpetually unfinished. They must always try to reflect on what to do at the right time in the right place. As with any attempt to imitate, challenges were a given. One conundrum of being ethical and just was that behaving the same way toward every person at every moment could potentially be oppressive. Therefore, what a howzevi does exactly, or what the Prophet Mohammad and his family would do, when X happens in life, was consistently in question. As I detail in the stories in the following chapters, doing life things with other howzevi, or making mistakes and being told what was acceptable and unacceptable, could reveal only some answers, not all. What they did know was that imitating the Prophet and his family was the proper way to be in the world.

The concept of personal connectedness, which I explain further in chapter 5, is part of the effort to imitate. Following a Marja'e Taqlid's interpretation of canonical texts, and a network of guiding teachers and mentors who modeled and instructed on these practices was necessary. Part of the reason the women joined the howzeh was to find out what these practices were and when to enact them, mostly by reading and disputing each other on the way scholars of the past read and disputed each other. In their seminal work on situated learning, Lave and Wenger illustrate the critical role of communities of practice in determining what is and is not successful: "Activities, tasks, functions and understandings do not exist in isolation; they are part of broader system of relations of which they have meaning. . . . The person is defined by as well as defines these relations."[30]

By being part of the women's howzeh, the women had howzeh teachers and mentors they could emulate at the granular level. I draw on Mauss's notion of "prestigious imitation" in that we imitate actions "successfully performed by people in whom [one] has confidence and who have authority over [one]."[31] But finding out from imitating teachers and mentors as well as Islamic text was not enough to find out when to do the right thing at the right time. Imitation also involves having to think about the proper context of application since howzeh teachers and mentors operate on these practices out of their interpretations of narrations.

Maryam described a practice among her friends who would sometimes experience the misfortune of riding the mixed-gender metro cabin instead of the women's-only cabin during rush hour. Some of them would avoid occupying a seat that a man had just stood up from. They would wait a few minutes for "the warmth of the seat" to cool down before sitting. She explained that avoiding any possibility of feeling another man's warmth from the metro cabin seat was part of their observance of proper distance from marriageable men.[32] I explain the creation of this proper distance later on. Maryam did not consider this to be an extreme practice.

What Maryam found extreme was a practice some of her other friends and her husband's friends abided by. When a man would call to speak to her husband, Mohammad, he would tap on the phone instead of asking for Mohammad directly. He would do this to avoid hearing Maryam's voice. For Maryam, this practice was impossible to carry out at every moment. There needed to be some room for adjustment. Therefore, the attempt to imitate the Prophet and his family was an entangled process of interpretation. Maryam needed to experience mistakes and misunderstandings in the gradual passing of time to find out what could and couldn't be applied in discrete moments.

What does *ethical, just,* or *justice* look like exactly in distinct moments? As a nonpractitioner, I did not know exactly what comprises an average, or in Aristotelian terms the mean, between success and failure in their practices because these were, in essence, a lifetime's worth of work that I did not perform. If the howzevi themselves were unsure, then I, as an observer, could not know what being an 'adil might even look like exactly in distinct moments except from my own assumptions about the way the world works.

What I hope to do is lay out the context of their practices because it is out of this context that their practices become emblematic of a person who is ethical and just. This will hopefully shed light on a part of their logic. One undeniable fact about being an 'adil is that regardless of what it might look like at any given time, it requires the presence of others. Being ethical and just requires social interaction. Being an 'adil is revealed not only by the way a person comes to a decision between right and wrong in the moment. Others must recognize the practitioner as such not just once or twice but as a cumulative experience of being around that person.

This recognition requires markers. I risk being misread that I am proposing that howzevi women strategize merely to appear to be just. It is difficult to disentangle this misreading because even a well thought out description implies that they were inauthentic in their acts of worship. To portray them this way is not my objective. I cannot see what takes place cognitively with anyone, not just the howzevi. Case in point, the women taught me that they were waiting for the Hidden Imam and his arrival. Although they made mention of preparing for his arrival by way of khod shenasi, I had no way of knowing if in fact they thought of the Hidden Imam's arrival at any given time. Waiting for him was simply part of the overall logic of their being in the world. Preparation for that is never lost in this conversation. I am unconcerned with gauging sincerity because regardless of intention, the human body and what it does will inescapably be entangled in what people stand for. Mary Douglas writes, "The human body is always treated as an image of society and . . . there can be no natural way of considering the body that does not involve at the same time a social dimension."[33] In the howzevi context, even if the women are heartfelt in their acts of worship, some will charge them with inauthenticity just as some will regard their actions as noble.

While these imitations facilitated bringing a constant awareness of God's presence, these actions were also part of a social register that necessarily involved other people, an audience engaged in similar practices, which includes what I referred to as social circles in chapter 3. I bring this point back to support the idea that the imitation of practices can lead to creating a sense of belonging. A social context in which many individuals are imitating similar practices eventually becomes a space where assessment of those practices becomes part of the interaction. Another way of putting it: the howzevi and her practices become communal property.

On this, Charles Goodwin shows that an audience and their varied interpretive work are constituted through a dynamic process of ongoing interaction. The howzevi gauged the way each of them imitated a practice by referring back to the Qur'an and the Sunnah as well as the scholarly interpretations of the past and present. On his work on talk in progress, Goodwin writes, "Through the use of participation resources available to them, members of the audience are able to not only interact with each other but actively influence the interpretation that will be made of the performance being witnessed."[34] There is unavoidable tension, but it is at this juncture that belonging to a group of people who are imitating similar practices becomes important. For the howzevi, belonging was first and foremost grounded in returning to the Original Self, a belonging to God, thus a belonging to those who are also belonging to God.

This warrants a brief discussion because it carries with it a connotation that a person's desire to belong can make them an automaton. I situate this idea of belonging in the rephrasing of Martin Heidegger's question, *what does it take for a house to be a home?*[35] What is it, then, that the howzevi act on to create a sense of belonging? I chose to frame it in this manner because Heidegger's work holds the closest resemblance to Mulla Sadra's work according to the howzevi. Heidegger proposes that we inhabit the world by *dwelling* or *wohnen*, creating a sense of belonging, for which self-knowledge and an awareness of mortality are crucial. My use of *dwelling* here is very much rooted in Jeffrey Malpas's rethinking of place and place making as dynamic.[36] Our need to constantly create and re-create belonging implies that it is unstable and fleeting, and there are all sorts of shifting around us. Thus, it is not a kind of belonging that overwhelms and determines human action.

On mortality, what Heidegger called *a totality of involvements*, in that our being is contextual and relational, is what constitutes a life worth living.[37] How we live is always in relation to the way those around us also make their lives whatever they wish to make them. Malpas explains, "To dwell is to stand in such relation of attentiveness and responsiveness, of listening and of questioning. The question of dwelling is never a question settled or finally resolved. . . . To dwell is to remain in a state in which what it is to dwell—and what it is to dwell here, in this place—is a question constantly put anew."[38] To illustrate this possibility, Edward Casey writes on the body's active role, the way place and body are mutually constitutive, a process that requires a phenomenological examination.[39] That is, we leave a place with one set of eyes, and we return to the same place with different ones. We also see this in Keith Basso's work among the Western Apache, where he shows the importance of stories and human action in creating and re-creating a sense of belonging with and in the desert.[40] Belonging in this sense assumes instability or a constant movement among people and between people and their surroundings at any given time. This sense of belonging therefore emphasizes a coming together, *a gathering of*, instead of an enforced sameness and uniformity.[41]

On this point, like any human action, the way a howzevi interacts with others is also inevitably a marker of their social reputation. For example, the black chador is associated with particular ways of interacting in public space, which in turn places moral expectations on its practitioners as a collective. If a chadori woman openly engages in morally shameful behavior, she will give other chadori women a bad reputation because observers would associate the chador with that immoral behavior. This kind of association is far from unique. US Air Force officers, for example, are not allowed to display affection in public while in uniform. Public displays of affection supposedly indicate of a lack of discipline, and showing this deficit diminishes the credibility of the collective. Being marked is consequential regardless of intention. In this context, because the Prophet and his family were considered the best examples of people who were ethical and just, the howzevi's labor also signified, at the very least, as an attempt to become more ethical and just than she had been previously. A howzevi's Shi'i religious practices signal to those who operate within this logic that she is attempting to learn and imitate her just predecessors. Through these actions, she earns a reputation for moral and legal expertise among her peers.[42] As I briefly noted in the introduction and in chapter 3, their social space was composed of factions along shifting lines—religious, political and beyond. This space of earning reputation is, therefore, unpredictable. But one obvious sign of this imitative effort is the howzevi's practice of wearing the black chador.

BEING UNSEEN

The chador serves as a way to receive divine merit in that God rewards those who labor to imitate the Prophet and his family. But it is also a useful tool in developing the right amount of self-surveillance to mold oneself toward a desired transformation of self—what Mulla Sadra referred to as moral perfection. While avoiding sinful actions that bring oneself further away from God is important, which I address later, the more difficult task is the way to maintain proximity to God—in other words, to be mindful of God's graces and presence in all actions. This in part involves both laboring to be unseen and knowing the proper time to be visible. This is where being unseen under the black chador is consequential.

The black chador is a moving part of a broader system of relations where being socially unseen or hidden is the objective. By *unseen* or *hidden*, I do not mean invisible or nonexistent. It is more a purposeful act to be unseen, referred to in religious text as *mahjoub*. An extension of this concept is *hijab*, or veil. This is worth thinking through. Growing up as a veiled Muslim in California, I spent my early years in college constantly enunciating myself in student organizations and in Muslim community projects, making sure that others would somehow understand that veiled women could visibly excel, organize, and lead. I assumed then that this was the only way to be heard. The howzevi taught me that being unseen is not equated with being prevented from being heard or understood by others. In certain instances, its opposite—being up front and center, competing with others to take up space, or being visibly public about one's thoughts and achievements—could do more harm than good as far as being heard or understood. I learned that taking up leadership positions is only one of the many signposts of power, not the primary indication of power.

For this reason, I want to take a step back here to further unpack the concept of being unseen or hidden. For many nonpractitioners, the black chador as part of the spectrum of veiling practices is a symbol of women's erasure because it keeps women hidden away from the rest of society. Women must be freed from it. With identities and personalities erased, the veil makes women "invisible."[43] The state of being hidden is assumed to be perpetually crippling because its opposite, public visibility, the space where men have dominated, is again assumed to be the only place where true power resides. Being unseen thus has become equated with being voiceless on the one hand and stuck on the other.

For some feminists, the entire spectrum of veiling practices is but a symptom of something pathological. Damani Partridge mentions a bit of this in her work on veiling practices in Germany. She writes that being "walled off created a frustration" for those who have to look at a veiled woman. Nested in this idea of frustration, gaining access to veiled women also means access to an "exoticized German production" of women.[44] During a speech, the feminist Elisabeth Badinter openly accuse veiled women in France of suffering from a pathological condition because veiled women see themselves as excessively attractive, to the point of always being in danger of being raped. She also refers to veiling as "the refusal of reciprocity" because they can see her but she cannot see them. Veiling for the veiled woman is thus a moment of "triple pleasure over the other: the pleasure of nonreciprocity, the pleasure of exhibitionism, and a voyeuristic pleasure."[45] Badinter's example illustrates what happens when the reasons for veiling are fixed. She assumes that all women veil for self-preservation from men or to reverse the power of the gaze. That's not always the case. She also fails to recognize that these categories are unstable for those who claim to do it for these reasons. Sometimes women veil for these reasons, sometimes not. Both reasons can exist at the same time.

Women in France or elsewhere may veil for all sorts of reasons, and none of them can completely control their audience's interpretation of the practice. I harken back to Goodwin's point on performance and its audience. Again, the way the audience interprets a particular performance has much to do with the way they interact with each other and what ideas circulate among them. Interpretation says more about the audience than the performance itself. Badinter stands for a kind of feminist assumption that life is about gaining power over others and that the world revolves around men. It also seems that a woman's body is a site for consumption that must be reciprocated, the vocabulary of which includes rape.

Here, in this specific howzevi context where being unseen was purposeful and practiced over time, I reframe the notion of being unseen as agentive. This possibility is not difficult to imagine. The question is where and when. Historically in Iran, being hidden under the chador had symbolic value. Being covered by the chador was a marker of "free women" and Persian kings and queens.[46]

The women were quite cognizant of the way being unseen can be a position of power. They were quick to school me on the power of being hidden by way of the Twelfth Imam's Occultation, a story they felt Sunni Muslims like myself could benefit from.

Although my work is not specifically about power, here I consider relevant connections between power and the position of being unseen to ground my argument. I want to begin by first thinking about Foucault's recapitulation of Jeremy Bentham's panopticon, the supposed all-seeing eye that then causes its subjects to internalize its work via self-surveillance. The panopticon is in fact powerful because it is unseen, and whoever or whatever is behind its workings is not always legible except through its symbols. Being unseen here is not a deficit.

Furthermore, its power is temporary and is not all-encompassing because its subjects are also capable of becoming unseen. Michel de Certeau theorizes the effect of the figure of the walker on the all-seeing eye from above. On the traces of walkers on a city map, de Certeau adds, "Itself visible, it has the effect of making invisible the operation that made it possible."[47] On the making of invisibility, one unrelated phenomenon comes to mind: writing graffiti. Graffiti writers derive their power and notoriety from being hidden and unseen. The more anonymous they are, the more power they have to evade law enforcement, and the more notorious they are within the graffiti community. We know they exist because of the visibility of their writing, but we cannot see them.

Having seen from afar a sea of hundreds of black chadors on numerous occasions, I can agree this is the case. I was moved yet bewildered at the same time. For de Certeau, what the walker does is illegible to the surveilling eye from a distance. On this, de Certeau writes, "Each body is an element down by and among many others, eludes being read."[48] I found this to be my experience within a crowd of women wearing black chador that, from a distance, resembled an enormous black blanket. The howzevi here, hidden under the black chador among hundreds and thousands of women like them, evade what de Certeau called the celestial eye.[49] We knew we were unseen, and yet we were more than visible as a whole.

SINCERITY AND HUMILITY

There are foundational Islamic teachings that are directly related to the function of being unseen. Much of what the howzevi learn, perhaps long before participating in the howzeh, were the Prophet Mohammad's teachings on bringing oneself closer to God. One of these was his teaching around the virtue of *ikhlaas*, or sincerity, to carry out an action or to do something only for the sake of God. For instance, to work to feed the family for the sake of God, to wear the black chador in support of an Islamic government, or to propagate Islam in Singapore all for the sake of God would constitute ikhlaas. This sincerity is nurtured by having *tawadhu'*, or humility, a recognition that God is the source of all. For the devout practitioner, tawadhu' is essential to developing ikhlaas, both of which are shown through examples from the Qur'an and the Sunnah. The opposite of tawadhu' is *kibr*, arrogance, considered the root source of all injustices. Kibr is the misrecognition that self—in this case, the howzevi practitioner—creates all possibility and therefore sees herself as greater than those who appear to have created less or have no possibilities for themselves.

With these concepts bounded in their specific definitions, I move forward using the words *sincerity, humility,* and *arrogance* to represent aspects of ikhlaas, tawadhu', and kibr, respectively. Although I risk losing depth, I use these to allow us to draw on some relatable characteristics of these concepts. In this foundational teaching, having humility means always being ready to surrender to any outcome in life beyond one's control. To be effective in developing sincerity, the howzevi practitioner needs to work hard on strengthening humility by constantly reminding herself that God creates the very possibility of her labor. In order to achieve sincerity, this reminder must always also be present.

A kibr seeing of self takes place in the heart—in other words, internally, which can manifest through action. Arrogance is thus considered a disease of the heart and the self, which leads a person to commit injustices and, if not curtailed, tyranny and oppression. Fueling anger and desiring, expecting, or eliciting praise and meritorious recognition from others are the most common symptoms of arrogance. One cure to having arrogance is to develop its opposites, sincerity and humility, again by imitating acts of sincerity modeled by the Prophet Mohammad and his family. The imitative repetition of self-imposed practices, which are active positions of the body, as well as avoidance of particular situations help to accomplish this development. The following are some examples.

AVOIDING EXTRAVAGANCE

One predicament that unfolded among the howzevi after the revolution was the impression of north Tehran as a place for privileged secular Iranians "who imagine they are in Europe," in the words of Maryam. Khanum-e Tabesh expressed a similar sentiment in a tone of apology: "Iran is a beautiful country because the people are kind and good, except just one place, north Tehran. I am sorry about the north of Tehran." Their ambivalence toward secular Iranians in north Tehran in part gives us an idea about the kind of work the howzevi participated in. In its very essence, their work involved seeking ways to prevent Iran from going back to the kind of exclusion the religiously conservative experienced before the revolution. But north Tehran was also notorious for expensive foreign cars, mansions, mixed-gender gatherings, men without beards, women with loose scarves, tight-fitting clothes, and makeup. My friends from south Tehran avoided visiting me when I moved to Gheytarieh. Despite the fact that Ayatollah Khomeini's compound was located in Jamaran, north Tehran, my howzevi friends avoided this part of the city unless it was to go hiking.

Most of the women considered accumulating material possessions beyond their basic needs as a detriment to their project of self. Excess for them contributed to various social and economic injustices and was incompatible with the Prophet Mohammad's and Imam Ali's life ways. This was the ideal. Although I did not find this among the women I spent time with, there were religiously conservative women who wore expensive headscarves and clothes. Case in point, the daughter of the former reformist president has been publicized as wearing Chanel under her chador.[50] Regardless of the way they defined their limitations, the women I spent time with avoided what they saw as unnecessary consumption. For instance, although Mohammad and Maryam were financially capable of elaborately decorating their home, we ate and slept on the floor in keeping with the narratives about Imam Ali's life. Although she was one of the most influential women among Ayatollah Khamenei's students, Khanum-e Alizadeh did not hire a chauffeur or drive a car like some of my friends from north Tehran. Instead, she took a shared taxi to and from work. In the instances I shared the taxi with her, no one knew who this powerful woman was under her black chador.

The women's ambivalence about wedding parties as spaces of possible excess illustrates this further. One afternoon, a student at Howzeh-ye Kowsar asked Agha-ye Sharifi the way to properly reject wedding invitations that involved displays of wealth and the playing of music. Rather than rejecting the invitation entirely, Agha-ye Sharifi suggested that they stand outside the door of the venue and at least offer their greetings to the wedding hosts. The students took issue with his suggestion. Instead of delivering a lecture on an edict as he had planned, Agha-ye Sharifi spent the entire period debating the women without reaching an agreement with them.

A similar tension marked the two wedding parties I attended separately with two howzevi. One party was held in central Tehran and hosted by a cleric for his daughter's wedding. Most of the attendees were students of the howzeh. Sara, who brought me along, assured me that men would be in a separate room, there would be no music, and it would not take more than two hours of socializing. The mothers of both the bride and the groom greeted the guests at the entrance of a dining hall that accommodated about twenty round dinner tables. Creating this space enabled the women to remove their chadors and headscarves. We were served dinner as members of the host family circulated around the room to talk to guests at each table. Unlike other gatherings I had attended in Iran, this one did not have music playing or, at least, the clapping of hands to a rhythm. After about two hours, we began to line up to say our farewell to the hosts. We put on our chadors one by one, and before exiting the double doors onto a staircase up toward the sidewalk, most of the women pulled their chadors over their faces.

The other was a wedding reception of two religiously conservative families closely linked to the family of a well-known revolutionary cleric. There were elderly howzevi in attendance at this wedding. A disagreement took place between the women sitting at my table about the host's choice to allow entertainment that used handheld drums, both large and small. The drum playing was put to a stop at some point. I suspected that news of this reached the groom because similar tense conversations began to take place at the other tables. The groom eventually took hold of the microphone and apologized to the guests for the appearance of excess (*efrat*)—more specifically, for holding the reception in an expensive venue, for the excessive amount of food, and lastly for the entertainment. He explained why they believed that playing small drums was a permissible way to publicly announce the union of two Shi'i Muslims. But at the end of his speech, he expressed that it was more important to make guests comfortable.

During my conversations with the howzevi about marriage, some of them spoke in detail about how important it was for them to have small and private weddings. Maryam held her wedding party in her home and wore an embroidered blouse and a shiny skirt. Three guests sat on the floor next to a basket of flowers and the wrapped gifts from Mohammad and his family. Fatimah had a similar gathering for her wedding, which took place in her home with only a handful of family members. She shared her wedding album with her friends during one of the short breaks at Howzeh-ye Kowsar. She explained what design inspired her in tailoring her own blouse and skirt. She also sewed her own ceremonial *sofreh*, the ceremonial tablecloth, and created the decorative items for it. Her friends congratulated her in the form of short invocations for God's blessings and protection. One described the way she admired Fatimah for having a wedding that resembled those of the *engelobi*, the revolutionary.

Observe Privately

The women took to heart particular teachings that encouraged them to do acts of worship in private or secretly in the hopes that sincerity and humility would become predispositions in other situations. One of these teachings came from the famous prophetic narration "When the right hand gives charity, the left hand is unaware."[51] The idea of having an audience or having the desire to have an audience was considered a flaw or disadvantageous to a woman's progress. The logic was such that by performing general goodness or acts of worship to an audience, she risked gambling away previously existing improvements to develop sincerity and humility—that is, to do only for the sake of God. Thus, part of developing sincerity and humility entailed removing the desire to have an audience.

Case in point, the women frowned upon wearing makeup or laughing loudly in public for reasons not necessarily linked to an aversion toward beautification or pleasantries. They avoided these for what these brought on—attention—and for what they pointed at: some *desire* to be the center of attention, *jalbe tavajo kardan*. Therefore, acts of worship were preferably done in private, with no audience except God.

However, being unseen inherently becomes an obstacle. Interacting with others is, more often than not, necessary for completing tasks. Thus, one way for a woman to keep herself in check in these instances was to avoid becoming *attached* to what that action might signify socially. Being the center of attention or simply having an audience was one of the ways this attachment was developed. I return to the role of the black chador. Here, the black chador makes it easier to avoid having an audience or to engage in an ostentatious display of her labor. Rather than being disabled in this context, the howzevi was creating possibilities by way of anonymity.

The practice of being unseen, which I have coined as anonymity, consists of self-initiated actions that render oneself as one of many participants rather than the one and only. It involves the purposeful attempt not to inform many people, if any, about what they have accomplished while simultaneously contributing to the workings of the Islamic Republic. Being unseen under the chador was coupled with certain initiatives that maintained this position. With exception, the howzevi women in the following examples would downplay their achievements to prevent developing an attachment to their social value. Before describing these examples, however, it is worth noting that the one space the women were expected to reveal their knowledge was during mobaheseh or disputation sessions. I detail this in the following chapter. In order to fully grasp mobaheseh as a social and political space, it must first be prefaced by the women's religious practices and the role of the black chador in this chapter.

Khanum-e Alizadeh, Tabesh, Maryam, and the other women generally avoided mentioning the books they had studied or continued to study, which books they had published, or which scholars they had studied with. I realized later that my inquiry about their accomplishments was putting them in an awkward position, and I had to find other ways of paying attention to their words, actions, and interactions. They took a long while before giving any indication that they had accomplishments. Sometimes they did so when it was no longer my focus. Khanum-e Alizadeh and Tabesh, often used "we," *maa*, to describe a collective attempt at something instead of the self-prioritizing "I," *man*. I asked Khanum-e Alizadeh and Tabesh one afternoon about their scholarly accomplishments. Rather than responding to my question, they changed the topic. A few hours later, Khanum-e Tabesh took me to a bookshelf to show me not her own books but some of the books Khanum-e Alizadeh had published. Indirectly praising Khanum-e Aliza-deh was her way of responding to my question about her own accomplishments. Several months later, they revealed together that they were hoping to someday reach the level of ijtihad.

The practice of downplaying positionality was also common among the men I interacted with. I asked Dr. Sajjadpour if I could be introduced to a mujtahid or mujtahideh. Though he would try, he could not make this promise. He facilitated a few preliminary meetings. Much later in my fieldwork, his students mentioned in passing that Dr. Sajjadpour's peers considered him a mujtahid. Being unnoticed was important for Maryam. Despite our long conversations about other howzevi women whom Maryam knew were in Ayatollah Khamenei's class when we first met, Maryam did not tell me she was also in his class. I overheard a conversation referring to her absence in one of the classes. When I asked her, her friend responded for her. In this attempt to balance between downplaying her position and attachment to the value of her labor, pronouncing achievements would have been detrimental to her project of self-transformation.

There were many instances like these. Although being hidden can be thought of as a way to prevent the curse of the jealous eye from affecting them, which is a common notion among many groups of people, it can also be an indication of the women's labor to remove the desire for an audience. Regardless of whether they were also concerned about the jealous eye, downplaying their achievements involved diverting an audience.

There are circumstances that are seemingly contradictory to the analysis; women from the howzeh do take up positions of power that are quite visible. They serve in the parliament, as heads of offices, or as media representatives. Being unseen, therefore, in this context inherently becomes an obstacle to fulfilling obligations. They must be seen, and their accomplishments must be known. At the same time, what these positions demand, being seen, can become a hindrance to their personal work of khod shenasi. This contradiction has some nuances worth engaging. First, in the framework of working toward khod shenasi, there is a difference between taking on public roles as a necessity or duty versus taking on these roles out of a desire for power. The former is desired more than the latter. My task, however, is not to delve into motivations, thus I assume both motivations to be present and also to fluctuate. I simply describe the logic in operation that influences the women's decision-making. Second, it's possible that by taking up public roles, the work of anonymity, specifically of downplaying their achievements when possible and of finding ways not to become attached to their power, becomes even more challenging, thus more spiritually rewarding when achieved. Finally, and more importantly, the fact remains—the women I spent time with were not interested in such publicly visible roles at the time.

Removing the desire for an audience and keeping "good actions" and signs of accomplishments a secret were only parts of a longer list of teachings howzevi tried to observe. A more challenging layer to this comes from Imam Ali's narration about arrogance: "The sin that makes you sad and repentant is more liked by God than the good deed which turns you arrogant."[52] That is, it is tempting to desire recognition for labor or any progress from the labor to be closer to God. Assuming that the absence of an audience dampens the temptation for social recognition, the real struggle emerges when the practices and tools like the black chador that are supposed to help achieve sincerity and humility become a source of arrogance. This desire for recognition and praise, referred to as *riya'*, contributes to a more virulent kind of arrogance that is related to acts of worship. This happens when a woman sees herself as better than those who appear to have less anonymity and other such pious actions, or, in summation, less sincerity and humility. In this way, prayer or giving charity, like other human actions, can become sources of arrogance.

Accordingly, the process of bringing oneself closer to God involves a never-ending practice of self-checking against arrogance, which in turn must also be checked as a source of arrogance. This self-checking process against arrogance was especially complicated by the work of teaching, guiding, or interacting with a generation of nonreligious Iranians who have a different vision for the future of Iran, reformists who believe that the Islamic government has failed on its promise, and those who neither relate to the howzevi experiences before and of the 1979 revolution nor understand their logic for working against the impact of the Soft War. Some howzevi women like Khanum-e Tabesh considered being positioned to address these challenges one of their greatest struggles, or *jihad*, of which, for the women here, the chador was only an instrument.

FORCING ONESELF AND CREATING RESOLVE

Wearing the black chador, however, was more than just a tool for remaining unseen. The difficulty of wearing the chador works on the body in certain ways. I return to the notions of *repetition* and *self-imposition*. I situate both in the process of molding one's proclivities as complex and laborious. Forcing oneself to carry out an action implies some form of self-surveillance, what Foucault would categorize as disciplinary techniques, and "the soul [becomes] the prison of the body."[53] I want to problematize the assumption that self-policing is necessarily always about power relations that create a deficit on one side and dominance on the other. I do this first by examining the scholarship around veiling. In the case of veiling, the formulaic critique is that women who veil have internalized the dictates of male authority through religious text, and that is why they veil.

If women can police themselves to veil, women can equally police themselves on the way to properly interact with those they anticipate would become agitated by their veiling practice. Some women find it more difficult to confront the un-favorable reactions of others toward their face veil than to engage in the practice itself. Some continuously defend themselves with explanations.[54] Their effort to explain require a sense of anticipation for the way people around them would in-teract with them. Some women see themselves as "ambassadors for Islam" whose responsibility is to dispel stereotypes about Muslims. Some police themselves to accommodate those around them, to make sure their practice of veiling does not become a hindrance to others.[55] Rather than seeing self-surveillance as always a deficit, it can equally be treated as one of the many things people sometimes do in order to maximize their chances at success in finding a remedy to an immediate or foreseeable problem.

I use the category *self-imposed practices* to indicate two general qualities of the howzevi's experience. First, they had to make an effort to remember to do many of the practices, especially the new ones. This was grounded in the way the howzevi saw life as full of unpredictability; to survive, it is necessary for us ignore or forget most of what we see, hear, or touch in the span of a lifetime. But forgetfulness also makes life unstable. Our propensity to forget thus makes the effort to remember ongoing. Second, the women were not as docile as they wished to be in order to meet their objectives.[56] They imposed disciplinary practices on themselves precisely because they recognized the impossibility of internalizing what they wished to internalize. At times they would have to force themselves to do what they did not initially want to do. Unpleasant physical experiences equally contributed to life's complexity. Not only would they have to make an effort to remember, but they would have to force themselves to do what they might not want to do at the moment. The desire to develop sincerity and humility in all ac-tions are thus moving targets. It is not a frustrated kind of labor, however.

The practice of praying five times a day without delay is one example of the challenges women faced in both remembering and doing. The sisters Fatimah and Hoda and other howzevi explained that their orientation of time revolved around the designated prayer times. Fatimah and Hoda thought this might have been because they had been doing the daily prayers since they were seven years old. But they still needed constant reminders when it was in fact time to pray. The call to prayer, or *azan*, served this purpose. Since a directive was issued to lower the volume of and to shorten the azan in Tehran, some women would set alarms on their phones using the azan. Not all, however, had advanced mobile phones.

In making our travel plans, we made certain we could reach a pit stop to avoid having to pray on the side of the road. Finding a designated place to pray was especially challenging with children in tow. When we were not traveling, the time for prayer frequently interrupted our activities when the women would get up in the middle of conversations, afternoon naps, cooking, or putting their small children to sleep to do the ablution. This involved washing their hands, head, and feet at the bare minimum. If they felt there was a slight possibility of having any urine on themselves or on their clothes, they would wash these off as well. Before positioning themselves for prayer, they would make sure to fix their garments so that they completely covered their limbs. The preparation for and the prayer itself took at least half an hour, a daily total of at least two and a half hours. The most challenging was the predawn prayer. It was especially difficult for married couples because a full-body ablution, *ghosl*, was required after having sexual intercourse before the upcoming prayer. This was particularly hard in the winter months when the water temperature was inhospitable at four in the morning.

Kobra, a howzevi from Madraseh Ali, remarked that she considered her prayer a one-on-one meeting with God, an opportunity to build on her personal relationship with God. Therefore, the moment of prayer must not feel like a habit, void of meaning and intention. She would try her best to focus and feel sincerity for every verse she recited from the Qur'an. I make a connection between this and a kind of experience that results from a laborious undertaking. The labor involved in remembering to pray and then acting on that remembrance despite the obstacles are evidence of the prayer's value. That is, whatever is worth remembering and whatever is worth doing despite the barriers must be important. The difficulties of doing each of the prayers were in many ways necessary to produce prayers that were not just habitual but meaningful.

For the howzevi, naturalizing virtues like "being just" or "sincerity and humility" through practice was very much about bringing about comfort from and in the discomfort—in colloquial terms, *owning the practices*. Here, the experience of the practice being laborious is fundamental. That is, one does not eliminate the discomfort; one pushes through it. That is part of making an experience all the more meaningful.

Let me return to the role of the black chador in developing sincerity and humility. As a Muslim woman, I am familiar with other forms of veiling like wearing the *jilbab*, the long coat over another layer of clothing, and the niqab, the face veil. Essentially, I had been desensitized to the veiling practices before arriving in Iran. But there was one incident at the Teatr-e Shahr metro station that forced me to pay closer attention to the complexities of the practice. There was an elderly woman with two men walking in front of me. She was holding her black chador over her face as we all moved with the crowd of commuters toward the escalator. The two men stood behind her as she stepped forward on the escalator. After a few seconds, her chador got caught on the side of the moving escalator. The escalator continued to swallow her chador as she desperately pulled on it. The two men held her while instructing her over and over again to let the chador go. She would not. The line of people and I standing behind her feared we might all fall downward. The escalator eventually stopped.

Like the elderly woman, many were protective of their practice. After this experience, I began to observe the howzevi's practice more closely. I noticed that women were constantly fixing their chador in place. I began to focus on one or two howzevi in specific interactions to count the number of times they would adjust their chador in a span of an hour. I also began to observe when and where they would create particular movements with it, holding it in specific ways with their teeth, hands, or elbows. Finally, I observed when and where they would take it off. I began to think of the different ways a certain kind of discomfort allows the chador to slowly work on the body as the body works on it.

During one of our classes with Agha-ye Sharifi at Howzeh-ye Kowsar, Fatimah adjusted her chador at least ten times in a span of two hours, despite the fact that it was already held in place underneath with a garter. Other women on other occasions fiddled with their chador more than that in a short period of time. During our conversation after class, she asked me what I thought about the lesson and the discussions. She was fascinated by Agha-ye Sharifi's lesson but felt tired because she may not have slept enough the night before. Fatimah did not have to adjust her chador. But she continued to do so.

One of the things a woman did with the chador was to pull it three-quarters over her face, or *ro migire* in Persian. They did this especially when they felt uncomfortable about their surroundings for all sorts of reasons. Many of us today might be familiar with this kind of response to what is around us—specifically, the habits we have developed around wearing masks during the COVID-19 pandemic. To lessen the difficulty of wearing masks all the time, my friends and I pulled our masks below our chins or our noses when we were outdoors or when no one was around us. But as soon as we felt unsafe, we pulled our masks over our faces again. It became a habit. During peak infection rates, we might have even estimated a distance of at least six feet between others and ourselves before feeling safe to pull down the mask. Our bodily movements work on the mask as the mask works on our bodies. A similar logic applies to wearing the chador.

Keeping the chador on the body was not easy, especially while using squatting toilets or carrying a child. The challenges of keeping the chador on the body forces, and thus enables, the practitioner to rethink, which begins with at least remembering, her overall purpose for the practice. As with moments with other women, it is possible to interpret Fatimah's repetitive attempt to keep it on as a constant renewal of commitment to the practice. The challenge of sitting through the lecture could be channeled into becoming a motivation to continue as Fatimah creates the movements necessary to adjust the chador using her hands and arms. That is, the feeling of not wanting to act on something could turn into a catalyst and then into a series of actions—in the words of Jose Ortega y Gasset, "To be astonished and to be always alert (when reading)."[57] A single moment of success enables the practitioner to recognize the possibility of overcoming other obstacles.

Anchoring Oneself and the Flow

Wearing the black chador helped the women develop a kind of spatial sensibility that could prevent them from behaving in ways that would sabotage all previous efforts to become the women they hoped to become. We see this in a later example with Khanum-e Bagheri and her interest in playing sports. Developing spatial sensibility included avoiding spaces of *gonah*, or sinful behavior, such as wedding parties where music was being played, as I've explained, or restaurants that offered *galyon*, molasses-based tobacco smoked in a water pipe. Avoiding parks where men and women mixed socially was always a factor in choosing where to meet each other or to take family walks.

The effort to avoid mixed-gender spaces was often prefaced by already existing gender-separated spatial arrangements made by individuals or institutions they frequented. Maryam spoke highly of one of her professors in Kashan whom she thought was conscientious about men and women interacting with each other. He explained to Maryam that men and women together were like cotton and fire, in that if they were to be left alone together "something will happen." Maryam added, "Even if they were not alone, something will catch on fire." The professor used to arrange for *jahadi* (reconstruction corps) excursions in a way that would facilitate ease of communication between the gender-separated groups. He would make sure there was at least one man related to at least one woman in the other group—for instance, a husband and wife, brother and sister, mother and son, or father and daughter. He did this so that if someone from one group needed something, they could communicate through those who were related to each other. For these reasons, Maryam went to do the *hajj* (pilgrimage to Mecca) and the *umrah* (minor pilgrimage to Mecca) and traveled to Karbala with this professor's group.

When spaces could not be completely separate from men, the chador was meant to accomplish this separation in the immediate, but also in ways that are not so obvious, in ways beyond its utility as a material barrier for gender separation. Observing gender separation and wearing the chador were only two of a long list of bodily practices that served to help the howzevi develop sincerity and humility. For this point to make sense, we have to assume that wearing the chador was sometimes about creating a barrier between oneself and unfavorable actions.

This point is illustrated best by looking at their bodily movement in relation to time. Farideh's practice of gender separation played an important role in the way she saw herself as a Shi'i Muslim woman. Farideh, her cousins, her two aunts, and I went on a picnic at a nearby park in the next town over from hers. After eating, we decided to go on a short hike in the woods while her aunts remained behind sitting under a tree. We walked through an old fort and into the woods. About midway on a trail, Farideh stopped and pulled her chador over her face. She signaled for us to keep still because she was trying to listen for sounds coming out of the woods. She slowly retreated in the opposite direction as soon as we heard men's voices further down the hiking trail. We walked an extra half hour to avoid that trail. But as we approached the picnic area, we had no other choice but to go down this one and only trail. There were three young men standing in our way. We did not have a choice but to walk past them as we all pulled our chadors over our faces.

Assuming that Farideh experienced time as a flow at whatever rate, the chador was an object that anchored time—a slowdown, a gradual decrease in the flow. The act of pulling the chador over her face drives home this point. It helped her create a proper distance from unfavorable situations. The act of pulling the chador over the face, or fixing it in place over the head, gives the practitioner a moment to slow down and consider the next move. In Farideh's example, it gave her a moment of pause to bring her body to attention before deciding on the next course of action. Her decision for us to take another trail became, again, a renewal to her commitment to something greater than that moment.

This effort to pause was especially evident when we were refused service or entrance into certain places or were harassed. This refusal of service happened several times in north Tehran because at the time it was common for people in that part of the city to reject the presence of people who appeared to be religiously conservative like the howzevi. The moments of pulling the chador over the face or having to manage keeping the chador over the head and the body allow for a pause to consider purpose and intention. I provide a more detailed example in chapter 6, in particular the way nineteen-year-old Zaynab controlled her temper against a man who was harassing us on the bus. But it is in this very moment of pause that wearing the chador helps women like them avoid behaviors such as backbiting, cheating, lying, wearing makeup, mixing with men unnecessarily, and, in Zaynab's words, all the "bad behavior." She used the chador to create a physical barrier between her and these actions, which may start off as small and unnoticeable but have the potential to become a way of life.

Becoming by Way of Clothing

As with any effort to imitate, imagining who we want to become is part of the labor. Depending on the context, it's possible to imagine ourselves differently as a result of what we put on our bodies. I suspect that there is something about wearing a suit to a job interview, camouflage fatigue in the battlefield, or a chef's jacket in the kitchen that focuses the wearer on the tasks at hand. Mauss interprets a similar phenomenon in his interest in "the confidence, the psychological momentum that can be linked to an action which is primarily a fact of biological resistance, obtained thanks to some words and a magical object." He describes that the tribes near Adelaide observe a chanting ritual while hunting the dingo. During the possum hunt, they carry rock crystals in their mouths while chanting. He adds, "It is with this support that he is able to dislodge the possum, that he climbs the tree and can stay hanging on to it by his belt, that he can outlast and catch and kill this difficult prey."[58] Just as wearing the black chador can make someone feel trapped and subjugated, it can equally make someone feel the exact opposite. The black chador can facilitate a momentary shift in who someone can become. It can enable the forgetful and expectedly resistant practitioner to become an idealized Shi'i woman for a moment in time.

It is useful to describe the occasions when the women did not bother keeping their chador on for what these might tell us. I attended a conference with Khanum-e Alizadeh one afternoon, and during a session break we walked outside the convention center to get some air. We sat on the lawn under a tree, and one of the senior women let her chador fall below her shoulders while the others made sure to keep them on. Other examples, however, involved traveling with a group of women. For example, on our way to their village, two women let their chador fall below their shoulders even though passengers in the other cars could see them. In another instance, a group of us decided to rent a room to rest in during our pilgrimage to one of the shrines outside of Tehran. The door was left slightly open to the point we could see people walking by. While we all put on our chador, one of the women did not. But she did not seem to be bothered by the situation. She eventually placed her chador over her head. This last example took place midway during a long-distance drive with a family whose matriarch, Tahere, was a howzevi. We parked on the side of the highway to rest and drink tea by a small stream. There were three men making food nearby. Tahere got out of the car without her chador and made her way to the small stream.

In each of these instances, the women put their chador on after a period of time to repeat the practice. These moments tell us that the practice was exhausting. Practitioners needed a moment to compose themselves. And though exhausting, these can also be turned into points of renewal of commitment. In the act of letting the black cloth fall on their shoulders, and then again laboring to keep it on, the chador became an on and off switch for the women, a signal that it was time to try again to become who they wanted to become.

The occasions when the women did not wear the chador at all demonstrate this point further. In the spring, Fatimah, Hoda, and I spent a day hiking up one of the trails in north Tehran. Hassan, their mother's husband, who had been a prisoner of war during the Iran-Iraq War, raised them to become expert mountain hikers for the time when a war with Iran's enemies becomes a reality. He had been taking them hiking every week since they were about seven years old. The sisters wore their chador in the car during the drive to the trail, but they did not wear the chador during the hike. Instead, they wore full hiking apparel. Each carried hiking gear, which included hooks, sticks, flashlights, blankets, an emergency kit, a portable stove, a foldable tarp, canned goods, fruits, nuts, sandwiches, and three canisters of water.

This example illustrates three points. First, wearing the black chador was not always about women protecting themselves. The sisters' practice all the more highlights the fact that the black chador accomplishes something else for them. Second, they did not wear chador in three spaces: inside their homes with their family or in trusted friends' homes without men, inside the mobaheseh circle in the absence of men, and on hiking trails. The two of them had been hiking weekly, rain or shine, for about twenty years at the time, which, perhaps to them, designated hiking trails as an extension of spaces like a home. Finally, the hiking attire and gear, along with the skills Hassan had taught them, helped them to be the expert mountain hikers Hassan trained them to be. Hiking in hiking gear became a momentary shift in the versions of Shi'i women they wanted to be, women who were physically active and took care of their health in a way similar to how the women in the Prophet's family have been described. If hiking attire can put them in this mode, so could the black chador in howzevi mode. By wearing the black chador, they can become like Fatimah, the daughter of the Prophet and wife of Imam Ali, who performs her prayers consistently, who carries out acts of worship and goodness, and who can overcome difficulties for the sake of God.

I explore the idea that these momentary shifts are aided by signals that allow practitioners to bring their bodies to attention. This can be observed when Iranian women who wear neither the black chador nor the proper hijab enter a shrine. They pick up a chador provided at the door, fix their scarves, place the chador over their heads, pull it over their faces, slouch their shoulders, and lower their gaze as they walk toward the burial room. We can see a similar call-the-body-to-attention moment in the opening vignette during the elegy at Khanum-e Ghorbani's home. The women flickered the lights on and off as a signal that it was time to bring Fatimah to that moment. But these moments with the chador are

Figure 4.2. Fatimah and Hoda set up their cooking equipment during our hike where they did not wear their chador. Tehran, 2011. ©Amina Tawasil.

not determinate toward one particular version of who they want to become. As I show in the following chapter to elaborate this point, wearing the black chador can enable a howzevi to engage in dispute for delaying marriage in order to do the religious work as Fatimah Ma'sume, the sister of the eighth imam, had done.

Putting on a piece of clothing associated with the idealized women of the Prophet's family, with Ayatollah Khomeini's wife, and with the women of the 1979 revolution makes it slightly easier to accomplish a task through a momentary shift of enacting who they are. Point being that through clothing, we, not just the women here, can make ourselves be that or become what we think exists outside of us. It becomes possible to dress the possibilities into being. This is, again, a work of educating the self to remember or to do what is not easy to do.

Inasmuch as the chador can facilitate imitation of women in Islamic history, "the who" that is developed through wearing the black chador also serves as a deterrence. It is as if to say, *A woman who wears the chador does not [insert unwanted action]*. At its core, this is elective self-surveillance that is, again, supposed to help achieve a goal. For instance, not all forms of movement outside the home were considered beneficial. Throughout my fieldwork, I did not meet one howzevi who would leave home by herself to go to a movie theater, to shop, or to roam the city streets for the sole purpose of having time for herself—actions we might consider uncomplicated elsewhere. They were ambivalent toward the idea of going on an excursion, a *gardesh*, alone. Leaving the house with permission from their fathers or husbands was often for the purpose of visiting family members, meeting a friend, attending a meeting, going to class, or doing a local pilgrimage to a shrine with friends or family. When they did not have other women to go food shopping with, their fathers, brothers, or husbands would carry out the task.

The time of day was an important factor to consider. "It is bad for a woman to be outside when it is dark," Maryam explained. The other howzevi told me that a woman who wears the chador simply did not go out after dark. "And a woman should not know all the places in the city. If she tells the people she knows this place or that place, they will think she is bad," Maryam added. The black cloth for Maryam was a way to distance herself from such actions. Thus, every pull, every adjustment of the chador, was a renewal that a woman who wears the chador does not stay out late. This does not mean that all the howzevi never went out after dark. Zaynab, in chapter 6, was among the few from Madraseh Ali who had experienced watching a movie inside a theater with her family and who had experienced coming home close to sunset.

Laughter and the Temporality of Remembering

One afternoon near the Abdol Azim shrine, I asked Khanum-e Refaei how her English class was coming along. "We are reading a book called *Old Henry*. It's a beautiful story," she answered. We were heading back to Khanum-e Refaei's office for refuge from the midafternoon heat for about half an hour. On our way out the door, we saw that the four-seater yellow seesaw in the courtyard was vacant. Khanum-e Refaei and her office secretary, Samira, led the way, running and jumping on one side of the seesaw. Maryam and I took our positions on the other side. We rocked back and forth a few minutes, laughing out loud while our chadors expanded into the air like balloons with every push higher.

The alignment between an ideal and a human action is not always clear. In the effort to bring oneself closer to God, there were moments that did not quite fit the script but also did not fall out of it. In this context, I explore the role of play, as in what Gregory Bateson writes "could only occur if the participant organisms were capable of . . . exchanging signals which would carry the message 'this is play.'"[59] Roberte Hamayon writes, "Playing is not true doing, but a kind of doing."[60]

Saba and Zaynab, whose friendship I detail in chapter 6, were both in their late teens and were students from Madraseh Ali. Early one evening, the three of us had just left Madraseh Ali and were walking on the unusually nearly empty

Mostafa Khomeini Street toward the metro. Just before reaching the chocolate shop on the corner, I noticed Saba was shivering. I asked if she was cold and she said, "Yes," with a smile. Zaynab did not feel cold because she was wearing a coat underneath her chador. I told Saba it was unfortunate that she had forgotten her coat at home. Saba and Zaynab looked at each other and laughed. They knew something about the situation that I did not. "I don't wear a coat," she explained in Persian, then quipped in English, "Because I will look very, very this way." While laughing, Saba then trudged a few exaggerated elephant-like steps forward with both her arms stretched out to the sides, thus appearing much, much larger in width from the back. Just to be sure that I understood the joke, Zaynab explained that Saba would appear wider in size if she were to wear a winter coat underneath the chador. We could not stop laughing as Saba continued to plod like an elephant.

Although this particular example is not about Saba beautifying herself, other than being concerned for the way she appears, it warrants clarification. This can be analyzed as vanity. But I hesitate to interpret Saba's concern as such for several reasons. First, motivations are not fixed. Vanity is only one of several motivations at once. Maryam and Khanum-e Refaei, like Alimeh and Farideh and other howzevi friendship groups, accessorized minimally. Recall Nahid and her friends playing with makeup in Behesht-e Maadaran. Sometimes the women modeled different chadors for each other or new scarves with matching outfits. Despite the strict observance of wearing the black chador, the howzevi also went to great lengths to wear headscarves of different shapes, colors, and sizes underneath the chador. An interpretation of each instance must be framed alongside or within the rest of my experiences with the women. Actions and their meanings cannot be decontextualized. If I want to do the work of interpretation, I cannot write about the meaning of an act without connecting it to other actions or other stories simply because meanings exist in a social field full of other meanings.

Second, it reiterates an understanding about womanhood that is heavily informed by evolutionary psychology's biogenetic framing of gender. It supposes that "males" are physically stronger, thus have better access to resources, and are concerned only about maximizing genetic success through reproduction. Given their reproductive capabilities, "females," on the other hand, are perpetually concerned about upward mobility for their offspring. Thus, they must compete for male attention.[61] Women's vanity is part of the narrative that beautifying oneself, whatever that may mean, is automatically linked to competition for upward mobility.

Releasing acts of beautification from the category of vanity allows us to consider other possibilities. For the howzevi, vanity leads to conceit, the desire to be the center of attention, and fuels lesser tendencies. But the enjoyment any person derives from wearing different colors does not always equate to conceit. The first time Maryam and I attended one of Khanum-e Tabesh's parties, we made our way to an empty bedroom upstairs so we could change our clothes to "party dresses." Maryam asked me if I wore makeup, and I said no. She proceeded to put makeup on my face. I did not interpret this as motivated by vanity. Rather, it was motivated by what was deemed an appropriate presentation of self to a circle of women who were also thinking about presentation of self to others. One needed to wear a party dress and put color on one's face to show respect to the host and to the rest of the guests at the party.

All of these examples, out of the many more I weave through the chapters, may or may not have been constituted by the desire to become the center of attention. In the time I spent with Maryam, Zaynab, Nahid, and others, I did not interpret their actions as forms of vanity, for reasons I have already stated. The example of Saba's concern about appearing large could be about vanity, but a vanity whose audience is Saba herself and that produces Zaynab's laughter. It's more probable that this example was not so she could be the center of attention when around others, based on my experiences with the two women. For them, being concerned about appearance is still within the workings of knod shenasi. One could even argue that appearing larger under the chador might actually draw attention to herself.

It's possible that part of the work they do on themselves includes trying to express an image of a Muslim woman as someone aesthetically pleasing, which they would like to develop inside themselves.[62] If the outside appearance is colorful, perhaps the inside can become colorful as well. Basso writes, "Deliberately and otherwise, people are forever presenting each other with culturally mediated images of where and how they dwell. In large ways and small, they are forever performing acts that reproduce and express their own sense of place—and also, inextricably, their own understanding of who and what they are."[63] But in the howzevi context, this could also lead to an attachment to the material. So, for instance, wearing different colors with each other was ideally situated in the remembrance of God by frequently saying "Masha Allah," or "What Allah has willed," whether this was effective or not in subduing the personal pleasure of colorful scarves.

Rather than treating the scarves as a contest of self against vanity, I consider these expressions a form of play that builds humor into the process of continually renewing commitment to a lifelong practice. Without contextual knowledge, one might also assume that Saba's behavior is evidence of a young woman's desire to disavow herself from the practice of wearing the chador. Yet Zaynab and Saba continued to wear the chador by choice. Wearing the chador was a longstanding practice among the women in Saba's family. She began her training at a very young age with the *chador-e arabi*, or chador with sleeves, because it was difficult for her to manage the *sonnati* chador, a chador without sleeves. Zaynab's family did not have such expectations. She decided to wear it when she was fourteen years old because it was the best hijab, as she explained. Before then, she wore only the school uniform to school. Wearing the chador was a self-imposed lifelong commitment until they decide otherwise. Regardless of their histories in the practice, this commitment, as with other long-term commitments, did not always produce a sustained desire to want to be in it.

I refer back to Mahmood's framing of agency, which implies the possibility of the subject completely internalizing or attaining "certain kinds of ethical and moral capacities."[64] This was not an obvious outcome for the howzevi. Zaynab and Saba must continue to do the work of khod shenasi because a forgetful and distracted subject is incapable of completely internalizing ethical and moral capacities. Had the women's work of khod shenasi been internalized in its totality, they would no longer have to do the work at all. Their existence would run on autopilot and lose its meaning. The howzevi's work of self-knowing is imperfect and unfinished in the presence of difficulties and challenges that are beyond their control. But they persevere in the near impossibility of the task, and still the endeavor is not a frustrated one. The work of khod shenasi is thus valued for reasons I examine in a later section.

Though it often became a struggle for them to persist, the women did not end their work. Rather, they productively struggled through the way the chador and other challenging practices sometimes made them feel. A renewal of commitment or a refamiliarizing process was necessary. Part of refamiliarizing oneself with a practice was to push up against it, to challenge it, to doubt it, and sometimes to laugh the experience away. Playing along with the continued interrogation of the sociopolitical order allowed them to further their commitment.

What the two close friends found humorous—that the black chador sometimes makes a woman look like an elephant—would have been offensive had our actions, like the laughter among us all and Saba plodding like an elephant, come from people they did not know. It would have also been offensive to those who considered the chador a sacred practice and certainly a political one. Bateson writes, "It may even be that the essence of play lies in a partial denial of the meanings that the actions would have had in other situations."[65] Perhaps because I had been spending time with them and yet was considered a stranger who would eventually leave, they decided that evening to let me in on the joke, inviting me to laugh with them about Saba's reluctance to wear a coat under her chador. This created a kind of feeling of being at home with the chador. Play was possible perhaps because they had experienced together the painstaking labor of wearing the chador and felt and witnessed the power and disempowerment of the practice.

Figure 4.3. Howzevi women share their food during a lunch break, where most of the side talk and laughter happen. Tehran, 2011. ©Amina Tawasil.

There were different kinds of play among women at Howzeh-ye Kowsar. We had just finished lunch. Some of the women were talking, doing impersonations, lying on the floor, or napping using their chadors as blankets before the next class. Notebooks, books, bags, scarves, and chadors were scattered around the room. The women began to shuffle in panic as soon as the administrator announced that Agha-ye Sharifi was on his way up the staircase. Laughter filled the room as most of them rushed to pick up their headscarves and chador. Some continued to play by blocking, tripping, and preventing each other from reaching their scarves. These instances were commonplace. Some of the women were not ready, still sorting through the pile of black chador on the floor. As Agha-ye Sharifi approached the door, the women began grabbing any chador and quickly put these over their heads. "Yaaa Ali!" he said three times before entering the room to signal his entrance. With some giggling, some breathing slightly harder than normal, many of the women knew immediately that they had put on someone else's chador. They scanned the room in search of the person who had their chador. Smiles and signals were exchanged among them as Agha-ye Sharifi introduced his topic for the next hour.

These kinds of interactions were not automatically funny and could even have been disastrous for the women involved. The difference between play and non-play becomes recognizable by successfully participating with and engaging other howzevi for a good amount of time. Since I had not been with them long enough to get a sense of what would be appropriate, the line between play and non-play was momentarily blurred to me. And even if I had been there for a longer period of time, it did not guarantee that I would be invited to play. But at that moment, it was clear to others and to me that it was not offensive for them to trip each other or mistakenly wear each other's chador. They signaled to each other in some way that what they were doing was play. It would have been a different story had I been the one to try to make someone fall over or tried to wear someone else's chador, because I had not done the necessary work to earn that privilege. This was an indication that different forms of play brought them together.

One-liner remarks that made us laugh spontaneously sometimes punctuated our conversations. At the end of a howzeh admissions interview, the assessors requested a ten-minute break and approached Maryam, Khanum-e Refaei, and me. "Let us practice our English with Khanum-e Amine," one of them said, laughing. Khanum-e Gholami, who was recently widowed, responded with more laughter and egged on the others to speak English with me. A light conversation took place about where I studied and what brought me to Iran. Maryam asked the widow how she and her family were doing. Seconds into the conversation, Khanum-e Gholami said, "Well, you know, I'm available now. If you know anyone...." We all laughed as one of the other assessors slapped her on the arm. Khanum-e Gholami turned to me and asked, "Are you married?" I said, "No." She said with a smile, "Ah, don't worry, better to be alone from the beginning because in the end you will be alone anyway."

Khanum-e Gholami's remark lurked around nonnegotiable gendered boundaries of moral decency. That is, a woman, especially of her stature, was not supposed to let people know she was looking for a man. But this remark was negotiated as a joke to us, her audience, by virtue of her marital status and age. Khanum-e Gholami was a widow and a woman in her late sixties who could no longer bear children so was therefore considered almost genderless. She no longer had to respond to the same expectations as a woman in her childbearing years. Women at this age were to be celebrated and respected because of, or despite, the outrageous remarks they would make.

Staying within guidelines of the practice did not imply the absence of physical activities in the women's lives. Playing sports was an important part of the lives of some of the women. Mona, one of the howzevi, competed as a sharpshooter in tournaments in Tehran. She went from beginner's level to the advanced level in a short period of time because she enjoyed the sport very much.

Sana and I were spending time with Khanum-e Bagheri one afternoon at the Imamzadeh Davood shrine. One of our conversations was about notions of beauty and the body. Khanum-e Bagheri, a howzevi at the Dars-e Kharij level and an administrator in one of the howzeh in Tehran, had an international black belt in tae kwon do. She was also giving tae kwon do classes to her students from the howzeh. She explained that the boredom of her study routine motivated her to look into playing some kind of sport. She first learned gymnastics, then she looked into aerobics. But she saw "the women dancing, and it's not good for me. They were wearing beautiful clothes and too much makeup. And then dancing, I don't like it, and I decided that I wanted to do sports that didn't involve these kinds of behaviors." She chose tae kwon do because its rules of discipline reminded her of her Islamic practices: "Tae kwon do has a good rule, for example, you must be polite with your teacher, respect for your classmates . . . respect elder students, especially those that have more experience than you . . . the same as rules of my religion." She also appreciated that tae kwon do did not require tight-fitting clothes. "This is very good for me," she said.

Khanum-e Bagheri attempted to make room for her interest in playing sports while observing the boundaries of her practices, mindful of clothing, dancing, and other inappropriate activities. Part of that enjoyment came from the alignment of disciplining their bodies to focus in the same way they would during their prayers. In Khanum-e Bagheri's description, she was remaking the practice into what suited her because the disciplinary practices of tae kwon do would help her continue her Islamic practices. Khanum-e Bagheri could not keep up with the regimen after she gave birth to her first child; she said, "I now play volleyball.

There were moments where ideology itself was under scrutiny, especially about gendered notions of personhood. The tension between what the scriptures and teachings say versus personal experiences with men could be located between the lines. One afternoon as we were sitting in Hoda's living room, one of the howzevi told a story of another howzevi who had received a phone call from a woman married with children, a friend of a friend. She was asking for Islamic legal advice on what to do about a wrongful surgery procedure. The caller's husband had brought her to a gynecologist for an embroidery surgery, a surgical overhaul of a woman's entire reproductive system, which made the woman "like a virgin again." The husband paid for the surgery as expected, but when the woman healed, the doctor had made the woman "too much" a virgin. The husband could not have intercourse with his wife. The woman who made the phone call was happy about the procedure, but she said her husband felt wronged, was depressed, and needed legal advice. When the storytelling ended, there was a short pause among us, without further commentary. Then there was howling laughter from all who heard the story.

During my time with them, there was plenty of laughter among a handful of a married howzevi who had been friends for years—laughter about men, *at* men, and about misfortunes in relationships. But this instance showed the way the howzevi thought of men as lacking, as having a weakness that leads them into making detrimental decisions. Khod shenasi here was the benchmark. Khanum-e Tabesh alluded to this weakness in one of her lectures: "Men have a good imagination—when they look at a woman, they will continue to imagine anything on earth. That look has an effect.... The look is the same in men and women, but in men with one gaze it is more intense. They become aroused.... They will continue to imagine anything on earth." This was a sign of weakness, a deficiency of self-awareness. Although arousal purely by the physical senses is natural, indulging it was a sign of neglecting moral development. In this story, the husband put his wife through vaginal reconstruction surgery to indulge his physical senses, indicative of his weak character as someone who had forgotten the struggle against his lesser tendencies. While the irony of the situation was funny to everyone in the room, it was also a reminder of the elephant in the room: men were not as capable as women of disciplining their bodies to damp down the impact of their senses.

PARTS AND THE WHOLE

These practices fit into the greater picture of things. While practices like enduring a hot, crowded living room while listening to an elegy or staying home after dark might seem independent of each other, each act shared a cumulative logic of moving closer to God. I look to Mahmood's work on agency as both a particular progression and "the capacity to endure, suffer and persist."[66] Developing the experience for the howzevi in one circumstance was potentially useful for other circumstances. That is, performing each act of worship, seemingly unrelated as they were, was supposed to make other acts of worship easier to do. While practices like wearing the black chador in addition to wearing the proper hijab, eating with the right hand, visiting the sick, saying a set of supplications before leaving and entering the home, fasting on certain days of the week, uttering "bismillah" before an action, avoiding eating walnuts by themselves, or avoiding eating raw peeled onions that have been out for too long seem disjointed, doing these was supposed to make the practitioner more amenable to more acts of worship.

The power of supplications to God is not lost in the formula. The seemingly insignificant words of praise for God, or prayers for the Prophet and his family, are felt like they had power to protect one's effort. *Salavat*, for instance, are the words of praise for the Prophet Mohammad and his successors to be uttered in unison when people who are present are in solid agreement, or at the end of a gathering. It has this power. Maryam turned to me during a rowzeh-khani we attended together at Bayt'e Rahbari and said, "Did you hear what he [Ayatollah Khamenei] said? . . . He said to say salavat out loud to remove and push away the hypocrisy and arrogance from the heart."

Since every act is an opportunity for a woman to say, "This is for you, God," then one act becomes a challenge to the self to do another. Other ways of putting it: "Today, if I recite the Ayatol Qorsi before the car starts, then I have no reason not to look after my neighbor's property when she travels tomorrow." "If I can keep wearing this chador in today's heat wave, then I can continue to keep my donation a secret." "If I force myself to cry at this elegy, then I will use the same force to wake up for the dawn prayer."

Returning to the notions of sincerity and humility, the idea is to continue doing the unrelated parts of a whole so that one develops the know-how to differentiate sincerity and humility from arrogance at any given time. By cultivating sincerity and humility through an action, one can then authentically claim, "I am doing this act for God, the one who created all possibilities." The aim is to be in a constant state of remembrance of closeness to God. Since this state is not guaranteed, a woman must work on policing herself so that in times of adversities and confusion she will have enough self-awareness to differentiate sincerity and humility from arrogance.

The stories and sayings of the Prophet and his family illustrated this work. A story about Imam Ali engaged in a sword fight provides insight to what sincerity and humility versus arrogance might look like in human action. In this story, while Imam Ali was drawing his sword for the final blow against his enemy, the enemy spat in his face. Imam Ali backed away and walked toward his soldiers. When he was asked, he explained that when he realized he was acting on his anger, which was a sign of arrogance, he stopped himself from killing his enemy. This story is important because it provides a glimpse of the objective to develop enough self-awareness so one does the right thing at the right time. In Imam Ali's case, he controlled himself at a critical moment, or had enough self-control to examine his sincerity and humility. In moments of high tension or aggression against the howzevi, whether we were riding in the taxi, debating a neighborhood merchant, or barred from entering buildings or stores in north Tehran, they would tighten their chador under their elbows or pull the chador over their faces, then pause.

I liken this practice to withstanding discomfort and recovering comfort with Ernest Hemingway's portrait of bullfighting. Rather than focusing on the matador and the ring as his boundary, I want to focus on the bull and his *querencia*. A querencia is a place in the ring where the bull prefers to go. The job of the matador is to lure the bull away from this querencia. The bull has two preferred places, the natural and the accidental querencia. The natural querencia is fixed and pre-dictable, giving the matador the strategic advantage. The accidental querencia, however, is the place in the ring where the bull begins to make his home in the course of the bullfight. Its location is not obvious immediately to the matador. It is often the place in the ring where the bull has had some success in past bullfights. The bull continues to visit and revisit this place until it becomes his *home*, where he is most dangerous. Hemingway writes, "In this place he feels that he has his back against the wall and in his querencia he is inestimably more dangerous and almost impossible to kill. . . . The reason for this is that the bull, when he is in his querencia, is altogether on the defensive."[67]

Just as the bull in a fight has his querencia, the boxer has his place in the ring where he is most dangerous as a counter-puncher. It is through the authoring of comfort out of discomfort that the howzevi women I spent time with feel most powerful and accomplished toward their goals. In hypothetical terms, they had been for decades imposing practices of self-regulation to bring themselves back to remembering God in their actions with others. When this labor of self, the signpost of which is the black chador, comes together, what is developed is an overall persona of Shi'i womanhood to herself, and perhaps seeming ethical and just in the eyes of others.

SHIRINI

Having a feeling they described as *shirini* was a sign that they had attained a certain level of success from their labor. Used as a noun, *shirini* refers to a con-fection or sweet delicacy. With regards to the howzevi's practices, the feeling of shirini came from a person's experience after doing the hard work to overcome the challenges that come with accomplishing a goal. One howzevi, for instance, explained that she absolutely dreaded learning the Arabic language. But after working through recurring thoughts of quitting and eventually succeeding in learning the language, "It was shirini," she said. Shirini in this expression includes overpowering the temptation to abandon an effort.

An analysis of shirini provides a way of translating the way the howzevi might experience success in their practices. The feeling of shirini here can be produc-tively analyzed as one manifestation of Heidegger's concept of dwelling. The idea of dwelling is essentially about the primacy of human relationships and an-swering the questions "What is it that makes us human? What makes life worth living?"[68] I relate these questions to Alberto Perez-Gomez's interpretation of dwelling that life is worth living because of its limitations. Life will end.[69]

Part of shirini is recognizing the overall labor of working with limitations such as mortality and difference in creating a sense of belonging. I draw on a metaphorical example of a Persian miniature painter's labor in order to describe the important role of limitation among the howzevi and their practices. The painter uses cat hair as her painting tool to paint inside a border that was created on a parchment. It enables her to stay within the border of a very small square or rectangle despite the availability of the larger surface that surrounds this border. The painter creates a sense of belongingness for every stroke of the cat hair without turning the stroke into a habit, or her into an automaton. If she did, the painting would be lifeless. For this reason, miniature painting styles vary. Some artists place a tiny object or two on the border of the painting itself where it slightly touches the area outside the border. Some place half of the painting outside one section of the border. This half spills out into the external space beyond the border, giving an impression that the artist could have extended well beyond the entire surface but did not. This draws attention to the painter's recognition of limitation and the spillover into the border shows it as a place of tension that is drawn into the picture instead merely containing it. The labor of staying within the border is what characterizes the artist's painting as a miniature, but it is also a kind of labor that makes the experience gratifying enough for a miniature painter to paint more.

Shirini is as much about feeling triumphant as it is about reifying a limitation that produced an obstacle to being triumphant. Shirini emerges from difficulty, from the slow play-by-play labor at the particular. But the experience is not just about difficulty in the individual's body and mind. This difficulty, whatever it may be, cannot be extracted from the social context. Although the feeling is intimate and experienced individually, and often a secret, the value of that labor, by way of encouragement from family, friends, and allies, and the markers of success are shared. Shirini, thus, is an intimation of dwelling, a feeling that comes from the difficulties of the constant effort to create a sense of belonging. Difficulty from the process is expected and is seen as perpetually present. In this way, shirini is not about putting a stop to the difficulty. It is about pushing through the difficulty. The effort to push through a difficult situation "will stick to you the way something sweet clings to a person," in the words of Maryam.

An experience can only be shirini if it is short-lived, always with a hint of incompleteness. The end of the feeling is always in sight. On this, death, the ultimate end, comes to the fore. For the howzevi, reminders of the inevitability of death were a constant, and as I've noted, the soul and the flesh have only a single opportunity to experience life before death and to become what one should be during this brief period. A noble death marked by sacrifice and martyrdom is narrated over and over again in their prayers, narrations, and elegies.

Framed within a life script in which the human being is seen as malleable and can be trained toward desired predispositions, having the right amount of self-surveillance was a source of power, not a weakness or defect. Self-knowing and all kinds of disciplines were necessary to this experience. Somayeh said with a nod and a smile, "Sometimes Iranian people say chador is hard. Hot or cold, there is little difference. You can stand the challenge because there is a purpose for you to wear chador." In this framework, Somayeh, under the black chador, became a visual reminder of the constraints she had placed on herself to become a good Shi'i woman.

For many of my friends, having the right amount of self-surveillance, therefore, became not a disability but an endless source of strength for other objectives. Becoming a master at self-restraint was a way to develop self-confidence. Rather than perfection and superiority, the howzevi under the black chador signified a woman who was still a self-work-in-progress, unfinished, a person who, again, at the end of the day, forgets and resists among other momentary experiences. Through time narratives about their demeanor, actions, manners, and decision-making processes circulated between individuals and social groups. In the context of such narratives, at some point Islamic scholars, colleagues, and students will find their work worthy of engagement and will in due time describe her as a mujtahideh.

NOTES

1. Mauss, "Techniques of the Body," 70.
2. Meillassoux, *Maidens, Meal*, 75.
3. Nafisi, "Tales of Subversion," 264; Partridge, *Hypersexuality and Headscarves*, 112–15.
4. Anderson and Greifanhagen, "Covering Up," 56.
5. Siavoshi, "Islamist Women Activists," 178.
6. Ibid, 57.
7. Papanek, "Purdah: Separate Worlds," 297, 322.
8. Jeffrey, *Frogs in a Well*, 55-64.
9. Piela, "Wearing the Niqab," 515, 517–18, 526.
10. Anderson and Greifanhagen, "Covering Up," 61; Piela, "Wearing the Niqab," 519–22.
11. Salime, *Between Feminism*, 137.
12. Torab, *Performing Islam*, 54.
13. Salime, *Between Feminism*, 135–36.
14. El Guindi, *Veil: Modesty*, 129-146.
15. Minganti, "Burqinis, Bikinis and Bodies," 42.
16. Salime, *Between Feminism*, 136.
17. Deeb, *An Enchanted Modern*, 16, 31-47.
18. Mahmood, *Politics of Piety*, 40–78.
19. Hatam, "Why Iranian Women."
20. Poya, *Women, Work*, 75.
21. Momen, *Introduction to Shi'i Islam*, 203.
22. Street, *Literacy in Theory*, 132–33.
23. Momen, *Introduction to Shi'i Islam*, 202–03.

24. Momen, *Introduction to Shi'i Islam*, 202.

25. Jambet, *The Act of Being*, 198–99 citing Mulla Sadra.

26. Mauss, "Techniques of the Body," 75.

27. Ayat Al-Qursi is translated as the "verse of the throne"; these are special verses in the Qur'an from Surah Yasin.

28. Mauss, "Techniques of the Body," 73.

29. Torab, *Performing Islam*, 178, citing Starrett's (1995) critique of Bourdieu's body hexis.

30. Lave and Wenger, *Situated Learning*, 53.

31. Mauss, "Techniques of the Body," 73.

32. Non-mahram men, or men they could marry by Islamic law. They exclude biogenetic parents' fathers, fathers, brothers, father's brothers, mother's brothers, men who were breastfed by their biogenetic mothers, son-in laws in marriage and past marriages, and father in-laws in marriage and past marriages.

33. Douglas, *Natural Symbols*, 74.

34. Goodwin, "Audience Diversity," 284, 311.

35. Timothy Ingold's rephrasing of Martin Heidegger's question. Ingold, *The Perception*, 230.

36. Malpas, "Rethinking Dwelling," 8-9.

37. Heidegger, "Being-in-the-world," 149–68.

38. Malpas, "Rethinking Dwelling," 14.

39. Casey, "How to Get from," 13–52.

40. Basso, "Stalking with Stories," 19–55.

41. Malpas, "Rethinking Dwelling," 8–9.

42. In part this involved "ordaining the good (al ma'ruf) and forbidding what is evil (al munkar)" based on several prophetic narrations and verses in the Qur'an, 3:104, 110; 9:71, 112; 5:78–80. Al munkar is read as *illegal* in the Shari'a or *immoral* as defined in Islamic text.

43. Ibid, 143.

44. Partridge, *Hypersexuality and Headscarves*, 117.

45. Mbembe, "Provincializing France?" 94, citing Elisabeth Badinter.

46. Ahmed, *Women and Gender*, 5, 4, 18, 26, 32; Encyclopedia Iranica, "Cador."

47. De Certeau, *The Practice of*, 97.

48. De Certeau, "Practices of Space," 124.

49. Ibid.

50. Sciolino, "The Chanel under the Chador."

51. Bukhari, *Sahih Bukhari*, Chapter 24, Number 504.

52. Imam Ali, *Peak of Eloquence*, 840.

53. Foucault, *Discipline and Punish*, 218.

54. Piela, "Wearing the Niqab," 521–23; Partridge, *Hypersexuality and Headscarves*, 123.

55. Piela, "Wearing the Niqab," 523, 527, 533.

56. Foucault, *Discipline and Punish*, 138.

57. Ortega y Gasset, "The Difficulty of Reading," 16.

58. Mauss, "Techniques of the Body," 75.

59. Bateson, *Steps to an Ecology*, 185.

60. Hamayon, *Why We Play*, 8.

61. McKinnon, "On Kinship and Marriage," 106–31.

62. Christiansen, "Miss Headscarf," 238.

63. Basso, *Wisdom Sits*, 110.

64. Mahmood, *Politics of Piety*, 149.

65. Bateson, *Mind and Nature*, 125.

66. Mahmood, "Feminist Theory," 217.

67. Hemingway, *Death in the Afternoon*, 150–54.

68. Conversation with Jeffrey Malpas after his lecture "Place, Space, and Modernity" at the University of New Mexico, Albuquerque, New Mexico, George Pearl Auditorium, November 14, 2016.

69. Conversation with Alberto Perez-Gomez after his lecture "The Primacy of Place for Architectural Meaning" at the University of New Mexico, Albuquerque, New Mexico, George Pearl Auditorium, October 4, 2016.

DISPUTATION AND PLAY

IT WAS NOT ALWAYS THE CASE that howzevi sought anonymity, downplaying their positionalities, activities, and knowledge, but revealing these took place in subtle ways. The more experienced howzevi revealed their Islamic knowledge slowly during conversations, the proper timing and place of which they somehow learned by making forgivable mistakes, or perhaps by watching others make irrevocable ones. Novices treaded more lightly. Within the conversational space of discussing research projects or societal problems at a religious gathering, the senior howzevi were expected to engage those around them with their Islamic knowledge. By necessity, these kinds of conversations required those in attendance to tag and mark each other's proximity. Guests at social gatherings might also be familiar with books and articles that the more senior women had published.

Two circumstances in which women did not have to observe anonymity were in the two practices of disputation: bahes, the dialectic between teacher and student, and in mobaheseh, disputation circles. Both were a *sonnati-ye howzeh*, a trademark practice in the seminary where, in colloquial terms, women could come out with guns blazing. Unlike the bodily practices associated with the black chador, disputation was where the women were expected to be very visible, and for good reason. As I've previously detailed, the practice of imitation as part of khod shenasi was tacit knowledge, never spelled out. Part of the work of imitation is to dispute about how to properly imitate. Therefore, in more general and theological terms, it was important for practitioners to deliberate about what to imitate and when and the way to imitate.

The practices of disputation are not unique to the howzeh. In form, both are similar to the disputation practice of *pilpul* among Jewish rabbis and their fellows in the nineteenth-century yeshivas of Eastern Europe, or the *drsh* in a House of Midrash or the synagogue in ancient Israel and medieval Europe.[1] During a pilpul, a rabbi or the head of the yeshiva makes a claim and is then challenged by those in the room as they collectively process text from the Talmud. Bahes and mobaheseh also resemble the disputation practices among Christian theologians in the Christian studium in thirteenth-century France when they had to participate in a "determination" by defending a thesis against an opponent to receive a bachelor's degree. To receive a master's degree, they had to engage in "duties of public disputations for forty days."[2]

In the howzevi context, this particular kind of deliberation was full of tension and the right kind of conflict. How a student consistently performed in mobaheseh defined the credibility of a future Marja'e Taqlid because disputation was considered to be for the good of all. This public airing of ideas and rallying of textual knowledge in the howzevi practice of disputation made it the antithesis of the hiddenness in the practice of wearing the black chador. In a way, each—the black chador or the mobaheseh—shone a spotlight on the other. The impact of each on the other was, for me, like the impact of a loud sound on a person when its source could not be seen. The experience, though fleeting, leaves one thinking, searching in the aftermath. In other words, the practice of wearing the black chador, anonymity, and all that comes along with the work of khod shenasi makes a howzevi's presence in disputation inescapably more pronounced.

The first time I joined a circle of women to observe their mobaheseh in Madraseh Ali, they kept their black chador on because I was a stranger to them. This was my first experience, so I focused my attention on one woman. To an outsider like me who was not accustomed to mobaheseh, there was an element of fascination and internal upheaval in that moment as I listened to a woman I could not completely see, by virtue of her black chador and her practice of anonymity, engaged in a disputation against other women like her. Because I did not speak jurisprudent language and heard very little that I could grasp in Persian, her words and the certainty of her tone of voice were the only things I could grasp. However, for those who were part of the group, the position of being unseen validated a howzevi's belonging and contribution to the mobaheseh circle, where she was no longer unseen. Her command of textual resources and interpretations during disputation would not be recognized without her credibility outside the circle as someone properly working on bringing herself closer to God.

This chapter explores the way the howzevi experienced disputation spaces and moments as part of a system of personal connectedness, as part of a collective effort to interrogate religious text. It looks at the way mobaheseh becomes the space where women create, develop, and expand their social circles. By looking at howzevi women engaged in disputation practices, we get a glimpse of their training, the utility of which was not bound only to the howzeh space. The following analysis also allows us to consider the variety of ways howzevi women approach khod shenasi and their commitment to it.

DISPUTATION AS PRACTICE

To understand this, some background is helpful. I begin by providing a very brief history of the way Aristotelian logic, an important part of howzeh disputation, became part of Islamic education. The Abbasid Empire (AD 750–1517) created a commonwealth of Muslim citizens with an ideology of universalizing equal rights and privileges. These claims based on Islamic text became the rallying point that brought the Abbasids to power as a way to salvage the deterioration of the Umayyad Empire, which was plagued by its previous exclusivist Arab rule. This had two consequences. First, non-Arabs or assimilated Arabs rose to power. Second, since its egalitarian ideology needed a large constituency, they began proselytizing Islam, which meant there could be only one version of Islam to push for. This created opposition from within the Abbasid Empire.[3] Out of increasing conversion rates, there emerged religious political opponents. Iran in particular experienced high conversion rates at this time. Because the legitimacy of the Abbasid Empire rested on religious and theological positions, the caliph Al-Mahdi, al-Mansur's son and successor to the throne of the Abbasid Empire, needed to find a way to address political opposition for generations to come. To combat this, Al-Mahdi chose the dialectic approach to confront those who challenged this legitimacy.

Around AD 782, Al-Mahdi commissioned Timothy I, a Nestorian patriarch, with the help of Abu-Nuh, the Christian secretary of Mosul's governor, to translate Aristotle's *Topics*. Found in Aristotle's *Topics* were approaches to debating for or against a thesis based on social norms. It contained three hundred cases that provided various models or approaches to dialectic, which refers here to the art of argumentation with specific rules of engagement concerning a question-and-answer process between two antagonists: the interrogator and his respondent. Al-Mahdi was the first to introduce to the Muslim world the method and social attitude of disputation for coming to terms with religio-political dissonance. This would have far-reaching ramifications like the rise of law as the dominant social expression of Islam as a religion. For instance, when jurists established Islamic schools in the tenth century, it was to teach dialectic and jurisprudence.[4]

Historical analysis provides context to the practice of disputation in the seminaries in Iran. Let us fast-forward to Iran 1975, inside the men's howzeh elmiyeh in the city of Qom, where Aristotle's guidelines on logic and debate had already been brought to life for hundreds of years in two kinds of participation—namely, bahes and mobaheseh. Fischer has shown that in combination with social, economic, and political conditions, the practice of disputation within the clerical circles led to the 1979 Iranian Revolution. The title of his work—Iran: From Religious Dispute to Revolution—aptly reflects this observation. Thus, being a howzevi, at the very least, required effective participation in a mobaheseh. It began with becoming a master in *mantiq*, or logic.

Mantiq, Logic

The Persian word *mobaheseh* comes from the Arabic *baheth*, which is translated as search, investigation, exploration, and disquisition depending on the context of its usage. The practice of mobaheseh is guided by the principles of what is called *mantiq* to examine text, which can be learned from Ayatollah Mohammad Reda al-Muzaffar's *Mantiq Al-Muzaffar*. The howzevi learned mantiq from the age of thirteen or fourteen, during their first year of joining the howzeh, and for those who joined after high school, in their first year of what would be equivalent to the undergraduate level.

Mantiq is grounded in Aristotelian logic with principles on forms of knowledge, semiotics, expressions, synonymy and dissonance, words and compounds, universals and particulars, affirmation and negation, and deductive reasoning. The howzevi are taught these principles as tools or lenses to make sense of Islamic text and to grasp the way human beings and their conditions differed. One of mantiq's basic formulations is predicated on the understanding that people are born into a world full of meanings. Through time, people learn about this world with the intellect, ʿaql, which the arts and sciences in turn develop. But all of these and more also made human beings different in the ways they understood the world.

Thus mantiq, as a guide for disputation, prevented the howzevi from creating a reason, explanation, or justification for an event and extending the same reasoning to other events. The example of the jurist who went to a barbershop was often cited humorously to show the futility of generalized explanations. The jurist went to a barbershop because he had white hair in his beard. He was told that if he were to pull out the white hair, more white hair would grow. Generalizing the act of pulling hair as the cause for hair growth, the jurist began to pull out the black hairs in his beard, because according to previous explanation of cause and effect, the black hairs would multiply in growth.

While many prohibitions, like matters pertaining to worship and belief, are immutable, or *taʾabbudi*, based on God's commands in the Qurʾan, some prohibitions are conditional and open to interpretation as to what they constitute. For example, the act of stealing would be subject to disputation and personal interpretation as to what constitutes stealing, especially if there is extreme poverty in a particular place. With this kind of leeway in mind, the women used mantiq to debate word usage and meaning from Islamic text to gauge what constituted an impermissible act, *haram*, thus a sin, versus an undesirable act, *makruh*, in varied circumstances. Inevitably, whatever argument and counterarguments they made had to be placed in the context of local social conditions.

Mantiq equipped the howzevi with tools to navigate between different social worlds and to understand lives of non-Iranians outside Iran without necessarily losing sight of their own concerns. One expression of such a concept was the belief that God sent prophets to different peoples and generations, people with discrete ways of worshiping God referred to as People of the Book, *Ahl-e Kitab*—namely, Jews, Christians, and Muslims. Although the Prophet Mohammad "completed the religion," the women acknowledged the differences between the prophets before the Prophet Mohammad's arrival. Hoda from Howzeh-ye Kowsar explained the idea of worship *as form* and different ways of worship *as content*: "We researched [for our assignment] and focused on how God had different prophets. All of the prophets taught their people to pray, but each one in a different way. The prophets didn't provide the same guidance for Deen-e Yahud (Jews), Masih (Christians), or Islam (Muslims) on how to live their lives exactly, except that they must remember to worship God."

Regardless of what the women believed to be the correct way to worship, and whether they excluded those who believed in many gods or did not believe in a god, the women were giving a nod to a common ground between themselves and those who were unlike them. That is, human experiences have formed and may differ in content because there are differing social worlds and generations. This recognition is important because even though they considered their form of worship as the ultimate form, coercion or forcing belief onto someone would be counterproductive. That particular "someone" might have been accustomed to different social conditions. Mantiq gave the women a lens to understand the importance of contextualizing human expectations and responses. Disputation, not coercion, was a better approach to reconcile differences.

The use of mantiq was what the howzevi did as who they were, students of the howzeh. The language they spoke was mantiq. James Gee writes, "Language scaffolds performance of social activities . . . and human affiliation within social groups/institutions." The howzevi used the language of mantiq to reaffirm their place in a specific sociopolitical and religious order in which they could be differentiated from the religiously conservative who did not have training in the howzeh. It was necessary to behave and speak at the right place and time, in which mantiq played a crucial role. As Gee writes, "You are who you are partly through what you are doing, and what you are doing is partly recognized for what it is by who is doing it."[5] That is, a howzevi cannot be a "real" howzevi without the use of mantiq, similar to how a sociocultural anthropologist cannot be a "real" one without the particularized ethnographic analytic lens that focuses on interrogating existing categories.

The first mini-ethnography I share here is a bahes that took place between a teacher and his students on one aspect of khod shenasi, imitating the Prophet Mohammad in marriage. It is a description that underscores the importance of challenging the teacher in a way that is bounded by Islamic knowledge.

BAHES, THE TEACHER-STUDENT DIALECTIC

As I've written elsewhere, Agha-ye Sharifi established Howzeh-ye Kowsar, which was divided into separate men's and women's sections. These were located in different parts of Tehran. Many of the students at Howzeh-ye Kowsar in both sections were in their mid- to late twenties and had finished their undergraduate and/or master's degrees. Many in the women's section were unmarried. This afternoon's lecture was on the importance of marriage. In this lecture, marriage is specific to reproduction, and the desirability of a woman is dependent on her bearing children. In this frame, men could marry at any age, women could not. Women's plans to marry were confined to their childbearing years. This meant that a woman who decided to get married toward the end of her childbearing years would have to compete with women who were at their peak of fertility. The fear was that women in their thirties would then become desperate to marry and would, out of that desperation, rush to judgment and be taken advantage of.

As I demonstrate, the scene is not one of a religious patriarch "banking" religious text onto unsocialized young women to talk them into surrendering their reproductive capabilities to the institution of marriage. I use *banking* here in reference to Paolo Freire's critique of education as an act of depositing: "Narration (with the teacher as narrator) leads the students to memorize mechanically the narrated content. Worse yet, it turns them into 'containers,' into 'receptacles' to be 'filled' by the teacher. . . . Instead of communicating, the teacher issues communiques and makes deposits which the students patiently receive, memorize, and repeat."[6] Bahes makes banking impossible.

Sitting at his desk in front of the class, Agha-ye Sharifi began advising the students against being too particular in choosing a husband, the consequences of which would eventually minimize their prospective pool of suitors. Agha-ye Sharifi provided suggestions on the criteria for choosing husbands. The students opposed him. Mohadese, sitting right in the front row, said something to the others sitting near her as he paused. The women laughed and began debating with him.

Sara responded, "Hazrat Fatimah Ma'sume [Imam Reza's sister] never married." To which Agha-ye Sharifi said, "And [Fatimah] Az-Zahra is married with who? With Imam Ali." To counter the implication that Sara would rather imitate Fatimah Ma'sume, Agha-ye Sharifi was basically arguing to look at a better example, Fatimah Az-Zahra, who was considered the best example for women and was married to Ali.

Leila then asked, "Hazrat Ali koo?" By asking this question—*Where is Hazrat Ali?*—she was pointing out that he was dead and long gone. There were no men like him. The students laughed again. Zahra agreed and asked, "And yes, what about Hazrat Fatimah Ma'sume? She was not married."

Agha-ye Sharifi again responded with humor. "You mean that there is a match for Hazrat Fatimah Ma'sume? If there is a match for someone, they should marry." Hazrat Fatimah Ma'sume was the eighth imam's sister. By asking this question, Agha-ye Sharifi argued that it was impossible to find a man who would match her level of piety. Therefore, she did not marry.

Hoda brought forth a third example. "What about Hazrat Asiyeh? It's better not to be married than to have a situation like hers." The students again laughed. Hoda was referring to Asiyeh, who was Pharaoh's wife in the biblical story of Moses. For Muslims, the pharaoh embodied the most brutal kind of tyrant. When he ordered the killing of all male children fearing the coming of Moses, Asiyeh took Moses from the river and raised him as her own.

Zohreh remarked, "What is the rule? What is more important? To be married and be like Asiyeh stressed?"

Agha-ye Sharifi responded in good humor, "I don't know why she married him." And everyone, including Zohreh, laughed.

Zohreh turned to me and whispered, "It is better now [unmarried] than to be like Asiyeh."

The students brought out examples about mothers-in-law and how there should be a checklist for the kinds of mothers-in-law they might end up with if they were to get married. Agha-ye Sharifi used these examples to explain that these were opportunities to increase one's patience. He then proceeded to explain the reasons for why there were women in Islamic history who did not marry.

"The reason Fatimah Ma'sume did not marry was because she had to take care of her brother [Imam Reza, the eighth imam], and she could not be under the responsibility or protection of a husband. Sakineh [daughter of Imam Husayn] never married because she was not someone who could be *shohardari* [married]. She was really devoted [*bande*]. She devoted her life to God."

He was referring to Sakineh Kobra, Imam Husayn's older daughter, who was eleven years old and was arranged to be married to Abdullah, son of his brother Imam Hassan, before the Battle of Karbala. Only to fulfill his promise, she was symbolically married off to Abdullah on the battlefield. He died in the battle, and she did not remarry.

On this, again, Agha-ye Sharifi was met with insistence as Hoda replied, "We can try to be like her instead of being married."

Agha-ye Sharifi again emphasized his last point by speaking of Fatimah Ma'sume. "She had no focus on the material [world, *alam-e tabiat o madeh*]—everything was *fisabilillah* [for the sake of God]." To which Leila retorted, "So, we can try to be like her."

Agha-ye Sharifi spent some time explaining why the students should not compare their situation to that of women like Fatimah Ma'sume and Sakineh, because these women had reached such a complete state of worship, *makam-e mahv* (the state of erasure of the ego) that they could see only God: "These kinds of people cannot see anything else. They cannot get married."

Leila requested that he explain this state of piety further. This was her invitation to see if he would mention a characteristic or logic to his argument that she could counter.

Hoda read a quote from Imam Ali about the way marriage completes a person, then she asked, "So this kind of lady cannot be complete?"

Agha-ye Sharifi responded by saying that Sakineh was complete, but in comparison to Fatimah Az-Zahra, daughter of the Prophet and wife of Imam Ali, who was married, Sakineh was not as complete.

Hoda asked, "How is that possible?!" Meaning, how could a person who sees God all the time be lacking in anything at all?

Agha-ye Sharifi responded with humor—"I don't know, she was in the makam-e mahv. I don't know how"—at which the students laughed again.

He was caught off guard. He clarified his last response: "It does not mean that *she is not* complete, it means she *could not be* complete.... We have a lot of narrations which say half of the religion is this or that, if you add them together, it will become more than one!" The students laughed again. By *could not be complete*, he meant she could not function as a person who could interact with others, much less in a marriage.

He explained his comparison of the two women. Sakineh was in the *makam-e mahv* (the state of erasure of the ego) because she was an ascetic who could see only God. But Fatimah Az-Zahra was in the *makam-e sahv* (the state of oversight), which was a level above makam-e mahv. The reason for that was Fatimah Az-Zahra was challenged by the struggle of living piously in the material world—for instance, by being married. Yet her state of being was already seeing God. Speaking in mathematical terms, "You are comparing infinite number one with infinite number two, so one is higher. But, we are one or two, and they are infinite one and two. Don't compare them [with yourselves]."

The women were not convinced. They referred to his speeches in the past where he had said that women must put value in serving other people through their Islamic education. Marriage would get in the way of doing that. Leila in particular shifted the argument into the right of a woman to place stipulations on a marriage contract: "I will not marry the boy if he has not read the seven books of Shahid Motahhari." Agha-ye Sharifi responded, "This is not correct. If this lack of reading will cause you to not grow, yes it could be. But the fact that he has not read enough Motahhari books, no, it is not an acceptable reason not to marry." And the disputation continued.

There are many possible revelations from this example. Though it was left unsaid, Agha-ye Sharifi and the women were disputing, in essence, the way to properly exist in the material world while Islamically educating themselves on the way to do so. Assuming that each individual in this bahes believed in what they disputed for, this example served to provide insight into a process of engaging others in bringing forth assumptions about women, marriage, and piety. By way of imitation, khod shenasi for Agha-ye Sharifi included the institution of marriage. For the howzevi, marriage was not a priority in their work of khod shenasi. What is evident in this example is that the women's participation sought to openly acknowledge that not all women, inclusive of those who were considered saintly, had the capacity or were suitable for marriage.

One could also argue that this specific circle of howzevi were resisting authority or specifically, by way of disputation, the necessity of marriage. Context is crucial here. First, Agha-ye Sharifi's role as both teacher and mentor to his students was far-reaching. About a decade previously, Agha-ye Sharifi had been an engineering student at Amir Kabir University when he left his program to study in one of the howzeh for men in Qom. Agha-ye Sharifi's reputation as a teacher was the reason many of the howzevi joined Howzeh-ye Kowsar. By spending extensive amounts of time in Howzeh-ye Kowsar, I saw the howzevi's deference toward him as well as toward his wife, who taught a class in Islamic philosophy. The students approached him as a mentor, as an advisor about personal decisions or matters. He could relate to them as a member of a different generation from their parents. The examples he gave in his lectures, they said, were about living in Tehran and often about the challenges they faced trying to be religious people. Mahsa described, "He would catch the young people's attention, and they would wish he would stay longer in the class to give a lecture." The students explained further that anytime he was giving a lecture in Tehran, university students would go out of their way to attend them.

Fariba, who has an engineering degree, said about him, "He is not like the other clerics you don't want to listen to, because they are so hard and they only see their way. He talks to us in a way that we could relate to what he would share with the class. And we try to do the same with him. He lets everyone speak." When there was disagreement, he used laughter to settle the tension. The women believed that the way he related to them came from his exposure to the social atmosphere in the university, rather than from completing all his education in a howzeh. The debate about marriage, marked by tension but also humor and wit, shows the way students tried to strike a balance between paying attention to his words and being assertive. It also illustrates the way he approached his students. He was a patriarch but not an unpleasant or disconnected one in the way some of the howzevi described other clerics.

Second, the howzevi engaged Agha-ye Sharifi in this debate as students of the howzeh especially because they observed a set of practices. Like Maryam, who I write about in a coming chapter, expressing what they know was not limited to debate—it was more importantly through practices like wearing the black chador and anonymity, as I previously detailed. These practices also included wifehood and motherhood, as exemplified by Fatimah Az-Zahra in this debate. Their credibility in the disputation had to be earned by being mindful of these practices. The fact that some of the students were married and some spoke about their ideal husbands must both be considered. Hence, what the students expressed in this disputation must be taken with a grain of salt. Questioning the institution of marriage did not by default equate to the women's beliefs or actions outside the classroom. These were only half the possibility.

Bahes, the dialectic between the students and teacher, was not carried out in one sitting. It was a daily practice within the howzeh that served to adjust, stretch, and shift the boundaries of Islamic teachings like the institution of marriage. Even if a student's participation was meant only to be an intellectual exercise, it is important to recognize the role of Islamic text, of past Islamic role models, of observing the howzevi ethics to have the voice to participate, and of those who facilitate these kinds of deliberations like Agha-ye Sharifi.

The following is an explanation of the other form of disputation, mobaheseh, which Khanum-e Yasseri described as the art of reasoning by way of engaging a carefully selected circle of friends with similar objectives. The following illustrates the way this practice unfolds.

MOBAHESEH (*DISPUTATION, DISPUTATION CIRCLE*)

There were two general formats to organizing a mobaheseh. The first format involved women from the age of thirteen onward independently dividing themselves into circles composed of two to five participants. They debated freely, anywhere and at any time of the day. In this format, the women already knew which lessons were more important to do mobaheseh on. This format was especially common among the more senior howzevi who had been doing mobaheseh for decades and had already established long-term mobaheseh partnerships. They held their mobaheseh in their offices or their homes on diverse topics but often focused on the materials recently covered in their classes. The women in Madraseh Ali held their mobaheseh every day after class on the day's lectures but focused on materials for their exams the day before. Like the more senior howzevi, they were less regulated because most of them had been doing mobaheseh before starting at Madraseh Ali.

The second format involved a *modir*, a manageress, who was either a more senior howzevi or one of the howzeh administrators, whom the students posed questions to if they needed help. For instance, Khanum-e Ahmadi, at Howzeh-ye Kowsar, produced a list of mobaheseh groups so students could rotate between them. Input from the instructor and the students informed this list. The women at Howzeh-ye Kowsar held two classes every day on weekdays and then mobaheseh in the afternoon for the material covered in those two classes. An extra hour on Tuesday afternoons was dedicated to reviewing for the two exams the following morning, which covered materials they were given the previous two weeks. Either Khanum-e Ahmadi or Agha-ye Sharifi moved between circles to assess what the students were doing. They guided the students toward a particular point from the previous class and mediated or added to the debates. Agha-ye Sharifi at times highlighted a point in order for the group members to arrive at a common ground or better understanding of each other's views.

Choosing Members of the Circle

Choosing members of a mobaheseh circle involved women assessing each other. While some chose friends or did not care who was in their group, many chose students with certain characteristics. At the very least, they preferred to be with those who did not appear to have "a very busy mind," women who could stay focused on the discussion. Amicability and politeness were important. One of the women explained the way she used a pilgrimage excursion to look for possible partners because she wanted to see the way individuals changed behaviors in diverse situations.

Beyond behavior, students ideally formed circles whose members saw themselves as somewhat on the same level of expertise, despite having different viewpoints. They also looked for at least one member who was slightly more knowledgeable than others in at least one topic and one who had more exposure to approaches to Islamic text, or they sometimes chose women they considered highest ranked in the class. This meant each member would have something to teach others, and someone could occupy the position of teacher, then become a student of another topic.

Figure 5.1. Howzevi women in their mobeseh circles after their classes. Tehran, 2008. ©Amina Tawasil.

What constituted being knowledgeable in this context? Having read more books was one part. The women frequently used the words *clever*, or *zerang*, and *intelligent*, or *ba housh*, to describe the ideal mobaheseh circle members or partners. One needed to be what nineteen-year-old Zaynab and her friends called "clever" in English. Though clever could be translated in many ways in Persian, they repeatedly used the English *clever* when speaking with me, in order to describe students who excelled in class. *Clever* for them was more than knowing how to retain words from a book and recite the words at any given time. A clever student was someone who was well read, analytical, and quick-witted at the right time and place. This proper time and place, at the very least, took place in classroom debates and in the afternoon mobaheseh. A clever student was especially impressive when she compared new lessons to previous lessons and if she asked difficult questions that forced others to draw key points from other courses. She was either born with the *it* factor or was not. But, fortunately for many, becoming clever was something that could be developed in oneself.

The bahes disputation in the classroom was one of the socially situated proper times and places they could assess potential circle members. They examined

Figure 5.2. The women typically have tea during mobaheseh. Tehran, 2011. ©Amina Tawasil.

the way each woman cited sources and questioned or debated the teacher in the classroom. In specific instances, the quality of a student's comparison of current and previous lessons or positing of difficult questions constituted being clever.

The Rhythm and Flow

I spent my afternoons with either Zaynab or Maryam as they explained to me the basics of doing mobaheseh. Although there were variations in setting and process, students were expected to follow three courses of action: study the material from the class before the mobaheseh, teach the material, and dispute the material. The session started with women sitting in a circle to deliberate first about what was previously learned in class during either that day or the previous days. They would then decide the specific topic to discuss from those lessons and who would lead each topic. They needed to make sure each would have a chance to take the lead. The disputation usually started off with the leader reading Islamic edicts previously presented in class, which were then challenged by the members of the group. Depending on the topic, the focus at first would generally be to decontextualize and contextualize the meanings of key words in the edict using the

Figure 5.3. Mobaheseh can take place in a more formal setting like a library. Tehran, 2011. ©Amina Tawasil.

principles of mantiq. To debate proper usage of words in specific Islamic edicts, they focused on answering the following questions: how does the meaning of this word change in other contexts or edicts? Why are these terms used as they are in this edict? They would also assess whether the Islamic edicts continued to hold contemporary currency.

Though the sequence was fluid and varied slightly, this was the overall progression. Students moved from one level of expertise to the next. At the novice level, *moqademati*, and the intermediate level, Sat'h, students brought books for reference. Students read the text and would go back and forth between the disputation and flipping pages of the text. At the Dars-e Kharij level, with the exception of notebooks, books were not brought to the mobaheseh. The same could be said about their classes. At this high level, students recalled the proofs and evidences for an interpretation from memory, expectedly in exact quotes.

The following session shows what mobaheseh accomplished for four nineteen- to twenty-year-old women, Marzieh, Hamideh, Zaynab, and Mahsa. Having observed over thirty-five mobaheseh sessions with different circles of women in Tehran, I still had difficulty grasping the complex terms used in rules of logic and those of Islamic jurisprudence. Thus, to be succinct, I have chosen a session for a class on contracts, which can be easily understood by an audience unfamiliar with juristic terms in Islam. In this account, the women were disputing, in essence, another aspect of khod shenasi: the way to exercise intellectual reasoning in determining right or wrong without an exact how-to instruction. In this case, it was the way to start a family unit according to the Qur'an and the Sunnah, a commitment that will eventually involve birthing children by way of a marriage contract according to Islamic law. The idea was that gaining this sort of knowledge and strengthening their reasoning would help reinforce their resolve in deciding against their lesser tendencies. This specific mobaheseh took place on an October afternoon in a howzeh library in Tehran.

Mobaheseh on the Overseer

There were several mobaheseh circles sitting at tables and on the floor. Each group had its own topics of discussion. Marzieh's group was going to dispute about the necessary components of a valid marriage contract, details of which are not common knowledge to those who have not studied Islamic jurisprudence. As background, it is important to know that in Shi'i Islamic jurisprudence the bride was the one who was supposed to make the declaration of offering herself to the groom, and it was the groom who was supposed to pronounce his acceptance in the formula, the *sighe*, of the marriage contract, or *'aqd*.

Marzieh read from the textbook *Al-Lum'e ad-Dameshqiya* by Shahid Aval, one of the great Shi'i jurists. She began with the marriage contract of a mute person and that it was important for the mute person to use a signal that all those present understood to mean *an acceptance* of the contract. Then, she summarized the qualifications of an *aaqed*, the one who would marry the bride and the groom, whom I will refer to as the Overseer. Marzieh read in Arabic and then explained in Persian that the Overseer must be mature in age, *balegh bashe*; of sound awareness or intellect (*'aql bashe*); with the power/authority to decide (*mokhtar bashe*); and with the intention to marry. Without these, the contract would be null and void.

She continued to read the text, proposing a conditional "IF"—if the Overseer was intoxicated at the time of reading the contract, which would eliminate the condition of sound awareness and power/authority to decide, would the contract still be valid?

The women began to argue against this proposition by questioning the notion of invalidity and teasing out the role of the Overseer. The text also indicated that if *a* man was intoxicated and in the aftermath declared his agreement again with the contract, the contract would be invalid. There was agreement on this point. But the text did not indicate what position this man occupied. Meaning, was this man the Overseer? Or was he the one who accepted the offer—in other words, the groom getting married? Could the same man hold the position of Overseer, given that he was also the groom, the person responsible for accepting or declining a woman's offer of marriage?

But before this, Hamideh had questioned why the contract would be invalid in the above context since it was not specified whether the aaqed was a man or a woman in the first place. Based on what she had learned in class, if a woman were intoxicated at the time of the reading of the marriage contract, the contract was still valid. Why this was the case was subject to further research. The question was, to whom did this condition apply? Since it was not specified whether the Overseer was a man or a woman, Hamideh at this juncture opened the floor to the possibility that the Overseer could be the bride, and in that case the contract would be valid, since a woman's intoxication did not invalidate the contract. She added, "But my notes say 'man'" to indicate she was confused.

Marzieh responded, "Look, the bride offers herself and the groom accepts. For this reason, the man cannot be [the aaqed] the one reading the contract to marry the two parties." Meaning it was not possible to be a recipient of an offer and be an overseer of the transaction itself, the implication of which was that he had foregone his right to decline the offer.

For the next hour, a debate unfolded as to who could occupy the position of the Overseer. Fatimah, thinking out loud, said the lesson in class had been about conditions for the Overseer. They all talked at once and over each other in disagreement about the definition of *Overseer*, each perhaps thinking out loud, rereading the text out loud, with pauses and jokes. Sometime in between, we noticed that Zahra was curled up, taking a nap on the floor in front of the radiator with her chador wrapped from her head to her feet. So we decided to move to another table across the room to avoid disturbing Zahra's sleep. Zaynab was explaining to the group what invalidated a contract that did not need a third-party witness or a lawyer. Zaynab, in an attempt to clarify the discussion for me, interrupted and asked the group, *"Vakil ba inglizee, chi mishe?"* (What is "vakil" in English?). "LOW-YER!" shouted Narges from another group all the way across the library floor. Everyone in the library laughed. Zahra woke up from the laughter.

Marzieh, Hamideh, Zaynab, and Mahsa narrowed down who could occupy the position of the Overseer to three possibilities: a third party, the bride, or one of the representatives of the bride or groom. Mahsa insisted, "No, these conditions are for the man and the woman themselves." Marzieh asked Mahsa to clarify which role the man and woman occupied, "as guardians? Or bride or groom?" Mahsa answered, "The groom and the bride." Zaynab continued to insist that the conditions for an Overseer were for both men and women, which would make the argument against the proposition conditional. Mahsa argued that the conditions applied only to the Overseer as a third party, with neither the bride nor the groom serving as the Overseer.

A consensus was not verbally reached until much later when they had moved on to another topic. To respond to Marzieh's argument, Hamideh analyzed the assumption that Marzieh and Mahsa had made about the bride—that the bride would verbalize the offer first, thereby defaulting to the groom's right to respond as an overseer of the transaction. But this did not have to be the case at all. Hamideh spoke softly to the group and explained that it was possible for the groom to accept the bride's offer by being the first to verbalize it. For instance, the groom could say, "If you offer yourself to me, I will accept." And the bride would then say, "I surrender myself to your pleasure." At which point, Marzieh smiled. "Oooh! That's right!" The women paused, sighed, and began to engage in side talk. This meant the Overseer could actually be the groom.

They brought the discussion back to the ruling on the state of intoxication during the reading of the marriage contract, specifically about the woman's contract remaining valid even though she was intoxicated. Marzieh read the ruling on the matter by Sheikh At-Toosi, another great Shi'i jurisprudent who established the seminaries in the city of Najaf, Iraq. Even though the contract was technically considered valid if a woman was intoxicated, it was not acceptable because of the first condition, which was that drinking alcohol was forbidden in the first place. They then briefly touched upon the difference between the state of intoxication as an invalidating factor and the act of drinking alcohol as an invalidating factor.

Before moving on to another topic, Mahsa noted that in Iran, it was common for a girl to have a third person, usually her father, to represent her in the ceremony. She explained, "But in the past, it was possible for the woman to read the 'aqd and the man accepts." She reiterated, "Without her guardian." Further along in the discussion, Marzieh explained that in a permanent marriage contract, there was no need for two witnesses to be present. However, under civil law, there must be two witnesses. She emphasized, "But again, in Islamic jurisprudence two witnesses are not necessary."

WAYS OF KNOWING

To sum up, in this mobaheseh, nineteen- and twenty-year-old women translated between Arabic and Persian as they showed commitment to the three pillars of mobaheseh—namely, preparation, to teach, and to dispute. It provides at least four fundamental learning points about mobaheseh. First, the way these three pillars came into view varied. In practice, not everyone came prepared, and not everyone came enthused to teach and debate. However, these three commitments outlined its ethos so that a howzevi could assert that teaching the material was the best way to learn, that the act of defending and questioning an assertion increased one's self-confidence to speak out, and that the collective questioning and answering opened up spaces for self-questioning.

Second, the mobaheseh also calls attention to the relational interdependency of the howzevi woman and her society beyond the howzeh social space. The women, as students of Islamic knowledge, were expected to relay aspects of the discussion content outside the howzeh. Though women do not take on the formal mujtahid position, they informally engage in similar social activities, especially when family members, neighbors, or friends of friends consult with them about religious matters. Mobaheseh is a space to learn the way to communicate Islamic knowledge effectively. Mobaheseh is where students come to know how to speak. On forms of talking, Lave and Wenger write, "Inside the shared practice, both forms of talk (talking about and talking within a practice) fulfill specific functions: engaging, focusing and shifting attention, bringing about coordination, etc., on the one hand; and supporting communal forms of memory and reflection as well as signaling membership, on the other."[7] But it was also a space where students learned and practiced listening skills.

Mobaheseh helped prepare students to become good teachers and students. Effectiveness in both roles demanded careful speech and careful listening, always in relation to someone else. The mobaheseh leader needed to find the most effective communication style to provide an explanation to the group so all members could better understand the material. Accommodating different ways of knowing among group members was realized through trial and error. Likewise, crafting questions and strategizing the way to best respond to specific inquiries with counter responses in mind were key components of disputation that required close listening. Challenges by the group forced a student to question her assumptions and consider other angles on the topic. These strengthened the ways the howzevi contextualized and interrogated the implications of their interpretations.

The consistent practices of mobaheseh normalized sharing old and new interpretations. Hearing one's words and the words of others opened up the possibility of deeper understanding. The discussions also furthered the aim of content retention or, as they described, "*qashang ja migire*," or to retain information well, especially because mobaheseh sessions were a constant.

SUSPENDED CONFLICT

The third takeaway is that mobaheseh created a particular kind of conflict that was itself a form of knowing. Students were not expected to know the answers to questions. Rather, going back to the definition of mobaheseh as disputation harkens back to its Arabic baheth, which has several meanings: *search, investigation, exploration*, and *disquisition*. Thus, mobaheseh was a specific kind of conflict between parties as disagreement in order to come to know something.

In the mobaheseh, the field of interaction was already leveled since each participant's own experience with the world was perceived as a source of potential contributions. The participants each expected to express thoughts, questions, and disagreements on the subject matter. Moments of opposition or disagreement were both sought and expected. Contributions to the group involved a collective effort in experiencing widespread disagreement or disputation. A continuous showing or sharing of something different from what was expected was a contribution all on its own.

Because of this purposeful disruption, the aim of these sessions was not reaching a consensus. An absence of a foreseeable coming together was expected. As a result, students became accustomed to embracing a suspended dispute. Finding comfort in the dislocation exposed the disparity between ideology, perception, and action. When questions remained unanswered, the mobaheseh circle reached out to other circles, if available. Therefore, deadlocks were not thought of as negative. These were learning moments. Proposed ideas stood still at that moment of conflict. Sometimes the women spread out the debate for weeks. Participation in mobaheseh was not just encouraged but a requisite for becoming an Islamic jurist. Hence, mobaheseh was a site of possibility, perhaps analogous to a place for a comma, which has a potential to transform the meaning of an entire sentence.

Implied in this process of conflict as a way to know is that mobaheseh is also a space of assessment. Everyone was engaged in some form of assessment, which began with choosing members of the group. Often, the assessment was about the way a student communicated about complex topics so that others could make sense of them. Islamic knowledge is meant to be shared. Another instance in which students of Islamic jurisprudence gauged each other's progress was a practice called *taqrirat*, or exposition, where a student provided an explanation of the previous lecture. One version of taqrirat took place before the start of class. Students held mobaheseh at the very start of their day in the howzeh, and just before the teacher's arrival, a student would sit in the teacher's seat to provide the class an explanation of the previous lesson. This helped students review material, prepared them for the teacher's upcoming lecture, and benefited students who were having difficulty. It also benefited students who needed to practice public speaking.

There were different ways of choosing which students provided taqrirat, which involved the instructor, the modir, or the students. In this context, being chosen to do taqrirat signaled prestige and proximity to the teacher, but the expectations associated with the task were strenuous. During taqrirat, the chosen student was expected to speak from memory, without a book in hand. But the way the student spoke was as important as the content itself. Understanding the depth and breadth of the subjects was just as critical as language style and use. The practice of mobaheseh contributed to any student's potential to do and be chosen for taqriqat. The woman chosen was expected to have mastered the various interpretations of the previous lectures and then, through her speech, turn this content into material that was relatable to students whose interests and backgrounds varied. Students who were seen as effective in their delivery gained immense credibility. Ayatollah Khomeini, as a young student, had initially gained his credibility through this taqrirat.

POACHING

Finally, mobaheseh forces the students to disagree with the text, to bring their own understanding to the text. In the mobaheseh session on marriage contracts, the women made their own assumptions about the Overseer based on gendered norms in Iran. They deliberated until one of them imagined a possibility beyond their prior assumptions: that there were ways to accept an offer without being offered: "If you offer me this, I will take it." They also recalled a bygone practice and one of the many interpretations of Islamic law on marriage contracts in which women did not need a guardian to get married, and two witnesses were not necessary for the marriage transaction to take place between a man and a woman. This move then called attention to the difference between current civil law in Iran and the older traditions of Islamic jurisprudence.

Fazia's and Sania's experience with mobaheseh touches on this. Fazia, whose grandfather was a cleric, was one semester away from finishing her Sat'h 3 program at a howzeh in south Tehran. She was thirty years old and a new bride and lived in Shahr-rey with her parents, siblings, and husband. She and Sania had been mobaheseh partners for about five years. Sania had an eight-year-old daughter and a husband who was serving in the air force. Sania was a few months away from completing her Sat'h 3 program, which she had some difficulty achieving because her grandmother had just died. She came from a family that did not regard a howzeh education as a worthwhile endeavor. One of her siblings was a doctor and another an engineer. One of her teachers at a study group in Pirouzi sparked her interest in Islamic studies.

Mobaheseh was very important to Sania because it helped her with subject matters that were difficult to understand. Mobaheseh's appeal for her was that the content being discussed did not dictate the way the members of the circle interpreted or processed the content. She pointed out that because conditions differed between locations, interpretations would expectedly differ as well. She said, "Just because the book says this, we should accept it. The more important question is, what is her [the student's] idea? The mobaheseh allows the student to find her own idea. . . . She will read the book and take ideas from the books, but after that she has to form her own ideas."

The way women experienced bringing their understandings forward in mobaheseh is important because a commonly held assumption about the howzevi like the women of this study *as* Islamist women, *as* vanguards of the Islamic Republic, is that they function as puppets or *as* reproducers of what is taught to them by the clerical establishment. Here we see that mobaheseh instead performed what de Certeau referred to as "poaching" or "reading" or what John Fiske refers to as "practice over structure."[8] Far from parroting what they memorized, the young women questioned the text, their own assumptions, and the ideas of their teachers. As a result, the norm was not exact transmission but rather disruptions, which inevitably made exact reproduction of ideology incomplete.

Depending on the student's experience, mobaheseh was also, therefore, a source of increased leverage, especially when interacting with those who were unfamiliar with disputation as practice. Maryam made this intelligible by explaining the way Ayatollah Khomeini demanded that there be a special court wholly composed of clerics for the clergy in Iran. The Special Court for Clerics was established in the early 1980s right after the revolution. The belief behind establishing this court was that clerics would defeat the judge in the Iranian courts because of their training in mobaheseh in the event of judicial wrongdoing. The implication is that the way clerics interrogate words and statements by having mastered the principles of mantiq made them powerful against those who were not familiar with mobaheseh.

The practice of disputation also existed outside the howzeh. I saw many instances where women interrogated definitions of categories such as transaction and consent to debate family members. Some debated friends, neighbors, taxi drivers, and others in everyday life about mundane topics. Farideh explained the way she "enjoyed mobaheseh very much," and she does it with almost everything she talks about. Other howzevi expressed admiration for it as tool for critical thought, which they used in learning English and debating for their rights, especially if they felt they had been wronged. For Khanum-e Tabesh, as I have already mentioned, mobaheseh had a life outside the howzeh when she hosted gatherings of influential women to create a space of discussion. Khanum-e Alizadeh and her mobaheseh circle from Ayatollah Bojnurdi's Dars-e Kharij class formed a working group as a result of one of their mobaheseh on women's rights and inheritance. She and her friends drafted a proposal to the parliament to change the law of inheritance for widows, which they found had no basis in Islam from any of the scholarly interpretations.

PERSONAL CONNECTEDNESS (RESTORING THE WORK OF KHOD SHENASI)

I return to the social interactions in mobaheseh in order to look at what cannot be lost in the analysis of personal connectedness: play during mobaheseh. The concept of personal connectedness in Islamic education has been researched historically. William Graham cites the concept of ittisaliyah in the Arabic language to explain the personal connectedness in Islamic education. Part of Islamic educative practices are the assumption that "the truth does not reside in documents" but in the personal connectedness of human beings. Although he describes ittisaliyah in the context of teachers transmitting knowledge one on one to students as "the need . . . for personal 'connection' across generations,"[9] we don't really quite know the nuances of what makes these connections personal, thus human. The howzevi's experiences provide a window to what that might look like.

Students had to participate in mobaheseh. Some used the opportunity to lead in mobaheseh to gain a better understanding of the class materials. Some saw it as a way to overcome their shyness to speak up, while some saw it as a good opportunity to ask questions they felt were not worthy of class time. Most of the women in Howzeh-ye Kowsar joined the howzeh out of their desire to strengthen their Islamic knowledge and sensibilities without familial pressure. Most if not all had already completed their master's degree at a university. A few of them did not particularly care for mobaheseh. For them, they used the space to review for upcoming assessments. For those whose mobility was confined to going to the howzeh from their homes and back, mobaheseh was a way to extend their time to socialize. There were a handful of women from Madraseh Ali who would have rather been married immediately after high school, but their families had forced them to study beyond high school before getting married. One of the few experiences they enjoyed in this situation was the opportunity to make friends and to socialize in the afternoons during mobaheseh.

For all, though, participation in mobaheseh was a social obligation, an unwritten contract, to contribute to the disputation. As I've noted, it was for the good of all to learn to decide what to imitate in the practices of the Prophet Mohammad and his family, guided by the Qur'an and Sunnah. Each member of the circle was considered a unique source of insight gained from each woman's individual life experiences. Given this uniqueness, each member was seen as a contributor at any given moment. It would be selfish not to do so. Even members who were unable to relate to the text were expected to contribute by asking questions. The rest of the group would then be expected, if not obligated, to respond. They had no choice but to interact with each other in the spirit of disputation every day, perhaps for years.

Inevitably there were heartfelt experiences during mobaheseh. Hoda, from Howzeh-ye Kowsar, described the way mobaheseh was sacred to her "because in mobaheseh you have to have eye contact and are face to face [negah kardan, chesh be chesh]." The facial expressions and the body language would show if the person in the group was experiencing difficulty with the topic. She added, "But

Figure 5.4. Women lying down on their stomachs with their books in front of them. Tehran, 2011. ©Amina Tawasil.

the amount of kindness [*mohabbat*] we show towards each other's strengths and weaknesses makes our friendship stronger. We learn how to be with each other.... Even if you are encouraged to dispute and not easily accept other's interpretations, you are friends in the end."

Hoda's experience was not unique without claiming that it represents all how-zevi experiences. Her experience, along with the experiences of other women mentioned in this chapter, give life to the concept of ittisaliyah. It shows that personal connectedness is part of the work of khod shenasi, which, remember, is layered. It is an attempt to know oneself in order to strengthen one's resolve against the lesser tendencies. This path strives to recover the self in its original form that naturally worships God. For the students, including those who did not care much for mobaheseh as a practice, mobaheseh was still a space where the work of khod shenasi did not have to be a singular effort. As I have detailed, sometimes it involved a good amount of play. Learning the way to respond to each other, to start a connection with someone, or to maintain a relationship that had been developed brought different women who were doing similar kinds of work together. There was constant shifting of perception of self in relation to the shifting perception of others, the way they saw themselves in relation to others, and the work they did to act on these perceptions.

The story of Zaynab and Maryam in the following chapters shows that they initially had difficulty making friends when they first started at Madraseh Ali. But they eventually developed meaningful friendships by way of mobaheseh. And as I have illustrated, Khanum-e Tabesh, Alizadeh, and Shahriari had been close confidantes for fifteen years when I met them. By being mobaheseh partners, they persisted through the system when others did not.

A brief description of what transpired between two senior howzevi gives us an idea of what this looked like. It was common for Khanum-e Mohammadi and Khanum-e Hosseini to discuss personal problems first, before starting mobaheseh. On this particular afternoon, Khanum-e Mohammadi complained about being tired and worried. She and her husband had just visited family the previous evening, and she had lost sleep over what she had noticed about one of the sons wearing a polo shirt. He presented himself with the collar popped up. She described that this might be a sign that they were lax in their practices. Khanum-e Hosseini made tea. She listened to Khanum-e Mohammadi, asked her questions, and then encouraged her to question her own assumptions about the family. It took them almost an hour to begin doing mobaheseh.

Laughter

As we have already seen, part of what constituted this personal connectedness was laughter among the howzevi and even with their teacher during disputation. Many playful moments took place during and around mobaheseh. The afternoon after-class routine started with some women spending about thirty minutes tidying the classroom, vacuuming the floor, and washing any dishes in the sink downstairs. Depending on the time, women said prayers in another room. Some gathered around in circles to socialize, some headed for the restroom, and some took naps. Khanum-e Ahmadi then gathered the women into two different rooms to form their mobaheseh circles. For about two hours, sometimes three hours, about sixty women divided into circles of four to five would do their mobaheseh on topics of their choice.

During mobaheseh, some women preferred to sit on the floor with their legs crossed and some with one leg folded to the chest, and some, when tired, laid down on their stomachs. The women flipped through their books to follow the lead discussant's explanation of terms. The voices in the rooms sometimes became louder, sometimes not. Fingers constantly pointed at the pages of books while others adjusted their eyeglasses. Some took notes using different colored pens in a notebook; most wrote on the textbook itself, with slanted notes on the sides of the pages. It was common for someone to come up to the second floor carrying a large round silver platter with freshly steeped black tea in tiny glass teacups. Sometimes someone distributed cookies or fruit from their book bags.

Every so often, there was silence in the room as they read or processed the points in the discussion. Every so often there was also laughter from each group. Sometimes when frustration set in for Fatimah, after reading the same lines over and over again for comprehension, she would break out in a tiny voice while reading the text. And the women in her circle would predictably laugh and give her encouragement. It was also common to see women hug each other, pat each other on the shoulder, high five each other, or hold hands.

Some interruptions were ignored and some welcomed, more like moments of restoration than interruptions. This was especially visible when women became newly engaged or married. One afternoon, Mohadese pulled a silk scarf from her bag that her fiancé had given her. Though she did not announce it, all the women in the room, including those from other circles, cheered her on, laughed, and teased her. It was perhaps her facial expression, the way she pulled it out from her bag, and the fact that it looked brand new. The women continued to talk among themselves for about ten more minutes while a handful of women from different circles approached to embrace her.

An old friend of theirs, Ziba, came to visit one afternoon. She had just moved to Qom with her husband, and by the looks of it, she was quite sad about leaving Howzeh-ye Kowsar. She cried, and Fatimah and the other women comforted her with hugs. They eventually sat together holding hands and telling stories until it was time for her to leave. It was Fatimah's turn to share her good news on another afternoon. While she shared her wedding pictures on her laptop, her friends commented on the ceremonial wedding tablecloth and blouse that Fatimah, with the help of her sister, had tailored. The conversation went on for about twenty minutes.

When Khanum-e Ahmadi joined in the conversations and then stepped back, the women moved right back to their circles. She frequently made announcements in the middle of the sessions about upcoming lectures in the city, exams, guest speakers, pilgrimage trips, and Jahadi Basij (Reconstruction Corps) excursions.

Breaks seemed to come at an unspecified time. The circles would simply disperse, and some members would lie down for a short nap while others took a restroom break or sought out other students who were also on a break. At one point during one of these afternoon breaks, Nahid began chasing Azadeh around the room to tickle her. They both slid on the carpet, and Azadeh's eyeglasses fell to the ground. Fatimah and others pleaded with them to calm down as the two of them continued to laugh uncontrollably.

The women shared jokes, showed each other funny gifs from their mobile phones, and spoke about politics. Occupy Wall Street caught their attention at the time. The day after they saw images of protests in New York City, Nahid gathered her friends around me to ask if I thought the United States government was about to succumb to the protestors. They thought discussing the protests was more important than beginning the mobaheseh on time.

There was also plenty of storytelling. Hoda, Fatimah's sister, narrated a story with a small voice as if she were the plastic grasshopper she held in her hand. She moved the plastic grasshopper back and forth as she told its story of being hungry and finding food in their bags. Her friends were amused and suggested that next time she video what she was doing. When I visited her at her house, she was doing exactly that with her laptop.

All of this and more took place around the mobaheseh. Hamayon writes, "We can both 'do' while playing and play in a manner that leads to doing 'for real.' Most importantly, these unremitting back and forths between *playing and doing* are part of our daily experience, for we are unable to refrain from playing."[10] In the mobaheseh space, play, humor, and laughter were undeniably striking features, along with the women practicing careful deliberation and challenging each other. Laughter brought them together and kept them together in the serious work of learning about themselves and God.

IN CONVERSATION WITH SUBVERSION

In a Durkheimian sense, transformations take place around us all the time. But we often do not notice because they happen slowly. Like any practice involving purposeful critique and debate, mobaheseh was a catalyst for change. What kind of change, where, and when were the more important details of this assertion. I want to argue against interpreting the mobaheseh space as "a light at the end of a tunnel," a space where women were trying to eradicate Islamic practices that we, from outside Iran, were uncomfortable with, or that we thought placed them at a disadvantage. If any practices were to be eliminated through mobaheseh, they would be rejected because they were un-Islamic, not because they were Islamic. Interpretations on the way to deal with problems, old and new, were framed within the boundaries of Islamic beliefs and evidence from the Qur'an and the Sunnah, the two main sources of critical analysis. For example in chapter 6, Zaynab's choice to wear her manto above her knee as opposed to one inch below the knee, the norm among her classmates, was still considered Islamic. That is, as long as a practice, an action, an event, and a decision were defined as *Islamic*, it would continue to exist, at the very least, as a choice of action and at best, a religious obligation.

On this, Fazia reflected on the role of women in the past as being kept inside the home. That was part of the norm where men, not women, worked outside

the home: "If a woman stayed at home, it was as valuable as the act of praying."
Society has changed since then, and she felt strongly about the need for women to
become educators and scientists. For her, women could no longer be expected to
stay home; they needed to contribute to society by way of their Islamic education:
"The new Islamic jurisprudence now says that women should get out of the home
and enter different parts of our society, of our community. This is power and we
should use it. We should continue with our education and produce ideas." She
differentiated abilities based on gender in that women for her tended to relate to
others better and were more detailed oriented. She said, "But men generally look
at issues on the whole, not by the details. Because of this, women can be more
useful than men." The women voiced that mobaheseh was more important for
women because women comprised half the population. Women's voices about
their struggles at home, in the workforce, and in public spaces were greatly needed
to develop religious edicts, not subvert them.

Though it was necessary for women's experiences to inform Islamic jurisprudence, they rejected pure reason and pure analogy without reference to the Qur'an
and Sunnah because of the endless conflicting interpretations that emerged from
these methods. On this, Sania said, "We are not talking about saying something
that is outside the frame, and we are not talking about 'big acts'.... We try to give
our own ideas, according to what we think would be appropriate for our society.
For example, like clothes, the body is still the same, but we change the clothes.
The shape of the subject is still the same, but the features are different."

Sania and Fazia, like the other howzevi here, hoped to strengthen their practice of mobaheseh to a point where they could examine new topics like genetic
modification, stem cell transplant, sex reassignment surgery, and artificial in-
semination, and possibly inform future Islamic edicts. Fazia put it into words:
"We need to check the conditions of our time and see if they are the same as the
past. If the conditions of the past are no longer the conditions of today, then we
have to find out which ideas [interpretations] are better." Fazia then emphasized
that in this work of comparing which interpretations worked best for the social
moment, the guide for the way to derive what was permissible or what was not
remained the same. She explained, "The frame should be the same as the past,
but its shape, its features may change or may have changed. This is the student's
duty, to take the frame from the old text and change the features, the shape of
it, maybe the codes, and bring them up to date. But we don't change the frame."
Meaning, addressing new social developments did not involve removing Islam
from the equation.

The second reason for why I move away from interpreting the mobaheseh as
an insurrectionary space was related to its inherent features. Mobaheseh was, in
essence, an exchange of words among individuals. It facilitated discourse, and

often that was all it was. It was legislative, centered on exchanging interpretations of Islamic laws on actions that were obligatory, recommended, permissible, impermissible, and reprehensible. Alimeh described, "Outsiders who do not know what mobaheseh is might interpret our half-hour debates as a serious fight, but we're actually just doing mobaheseh. In mobaheseh we are supposed to explain our interpretations, especially if they are different from the idea of others." Participants were sometimes impassioned about their opinions and, more often than not, carried the discussions for months and years.

Sania clarified this point, that ijtihad is inherently full of disagreements: "This is ijtihad. . . . The mujtahid in Iran differ in their interpretations even if they have been taught the same books. Their ideas, their interpretations were developed from doing mobaheseh, because the purpose of mobaheseh is to dispute your own ideas and the ideas of others. You are encouraged to develop independent thinking and then express them." However, interpretations often remained within the clerical circles. If one participant developed a more liberal interpretation of one text, it was equally possible for another participant to have developed a more conservative interpretation than the ones before it. Perhaps because of the constant push and pull, mobaheseh was legislative without necessarily resulting in legal or social change.

With enough credibility, senior howzevi published books and articles in religious journals, converting their interpretations from the practice of disputation to written form. Some of the women, like Farideh, worked for mujtahid on publishing their work in legal journals and coming up with ways to disseminate the information to the public outside the clerical establishment. When I spoke to my secular friends in north Tehran about this occurrence, they were clueless to the fact that howzevi women could publish in religious journals and make a case for their interpretations. That is, different interpretations stayed within the circles in the clerical establishment.

As with practice that involves deconstructing categories, mobaheseh is time-consuming. When they occurred, the visible outcomes were slow to come. There was quite a bit of politicking for an interpretation to pick up ground and gather enough characters to stand behind the interpretation, requiring a sort of "Broadway production" for it to make it to the legislative floor in Tehran. One such example was the law on polygyny. Initially, men could take a second wife without the first wife's permission. Tooran Valimourad and her allies approached the women of Jami'at Zaynab, which was headed by Maryam Behrouzi, in the early 2000s. Maryam Behrouzi also came across this same issue in mobaheseh. They eventually joined forces, and their attempt was partially successful. After several attempts they succeeded in passing a law requiring a man to inform his first wife before taking a second wife. However, the policy did not include a clause on penalizing the man if he chose to ignore the new law. At the time of my field-work, the women had been working on getting the votes in to include a penalty in the clause, but to no avail. Maryam Behrouzi died right after I left Iran without having seen the penalizing clause in the law. My sense is that mobaheseh circles were not spaces where radical sociopolitical transformations occurred in a short period of time.

If legislative and social change were the women's objectives in doing moba-heseh, it was slow labor to the point of obstruction. This is not to downplay the strides women have made in changing Iranian laws about women and families. The fact is, it takes just one legislative change to marriage or veiling laws to trans-form an entire social landscape. Changes to a handful of laws such as inheritance, blood money, and polygyny came as a result of senior howzevi initially doing mobaheseh. However, my point is, while mobaheseh was a stimulus for change, the amount of mobaheseh that took place on a daily basis in Iran was not com-mensurate to the number of legislative bills introduced as a result of mobaheseh. Most of the mobaheseh I observed among students at the early and later stages of their education had to do with deciphering Arabic text, Islamic philosophy, and Islamic jurisprudent rulings that had been debated among renowned scholars for hundreds of years. They were not always contentious subjects like divorce, child custody, abortion, temporary marriage, and so on.

Mobaheseh was a constantly shifting space. That is, women's interpretations of text and materials were not expected to be conclusive. More often than not, as more voices, more evidence, and more historical interpretations were brought forward over a period of time, interpretations were expected to change. Women explained that many of their mobaheseh topics have remained unresolved—some topics continued to linger through time and outside the mobaheseh space.

If the purposes for doing mobaheseh were about self-knowing, whether to master the various approaches to Islamic text, to think about the world analyti-cally, to become a good teacher, to overcome shyness, and the like, mobaheseh seemed to have facilitated these. In the previous words of Sania, "the mobaheseh allows the student to find her own idea." As Maryam advised her students, "You must do mobaheseh because you will be very strong in speaking." Mobaheseh was equally about the student as it was about the content and the skill sets. The value of each shifted depending on the context.

Disputation was a form of practice that served to perfect a student's way of re-sponding to inquiry using knowledge that was calibrated to take into account the current conditions of time and place. In the context of their education, they could not become exact replications of their practices. Despite the entanglements with the state, what the howzevi gained from this experience was not confined to the small circle of their mobaheseh. Today, the howzevi women continue to conduct research on past interpretations of the conditions of marriage, interpretations that had not yet reached common knowledge. As I've written, it is now being debated as to whether a woman can become a religious authority for all people, thereby opening up the possibility for a woman to become a religious leader like the Marja'e Taqlid. By way of long-term participation, mobaheseh was a space where women eventually developed forms of relatedness, where being ethical and just played out. These included moments of play. Laughter kept them together, a signal that the work of learning about themselves and God, a search for the self in its original form, though a journey by oneself, can also be done with others.

NOTES

1. Fischer, *Iran*, 47–48; Boyarin, "Placing Reading," 18.
2. Fischer, *Iran*, 53–54.
3. Gutas, *Greek Thought*, 61–69.
4. Ibid.
5. Gee, *An Introduction*, 1, 14.
6. Freire, *Pedagogy*, 71–72.
7. Lave and Wenger, *Situated Learning*, 109.
8. Fiske, *Understanding Popular*, 108.
9. Graham, "Traditionalism in Islam," 501.
10. Hamayon, *Why We Play*, 2.

PART III

**HOWZEVI WOMEN RECONSTITUTING
PRACTICES**

—⟋⟍—

PRELUDE, PART III

A CLASS IN ARJANTIN SQUARE:
DISCUSSING WAVES OF FEMINISM

The responses to Maryam after her speech in the English class at Arjantin Square intensified. Across the room, Khanum-e Moallem turned on her microphone and tapped it. She held both ends of the chador right underneath her chin and spoke in English: "But to me, I think this is a boring topic. This is old feminism. It does not say anything about third-wave feminism." Khanum-e Amjad, across the room, interrupted: "*Bebakhshid* [excuse me], what do you mean? She is speaking about radical feminism and how it affects the family and society. She is not talking about other feminisms." Khanum-e Moallem, who originally made the comment, replied, "Yes, I understand. But now people are not talking about this because it is an old [idea of] feminism. Now there is third-wave feminism that is about not having the same effect on society as radical feminism." Maryam sat quietly, listening to the discussion sparked by her paper topic. After a pause, she adjusted her eyeglasses and continued reading the main points of her paper until the end. "Thank you," she said. The women in the room applauded.

Dr. Hassanpour proceeded to introduce me to the class and asked me to say a few words about my purpose in visiting Iran. The women then began introducing themselves to me one by one, stating their names, educational backgrounds, and current positions of employment. At the end of the session, the professor gave me time to pose a question to the class. I asked for clarification on what was meant by the word *mysticism* and the historical role of women within Islamic mysticism, since I had heard some of the women introduce themselves as part of that field of study. Najmeh Khanum explained what mysticism meant: the dimension of

Islam that emphasized self-knowledge and one's relationship with the Divine. As for the role of women in Islamic Mysticism, Khanum-e Moallem turned on her microphone to say, "Because women have more of the emotions like mercy and compassion than the men, women are more 'mystic' than men." Khanum-e Tabesh turned her microphone on and spoke in Persian, then asserted in English, "This is from feminism thought—we have to be careful." Sara and Maryam turned their microphones on, interrupting each other to respond in English; "Islam is not feminism." In response, Khanum-e Shojaei interrupted. "But she [Khanum-e Moallem] is not saying in Islam there is feminism." A debate followed. Dr. Hassanpour interrupted to say class was over and gave the assignment for the following week.

SIX

—ᴍ—

MOVING THROUGH EXCLUSION

I HAVE DESCRIBED THE WAY howzevi women conceptualized the role of the 1979 revolution in their access to the women's howzeh elmiyeh and that through this access, the invisible work of women transformed the institution. I have also demonstrated the importance of including the work of khod shenasi when examining forms of success among the howzevi. By detailing the women's use of the black chador, I have illustrated what khod shenasi requires from the howzevi in bodily and social practices. Through the years, these continued practices potentially result in her being identified as an 'adil, a just individual. On this, I have also detailed the crucial role of these practices in the spaces and moments of mobaheseh, or disputation, a pedagogical tradition of the howzeh elmiyeh where social circles form and are developed.

The personal connectedness in and between these social circles comes with experiences of rejection and exclusion. This chapter examines what the work of belonging in these social circles looks like. I do so by describing the educative paths, or the movement from the periphery to the center, of two unmarried women who were at the early stages of their education. Both women introduced me to the strong women in their families and showed me that religious rituals were important to them. They spoke greatly of politics and religion, motivational teachers, discovering their interests, and about how they wanted to use their Islamic education to create an understanding between Iranians who found themselves on opposite sides of the sociopolitical spectrum.

Farideh wanted to Islamicize teacher training and create a legal system that normalized different interpretations of Islamic edicts while Zaynab wanted to make her Islamic practices relatable to whomever she encountered. Each went about their goals in different ways, but both saw their learning opportunities at

Madraseh Ali as a path to achieve these goals. Zaynab chose Madraseh Ali because "there was a lot of work to do in Iran to make it more Islamic" and because it would place her on the appropriate path towards a PhD. Farideh's master's degree from Madraseh Ali was one step away from its PhD program. Attending Madraseh Ali would increase her chances to work in universities and government offices.

Although the work of khod shenasi is personal, it is put to the test in social interactions. Participating in a project that seeks to develop a society that is conducive to khod shenasi while trying to observe practices of khod shenasi is difficult work. Differences between people emerge. Rejection and interpretive misalignments on "what should be" become inevitable. Farideh's and Zaynab's ethnographies about their challenges to belong give us an idea of the established norms around them. Having the intention to use their Islamic education in support of the Islamic Republic does not protect them from the rejection and exclusion that are inherent in social interactions or, in the language of khod shenasi, inherent in *alam-e tabiat o madeh*, the material world. But the way they each respond to their exclusion reveals that the work of creating a sense of belonging is also a relatable response to exclusion. Farideh and Zaynab do the work of reinterpreting behavioral boundaries, of prioritizing principles and codes of conduct that are of value to them, and of turning to family and friends for support. Finally, the way their surroundings adjust to their presence also informs us that these established norms give way and and are dynamic but always in accordance with Islamic teachings and practices.

FARIDEH'S SOLUTIONS

I return to June 2008, when I first visited Madraseh Ali, where I met Dr. Sajjadpour and his students. I sat four rows away from the windows in the back of the classroom. Three women holding their chador over their faces walked through the door. Another woman walked in several minutes later and sat in the very back of the class near the windows. A woman about five feet tall walked into the room with another woman walking right behind her. They greeted me and sat in the row directly in front of me. Turning my way, they asked me a question in Persian. I excused myself for having only basic Persian at that time. They both smiled, appearing as if they wanted to tell me more. They introduced themselves, "Farideh and Arezu," and laughed about the way they tried to speak English with me.

Farideh, to my left, had a striking unibrow. She asked me where I came from and whether I was a new student. Right before Dr. Sajjadpour entered the classroom, Farideh wrote her mobile number on a piece of paper and handed it to me. The class was on comparative family law and lasted for almost two hours. The dry summer heat in that classroom with very little ventilation seemed unbearable. Dr. Sajjadpour wiped his forehead many times with a handkerchief, as did the other men sitting in the front wearing their business suits. In these two hours, I observed what appeared to me to be an intense debate between Farideh, the men, and the professor. Dr. Sajjadpour gave me the time, telephone number, and location of where to go two days later to introduce me to the first group of howzevi from Tehran's Madraseh Ali. Farideh was not one of them.

Farideh's story is an example of a young woman who wanted to learn more about Islam and the way to think about Islamic morals by becoming part of the howzeh. Farideh's unibrow marked her as a *dokhtar,* or virgin girl who had never been married. She was in her mid-twenties. For Farideh, a degree from Madraseh Ali in Islamic theology and Islamic philosophy would enable her to eventually become the kind of influential teacher she wanted to become, one with a focus on religious morals. And in her calculation, a master's degree from Madraseh Ali was one step away from a doctoral degree, which would then give her the credentials to teach in both the howzeh and Iranian universities. Madraseh Ali, for Farideh, had "the best of both worlds." She began to reflect on what was happening in her hometown as a sign that Iranian society was falling away from the revolutionary ideals of creating a society that would be conducive to the work of khod shenasi. She realized that in addition to learning Islamic morals, she needed to work on protecting the project of creating that society. Her educative experience, which samples the social interactions in the women's howzeh, was full of difficulties but also the genius of finding solutions. I begin her story with the women in her family.

The Question

On one of our walks in Tehran, I asked Farideh about what the women in her family liked to do. It was one of those fieldwork introductory questions I had hoped would generate more questions, not realizing how complex a question it actually was. Farideh paused, laughed, and changed the topic. A few days later, Farideh and her family invited me to spend a few days with them in their town, which was six hours away from Tehran. They invited me to attend her aunt's *Sofreh-e Nazr,* a women's religious gathering that involved feeding guests as a votive offering to God.

When I arrived, we spent the morning preparing food for the Sofreh-e Nazr that was going to take place the following day. Farideh's mother, Khanum-e Khorasani, took charge of guiding the women for the food preparation, including her daughters, her sisters, their cousins, and a handful of neighbors. Women from in and around the neighborhood attended the gathering the next day, filling their basement with sounds of women taking turns reading Qur'anic verses from the chapter of Saad, known as the chapter of David, as well as praises of the Prophet Mohammad and his family between the turn-taking. After the reading of the last verse, we prostrated in prayer, greeted each other with blessings. We headed upstairs to take our place on the sofreh, a ceremonial tablecloth that reached the full length of the room. A handful of women approached Farideh to ask about Islamic edicts that applied in their personal lives. While sharing mostly humorous stories and experiences, we ate the votive food together as if we were consuming our prayers, in the hopes that these would be heard and answered.

Farideh's great grandfather from her mother's side was a mujtahid, and her grandfather from her father's side was a tolab. The role of Islamic education was important in her family not just in terms of family identity but also in ways of understanding the way people arrive at decisions about justice and injustice. Although she never spoke of this, it seemed as if Farideh was carrying on this legacy since she was the only one in the family who pursued an Islamic education. She was determined to make future changes in her town with work that was related to improving people's access to Islamic knowledge and advocating for bringing this knowledge to the practicalities of daily life.

Farideh was the eldest of three daughters, one of whom, Farhana, had just completed a degree in computer science but began working in a sewing factory because computer-related jobs were hard to come by in their hometown. Farideh's youngest sister, Hamideh, still in high school, was practicing for her tae kwon do black belt exam when she suggested we visit their grandmother, Khanum-e Jamshidi. Farideh, Hamideh, and their cousins walked me through unpaved streets and alleys and, at one point, along the side of a highway to their grandmother's house. On one of these unpaved streets, a large black bee suddenly buzzed above my head, making its way toward my face. Hamideh pushed me to the side and stood in harm's way. The bee unfortunately ended up stinging Hamideh's eyelid. Farideh removed the stinger and we rushed immediately to their grandmother's house as Hamideh deflected the pain. Hamideh insisted she was in a hurry, not so much in search of relief but because she was excited for me to meet their grandmother.

Khanum-e Jamshidi's husband, Farideh's grandfather who died long ago, had built a swimming pool in the backyard. It had been the first swimming pool in town that was accessible to the public and, on certain days of the week, exclusively for women. People paid a small fee for maintenance expenses. Its popularity gained traction because it was also the first public swimming pool in town that women could access since the revolution. Unfortunately, the local authorities caught on and demanded money from their grandfather. Farideh's grandfather eventually closed it down because he refused to take part in the bribery, which was considered a sin. The swimming pool was left stagnant for quite some time,

Figure 6.1. Farideh with her sister and cousins, walking me to their grandmother's house. Iran, 2008. ©Amina Tawasil.

a reminder for everyone in the family as well as the townsfolk of what could have been. Their grandmother eventually converted the swimming pool into a fish pond and cultivated the plot of land behind it into a luscious garden of vegetables and fruit trees.

When I asked Farideh what the members of her family liked to do, I assumed to a fault that she would simply provide a brief response, say a list of activities, to a question that in fact forced a more complex answer about women, society, and revolution. Farideh and her family invited me to join them for the Sofreh-ye Nazar and witness all the labor that it entailed, for the long walk to their grandmother's house, and for other things we did during my visit to provide an answer that best represented their values. There were the nuanced moments I cannot fit in these pages, like Hamideh getting stung by a bee, that taught me about what it meant for them to be dignified and generous. They made certain that I not only documented but also understood the kind of pride they had for their grandfather's effort to include women in his initiative and celebrated their grandmother's work to give life to his work in another form. For Farideh in particular, the swimming pool was a symbol of possibilities and of work to be done in Iran.

Farideh's Education

Farideh had always been interested in mathematics and science, but studies in Islam equally piqued her interest. Unlike others in this book, Farideh attended a Madraseh Ali high school in her region. In addition to the standard academic coursework required in Iran, the Madraseh Ali high school required students to do more coursework on Islam. Books that would normally be taught in other schools for four years were taught in one or two years at Madraseh Ali. The curriculum for the last two years of high school consisted of coursework at the university level. Though the workload at the high school was heavy, she discovered a sense of purpose along the way. Farideh credited her teachers for this good experience. The high school administration and teachers worked hard to encourage students to believe that "if you are successful, you can do anything for society." One teacher in particular encouraged her to continue her studies in Islamic philosophy and theology. "A field related to morality is good for religion," this teacher told Farideh.

Her teachers played a significant role in developing the idea that she, as an individual, played a meaningful role in transforming and strengthening an Islamic collective greater than herself. Through a combination of positive experiences, of having good teachers with a morals-focused curriculum, she began to see the way teachers played an important role in the development of Iranian society. Farideh imagined her future self as a professor who would have the same motivational impact on her students and conduct research toward improving the Iranian education system, and she hoped to return to her hometown to help develop a teacher-training program.

The decisions she made about her education were telling of her relationship with her family, her friends in Tehran, and the transformations of the system. Farideh's father questioned her decision to do a master's degree in Islamic theology and Islamic philosophy given that the program would take her three years to complete. He tried to encourage her to at least study Islamic law so she could qualify to work in the courts, but she disagreed with him. Farideh's father was part of her decision-making process, but he did not make decisions for her. He was aware that she hoped to work in changing non-Islamic laws into Islamic laws, inclusive of the full attainment of women's rights. He supported Farideh's decisions about her education and gave her more mobility compared to her sisters. This was in part due to Khomeini's push for a revolutionary ideal that a woman must not be prevented from seeking an Islamic education.

After graduating from high school, Farideh made her way to Tehran to study at Imam Sadeq University, which offered programs that qualified students to apply for a Madraseh Ali master's degree. After graduating, Farideh enrolled at Madraseh Ali's master's program. Farideh had a similar revelatory experience from her Islamic education about the role of Islamic laws in developing a Shi'i nation based on establishing justice. Islamic law offered more possibilities to Iranian society than the European laws that prevailed in Iran before the revolution.

Iranian laws, she said, had not yet fully accommodated for these possibilities for two reasons. Iranian laws were not entirely based on Islamic text, thus affecting the way the government operated. She hoped to work toward changing this. Like many of her peers, for example, she argued that if the Islamic Republic considered itself an Islamic state, then being a mujtahid needed to be one of the qualifications for Iranian judges serving in the judicial system. Also, Islamic-based Iranian laws were not inclusive of other scholarly interpretations because only one interpretation of Islamic jurisprudence continued to dominate the law-making mechanism in Iran. Therefore, many of the laws were outdated because they did not allow for the flexibility that diverse interpretations offered. For Farideh, in order to effectively replace borrowed European laws, valid yet varying interpretations of Islamic text needed to be recognized, especially when evaluating the utility of contemporary laws in an evolving society.

She provided several examples, such as child custody and marriage contracts, and in particular the issue of *vilayat bar nikah*, the consent for marriage from the father as the guardian. The dominant interpretation of this law was that a father's consent was a required component of a valid marriage contract. Without one, marriage was not possible. Farideh explained her interest: "But some mujtahid have other interpretations: that there is no *vilayah*, or guardianship, for virgin women. After doing research, there is much consideration for what is best on a case-to-case basis. All of these ideas or interpretations are needed in society." Farideh hoped to educate the public about these diverse interpretations of Islamic text so that people could advocate for themselves when necessary. She wanted the new generation of Iranians to know that many laws in Iran were not Islamic, as they assumed them to be, and that there were many valid interpretations of Islamic law that they needed to educate themselves about. But what she was most concerned about was maintaining a social atmosphere in her hometown and other small towns conducive to the work of khod shenasi.

All the women I met in Farideh's family wore the chador except for one aunt whom she was very close to. Farideh was clear about her stance on not forcing women to wear the chador. Her concern was that the practice of wearing the chador would become marginalized as it historically had been before the revolution. Part of her concern was related to women removing the chador and becoming a *bad hijabi*, a woman who wears the veil loosely and without care, to the extent that it would transform the visual and social landscape of her town for no other reason than imitating American and European women. The chador was part of the norm, and she wanted to use her education to keep it this way. She wanted to keep the markers of religiosity a constant presence—at the very least, to be visibly reminded that most were not losing sight of the importance of remembering God. The practice of wearing the chador was an important marker of this: "Now we see that as the time passes, the more we lose more Islam. Our mothers wore chador and our children don't wear chador. Hijab is not bad, but the children of our children will think Islam is not for them." Its visible predominance or lack thereof in public space was her way of gauging whether people were forgetting.

Farideh told a story of a childhood friend's transformation to becoming a bad hijabi, which began with no longer wearing the chador when she moved to Tehran to attend university. Her friend began wearing makeup soon after and through time became comfortable with partially showing her hair. Another woman who intended on becoming an Islamic sciences teacher and whom she knew from another small town went through a similar process. This woman, however, had a *doost pesar*, a boyfriend, though they were not engaged. "This is not from Islamic law. It is very bad," Farideh commented. The emergence of bad hijab was a sign that the women had forgotten their life's purpose to worship God and that they had forgotten the kinds of experiences of exclusion their families had endured throughout Iran's history by maintaining religiosity. "These women forget everything," she added.

She saw two problems with this situation. She said women like her friend would return to their towns and try to change the customs of that town. This affected women from religiously conservative families. While the bad hijab was a sign of encouragement for some women, the phenomenon created barriers for religiously conservative women who wanted to pursue an education in Tehran. Their families would discourage or prevent them from attending a university in Tehran for fear that they would return home a bad hijabi. Farideh explained that religiously conservative families saw the act of abandoning the chador and the hijab as a sign of deteriorating morals and beliefs.

Farideh saw the phenomenon of the bad hijab as symptomatic of a larger problem, of people allowing their lesser tendencies to dominate their character. Iranian families and the Iranian education system were the root causes of the problem. Although the families in her town attributed such a change to women moving to Tehran to attend university, Farideh placed the blame partly on the families in her town and other small towns, since many did not know much about Islam outside of their rituals. They were not educating themselves about Islamic teachings. She explained that if parents and other adults in the family were deeply observant and understood that Islamic practices could bring them closer to each other and to God, the children would hold on to practices like wearing the chador.

Furthermore, some religiously conservative families were forcing their women to study Islam, which corrupted the intention to carry out a sacred act. She did not quite know what do. But even with this, she had difficulty embracing the idea that families were entirely accountable for the bad hijabi problem. After all, not very many had access to the kind of Islamic education she had been receiving. Thus, she also held the government responsible for neglecting to develop teacher education programs for the Islamic sciences early on at the high school level. Thus, another anxiety over the situation was, more importantly, about protecting Islamic knowledge from those without proper training in the Islamic sciences. That is, the teacher as the carrier of knowledge must be someone who takes care of the sanctity of teaching sacred text to others. This warranted a careful selection of upright teachers.

Teacher training was an important part of Islamic education, according to Farideh: "I hate geography because I had a bad teacher. In Islamic lessons, if the teacher is angry or does not behave properly, the students will think this is Islam. The teacher is so important. And it is so important for Iran that there are good teachers in all Islamic courses. If it's a good system in education, they should see good behavior in Islam, in society, where we see society."

Islamic education was a tool to do the educative work that she believed needed to be done with teachers. She advocated for making Islamic education more widely accessible for Iranian families. In essence, she wanted to contribute to Islamizing teacher education in her town and the rest of the country, a desire informed by her experience as a student in the Iranian education system. Her criticism was more about strengthening the education system, rather than undermining it. According to Farideh, the system needed a pedagogical and curricular overhaul so it could play its part in developing a Shi'i nation. She was keen on enabling students to think critically and not just to memorize material for high scores, and on training teachers to teach with passion rather than "with boredom or harshness." Farideh saw herself as someone who could do something about all this through her education at Madraseh Ali, which began for her in high school.

Challenges in Teaching Islam

Farideh and I spent time meeting in the early afternoons and evenings in different parks in Tehran or at my apartment. She never failed to bring her own food and make herself feel at home. When our conversations went past midnight, she stayed with me overnight in Pirouzi. The first evening she and her roommate, Aliyeh, came to visit me I was immediately reminded of Farideh's humor. We hadn't seen each other for two years. When I opened the door, she and Aliyeh were drenched from the rain. She greeted me with a wide smile, pinched my cheeks, and said, "Salam! Amine! Your face grew another face!" She noticed that I had gained weight from the last time she saw me. We laughed loudly as she embraced me and handed me a bag with ice cream sandwiches and cheese curls. "You did not have to bring anything," I said. Farideh responded as she proceeded to take her wet socks off and place them on the radiator in the living room: "This is what girls love to do—bring food they aren't supposed to eat, and then eat late at night!" There was plenty of laughter for the rest of the evening from speaking about our families, the cost of living in Tehran, the commute with the pollution, and our daily struggles of climbing the staircases.

Farideh had a small circle of close friends. Arezu, whom I wrote about earlier, and Aliyeh were consistently present in her life. Like Farideh, Aliyeh was the only one in her family to have studied in the howzeh. She was one year older than Farideh and was from a small town in northern Iran. They had been roommates since their first days at Imam Sadeq University, and they supported each other through the years, including confronting the challenges in their studies, as they had been mobaheseh partners for years. The two women had just moved out of their apartment and were staying at Aliyeh's brother's apartment in the meantime. This was Aliyeh's first week working in a government office. She had explained to her manager that she was uncomfortable being the only woman on her office floor. Based on her rights in the workplace as a Muslim woman, Ali-yeh requested that the government office hire more women and build a door to separate her from the men on the floor. The room had just been completed when they came to visit me.

That evening, Farideh was excited to tell me that she had finally made it into Ayatollah Khamenei's and Larijani's Dars-e Kharij classes, which she attended three times a week. Farideh had worked hard to reach this goal. First she had to establish proof of which books she had finished studying. She also had to get a letter from a professor who could attest to her level of knowledge. She then had to go to the Ministry of Intelligence and National Security for proof of a clear criminal record. Although she had no way of knowing the yearlong process involving her record, she was aware of the clearance process to be accepted into this class because Ayatollah Khamenei and Larijani also held political positions.

She further explained that important in this process was having established good credibility, a life lived according to Islamic rights and wrongs. The offices conducted investigations into a student's behavior, which included talking to the student's neighbors, teachers, professors, friends, and acquaintances. The office looked into the student's activities in the neighborhood, whether the student taught vocational skills or engaged in community services like feeding the poor, cooking meals for the neighborhood during Ashura, and other activities. Playing loud music, wearing incomplete hijab, or behaving in a "bad" way with men or women and so on would prevent one from gaining acceptance into the class. If all the conditions were met, the student received a special identification card that gave clearance to enter *Bayt-e Rahbari*, the compound of the supreme leader, to attend class. Acceptance into Ayatollah Khamenei's class automatically qualified a student for Ayatollah Larijani's class.

Farideh's infectious laughter often concealed her struggle. Of all the women I spent time with, Farideh seemed to have experienced the most obstacles. For one, her clearance had taken one year as opposed to the usual three to five months like the other howzevi. Farideh was also not accepted into the doctoral program at Madraseh Ali in 2011. This was due in part to timing. The year Farideh finished her master's degree, changes in the procedure for doctoral admissions were imple-mented nationwide. Admission for doctoral programs was no longer entirely at the discretion of individual institutions. It involved taking an entrance exam, which Farideh had not taken yet. Maryam explained to me that these admission changes were extended to the Islamic science–related fields in order to avoid *parti bazi*, or insider networking, to get ahead. To make matters more challenging, the doctoral entrance exam for Islamic sciences was focused more on the study of theological discourse and Qur'anic interpretation, thereby placing students of Islamic jurisprudence, theology, and philosophy at a disadvantage. After spending over half a decade studying the latter, students like Farideh found themselves needing to study subjects that would take about another five years to complete in order to do well on the entrance exams.

Finding Solutions

Farideh was resourceful and figured out ways to circumvent being shut out. She often took it upon herself to sort out the logic behind the rules, social or otherwise. Most of these were unwritten codes of expectations. Some of her strategies involved taking the stated rule literally and then figuring out the opportunities its precise wording failed to cover.

To illustrate the way Farideh navigated rules and unwritten expectations, I use examples from the way she, like the other howzevi, handled my presence among them. This required trying to strike a balance between "knowing Amina as a person" and "knowing Amina is a stranger." Farideh belonged to a ruling group that held foreigners suspect of espionage. This concern was not without reason, as there were assassinations in Tehran during both of my visits. Although she and the other women determined that I was not a security threat, this did not negate the fact that I was still a foreigner. Some of what we discussed about the 2009 election protests and the harassment she and her friends had encountered in the aftermath reminded me of the way she consistently made an effort to educate me on spaces to avoid. Perhaps I was a friend, but I was also a stranger in a sociopolitical space that rightly harbored suspicion of foreigners from the United States. In this context, my presence and her desire to share her experiences with me posed a problem. How could she take me to the different spaces she wanted me to experience with her? The solutions to this dilemma taught me about the way she assessed rules in deciding to take certain actions.

My first visit with Farideh at Madraseh Ali is one example. I was body searched, and my digital items were placed inside a locker as Farideh waited for me on the other side of the curtain. I assumed at that point that security had been informed about my presence. Farideh met me on the other side of the check-in curtain to make sure I was allowed inside the campus. She said to me, "If you told me about your items [camera and cell phone] ahead of time, I could have taken them from you [before coming here]. They would not have taken it. I forgot to tell you. I am sorry. But next time tell me." Farideh was suggesting that we should have met outside campus beforehand so she could bring my audio recorder, camera, and mobile phone inside with her. Because she was one of them, and she would make sure that I used these appropriately.

At the end of this visit, Farideh had to leave to meet other friends and asked her close friend Arezu to walk me through the courtyard, a space where women were not allowed to be. I worried and told them I did not want to put them in harm's way. Both of them placed fingers on their lips to signal for me to keep silent because men on the other side of the wall would hear us. It seemed at this point that we would make our way to the courtyard anyway. Arezu and I walked briskly from one corner of the tiled walls and arched domes to the other. She said, "It is a bad idea for a woman to sit here because look [pointing at the windows above the arched walkways towards the men's rooms and offices]." In other words, we were not supposed to make ourselves vulnerable to the male gaze by sitting in the courtyard. Requesting for Arezu to walk me through this courtyard was an example of assessing the rules and their practical application. While Farideh and Arezu stood behind the unwritten rule that women could not loiter or sit in the men's courtyard, they acted on the obvious premise that admiring the architecture while walking right through the courtyard was not the same as sitting or loitering.

Farideh also instructed me on the way to do what we were allowed to do, without attracting the attention of individuals who could shift the context, throw an unrelated rule at us, and call it a violation. On our way back to Tehran from her family's home, Farideh decided to take a short detour. Already near the building, she told me we were about to enter her father's workplace to pick up a set of children's books for one of her volunteer activities in Tehran. At the time, her father was working for the government as a civil engineer, which meant we would eventually have to come face to face with security guards, if not Revolutionary Guards (IRGC), in order to get to the books, which were located in a stock room on the fourth floor. Taking the books was not a problem, and I was not a threat for Farideh. But my presence in a government building could have alarmed others because of what my legal citizenship stood for—an imperialist project that carries the might of weapons of mass destruction as well as economic sanctions. Before entering, Farideh instructed me not to look up at anyone and not to speak; if speaking were necessary, I was to speak only in Filipino, not English or Persian "because they might cause problems for us and also my father, because he is a government worker." This was a very stressful moment, one that hinged on the ethics of doing fieldwork. I hesitated and insisted that I stay away and wait for her elsewhere, but Farideh was certain there was more potential for trouble if we were to part ways. Farideh was determined that we could achieve the task together, and we did.

Farideh and I decided to meet at Chahor Rah Vali Asr one afternoon. I crossed the street to the Vali Asr metro station and found her standing at the edge of the sidewalk looking for me, her hand pulling her black chador halfway over her face. She had been calling me because she could not find me in the unusually packed crowd. There were police cars and vans in each corner of the intersection. Five security force members stood in helmets, fully geared with assault weapons. Security forces had been on alert since the 2009 protest here and in nearby Maydan-e Engelob two days earlier. Farideh and I looked on as the Basij passed us, two on each motorcycle, some in dress shirts and pants, one in a ski mask. Flustered, I told her I had intended to take her to Cafe France, on the other side of the security lineup. She promptly said, "No, this way" as we turned the opposite direction toward Maydan-e Ferdowsi. She asked if I knew what was happening. I told her there had been a protest two days previous, but, like her, I was caught off guard with this one. Halfway past Park-e Daneshju she warned, "It will be very bad, Amine, if you go to there. Very bad. You are not Iranian, and maybe they think bad about you, [that] you are doing something bad. We should go this way." We walked far from the intersection and sat in a small ice cream shop. She was referring to the accusation of citing unrest against the state, tantamount to espionage.

As a student of the supreme leader, Farideh had access to extensive networks bound ideologically to the shaping of a particular Iran, networks perhaps beyond the reach of a man with an assault rifle that late afternoon. I assumed that Farideh had nothing to be afraid of because of her associations with those in positions of power. I thought, if needed, Farideh could vouch that I was not inciting unrest against the state, and that would be enough. I found the opposite to be true. Her position limited her options. Farideh's privilege did not exempt her from its requisite charge: to take care of the privilege she had. Her family did not know she had made it into Ayatollah Khamenei's class. If people in her town found out she had direct access to two important political figures, they would request favors from her family. If she failed to deliver, which she said was a given, she and her family would have to face the backlash. Hence, for Farideh, continued access to this space demanded a great deal of discretion. She could not reveal her secret, and she could not lose the very reason for keeping that secret—her access. Certainly, in this situation she could not risk this privilege by being with me at a protest against the regime.

That was the ethos, of constantly evaluating expectations, weighing out options and considering what was at stake, in which Farideh took action to increase her chances of passing the doctoral entrance exam without violating the rules. Because the new doctoral admission policy required additional training in interpreting Qur'anic verses, Farideh needed to overcome this obstacle. Farideh and her friends relied on their resources and networks to develop strategies to study for this exam without having to return to the howzeh for another four or five years.

Farideh solved her problem by engaging the unwritten rule about taking exams. While using a cheat sheet or looking at other students' papers during an exam would be examples of violating the explicit written rules of taking an exam, interviewing and taking advice from people who had already taken the exam were not. Thus, she and her friends looked for a handful of people who had already taken the exam so they could learn about its patterns. Most of this effort hinged on acceptance and respectability—in other words, the way other howzevi would cooperate and be willing to share this information with them. But the effort was not in violation of exam policies.

Based on what they were told, the exam apparently recycled verses from the same chapter of the Qur'an. This pattern was common knowledge, Farideh said. This meant that even if the exam contained different verses for each exam, the verses were from only one chapter rather than random chapters. They did not know exactly which chapter was going to be used that year, but they were determined to work and study together. Farideh and her friends took their chances and chose one, then added three chapters before and after it, to cover their bases, a total of seven chapters of the Qur'an. This way they would not have to study the entire Qur'an. Her final strategy involved studying the work of two scholars with similar interpretations of the seven chapters. If one of these texts happened to be on the exam, it would be similar to the other. Farideh hoped that by the time she was ready to take the exam, the format would have changed to include her disciplines—theology, philosophy, and Islamic jurisprudence.

Another challenge for Farideh had to do with gaining teaching opportunities. She wanted to teach undergraduate classes while studying for the exam and waiting for better opportunities. As a student in Dars-e Kharij and after finishing a master's degree, Farideh could already teach in the howzeh. However, she had a very difficult time getting a teaching position. She was told that she was too young and needed more experience. So, to make ends meet, Farideh worked at a student campus-life office at a university in Tehran. She felt undervalued at her job because, as she explained, people she worked with did not understand her situation. She requested more engaging work than stapling notices on bulletin boards and making appointments for classes, but her request was ignored. "I want to teach classes . . . and they are not letting me teach." The woman in charge of assigning courses to teach told her she needed to study extra classes first.

"I want to teach so bad," she said while laughing. Although her credentials were limited to teaching in the howzeh, she found a way to teach elsewhere. Since she was put was in charge of finding teachers to deliver special and extracurricular lectures, she assigned herself a slot to teach a session on the principles of Islamic jurisprudence at the university. In addition to working at the office, Farideh began giving lessons to housewives at a howzeh in northwest Tehran on Tuesday mornings for forty-five minutes. These solutions were temporary and not sustainable. Not only did these kinds of teaching take time away from her responsibilities at work, but the financial compensation was not enough to pay her rent.

I later learned that other women who had not completed their master's degrees were already teaching classes in different locations. The exact reason why Farideh was not given teaching duties remained a mystery. I rarely heard women talk about negative characteristics of other women or the unfortunate circumstances of others. Complaints were often expressed in general terms. I thought that perhaps administrators favored those who were urban, but there were other howzevi who, like Farideh, also came from small towns. In Farideh's case, I could only suspect. Farideh was keen to learn new perspectives, and her approach to this learning was through disputation, by doing mobaheseh. It was a part of her everyday interaction with everyone. In one particular lunch invitation, the host, a more senior howzevi, whom Farideh debated with for several minutes, stopped responding. The host sat still, took a sip of her tea, and changed the topic. Perhaps an accumulation of these kinds of interactions marked her as over-eager or too contentious and prevented her from expanding her circle to the size that could help her with the work she wanted to do in Iran at the time. She did not know.

Farideh explained that even if she did pass the doctoral exam, the administrators who assigned classes she might teach would still have to factor in the total cost of the doctoral program, which was estimated at a cumulative $30,000. Maryam, like the other doctoral students, had been exempt from their fees because they taught courses at the lisans level and in the various howzeh in Tehran. If Farideh could not teach, passing the entrance exam would not matter at all because she could not afford the fees.

Farideh did not know exactly what administrators meant when they told her she needed to learn more before she could teach, except that one of them told her to take more classes. What I did know for certain was that as a single religiously conservative woman from a small town living in Tehran, Farideh did not have as much financial and emotional support as the other howzevi women. And for this reason, Farideh built and maintained a support network of friends and confidantes. She relied on relationships with friends like Arezu and Aliyeh. Farideh and Aliyeh had been roommates for almost seven years. They saved money together for a down payment for an apartment. In addition to working in a government office, Aliyeh traveled five hours by bus to Esfahan twice a week to teach rights and Islamic jurisprudence at an adult education program.

Farideh aimed to make it into the Dars-e Kharij classes, and she did. Completing a doctoral degree so she could teach in universities was next on her agenda. Afterward, she wanted to work on teacher training in her hometown. She could do neither at the time. Having reached this level of embeddedness in the clerical establishment by becoming a student of two of the most powerful men in Iran did not give her guaranteed access to a doctoral program or to the network of women who were responsible for assigning courses to teach in the howzeh.

Farideh continued to make ends meet and created opportunities for herself. In addition to working at a student life office and part-time teaching, she began conducting paid research for two of her former professors. She did research for an encyclopedia entry on *ojratol mesl*, a woman's right to financial compensation for work beyond sexual intercourse and asking permission from her husband in the duration of her marriage. The demand for right takes place during divorce proceedings and is owed by the husband to the wife. The amount, determined by the judge, is calculated on an hourly wage commensurate to the woman's level of education. For another professor, she was conducting research on the woman's *nafaqeh*, the husband's complete financial support of the wife throughout the marriage, and the legal steps to take that favored the wife in the event the husband abandoned the family or could not provide for the family. Although the networks of administrators and the offices of both ayatollahs recognized her, she had very little power to bend the other demands of that privilege. She still needed to "study more," in the words of those who were denying her access, to sort out what those demands might be.

Zaynab joined Madrase Ali in the hopes that she could become better educated to do the work of khod shenasi by studying Islamic jurisprudence. She also hoped her Islamic education would eventually contribute to the project of maintaining a society that is supportive of that kind of self-work. She assumed that by being in an institution that sought to produce students with similar objectives as her, she would not face similar challenges of exclusion as she experienced outside Madraseh Ali. But by identifying herself as *mazhabi motavaset*, a middle-of-the-road religiously conservative, Zaynab became the odd one out.

ZAYNAB: "WE ARE MAZHABI MOTAVASET"

Nineteen-year-old Zaynab wanted a graduate degree, a career as a lawyer, and eventually to become a wife and mother, in that order. She also saw the work of khod shenasi not only as an individual struggle but as the struggle to live morally with those who, according to Islamic teachings about the self, were naturally in the same lifelong struggle as her. Zaynab joined Madraseh Ali in the hopes that she could become better educated in the proper ways of imitating the Prophet Mohammad and his family by learning about Islamic jurisprudence. But Zaynab faced the challenge of having to overcome being different from the rest of her classmates. In Zaynab's case, this difference came from the way she practiced her understanding of Islamic teachings and the way those actions registered to those around her.

This story looks at the way Zaynab tried to create a sense of belonging. Equally important, looking at the way in which she addressed her challenges allows us to take a closer look at the parts of Zaynab's life that were most impactful to her. Zaynab was both spiritual and political in that she saw herself as someone who could influence change in her immediate personal interactions, not just in the future. While her experience tells us that the decision to be a howzevi carried with it a set of limitations and pressures to conform, it also allows us to think about the way social relationships expanded what could be accommodated for in the howzeh.

Growing Up in Tehran Pars

Zaynab spoke about her mother's wedding while showing me a photo on her phone. In it, Azadeh was in her twenties. In the following photo, Azadeh, at fourteen years old, wore a white dress as she posed for the camera standing next to her wedding sofreh. Zaynab's father, Mohsin, was twenty-two at the time. Azadeh and Mohsin were from Hamedan, but they eventually built a life for their children near Tehran's Azadi Square and Tehran Pars. Mohsin owned a small furniture shop he eventually entrusted to another party in order to drive a taxi. This doubled his source of income, which he needed in order to support his wife, children, and parents. Driving a taxi and overseeing the furniture shop barely left any time for him to be with his family except in the evenings. Azadeh embraced becoming a housewife and eventually a mother of now two grown women who, at the time we met, were taking advantage of every educative opportunity available to them. Mahtab, Zaynab's sister, had just finished her first year of a mathematics master's program at Al Zahra University, and Zaynab was completing her second year at Madraseh Ali, focusing on Islamic rights and Islamic jurisprudence. Azadeh, not too far behind her daughters' educational aspirations, was taking correspondence courses in theology and was attending afternoon classes at the local howzeh.

Zaynab shared fond memories of growing up in west Tehran. Whenever her mother and aunts traveled together to perform pilgrimage in Mashhad and Karbala, she and her sister, Mahtab, being the eldest of the cousins, would look after the younger cousins left behind. Thursdays were important to them. Following Imam Husayn's example, Zaynab and her family spent time reading the Qur'an and praying. She, her parents, her sister, and her cousins, along with aunts and uncles, would attend the rowzeh-khani, a gathering to read an elegy, and the *sine-zani*, beating of the chest in mourning, every Thursday morning after the *Fajr* (predawn) prayer at the famous hosseiniyeh in Azadi Square. Having the opportunity to be present every Thursday morning to commemorate Imam Husayn was very meaningful for Zaynab later on when her family moved to Tehran Pars.

Bringing the Islamic Past into the Sabalan Present

Although she loved the sciences and mathematics, Zaynab wanted to understand how those she emulated from the Islamic past made sense of their relationship with God. Like some of the women here, Zaynab's decision to pursue an Islamic education was in many ways influenced by events that took place in specific locations and their relevance in the present. Zaynab had traveled to Mecca and Madina with her class while she was in high school. It changed the way she imagined her life's purpose. Karbala was the other. "Karbala is the best place on earth," she said while showing me photos stored in her phone from her first visit. What had happened in Karbala over a thousand years ago for her served as a daily reminder about the nature of life's struggle, that there were going to be forces beyond what she could control, and that victory was defined not only by ending the struggle but by the way one experiences the struggle. Finally, it showed there were figures in Islamic history, the tyrant Yazid and those who betrayed Imam Husayn, whose stories of brutality could teach her important lessons on what happens to people who allow their lesser tendencies to overpower them and cause them to lose their relationship with God.

For this to make sense, a brief story of Karbala is necessary. The companions of the Prophet Mohammad became divided as to who would be his successor after his death. One group believed that his successor needed to come from his family, or his lineage, which would have been Ali Ibn Talib, his cousin. Another believed it needed to be his closest companion, Abu Bakr Al-Siddiq. The latter had succeeded in taking over the succession. The group that supported Ali as the successor resisted and came to be known as the Party of Ali, Shi'at Ali. Married to Fatimah, the Prophet's daughter, Ali had four children: Hassan and Husayn, Zaynab and UmmKulthum. While in Medina, they and the party of Ali in Kufa became marginalized. It was not until the fourth succession that Ali came to power. After Ali's death, Mu'awiyah Abu Sufyan became the caliph. Prior to his death, Mu'awiyah then appointed his son, Yazid, as his successor. Yazid was known to have been a ruthless tyrant, described as "a drunkard, who openly ridiculed and flouted the laws of Islam."[1] Soon after he came to power, the Party of Ali in Kufa began sending messages to Husayn to relocate to Kufa to take leadership. Though he was warned of the great danger of doing this, Husayn, with his family and some supporters, made their way for Kufa passing through Karbala.

An army was sent to Karbala to force Husayn to sign a pledge of allegiance to Yazid. This army cut off access to the Euphrates River for at least three days, and on the ninth of the month of Moharram, known as *Tasu'a*, Yazid's forces began to march toward Husayn's camp. While the women and children remained at bay, one by one his supporters died until he and his brother, Abbas, were the last ones standing. After the water supply had been blocked off, the children in the camp could no longer tolerate the hunger and thirst. Abbas approached the Euphrates to fetch water for them and was killed, but more than that, many interpretations tell of a martyr who fell to the ground first before allowing Imam Husayn's flag to fall. Carrying his infant son, Ali Asghar, Husayn pleaded for water. The troops closed in and shot an arrow, killing Ali Asghar. It was at this moment Husayn fought and was killed on the tenth of Moharram, famously known in Islamic history as Ashura. Yazid's men decapitated him. His head was to be delivered to Damascus. The women, the servants, and a few elderly men who could not fight in the battle were eventually captured and brought to Yazid. Zaynab, Husayn's sister, addressed Yazid in his court, admonishing him for his arrogance against God to cause suffering and spilling the blood of the innocent. She told Yazid that his body would bear witness against him and promised that the memory of Karbala would never be forgotten.

The Battle of Karbala moved Zaynab, a newcomer at Madraseh Ali, in a profound way. What happened in Karbala informed her decision to take up studies in the Islamic sciences. She and her mother, Azadeh, replayed the story of Ali Asghar and the martyrdom of Husayn annually in an event called *Shir Kharegan* in Tehran's Mosalla until she was fourteen years old. This was an annual gathering of mothers with nursing infants where they would sit and listen to an elegy about Ali Asghar. Even though Zaynab was not in Karbala, it was as if she had seen these events herself. *Tasu'a*, which takes place on the ninth of Moharram and the night before Ashura, was one of Zaynab's favorite evenings of the year in Tehran Pars and Sabalan. It was devoted to commemorating Abbas ibn Ali for his martyrdom during the battle. For her, Imam Husayn and his family had fought a good fight beyond the moment, beyond Karbala, for the generations of Muslims who had not yet been born.

Memorializing these historical events was especially important for Zaynab. How she and her neighbors interpreted the Battle of Karbala could not be removed from Iran's geopolitical reality of being surrounded by over thirty US military installations and over forty years of US-imposed sanctions. Though the battle of Karbala took place long ago, it was still relevant to the way Zaynab thought the world worked. Resisting tyranny went hand in hand with suffering, and out of that suffering came tremendous virtue and dignity. Specifically, for Zaynab, the battle resonated with the way the United States and its allies continued to torment and strong-arm Iranians, causing tremendous hardship for generations of Iranian families including those in Sabalan. From the time Zaynab was born, the geopolitical rules were rigged against them. No amount of diplomatic talks and agreements gave the kind of comfort that Ashura rituals afforded Zaynab. Victory for her was unimaginable except by embracing the process of helping her government lay the foundation for future generations who would eventually come to know of past struggle. That was the hope. She could achieve this through her Islamic education in the howzeh.

Conditioning Herself

Being a good Shi'i woman to those around her meant being mindful of a combination of practices based on Islamic teachings and social norms—in particular, how much space she occupied around others and striving to be the best in all her endeavors. But it was also about other things like fulfilling her Islamic obligations in practice. Wearing the black chador in the varied ways this practice symbolized was for God. Zaynab sometimes wore the black chador for both religious and political reasons, as a symbol of strength against those who wished to dominate Iran, and as a symbol of celebration that Iran had freed itself from American hegemony in the region. Because of the revolution, she now had access to an education that could give her a voice to discuss Islamic law with those who had power to impact the future of Iran. But Zaynab also wore the chador to help her develop, as she described, "a kind of discipline to follow the rules of Islam," to condition her body in ways that would help her against her lesser tendencies.

Many women explained to me that wearing the chador protected them while enabling them to gain respect from men. Zaynab took issue with this. There was more to wearing the black chador for her, reasons that did not imply that men had that much power over her choice of clothing. Wearing the chador did not guarantee respectful behavior from men. This became evident to us one November evening. Zaynab and I were on a bus to Maydan-e Engelob. A young man in his early twenties began asking me questions above the transparent three-foot pane that separated men and women. When I did not respond, he called out toward Zaynab, who took offense. She turned her head toward me and slung her handbag over her shoulders, which were covered by her chador. With her other hand, she pulled her chador over her face. But the young man continued to make attempts to talk to us until we got off the bus.

Zaynab felt harassed and became increasingly upset. But becoming angry for every time she experienced harassment during her commute was not going to solve the problem. She identified these instances as symptoms of greater social problems that could best be solved by developing Islamic-based programs to educate the Iranian family on Islamic teachings about respect for women. The chador was a significant part of the way Zaynab handled the situation. Zaynab felt the need to control her anger at that moment. By pulling the chador over her face not only did Zaynab create a barrier between herself and the man harassing us on the bus, but it also gave her time to consider the way to manage her emotions and her words.

This aspect of her practice was useful in her work of khod shenasi, including moments when she felt provoked. I had seen Zaynab pull the chador close to her face on seemingly insignificant situations, but I focus on this instance because it tells us a lot about Zaynab and the things she did to develop the internal strength to go through hardships in life like her first few months at Madraseh Ali. While wearing the black chador was something she had in common with the students at Madraseh Ali, it was also a practice that helped her develop a kind of resilience against unforeseeable challenges.

The Politics of Personal Connectedness

Zaynab and I met for the first time in early spring 2011, after months of Maryam trying to contact the women I had met in the summer of 2008 to see if they were willing to meet with me, but to no avail. With Maryam's feedback and approval, I decided to draw up a very basic questionnaire that Maryam could hand out to students at Madraseh Ali. Zaynab volunteered to hand me the stack of completed questionnaires. We exchanged phone numbers as she joked about finally having the opportunity to practice speaking English with me. Soon after, she and I began visiting shrines and attending elegies together.

Zaynab and I began meeting at the Madraseh Ali library in the afternoons, a time of day where students gathered into different circles to do mobaheseh. This was also the time of day when private taxis lined up outside the gates, as many families hired taxis to bring their daughters home safely from Madraseh Ali. A handful of taxis were sometimes forced to wait longer than necessary since many students used this time to stay and socialize. During these afternoon meetings, Zaynab practiced speaking English with me while I learned mantiq from her. I was also allowed to observe mobaheseh among students. Zaynab's friends and other students, too, would sit around us and talk, laugh, and sometimes chase after each other. But this kind of ease in moving through Madraseh Ali's social space had not always been Zaynab's experience.

Her difficulties during her first months at Madraseh Ali were rooted in a combination of factors she described as a lack of understanding herself, being unprepared, and the institution's social atmosphere. During the start of her first year, Zaynab did not care much about earning high scores in her courses. She was content with a good average as long as she could understand the material. When she went to Karbala with her family for two weeks, for instance, she was not concerned about missing classes and that this would affect her marks. But that pilgrimage was actually momentous for Zaynab. Unlike her previous trips to Karbala, on this occasion she unexpectedly became her family's Arabic language translator. She explained the importance of rituals and their histories in more detail than ever before. Women from her neighborhood would call her house to ask her for advice on religious matters when they wanted to make sure their decisions were not violating Islamic teachings. It was in these moments that she realized it was important to focus more on her studies so she could continue to use her knowledge to enable people to gain a deeper understanding of and appreciation for Islam.

By the time she gained this insight, she realized she did not have the proper training needed to excel. Zaynab did not see herself as someone who was born gifted with retaining information quickly without studying; she saw herself as the studious kind of clever, someone who needed to work hard. And that she did. Zaynab eventually caught up with the rest of her classmates, making every effort to speak up and ask questions in her classes, to use a dictionary, and to take detailed notes. She also began approaching her teachers before and after class to ask questions on the readings she felt she could not address in class. Her teachers, who implemented the classic dialectic approach commonly used in the howzeh, played a significant role in her progress.

Though she was gaining traction academically, she was not doing so socially. Zaynab assumed that an Islamic institution like Madraseh Ali, whose students were learning about the Prophet Mohammad's life, would have a kinder, more compassionate atmosphere. She had assumed that the students at Madraseh Ali would be more accommodating. But her everyday reality for the first few months at Madraseh Ali was far from what she had imagined about an institution that sought to produce scholars and practitioners of Islamic teachings. It took her months before she could meet students who would welcome her into their social circles.

She was seen as someone who could negatively affect Madraseh Ali's social environment. How this came about became slightly clearer to me after spending some time with Zaynab outside of Madraseh Ali. It became routine between us to part ways around sunset after eating *meksiki*, a corn delicacy, together in a small shop inside the metro station. Most if not all of the women I spent time with often worried about being home, or at the very least being indoors, by sunset. So on one of the early evenings we were crossing Maydan-e Baharestan, I asked Zaynab if her mother worried because the sun had already set and it was dark outside. Zaynab explained that her mother trusted her, that all she needed to do was call her mother to let her know where she was and what time she would come home. She said part of the reason her mother trusted her was because she tried her best

to follow her mother's instructions, which were often given with Islamic explanations. She made an effort to be home not much longer after the sun set, even when
she was with her sister or her cousins.

What Zaynab did in these moments was unconventional for many of the
howzevi I met across the various institutions, and Zaynab knew that saying the
"wrong" things around her classmates would put her at a disadvantage, so she kept
these experiences to herself. But these kinds of decisions eventually became the
subject of conversations between students at Madraseh Ali. "It was a problem for
them," Zaynab explained. Students did not want to associate with her because of
the way she identified her and her family's religious practices. "We are mazhabi
motavaset," she added without hesitation. In other words, they positioned their
Islamic practices somewhere in the middle of being religiously conservative—not
too extreme and not too reformist.

As I noted previously, I use the category *mazhabi* to prioritize the way the
howzevi used it to describe themselves. But the concept can take on different
meanings depending on the interaction. Sometimes antigovernment Iranians
used it interchangeably with the words *hezbollahi* and *basiji* in derogatory ways.
Among many reference points for the howzevi, however, it was used to refer to a
person's level of adherence to Islamic practices. It was also used as a way to mark
a person's belongingness to a population marginalized before the revolution because they were thought to be too conservative, or not modern enough, for the
shah and his elite circle.

Madraseh Ali was composed of administrators, faculty, and students who observed Islamic practices in ways that would be considered by Iranians as mazhabi.
But that idea of conservative was constituted differently depending on context.
Zaynab's experience at Madraseh Ali illustrated the way the category of *religiously
conservative* and *mazhabi* or *hezbollahi* were in essence quite unstable. Demarca-
tions were made even between those who were considered religiously conservative in their practices based on the conservative way they were assumed to be.
What students considered at the center of their practices determined what they
thought of as part of the norm. Where they located the center at any given time
was not always predetermined. But at any given time, there were those among
them who were considered not religious enough. A student's position in all this
depended on markers such as the way she behaved, dressed, spoke, and was spoken of, and the way individuals or groups read these markers in relation to their
own. We saw the way these were relative in Maryam's examples in a previous
chapter. She would wait for a few minutes before sitting on a seat in the metro that
a man had previously been sitting on, a practice she did not consider to be extreme
in the spectrum of actions. Yet she considered the practice of a man tapping on
the phone when a woman answered to be extreme.

By identifying as a mazhabi motavaset, Zaynab was also acknowledging the sociopolitical polarization taking place in Iran since the end of the Iran-Iraq War based on markers of religiosity or lack thereof, like the black chador versus the bad hijab or a full beard versus a bare face. These markers were then translated into the pro- versus anti-government binary, pro-government as those who appeared to be religiously conservative and anti-government, in Zaynab's words, as "the ones who are fashion." More specifically, she identified Madraseh Ali students as religiously conservative, mazhabi, and her friends in an English language class as either political reformists or secular. Although these designations, reform and secular, are quite complex terms, she combined them under the label *secular modern*: Iranians who wanted to be like Americans and Europeans. In this framework, mazhabi and secular modern were on opposite ends of this Us versus Them divide. But as I explain, for Zaynab all of these designations were constantly moving points, with Zaynab's motavaset positioned in the middle of any two points.

Although Zaynab's explanation teetered on a mere caricature of a phenomenon that was clearly more complex, her story was actually evidence of this complexity. As arbitrary as these designations may have been, they were divisive. Having spent time with both the howzevi and their families and my friends who identified as reformist or secular modern, I was made aware that they did not like each other much. Each imagined the other as unfit to determine the future of Iran. Both imagined the other as The Other, as uneducated and not nearly as human as themselves. Located in this othering process, Zaynab often found herself cast out by either side. She tried her best to, in her words, address this polarization Islamically by confronting the problem of exclusion wherever she encountered it. She saw these moments as a testing ground for her years of strengthening her resolve to develop sincerity and humility toward God.

Positioning herself as motavaset—that is, average or in the middle—gave her enough leeway to be inclusive of either side of the pole, but she was not everyone's friend. Rather, she became friends with people who wanted to become friends with her. There was a difference. She didn't see herself as someone who compromised her principles in order to belong but rather as a person who knew the way to highlight aspects of her practices in a way that people from both groups could relate to. Thus, identifying her practices as motavaset signaled them as relatable.

Figuring out the difference between what constituted mazhabi and secular modern often involved people identifying themselves as nonreligious by pointing out the dress code they abided by or that they hated the government. Trying to read the difference between being mazhabi and mazhabi motavaset was not as straightforward to me. There was not much in Zaynab's practices that were particularly different from the lifeways of other students. I could not see much of a difference between the two, except in what Zaynab and her family would decide to do with their bodies in certain spaces and moments, in what Mauss referred to as the miscellaneous moments that appeared to be insignificant or minute to untrained eyes like mine.

During the weekends in the summer months, Zaynab and her family picnicked in the evening at their neighborhood park where she and her cousins spent time riding bicycles. Having men in the vicinity was not much of a concern for Zaynab and her family, unlike the other howzevi families. She was with her family, and they were all properly clothed according to Islamic teachings. Zaynab's mother and aunt would sometimes take her and her cousins to the movie theater, given that the government vetted publicly shown films. There was no harm going to the theaters as long as they went as a group, observed what they considered modest behavior, and, again, were properly clothed.

Zaynab described these choices as "acting upon the narrations of the Prophet and his family in everything, even in herself . . . in a logical way." That is, while she observed rituals and practices and sought Islamic knowledge, she made an effort to be effective in properly applying Islamic practices at the right time and place. The problem, of course, was that the right time and place were neither fixed nor universal. Riding a bicycle was considered shameful for many of the howzevi, much less riding in the vicinity of men who were not family members. Going to a movie theater was uncommon for howzevi families unless it was part of a Madraseh Ali field trip to view a religious-themed film.

Although it was Islamically acceptable to do or not do these things, in practice, Islamically permissible actions did not trump individual preference for whom or whom not to be friends with. The students were wary of Zaynab's influence over their practices. Like Farideh, who described her childhood friend as someone who became bad hijabi when she left for Tehran, perhaps they feared that Zaynab would eventually influence them to disregard their religious practices, to the point of diminishing the importance of sincerity and humility toward God. Through this line of reasoning, the students were unable to consider how similar Zaynab's family life had been to theirs. By focusing on the way she was different from them, they were not giving themselves a chance to see what they had in common. As a result, Zaynab felt rejected.

The Response

Some students openly admonished Zaynab for her views, especially when it came to her choice of clothing. Mahboobeh was one of those students. The teachers, staff members, and students at Madraseh Ali wore their manto, the long coat worn over the pants and underneath the chador, at least one inch below their knees. Zaynab arrived one morning wearing the black chador as usual, but her manto fell just above her knees. Although Zaynab was fully covered with her headscarf, pants, and manto and the black chador, Mahboobeh challenged Zaynab to provide legal justification for her decision. She and her friends pressed Zaynab to never to wear something above the knee ever again.

Zaynab did not budge. She argued that she was within the bounds of the proper dress code because she was fully covered, in loose-fitting clothes at that. Wearing the manto below, at, or slightly above the knee were choices within what were considered Islamically permissible since her manto was not tight fitting and it exposed only her hands. Zaynab explained that it was difficult to constantly defend herself. She shrugged her shoulders while explaining, "If you don't like it, okay. But this is me. I am Zaynab."

Instead of folding to the pressure, Zaynab continued to identify herself as mazhabi motavaset. She did so with an emphasis on motavaset, leaning slightly in the opposite direction of mazhabi. Meaning, she acknowledged that the norm in Madraseh Ali was to be mazhabi in ways that differed from hers as students around her made decisions about what to do with their bodies, like wearing a longer manto, not walking through areas full of men, not riding bicycles, and so on. She did not consider that her practices should be the norm but only relatable to the existing norm. But at the same time, she would highlight their commonalities.

To illustrate, she, like the other howzevi, avoided laughing out loud in public to avoid "catching attention," as they would say. Yet on her own, Zaynab did not avoid spaces where unrelated men and women socially interacted or exhibited public displays of affection that the other howzevi would avoid. She would not have been able to stake a claim at the *mazhabi* of mazhabi motavaset without the black chador. Therefore, even though she continued to wear different lengths of manto, she consistently wore the black chador, the most obvious signifier of what they had in common. Again, her purpose was not necessarily to uproot the norm. She hoped that those around her would expand what they considered Islamically acceptable practices. By merely being present among them, she was asking them to acknowledge the possibility that being motavaset was still part of being mazhabi. Regardless of whether her manto was one inch above her knee or below midcalf, together they were still women who sought to be close to God, loved the Prophet and his family, cherished their families, and worked toward safeguarding the ideals of the revolution.

Though disappointed, she believed there were students who would be open to accommodating her presence. One way to meet them would be to continue drawing a distinction between her and the existing circle of exclusion that made her social life difficult. Therefore, she also knew when and the way to differentiate herself from those who excluded her, particularly those who were closed off to the different ways people observed Shi'i religious practices. In this formulation, she needed to authenticate her knowledge of Islamic text through her actions, not by blindly following. She needed to trust her years of practice to strengthen her knowledge or test out which scholarly interpretation of Islamic text applied to which situation. In other words, to put into practice what she was actually training for: perform ijtihad, interpret Islamic text, apply it to herself first and foremost, and find "the average" between two courses of action. Considering when it had been appropriate to do so, she drew this dividing line by being vocal about two issues: marriage and her effort outside Madraseh Ali to develop friendships with women who were not religiously conservative.

MAKING FRIENDS OUTSIDE THE HOWZEH

Zaynab was outspoken about making friends with people from different religious practices and with people who did not identify as religious. Many of her friends at Madraseh Ali avoided Iranians who were considered not religious, or not religious enough. But not Zaynab. Unlike her friends who would use *bad hijabi* as a way to describe women who were not mazhabi, Zaynab used the words *modern*, *fashion*, or *vogue* to describe women who publicly interacted with men and did not wear the hijab like her, not so much in admiration but as a way to avoid considering herself more favored by God than they were.

Zaynab made these kinds of friendships a major part of her educative purpose and, more importantly, her religious practice. Inspired by Shahid Aval's Islamic teachings on the importance of seeking Islamic knowledge and nurturing unity among Muslims, Zaynab hoped to inspire others to guard themselves against the divide-and-conquer techniques of the Europeans and Americans. Shahid Aval (d. 1385), born Mohammad Jamaluddin al-Makki al-Amili al-Jizzinni, studied throughout his life with Sunni and Shi'i scholars in different regions of the Islamic world and excelled in the scholarship of both traditions. The only way he could gain Islamic knowledge from Sunni scholars was through *taqiyya*, the denial of his religious belief in the face of persecution. Although Shahid Aval taught unity among Muslims, in the end he was imprisoned, where he would write his book *Al-Lum'e ad-Dameshqiya* in a short period of time. He was then beheaded, crucified, and stoned. He was called Shahid Aval, the first martyr, because of the brutality of the way he was killed.

Zaynab explained that if Iranian youth in the universities learned about his struggle against persecution as a Shi'i jurist and his martyrdom, they would understand that the Soft War (the Western onslaught to corrupt Iranian society through the media) was a similar kind of persecution. She saw parallels with the way the Islamic Republic and its supporters were being persecuted through economic and political sanctions while being bombarded with anti-government programming on satellite channels and compared this with Shahid Aval's experience of having to avoid discrimination in a predominantly Sunni Islamic world. But that conversation would not be possible if religiously conservative Iranians were to continue excluding and disavowing themselves from those they thought were not religious enough. She explained, "If someone is mazhabi, trying to be correct in everything, and avoiding talking to men or avoiding talking to women, it is acceptable. But in today's society, it is necessary for us to have some connection with everyone in order to share our reasoning with each other." So she purposely made an effort to make friends with women who did not appear to have something in common with her. Although she had already been learning English during her first two years at Madraseh Ali, Zaynab enrolled in an English language institute in Sabalan in an effort to make these kinds of connections. Knowing how to speak in English would allow her to connect, as she said, with other girls her age who were not mazhabi.

To her friends in her English language class, Zaynab was also a mazhabi motavaset. But, unlike her interaction with her classmates at Madraseh Ali, where she highlighted being motavaset, here she leaned toward being mazhabi. Zaynab was open to becoming friends with women in the English class as long as they continued to acknowledge that practices like her prayers and wearing the chador were a part of her presence with them. "I have confidence that I have the ability to get their trust," she added. By becoming a familiar face among them, she was asking them to consider the mazhabi part of the motavaset. "At the first session, no one spoke to me, no one answered my greeting, because I wear chador. After that, when they saw that I could debate them in English, using logic, we agreed and they slowly accepted me. After four or five sessions we became friendly with each other," Zaynab described. Having an understanding of differences of opinion and ways of life was important in her practice. After all, she was not alone in this endeavor. She had a loving family who understood what she was trying to do.

"Saba Is Full of Surprises"

The other issue Zaynab held strong opinions about was delaying marriage in favor of a good Islamic education. For her, having completed some form of higher education was an important component of raising a family, and she did not hold back when debating other students about this. "I want to be married, but my father forced me to be here," one of them said to Zaynab. Many had already wanted to be married in high school or right after high school, before starting courses at Madraseh Ali. They expected to be married as soon as it was possible for them to do so. Zaynab rejected the marital expectations some of her classmates placed on themselves at a young age: "not everyone could be as fortunate as my mother, who got married to a good Shi'i man at a very young age." She was hopeful that in the years to come, her friends would change their minds: "When I was in high school, I used to think this way [like them]. When I came here, I changed my opinion. I think this will also change for them. I think when people study more, they find something that changes their aims in life."

By being firm in her stance on these two issues, she hoped that other students would eventually understand her, or that other students who shared her views would also come forward. It worked. Her situation would soon change after meeting Saba. They came together on one issue—they did not want to be married. Not just yet, at least. And although they did not completely agree on everything, Zaynab and Saba thought highly of each other. Once they joined forces, they no longer felt like the odd ones out. Zaynab described Saba as "full of surprises, and unlike the other students." Many students did not have plans to further their education and wanted to be married. Not Saba—she was not planning to get married right away after finishing her program. The students who planned to further pursue their education intended to continue studying the Islamic sciences. Also, not Saba. She wanted to become a highly respected journalist in Iran.

Zaynab and Saba were the same age and shared many interests outside their focus of study: chocolate, candies, and different colors of pens, ice cream, and fashion sensibilities. The inside jokes they shared indicated continued interrogation of the value of their practices. It helped them to press forward. They became mobaheseh partners from the start of their friendship and moved through social spaces together. Together they began expanding their social circle. Theorizing on the events leading up to Arab Spring also became a popular topic of conversation. Sharing food with other students during break time provided opportunities for conversations. They spoke of their mothers' cooking.

Zaynab would tell her newfound friends stories of her mother, Azadeh, with pride. That every year Azadeh would host an *eftar* dinner, the breaking of fast, several times during the month, where she and her daughters would decorate their house and prepare the large sofreh for her cooking. Zaynab shared stories of the way Azadeh took her places where they could experience a kind of closeness to God together, to contemplate and pray. Zaynab was very open with others on the way she confided in Azadeh about her feelings, challenges, decisions, and future plans without the threat of rebuke. "Whenever I encounter a hard situation in life, I remember whose daughter I am: my mom's. Because she is a strong Shi'i woman who does everything to educate herself in Islam and then bring it to real life," Zaynab explained one late afternoon. She did not want to disappoint her mother. Perhaps it was at this juncture, with the spotlight on the importance of Azadeh in Zaynab's life, that through time the other students began to understand the way Zaynab made decisions about what to do with her body in those moments when they would decide otherwise.

Figure 6.2. Azadeh's cooking; Zaynab initially developed common ground with her classmates by talking about her mother's cooking. Tehran, 2011. ©Amina Tawasil.

With Saba standing by her side, Zaynab brought the motavaset to the mazhabi. She was not the only one. As time passed, she realized there were other women like them in the more senior cohort, women who did not quite fit in because of their varied conservative practices but who eventually made their way through Madraseh Ali and created their own circles. By the time I met Zaynab and her friends, Mahboobeh and her friends were joining us in the library every afternoon.

Figure 6.3. One side of Zaynab's room. Tehran, 2011. ©Amina Tawasil.

They had been attending different elegies together with women who were given permission to do so. Sitting on a park bench one afternoon, Zaynab explained to me that she was excited to start reading books that were required to become part of Ayatollah Khamenei's and Larijani's Dars-e Kharij classes. She was enthusiastic about the possibility of reaching that level of study and her overall future. Beaming with a smile, she said to me, "Iran is the best democracy."

THE CHALLENGES OF BELONGING

This chapter looked closely at what the work of belonging in the howzeh social circles entailed. These two narratives reveal two key points. First, the Madraseh Ali social atmosphere expands. It is not fixed in place and time because of the social interactions that take place between howzevi women that, in turn, are also influenced by the systemic transformations I explained in previous chapters. Second, it tells us that the work of khod shenasi is not predictably linear. The way howzevi women consider the work of khod shenasi differs depending on the circumstances and the nature of their difficulties.

Both women experienced exclusion and rejection, but the context of their experiences and the way they confront these challenges differed. These differences teach us about their surroundings, the people around them, and what aspects of their codes of conduct are important for them. The work of khod shenasi for them is both a personal and a collective endeavor. Farideh's initial interest in improving her character developed into an interest in solving a social problem. She took action by moving to Tehran and educating herself through a master's degree at Madraseh Ali. In the process, she gained credibility among her family members and neighbors back in her hometown but also had great difficulty with gaining access to opportunities. Keen to the differing interpretations of regulations, but also staying within the bounds of moral expectations, she often came up with creative solutions to address her challenges. Without familial support in Tehran, she and her roommate, Aliyeh, relied on each other.

Having had the experience of living in Tehran and interacting with Iranian youth of her generation, Zaynab's khod shenasi involved the struggle of living morally with those who did not share a similar religious background as her. She sought to develop a common understanding between them—that is, to pull both the religiously conservative and nonpracticing Iranian youth to understand each other on common grounds. To make her way through Madraseh Ali's social circles, Zaynab depended on the fluidity of interpretations of Islamic rulings regarding bodily practices and hoped others would recognize these. Zaynab's mother, Azadeh, was an important figure in motivating her to continue pursuing her goals. Through continued participation, she and those around her recognized their commonalities and eventually became friends. She, along with her friend Saba, created and, in time, joined other social circles.

A deductive approach would not have captured the nuances that make the experiences of women relatable. As we have learned, not all experiences, histories, and contexts are the same even within one social grouping. In the following chapter, I look at another category of experience—the howzevi marriage. Married women experience the work of khod shenasi in the howzeh with added responsibilities such as fulfilling marital obligations, maintaining the household, and raising children.

NOTE

1. Momen, *Introduction to Shi'i Islam*, 28.

SEVEN

—✵—

A HOWZEVI MARRIAGE[1]

WE LEFT THE VILLAGE OF Mashhad-e Ardehal en route to Kashan about forty-five kilometers away. We had just exited a one-lane road onto a freeway soaked in illusions of water bouncing off the asphalt. This heat wave in mid-October made it unbearably hot. The Saipa's air conditioner did not make a difference. When I fell asleep, Maryam, sitting in front of me on the passenger side, had been breastfeeding Fereshteh. I could feel the hot air on my forehead because the car windows were slightly open. When I woke up, Maryam was peeling an orange, tearing a piece, and removing its pith with her small fingers. She leaned slightly to her left to place the orange onto Mohammad's lips. Mohammad opened his mouth, and his bearded jaw moved about while eating the orange. A few seconds later, Mohammad unfolded the palm of his right hand to signal for another piece of orange. Maryam put two in his hand, and as she had done earlier, he tore a piece and placed the piece of orange to her lips. The baby was fast asleep even as the wind blew through the top crack of the window. The wind blew onto Maryam's chador, making it appear larger than it should from where I was sitting in the back. Sensing my movement, she turned her head. "Amine, did you sleep okay?"

Maryam had once mentioned to me that traveling was a good way to get to know someone because the challenges of a long journey expose a person's core, their character strengths and weaknesses. We learned a great deal about each other on this trip. I saw moments of tenderness between Maryam and Mohammad often hidden from strangers. Public displays of affection between husbands and wives were considered shameful among many Iranians I knew, but especially among the religiously conservative. Rather than husbands expressing care, I had seen more making pesky comments to their wives in front of other relatives in order to prevent their mothers from feeling jealous toward their wives. On this trip to Kashan, I also became acquainted with Maryam's brothers in the Qom seminaries, their families, and her younger sister who was studying English literature in the city of Yazd.

Maryam had been married seven years to Mohammad when we took this trip. She had given birth to her daughter the previous year, which she described: "When I was younger, I did not think it was possible for a woman to fall in love with her child, but when I first saw Fereshteh, I fell in love with her." Maryam was a doctoral student in the field of Islamic jurisprudence and civil and private law at Madraseh Ali, where she also taught courses in Islamic law. When I asked Maryam why she had chosen to study private law, she said, "Private law is a safe field for women. Many things about family and society can be changed in private law." She stood five feet and one inch tall, shorter than many of her colleagues and students. Yet when she entered the room, she commanded attention by her mere presence. When she spoke, women listened. It was difficult to ignore the way other women, her colleagues and students, spoke about her and her knowledge with high regard. One source of her strength was the arena of mobaheseh and bahes in the classroom. She was quick, fiercely detailed, and precise. She had also earned a reputation among her students as a stern and highly knowledgeable teacher. When Maryam and I met in 2008, she was one of only twelve women and one of the youngest women in Ayatollah Khamenei's Dars-e Kharij class. By the end of 2011, Maryam had already been a student in the howzeh elmiyeh for fourteen years.

In the previous chapters, I provided examples of the way the howzevi discussed matters related to marriage in moments of disputation. I also noted that husbands and family were important for the educative mobility of many. This chapter looks at what the work of khod shenasi looks like when a young woman from a small town aspires to do her best both as a student of Islamic knowledge and as a wife and mother. I describe her actions to meet social, familial, and self expectations and what was made possible out of those actions.

The chapter is also about her family: what they did with and for each other. In Maryam's daily life, both aspirations became a source of frustration and hardship. Pregnancy and then childrearing, student teaching, and studying for her classes eventually became strenuous. But while I understood these to be in competition with each other for her time and energy, Maryam considered them to be part of her lifelong struggle of khod shenasi, to live in the material world, alam-e tabiat o madeh, while attempting to become part of the howzeh where she, like Farideh and Zaynab, experienced and overcame exclusion. Much of what follows is about Maryam's work to abide by Islamic teachings that seem incongruous. She regarded marriage and bearing and raising children as deeply meaningful aspects

of her life but also deemed Islamic education as a requisite to becoming an effective educator in the home and for future generations, all in remembrance of
God. Maryam's attempt to balance these aspirations reflects both the regulatory
and the emancipatory aspects of the human condition and again are relatable to
women in general who aspire for both motherhood and having an education.[2]
However, the way Maryam navigates the complexities of her practice and her situation demonstrates her resolve in her commitment to her Islamic practices. She is
not interested in other forms of womanhood. This is critical in our understanding
of howzevi women like Maryam.

WHERE I ARRIVED FROM

Maryam was born and raised in Najaf Abad, considered one of the most religiously conservative towns in Iran. It was unlike the other towns and villages I
had visited when it came to the practice of wearing the black chador. Although
the black chador was a marker of religious conservatism, my status as a foreigner
in the other places I had visited exempted me from having to wear it. This was
not an option during my two visits to Najaf Abad. Maryam was required to wear
the black chador and strictly observed gender separation in public settings from
a young age. Like many young girls who grew up in Najaf Abad, she observed
certain behaviors when walking down the street. She would keep her head down
if there were men in the vicinity. She would avoid looking inside the stores as she
passed in case a man was standing in the doorway, who might misunderstand her
quick glance as an invitation to speak to her.

Najaf Abad was infamous for being religiously conservative but also for being
openly anti-government. Its identity as both proves that the religiously conservative population in Iran is not a monolith. Many do not support the Islamic Republic as it stands. Prominent figures continued to challenge the religious legitimacy
of the Islamic Republic and the institution of Vilayet-e Faqih, the guardianship
of the Islamic jurist—the position occupied by Ayatollah Khamenei and, before
him, Ayatollah Khomeini. This was visibly demonstrated in public space. The
pictures on street corners, billboards, and behind-the-store-counter walls did not
have Ayatollah Khamenei's photo as they did in Tehran and other cities. In his
place were pictures of Ayatollah Hussein Ali Montazeri (d. 2009), a high-ranking
cleric who disagreed with Ayatollah Khomeini in 1989 over government policies.
Montazeri's seminaries were closed sporadically after this disagreement as he
remained one of the main critics of the Islamic Republic's policies. Montazeri
argued that Iran was not being governed as the Islamic state it should be.

Maryam rarely commented on Najaf Abad's political resistance. Instead, she
called attention to its strong Shi'i identity and that it, like the city of Qom, had

been a hotbed of uprisings against the shah in 1979. She was proud to point out that it had the highest number of martyrs during the Iran-Iraq War, and one of its villages, Hajiabad, had the highest number of martyrs of all the villages in Iran. It also had the highest number of volunteers per capita, second only to Tehran. Thirteen men in her family died during the Iran-Iraq War. She kept a photo of her mother's youngest brother wrapped in a green cloth. One of her uncles almost died and underwent chest wall reconstruction. He explained that the men in Najaf Abad during the war would use *peshkel mochalag*, a pregnant female donkey's dried manure, to disinfect their wounds because it had a high content of antibiotics. They burned the *peshkel* and fanned its smoke over their wounds. They resorted to this because the United States' sanctions against Iran prevented the import of medicine during the war.

Maryam's family was her cornerstone. Her father, Abbas, was a professor of Islamic philosophy who had published a book on Allameh Tabatabei's work right before I left Iran. He had been an ardent follower of Ali Shariati in his youth, and before the revolution, he had memorized Shariati's speeches to recite them to others. Whenever Maryam mentioned this about her father, she often followed with words of admiration for the way her father had risked his life in spreading the words of revolution against the shah, whom they considered a tyrant. Maryam thought that Abbas was not at all unreasonably conservative. He supported decisions within the family as long as they remained within the bounds of Islamic law. For instance, he often gave Maryam's mother permission to travel to Qom and Tehran to learn Islamic-based healing methods. Maryam's mother, Hojar, became an expert healer using methods like cupping and medicinal leech applications.

Maryam attended a mathematics and science high school and thought she would eventually pursue a career in either one. Her father encouraged her to do so. But when her older brother, Hassan, left home to study in a men's howzeh in Qom, she began to change her mind. His visits back home impacted the way she envisioned her future self. Kindness and gentleness were at the heart of what attracted Maryam to her brother Hassan's demeanor: "When he would come home, he would always show my mother kindness, and his manners were very beautiful. . . . And he would teach me new things he had learned about the manners of the Prophet's family. It was unusual for me . . . and I knew I wanted to study what he was studying. So, I did."

During Maryam's third year in high school, when she was about fifteen years old, Abbas gave her permission to apply to a reputable howzeh in Tehran. She was eventually accepted into Howzeh-ye Chizar, where he accompanied her for an interview. When Maryam became more informed about student life at Chizar during that interview, she worried she might not excel because of the course load and because she felt she would not be mature enough to live away from home. The thought of living in Tehran by herself was a source of apprehension. She asked the administrator for advice on what would be best for a girl her age. The administrator advised her to return to Najaf Abad to complete high school and to explore other interests while she was young. After careful consideration, Maryam could then decide if she still wanted to study in the howzeh.

THE SHARPNESS OF BEING SUBTLE

After graduating from high school, Maryam was accepted to Jami'at Al-Zahra in Qom and Madraseh Ali in Tehran. She visited both places and had a difficult time choosing between them. Abbas made phone calls to his colleagues to ask for their opinions. She eventually chose Madraseh Ali because it provided a small but significant pathway for its students to practice law. While she wanted to use her Islamic education to better herself and her family, she was also deeply influenced by her father's work during the revolution. She wanted to use her education for the betterment of creating society that prioritized the worship of God and mutual respect over accumulation of wealth and imitating Europeans and Americans.

Maryam explained her delight when she learned that in the year she was accepted, Madraseh Ali had just opened a campus in Yazd, a smaller city southwest of Najaf Abad. She no longer worried about having to live in Tehran. But choosing a campus was the least of her problems. Since she came from a mathematics and science high school, she did not have the fundamental skills to do well in the howzeh system. Maryam had two significant challenges: unfamiliarity with the contents of the readings and reading jurisprudent Arabic.

Students initially would not include her in their mobaheseh for these reasons, but very early on it became clear to Maryam that the space where one learns about khod shenasi could also be a space of exclusion for all sorts of reasons. Fortunately, Maryam had been learning Arabic grammatical structure since she was in fifth grade from her father. To review Arabic for his own research, Maryam's father would go over his lessons with Maryam, her siblings, and sometimes his younger brothers-in-law for a few minutes after every *Fajr*, the pre-sunrise prayer. One unintended consequence of this was that years later it allowed Maryam to build on what she already knew. Maryam then requested a list of foundational books from her brother Hassan in Qom. She labored independently through these books during her first year in Yazd, often making phone calls to Hassan, who would take time to explain jurisprudent language and philosophical concepts. It was extremely challenging. There were times she could not reach Hassan for days because he was busy, and access to a telephone was hard to come by. There was only one telephone in her dormitory, and mobile phones were not yet available. I found out from Mohammad later on that Maryam eventually ranked first in her class until she graduated.

Although socializing and making friends were not her immediate priorities, Maryam also found it hard to gain acceptance into the existing social circles at first. Some students wrote comments next to her name when the list of rankings was posted. She ignored them at first, but she eventually became friends with some of the women who wrote them. As a young woman from a small town with very little exposure to social interactions outside her extended family in Najaf Abad, she also came to realize that people attempting to abide by Islamic teachings were struggling with themselves and their propensities in different ways. Some worked against their tendencies to become complacent in being led by others, some to see themselves as better than others. Some struggled to force themselves to do what they did not want to do beyond Islamic practices. Out of these friendships, she came to understand that some students were forced by their families to be in school. At least two students wanted to be married instead. One student who eventually became her good friend purposely did things to get expelled from Madraseh Ali.

Finding a sense of belonging in Madraseh Ali in Yazd was an ongoing project. Having been raised in Najaf Abad with all its complexities, Maryam sometimes had to put in extra work to signal where she positioned herself in relation to her town's conventional image. For instance, because of Najaf Abad's anti-government stance, she sometimes had to drop clues about which Marja'e Taqlid she followed—Ayatollah Khamenei. Conversely, by being a supporter of Ayatollah Khamenei, she engaged in similar kinds of signaling work when in Najaf Abad to show that she held the same Shi'i morals and values against the threat of foreign enemies. Beyond navigating political identities, however, Maryam's detailed knowledge of the rules of acts of worship and the way to appropriately relay this knowledge enabled her to make her way from being a howzevi at the edges of Madraseh Ali's social circles to becoming a respected howzevi. Her actions, and her attempts to imitate the Prophet as best as she could, marked her as an individual who placed the work of khod shenasi at the center of her everyday experiences.

"I am very detailed," Maryam once mentioned in passing. She had a knack for paying close attention to the finest details of her worship practices, from performing her prayers to feeding her guests. She took her time to do ablutions before each prayer and made certain that both her prayer area and clothing were clean beforehand. Her discussions with her father and brothers on the way to properly carry out daily rituals fueled this serious concern for meticulousness. Maryam felt that this kind of concern warranted an explanation. The expression of sincerity in a prayer included the thoroughness involved in its preparation, thus its production. For instance, neglectful behavior or a lack of attention to its preparation and

delivery might cause a prayer to become invalid. This kind of attention was especially important when she prayed behind a prayer leader. She held them accountable in a similar way as she held herself accountable. Making sure that each of her
daily prayers was in order was part of her self-surveillance to achieve self-knowing.

She told me a story about the time she realized the power of knowing the
proper ways of doing acts of worship. She and her high school classmates once
traveled to north Iran for a fieldtrip, where a clergyman ended up leading the
group prayer. Maryam at one point heard him pronounce an extra letter, *vav*,
after the *sajdah* (prostration). This concerned Maryam because she knew that a
leader's mistake in prayer was also considered a follower's mistake in prayer. She
approached him after the prayer and asked him to repeat what he had said after
the prostration, and he again pronounced the extra *vav*. Maryam informed him of
his mistake. By her correcting him, both of them knew if he had indeed made this
error, he might have also invalidated everyone else's prayer. Embarrassed, he disagreed with Maryam by reciting the line repeatedly. But he continued to commit
the same mistake until he finally admitted his blunder. This, for Maryam, was an
example of the way gaining Islamic knowledge strengthened one's determination
against any disposition to become lazy in worship. It was through the knowledge
of these details that she began to realize the dangers of following and imitating a
leader blindly. In addition to the examples I've mentioned, she also realized that
sometimes, in order to protect her previous efforts at khod shenasi, she needed
to challenge others, including men in positions of authority.

A similar event took place at Madraseh Ali. Maryam once joined a group of
women in prayer and, again, she heard the clergyman mispronounce one letter
in Arabic over the microphone. She doubted herself, worrying that perhaps she
had heard wrong because she was in the women's section. Out of concern that her
prayer would be invalidated, she did not join the group the next day. She listened
to the clergyman's prayer recitation instead. Maryam found a pronunciation error and checked the books for the rules pertaining to it. From that moment, she
stopped taking part in the group prayer. One of the students noticed this and
asked why she no longer joined them. Maryam explained his mistake and that
she worried her prayer may be invalidated because of that. Although this student
accused her of wrongdoing, of arrogance in thinking she knew better than the
clergyman, other students listened to her explanation. Maryam went on her way
after she explained her decision, but she also gained a kind of recognition from
other students afterward. This was so, in part, because she did not insist that she
knew better than anyone, only that she had caught an error and did not want to
risk invalidating her prayer. She left the option for others to do their own inquiry.

The number of students who prayed behind the cleric dwindled through time.
Maryam presumed others might have also discovered his error on their own.

In the handful of conversations about this occurrence, Maryam deflected any responsibility for the way other students began to pay attention to the cleric's recitation. When I pressed her for clarification, she merely expressed uncertainty about whether she had made an impact on the other students' decisions. "I really don't know," she quipped.

This point is critical for what I may have missed because of my own predispositions as a Muslim woman from the United States raised with the imagination that Muslim women must take credit and lead in order to show white middle-class Americans that we could. My urge to interpret, at this point, to diagnose such efforts to reject taking credit for upending a man's authority as low self-esteem, no doubt comes from my assumption about the way women should exist in the world. I had previously assumed that if women must do for themselves to cause change, then they should take credit so other women would follow. Imposing my bias would not have made sense because by the time I met Maryam, all eyes and ears were on her whenever she entered a room. Had I gone in this analytical direction, I would have missed the opportunity to understand, or to experience for myself, the way she developed this presence by imposing forms of self-discipline that came from her understanding of morality and ethics.

Putting together most of my experiences with Maryam, I became more aware that khod shenasi for her included expressions of uncertainty that signaled to herself, and perhaps to me, that she was attempting to reinstate her sense of humility. This reminds us that practices around anonymity can be carried out while being visibly present and impacting those around. This includes being in a publicly visible role. Questioning one's conclusions, hesitation in certain moments, keeping verbal pronouncements of achievements to the self, and avoiding taking credit for an action were markers of someone working against their lesser tendencies to become attached to the outcome of their actions. This was an important aspect of Maryam's work of khod shenasi and very much tied to the practice of anonymity among the howzevi, a concept I explained in a previous chapter.

It was impossible for me to determine whether Maryam was in fact experiencing feelings of humility. But by questioning the impact of her decision to stop following the clergyman in prayer, Maryam was simultaneously expressing her understanding that a godly Shi'i would be very careful to stake a claim of having led some kind of collective resistance. In the howzevi constellation of practices, taking the lead became palpable only in the context of humility as practice. The consideration of whether others saw Maryam as someone with authority to lead was made possible only under the rubric that she did not see or consider herself qualified to take the lead. Maryam did not see herself as a leader of that moment. She expressed self-doubt numerous times. This was a check on herself: Am I thinking I am better than others? Am I forgetting that all possibilities come from

Figure 7.1. Maryam and Fereshteh. ©Amina Tawasil.

God? Am I doing this for the sake of God, for me, or for people to praise me? In everyday occurrences, expressed self-doubt became an unintended invitation for others to claim certainty of her credibility, which is itself rooted in self-doubt.

AN ECONOMIC TRANSACTION

Mohammad and Maryam considered themselves an unlikely couple because they came from opposite sides of Iran. He was Azeri, and she was Esfahani. Maryam chose to marry Mohammad for the same reasons he chose her: to struggle to do the work of khod shenasi together and to raise a family that would do the same. This included becoming prepared to defend Iran with a government that ideally sought to foster this approach to life. Taking advantage of having access to a religious education was one of the many avenues to do so. Like Maryam, whose research and work were geared toward bolstering an Islamic society, Mohammad was also involved in Islamic-based projects. When I arrived in Tehran in 2010, he was helping to produce advertising materials for a religious film he and his friends had helped to finance.

Maryam's father added a stipulation to their marriage contract that obligated Mohammad to make certain Maryam completed a PhD and other advanced degrees in a field of her choice. This meant he needed to provide full financial and physical support. More specifically, the stipulation required that Maryam must finish a doctoral program before having their first child. With like-minded goals to help support the creation of the Islamic Republic, Mohammad and Maryam's father agreed on this condition. When the couple returned to Tehran, Ayatollah Emami-Kashani, the head of Madraseh Ali and a close advisor to Ayatollah Khamenei, led the marriage ceremony in his office in the presence of a handful of their friends. Six months after Maryam's father signed the marriage contract, she and Mohammad traveled to Mashhad to consummate the marriage and begin living together. Maryam sometimes reminisced while looking at photos of their early years together, picnicking in her grandfather's orchards. She sometimes posed with her hijab, sometimes without, and sometimes they were in each other's arms. Mohammad considered himself a Tehrani, or a person from Tehran, but specifically a native of Pirouzi. But his family was from a village near Tabriz in the Azeri region. Mohammad's mother was twelve years old when she married Mohammad's father, who was twenty years old. She was a carpet weaver and had her first child at sixteen. She moved from the safety of her village home to the isolation of living in Pirouzi without other family members nearby. She cooked, cleaned, and took care of toddlers all at once without any help. "She is rare in today's Iran," Mohammad described, "a symbol of strength."

Mohammad shared stories of playing in the streets of Pirouzi and attending Alborz high school, which used to be an American educational institution before the revolution. A picture of Mohammad at eleven years old hung near Maryam's doorway. When I mistakenly guessed his age in the photo as fifteen, he smiled from ear to ear while correcting me: "Eleven." That prompted our conversation about his experiences during the Iran-Iraq War when he was eleven years old. He heard that boys around his age were already in service. He tried to enlist himself by going to the military barracks. He was ultimately turned away for his age but eventually was assigned to serve food and deliver supplies to the soldiers.

At times, when we drove past the defunct US embassy, Mohammad would point at one of the buildings across the street and recall the times he and his friends had climbed to the top of the building to see the garden on the embassy grounds, what they used to call "the den of spies." One of his older friends who also grew up in Pirouzi had been one of the university students who climbed over the gates to ransack the embassy in November 1979. They wanted to find evidence of the espionage network that operated out of the embassy, but all the papers had already been shredded. That friend eventually became part of a team to piece together the shredded documents, something Mohammad thought was a noble endeavor.

Mohammad grew up helping out in his father's fruit stand at the *maydoon* of the Tehran bazaar. When kiwi made its first appearance in the distant fruit stands, he convinced his father to include kiwi in their fruit selection. This brought in more money for the fruit stand. He gave this experience much credit for his economic endeavors as an adult. He mentioned some of his readings on being an entrepreneur and spoke about Ross Perot's book *My Life and the Principles for Success,* and that he learned from it. He explained to me in very loose terms that he was part of a guild of bazaris—men who pooled their money together and invested in a specific sector of the economy. His guild traded minerals in and out of Iran. At the time, he and his brother had just opened their own laboratory where they could work part-time on mechanical inventions. It was a small room located on the second floor of an almost dilapidated building located south of Tehran, in an area known for collection and distribution of scrap metal.

Mohammad played a pivotal role in continuing to motivate Maryam to pursue her goals. Juggling between being a mother, wife, teacher, and student was extremely difficult for her. The first few months we were together in 2010, she was swamped with household chores, inconsistent sleep patterns, and staying on task with the classes she taught. There were times she lacked focus and confidence in her studies, especially after having the baby. When she felt stagnant in writing her dissertation, Mohammad would remind her, "There is no one else who has studied what you are interested in for years. So you are the master of your research. You must believe this. If you believe this, everything will change."

Etaa'at: A Wife's Obedience

But in all this witnessing of spousal and familial support, I experienced situations I wanted to change. Throughout my time with Maryam and her family, Maryam consistently asked Mohammad for permission to leave the house and other such actions involving her body and her daughter's body. The same held true for the other howzevi. I am quite familiar with the practice of unmarried daughters asking permission from fathers and wives asking permission from their husbands, having been raised in a Muslim family. But I was not used to the extent to which the howzevi observed this practice. I had, for most of my adult life, associated asking permission from a father or a husband with being treated like a child. I make note of this because my urge to save my howzevi friends in those moments resonates with the motivation to save the Muslim woman, oppressed but also dehumanized by benevolent saviors, as Abu-Lughod described in her work. It was not until I returned from Iran that I reflected on this confluence between my impulses and the savior pattern.

As I will explain, Maryam's practice of regularly asking Mohammad for permission was based on a commitment she agreed to when she entered into the marriage contract based on Islamic law. It was an obligation, part of a system of mutual exchange. I position my description of this mutual exchange in the work of khod shenasi as life's purpose. I do so because the outline of "becoming good Shi'i Muslims together" for Maryam and Mohammad constituted the work of khod shenasi. The purpose of marriage in this context was to enter into a union with another person who was also doing the work of khod shenasi.

Part of khod shenasi is becoming learned in interpretations of Islamic law because Islamic law, in its essence, is what prevents the social normalization of the self's lesser tendencies like greed, anger, envy, arrogance, and so on. To abide by Islamic laws is to help turn oneself against these pitfalls through growing self-awareness. Thus, Islamic jurisprudence informed the marriage contract, Islamic conceptualization of the reproductive system, and the way the howzevi reconciled these and other parts of their lives.

Maryam explained matter-of-factly that in Shi'i Islamic law, the marriage contract was considered an economic transaction. There were two kinds of contracts for marriage, permanent and temporary. By entering into a permanent marriage contract, the woman was likened to the seller of access to her womb. In other words, she would be offering the buyer, the potential husband, access to her womb, by which she meant sexual intercourse that involved the husband's penis penetrating the wife's vagina. This was not a contract of sale for the entire body of the woman, only of access to her sexual and reproductive organs. Two forms of payment for this access were the *mehriye*, or the bridal payment, the amount of which was predetermined by both parties, and the nafaqeh. That is, by purchasing access to the womb, the man is obligated to give the woman nafaqeh, the full financial upkeep throughout the marriage at the socioeconomic standard she had been brought up in as a child, as well as other material requests she stipulated in the marriage contract. The logic is that since the wife is the carrier of the womb, the husband is therefore obligated to provide full financial maintenance. The man, who was considered the buyer, would be the one to accept that offer by paying the price of the bridal payment. The woman's acceptance of the bridal payment validated the contract. Without this, the contract would be invalid, and sexual penetration, the necessary legal term for intercourse, would be punishable by law.

The force of these contracts exists between the lines in the immense social cost of the contract for the lives of both the man and the woman. In selling access to the womb, the woman, as the carrier of that womb, also gives the man a lifetime of *etaa'at*, a wife's obedience specifically pertaining to her body. I explain its confines in the following sections. Once the woman is given the bridal payment, the man has sole ownership of access to her womb. This ownership of access means that he is entitled to sexual intercourse. The wife's obligations for the entirety of the marital union are couched in this logic. Thus, there are only two marital obligations—sexual intercourse and etaa'at. Everything else she does in the marriage outside of these two is voluntary. Should a married couple ever decide to end the marriage contract, the court is supposed to calculate an hourly rate for any labor beyond these two obligations and force the husband to pay this amount to his wife. This is referred to as *ojratol mesl*. The rate of payment must be commensurate to the woman's level of education. The howzevi were involved in doing extensive research on the legalities of ojratol mesl in response to increasing divorce rates. Whether this was actually carried out by Iranian courts is beyond the scope of my work, but based on what many howzevi explained, this is what an Islamic marriage contract entailed.

Although the second type, the temporary marriage contract, falls outside the focus of my project, briefly touching on it will give us more insight into the way a woman's reproductive system is consequential to the transaction. Both types of marriage contracts and the sociality that comes with them are at the center of anthropologist Shahla Haeri's work. Here, I will focus on what she argues about the temporary marriage contract, which is a written or verbal agreement between a man and a woman being married only for a specific period of time. The agreement includes a starting and ending date or time of the marriage. Therefore, if the permanent marriage contract is a contract of sale of sexual intercourse, then the temporary marriage contract is a contract of lease of sexual intercourse. In this version, the husband leases sole access to the woman's reproductive system only for a designated period of time. Therefore, he is neither entitled to a woman's lifetime of obedience nor financially responsible for her upkeep and well-being. Instead of paying a bridal payment, the man pays the woman an *'ajr*, a payment of consideration that must be clearly stated in the contract along with the duration of the temporary union. Without this payment of consideration, the contract is invalid, and sexual penetration would be punishable by law. In all, Haeri argues that while temporary marriages are advantageous for some women, they are essentially economically detrimental and socially damning to many more, especially women who are unable to establish paternity and inheritance rights for their children from a temporary marriage.[3]

Maryam's transactional description of an Islamic marriage contract appears rigid and stripped of possible emotions between a man and a woman in a legal union. But that is what an economic contract is: sentiment-free. The excesses of marital life, the relatedness between two people and their families, unfold between the lines. This unfolding includes people freeing themselves from the contract because these conditions allow for enough ambiguity for men and women to leave the union and get a divorce. In Iran, infertility is one of the reasons marriages end in divorce. In other ethnographic work about Saudi Muslim women by Amélie Le Renard, women in Riyadh returned to their fathers' homes for a period of time to signal the formal process of divorce.[4] Similarly, Anne Meneley describes that Yemeni women in Zabid return to their fathers' homes to do the same.[5]

Like a Potato

I want to return to the idea of obedience and look at what it can teach us about the howzevi. Marriage necessitated being observant of a system of exchange between a husband's responsibility for financial upkeep, nafaqeh, and a wife's obedience regarding her body, etaa'at. There was enormous ambiguity for what etaa'at exactly entailed or the extent of the husband's domain in the matter. But during my time with the howzevi, I observed patterns in the context of when and about what etaa'at was consequential. Almost always, the action of asking a husband for permission was related to decisions about where she was taking the womb and children birthed from the womb. Examples of when a woman asked her husband's permission included whether she could leave the house for any reason, who was and who was not allowed to enter the home, and with whom the wife was allowed to interact. I will return to this later.

Obedience to the husband was only half the system of the mutual exchange in a marriage contract. The other half required the husband to do his part. During the courtship period, *khastegari*, women looked for signs that a potential husband would fulfill his side of the contract, indications in his behavior and speech that he deserved to be asked permission from. One important indication was for a man to have the quality of *gheyrat*, a protective emotion of responsibility.[6] Gheyrat can best be defined by describing, according to the howzevi, what men with a protective emotion of responsibility do. In the following, I provide examples of the way the howzevi described gheyrat, and I situate these in Islamic text. I then provide ethnographic examples of what it might look like.

For Maryam, Mohammad was first and foremost a *gheyrati*, a man with a protective emotion of responsibility. Mohammad was a husband who, at the very least, expected her to be obedient and to ask him for permission about her decisions. She chose him because she felt he would help her stay the course with working on herself against her lesser tendencies. She hoped they would help each other become good Shi'i Muslims. Maryam would not have taken an interest in Mohammad otherwise. She spent a good amount of time during the courtship period collecting background information about Mohammad from her network of friends and colleagues and interviewing him to determine this. Mohammad chose Maryam for the same reasons. But this was not unique to Maryam; even those who thought they were past marriageable age said that if they were to ever get married, the man would have to be gheyrati. They could divorce if either one of them failed to live up to the commitment.

While gheyrat for Maryam and Mohammad was framed in the work of khod shenasi, it was experienced in diverse ways. There were other emotions, such as wanting to be desired, cared for, and paid attention to, infused with the idea that a husband would help them in the work of khod shenasi. "I don't want a husband who does not care where I am," Zahra, twenty-three years old, commented. She described gheyrat by describing its opposite, *bi gheyrat*, a man without gheyrat: "He does not care who I talk to. He does not think about me. It means I have no value for him." Elham, on another occasion, explained the concept as a term of endearment: "[Gheyrat] means *mal-e mani* [you are mine]." The husband feels and behaves as if the wife belongs to him. In this context, I also heard women say, "He loves you," "He cares for you," "He always knows about you." Mehdiyeh, twenty-five years old, explained, "He just misses her all the time and wants her by his side all the time, and pays attention to what she needs, and protects her from harm."

Like Zahra, who said, "Gheyrat is good, and the Iranian man, I think it is in his blood to have gheyrat," Maryam pointed out that having this protective emotion of responsibility was not unique to religiously conservative men. Iranian men who did not appear to be religiously conservative also exhibited gheyrat. While Maryam, the baby, and I were walking to the park, a newlywed couple drove by with flowers and writing on the hood of the car. We could barely see the bride because of the tinted windows, but she wore a white wedding gown and held a bouquet of flowers on her lap. She had a silky white cloth draped over her head, with enough space for her to breath as it hung over some apparatus jutting over her forehead. The groom's appearance, with spiked hair and eyeliner, signaled he was not religiously conservative. Maryam laughed and said, "You see, even if he is this way with some bad hair or 'modern,' he has gheyrat. He does not let other people see his wife. It is the best." In other words, a man with gheyrat would shield his wife or any woman in his family from the public gaze. "He shows everybody he protects you," she explained further. On this idea of shielding from the public gaze, one howzevi mentioned that men her grandfather's age would avoid calling their wives by their names in public. They would call them by another name because they did not want other men knowing or saying their wives' names.

Mehdiyeh explained, "Women like gheyrat because the men pay attention to them carefully, and they [women] get full attention from the man. They want a man with gheyrat for this reason. If a man does not have gheyrat, they know the man does not care about them. She is not important for him. Having gheyrat is a way for the man to show that the woman has *arzesh* [value]. . . . *Bi gheyrat mesle sib zamini!*" This could be translated as "a man without gheyrat is like a potato." A gheyrati was a man who would, at the very least, expect to be asked by his wife for permission and would not allow his wife, daughters, or sisters to come and go as they wished.

As the logic goes, if a man had gheyrat for his wife, it also meant he would have gheyrat for his children. By accompanying Maryam to her interview in Tehran and calling his colleagues about which howzeh would be a better fit for his daughter, as I described earlier, Abbas was exhibiting the nuances of gheyrat for his daughter. This was a desirable characteristic for a man because it contributed to having stability and feelings of security in the family. Security would be one less concern for a future mother, and she could then focus on raising moral children. As we were sitting outside the shrine of Abdul-Azim in Shahr-Ray, Leila and Aatike both explained that a father also had gheyrat for his daughters and the other women in the family. They always had to ask him for permission to leave the house or for who they could allow inside the house. Neda and Amine provided a similar explanation about brothers toward their sisters. Yet, having a "jealous emotion" is only one of its many attributes.

Gheyrat is much more than emotion and can extend beyond family members. The final example of gheyrat comes from my own experience during my time off from doing research. I decided to go on a two-day hike in the Alamut Valley with a hired hiking guide and a mule driver. When we reached the end of the hike, the guide and I took a two-hour shared taxi ride from a village at the top of a mountain located near Do and Se Hezar forest to the transportation station in Tonekabon. The guide insisted on finding me a ticket to Tehran since he was a local and would have more success in doing so. By sunset I finally left for Tehran in a shared taxi headed for the nearest transportation hub in Tehran, about four hours away.

Sitting in the passenger seat, I struck up a conversation with the taxi driver, whose name was Amir. I asked him about gheyrat and asked him to give a definition if he could. Instead, he told me what had happened behind the scenes in Tonekabon with regard to my travel. There were no tickets left for Tehran. One of the men I had shared the taxi with from the village overheard my travel guide at the ticket counter. This man then helped my guide purchase my ticket. Unbeknownst to my guide, this man from the village went looking for Amir and introduced himself by providing information about his family and where he lived. He asked Amir for the same information. He then told Amir that I was under his care, that I should be seated in the passenger seat, that Amir should not lose sight of me during the rest stops, and that he should drive me directly to my front door in Tehran. He ended his conversation with Amir by saying that if any harm were to come to me during this ride, he and his brothers would look for Amir in his village. Amir concluded the story, "This is gheyrat." Amir dropped me off in front of my building in Tehran.

In these examples, we can see that the attribute of gheyrat can enable a woman to do the work of khod shenasi because someone else, in this case a male authority figure in the family, is always holding them accountable to what they do with their bodies. But it's necessary to situate the idealization of a gheyrati man in Islamic text because Islamic teachings inform the way a man is to properly possess gheyrat, which is then reconstituted through social interactions. The word *gheyrat* comes from the Arabic word *ghira*. In both Persian and Arabic languages, it connotes some kind of honorable attachment to something. The word is commonly used in the context of choosing a spouse as well as in commentaries on marital or familial responsibilities. As I will explain later, it is desirable when men have the right amount of ghira for women. But it is considered a detriment for women when women have ghira for men. This is not to say women did not exhibit actions that looked like a man's ghira, but they would not call it gheyrat. This deserves a more detailed engagement beyond these chapters but is outside the scope of the book's project.

When read from Islamic text, ghira is characterized by a type of protective emotion of responsibility. The idea of responsibility implies that possessing the right amount of ghira is subject to both self-evaluation and social appraisal. Ghira manifests in action. First, having ghira is considered part of faith. Ghira begins with God, who has the most ghira of all. In Sahih Bukhari, the Prophet Mohammad describes God's ghira in comparative terms of intensity by first quoting one of his companions, Sa'ad, about his own ghira. The Prophet then remarks that although he and his companions are astonished by the intensity of Sa'ad's ghira, God has more ghira than he and others combined. Second, ghira can also refer to a heartfelt attachment to place in that all human beings naturally have ghira toward land, nation, or religion. The prophets in particular possess ghira for their people.

The use of ghira in the context of marriage is found in Sahih Bukhari's chapter on the marriage contract. Without proper training in reading Islamic text, it is easy to assume that ghira fosters a man's inability to trust. The nuance of Asma bint Abu Bakr's narration, however, shows a more complex concern beyond the inability to trust. Asma was married to Az-Zubair. He did not own property and did not have a helper. But he did own one camel to carry well water for the household, as well as one horse for his daily affairs to make a living. Because of his limited means, his wife, Asma, had to carry date stones to the house, a distance of about two miles. One day the Prophet Mohammad and his companions saw Asma carrying date stones on her head while walking home. Out of his sense of ghira, the Prophet stopped his camel to offer Asma a ride for the remaining distance. She then recalled an uneasy feeling of embarrassment or shyness in remembering her husband's ghira.

The Prophet, noticing her embarrassed state, moved on along with his companions. Az-Zubair later responded to Asma by saying, "By Allah, you carrying the date stones (and you being seen by the Prophet in such a state) is more shameful to me than you riding with him." Az-Zubair felt ashamed that he did not take care of her as was expected of him, and she was forced to walk two miles carrying date stones on her head.[7] His ghira, his protective emotion of responsibility, was not out of feeling threatened that his wife would be riding on a camel with someone other than himself. It was out of his inability to meet the community's expectation of a husband to fully provide for his wife. In this example, ghira is more than just trust or jealous emotions. As I've mentioned, according to Zahra, gheyrat was something Iranian men were born with. Some were born with an excessive amount of it. This excess was no longer considered gheyrat but ta'asob, an extreme and intolerable temperament. Mehdiyeh clarified, "The difference between gheyrat and ta'asob is that the one with ta'asob is sick. He has a problematic heart (inner self) or inside. He has some sickness and hurts the woman. This is not caring for the woman anymore if he is hurting her. . . . A man that has gheyrat does not hurt the woman." The right amount of gheyrat was measured against a set of unwritten rules. To violate these would make him an intolerable failure. Stories of brothers getting into fistfights with men who glanced at their sisters was a common example of ta'asob.

The women acknowledged that the attitude toward gheyrat had changed through time, and they looked to Islamic text to differentiate between a man with gheyrat and a man who was ta'asob. Khanum-e Tabesh emphasized that Islamic teachings provided a general blueprint for a middle ground. For instance, Prophet Solomon was said to have advised his son to be weary of this excess because it could result in making false accusations against family members. Quoting the Prophet Mohammad, Khanum-e Alizadeh explained there was ghira that was desirable in the eyes of God and ghira that was despised by God. If a man became unreasonable, Islamic teachings would "tell the Iranian man what is correct," Khanum-e Alizadeh explained. Ta'asob was something to be ashamed of, a sign of failure. Nurturing and disciplining oneself to have the right amount of gheyrat did not come with an instruction booklet. It was something to be settled by way of practice through social relationships as a son, a brother, or an uncle.

I return to the example I explained previously about Asma bint Abu Bakr and locate an intriguing aspect of ghira at the end of this narration. Asma explains that she continued to walk these miles and other kinds of work for a period of time until her father, Abu Bakr, sent a servant to help her. In this narration, both her father and her husband were expected to provide support for Asma. The concept of gheyrat plays out similarly in Maryam's educative mobility. I now return to the notion of etaa'at.

Obedience (Etaa'at) and Gheyrat Are Intertwined

Part of signing up for marriage and motherhood involved asking for the husband's permission regarding her and her children's mobility. Asking their husbands for permission about who could enter their homes, about leaving their homes, and about their children were displays of their observing etaa'at. I originally interpreted this practice as mere consultation with their fathers or their husbands. But married women clarified this for me. Asking their husbands for permission was a religious obligation that was worthy of attention and care, and they did so with the acknowledgment that their husbands were responsible for the final decision. As an outsider, the appearance of patriarchy's chokehold seemed obvious to me. The requirement of obedience is generally considered one of the features of Islamic marriage that reveals its deep inequality. However, Maryam and the other howzevi did not see this practice as disabling or a source of inequities. The practice was part of a larger set of obligations and commitment to something greater than oneself. I liken this larger set of commitments to a sequence of choreographed dance steps later on. It is a problematic analogy and cannot be used for every moment of etaa'at. But I find this analogy to be helpful for the following descriptions of what the concept of obedience looks like for Maryam.

One evening in October 2011, Mohammad, Maryam, the baby, and I were on our way to the toy store to look for a pair of plastic toy eyeglasses that the baby could play with instead of Maryam's eyeglasses. When we stepped out of the car, a woman with makeup, loose-fitting hijab, and eyeglasses asked me, "Khanum, what happened to my mobile? Did you see my mobile that day?" I then remembered who she was, a customer who left her mobile phone on the glass counter at the optician's store while I waited to see a pair of glasses. The woman told Maryam that she remembered me and asked if we could help her find her phone at the optician's. Shortly after, an argument then ensued between the woman and the optician. The optician's daughter later explained to me that the woman was "bad." The optician had taken the phone to the police station because he had found in it inappropriate pictures of her with a man from the neighborhood. He had given the phone to the police.

Maryam became upset by this incident and expressed that even if the optician's story were true, the optician did not have the right to look through the woman's phone, make those conclusions, and then surrender the phone to the police. Maryam wanted to find the woman to let her know that her phone was at the police station. She also wanted to hear the woman's side of the story and then speak to the optician. Maryam waited for Mohammad to come home to ask for his permission to leave the house and take action. Mohammad did not give Maryam permission to do what she intended to do.

Being married to a gheyrati man clearly placed limitations on members of the household. Apart from asking permission about her own activities outside the home, Maryam also asked Mohammad for permission concerning activities outside the home involving her daughter, Fereshteh, who at the time of fieldwork was one and a half years old. When the weather became warmer in the spring, Maryam began dressing Fereshteh in colorful dresses she had been waiting for a year to see Fereshteh wear. Mohammad felt this grooming would cultivate a sense of materialism in Fereshteh. He felt it would develop a habit of beautifying herself in public to draw attention to herself. Developing the habit of beautification would also then place Fereshteh at risk of drawing envy toward herself. Though not in these exact words, he eventually explained this to Maryam, who no longer had permission to dress the baby in colorful dresses unless she was at home when guests came to visit. He told Maryam it would be much better if the baby were to dress in "clean but old clothing." Maryam followed through with what Mohammad wanted. She explained to me, "Mohammad does not like it."

The following month, Maryam and I began taking afternoon walks to the park, pushing the baby in the stroller. This usually involved an hour of sitting on a bench and talking. One afternoon, Maryam explained that Mohammad no longer gave her permission to take the baby to the park because of the gonah of men and women who were flirting with each other in the park. Maryam stopped taking Fereshteh to that park. I will return to these examples later. What I want to point out for now is that as a student in Ayatollah Khamanei's Dars-e Kharij class, Maryam clearly knew about Islamic edicts on what she could and could not do, perhaps more than Mohammad. However, the requisite to ask for her husband's permission about her and the family's social relations transcended the fact that Maryam had more Islamic knowledge than her husband. Maryam consistently asked Mohammad for permission regarding whether specific guests were welcome in their home, whether she could visit certain individuals, and what appeared to be any decision that involved leaving or entering the house.

Figure 7.2. Maryam's sister, Maryam and Mohammad carrying Fereshteh during our visit to Kashan. Kashan, 2010. ©Amina Tawasil.

Half the Contract

The idealized gheyrati man was linked to an entire set of ethics about manhood, especially nafaqeh, which men were called upon to uphold. Those ethics that play out in the social relations of the bazaar, the local neighborhood, the streets, and larger Iranian politics may be located in the constellation of what Aldekhah referred to as the *javanmardi*. A man cultivates virtues of courage and open-handedness, both of which were defined by and emerged through a man's ability to develop a posht, a network of alliances and followers.[8] For Mohammad and Maryam, being a man with gheyrat among other men who were constantly maintaining their positions and alliances within and between networks, such as neighborhood study groups and the different guilds of bazaris, was both expected and found worthy of respect. These expectations of men do not end with Mohammad. I return to Maryam's father, Abbas. It was out of his protective emotion of responsibility for Maryam that he placed conditions on her marriage contract, conditions that would almost guarantee her educative mobility after she left his household. In this instance, it contributed to bringing her to the supreme leader's circle, literally.

Mohammad was devoted to Maryam's goal of pursuing her education along with assuming full responsibility for the household. It was out of Mohammad's entrepreneurial work that he subsidized Maryam's education. Because of Mohammad's support, Maryam's situation was palpably different from her brothers' financial positioning, as I will now explain. Both of Maryam's brothers became students in Qom after graduating from high school. Their father purchased an apartment for them in Qom, which they could share. Her father was aware that his sons would not have enough financial means to live in Qom. Yet even this financial support was not enough. Articles have been published in Iranian newspapers to describe similar difficulties. For instance, seminarians from Yasuj reported that despite the continued increase in inflation, their allowance had not been increased and was no longer enough to cover the basic needs as a student. Unmarried men received 60 hezar touman (at the time equivalent to $40) per month on average. Moreover, the allowance they received from the howzeh via the vaqf was not enough to support a family. Married men received between 150 and 250 hezar touman (in 2011, equivalent to $102–$250) per month on average, depending on the number of children. The rent cost located in a less congested area in Qom was 100 to 250 hezar touman.

In order to financially maintain their families, Maryam's brothers, who were also expected to uphold the virtue of gheyrat and by default the ideals of javanmardi, ventured into their own small private businesses. Maryam's older brother, Hassan, distributed snack items to a few retailers in Qom while studying at the howzeh. Her younger brother, Hamed, took on an apprenticeship in traditional Islamic forms of healing from a well-known healer in Qom. Through this apprenticeship, he became a healer using bee venom, bee calcium, and honey. When I met him and his wife, he had just started to cultivate three cages of bees in a small co-op bee farm north of Tehran. It had been a project he first experimented with by curtaining off a small section of his apartment in Qom.

From seeing that it would take students five to six hours to study outside of classes, time that would take away from the possibility of taking on any sort of labor for wages, I had a better grasp of why men in the howzeh needed a monthly living stipend. This stipend was often a source of public ridicule, which included stories of freeloading seminarian men finding ways to acquire a monthly allowance from different howzeh as well as high-ranking clerics buying expensive cars. Although some howzeh would provide small stipends to women, women were generally not entitled to a monthly stipend because the men in their families were expected to fully provide for and support them. Without disregarding the limitations placed on howzevi women, I became aware of the way Maryam's father's stipulations on her marriage contract, based on the expectation placed on fathers, husbands, and/or brothers as providers for their families, freed Maryam from the load of financing her education and taking on the full responsibility of her success as mother, as wife, and as student.

I first met Mohammad in 2008 as he was picking up Maryam from the howzeh. She was finishing her doctoral coursework and had not yet had the baby. Maryam was always on the move to make sure her tasks were carried out properly. She participated in English classes, local pilgrimages, social gatherings, meetings, and sports activities. Mohammad would drive Maryam at 5:00 a.m. three days a week to Ayatollah Khamenei's class. However, when Maryam had the baby two years later, she struggled. Mohammad blocked out his early morning hours to take care of the baby while Maryam taught her classes three days a week. Only when pressed for time to run last-minute errands would he leave the baby with me in my apartment.

Mohammad was an active participant in taking care of the baby to the extent that a slight competition developed between Mohammad and Maryam for the baby's affection. It seemed the baby would often look for Mohammad's attention and not hers. Mohammad could not tolerate the baby's crying and would stop the car by the side of the road just to hold and carry the baby until she would stop crying. Maryam, on the other hand, tolerated the baby's tantrums. Many of my interactions with Mohammad involved him being of service to Maryam and driving us to the doctor, family visits, and religious ceremonies or the howzeh, which sometimes entailed waiting long hours for us in his car. Mohammad often left work at will in order to drive Maryam and Fereshteh to appointments. Maryam shared stories of the way Mohammad would cook and clean during her difficult months of pregnancy and said he often had to explain to his friends what he was doing. Mohammad continued to take an active role in serving the guests, cleaning the kitchen when Maryam could not, and making *kuku*, a frittata made of green vegetables, when Maryam could not make dinner. By springtime, both their schedules had become unmanageable. Mohammad decided to hire a woman to help Maryam three days a week.

Mohammad's efforts to fulfill the conditions of his marriage contract were also about working for Islam by way of his wife's research and occupation. It was an exasperating obligation he took to heart. Mohammad's relationship with his mother and sisters, which I have not described, also involved labor not too different from that of his own household. He visited their apartment weekly to help them run errands. Mohammad and his older brother, who was also married to a howzevi at the time, described the pressure they felt. Mohammad at times wished he could split his body into three to tend to obligations toward Maryam, his mother, and his business. He could not be in two places at the same time but wished he could. But he, like his brothers, continued to do what they do. "He is being gheyrati," Maryam said.

Between the Lines

There is more to describe about gheyrat and etaa'at that goes beyond the utility of mutual exchange. There is the intimate aspect of the practice. Without losing its purpose as a religious obligation, the howzevi's motion of asking for permission from their husbands, whom they often addressed as *agha*, the man of the house, at times appeared to be part of a sequence of ordered operations. I describe later on what this term signifies. In this context of usage, there was a sense of anticipation. The words, the tonality when Maryam says, "Agha," served as a contextual cue, not just for Mohammad but also for me as part of their household for that period. Over time, I became more attuned to this anticipatory tone. Khanum-e Tabesh and others calling their husbands from their offices to ask for permission had a similar effect. The same could be said when the younger howzevi would call to ask their fathers for permission. I liken the motions to the way dance partners repeat partnering techniques before effectively moving onto the next sequence of dance steps. In Casino Salsa, when the lead brings his arm waist level, opens his palm, and folds his fingers with a slight tug at the follower's hand, the follower will know the sequence of steps to follow, known as *enchufla*. The follower's right foot stomps, and the left foot moves forward.

I draw on this analogy because Mohammad seemed to anticipate Maryam's question, and Maryam in turn seemed to know her husband's answer in advance. There were moments when it seemed like the husband expected his wife to find a way to modify her plan of action, to find a compromise between both his decision and what she wanted to happen. Maryam sometimes made slight adjustments to her plans so she could obey Mohammad but also do what she needed to. Mohammad did not give her permission to dress Fereshteh in decorative dresses when going outside the house, but Maryam dressed her in pants with light-colored designs and a sweater with a dainty flower or two. For Maryam, her choices were still within the bounds of etaa'at since she did not dress Fereshteh in dresses or elaborately designed clothes. Mohammad no longer gave her permission to take the baby to the park, and Maryam stopped doing so. But she took up a new routine. Instead of going to the park, Maryam began taking the baby in the early evenings to the larger mosque about ten blocks from her home. The baby could sit and watch or imitate women performing the evening prayers and afterward socialize and play in the back of the room with other children.

I often wondered why women bothered going through the motions of asking for permission if the outcome could almost always be determined. Maybe they wanted to, plain and simple. But with just about any human action, we can assume that whatever we act on is out of desire. That is, Maryam consistently asked for Mohammad's permission because she wanted to. Underpinning much of what we want to do might also be wanting to survive, express, or become mobile. And this desire, this want to, becomes difficult to describe because it's archaeological work. Desire as an analytical angle forces me to establish that something inside Maryam at that very moment motivates her to ask for Mohammad's permission. I do not know for certain what went on inside Maryam when she asked Mohammad for permission other than what she wished to tell me, so I am assuming all forms of motivation—desire, non-desire, unconscious desire, and so on. And what I hope to do is describe what is less problematic to establish, what these moments produced.

The motion of asking permission points to a moment where theory and practice meet, a moment that turns Maryam's knowledge into practice. The motion of asking for permission came with cultivating sensibilities that appear as a disadvantage in the moment such as *tahamol kardan*, or to bear down, endure, or withstand, but could also be advantageous when used in other social circumstances. Central here is the notion of deference as one of many symbolic languages for Maryam communicating her knowledge of Islam to herself and her family. In this context, deference meant submissiveness in appreciation, or *taqdir*, and admiration, or *ihtiram*, of her family.

The motion of asking for permission from Mohammad was the very evidence to Maryam that she was a knower of Islamic practices and their logic, that she was doing the work of khod shenasi. I harken back to Khanum-e Yasseri's explanation that there are no gendered differences between souls, between the ruh. But difference between God's creations is a necessity in the material world, where the work of self-knowing becomes most relevant. Maryam's motion of asking for permission is one analytical moment that tells us what it is she does with this idea of necessary difference in doing the work of khod shenasi in the material world. According to Maryam, not asking Mohammad for permission would have taken away from her self-perception that she knew Islamic practices, perhaps better than her husband. She was concerned not only with the opinion that others would form about her but also with an image of herself with herself as the audience. She held that power of evaluation, where a positive evaluation serves as an incentive to continue.

In her work among South Asian Muslims, Barbara Metcalf writes, "Knowledge . . . is not true knowledge unless it is realized, for there is no concept of the detached intellectual. Nor can one's inner self be untouched by what one knows and hence by what one does. . . . Knowing, doing, and being are inescapably one."[9] Deeb describes a similar situation among the women of al-Dahiyya. Piety for them was authenticated not only through educating oneself in classic Islamic texts and the various interpretations of Islamic scholars but also through community service. Making Islamic practice public was an expression of one's Islamically informed ideas of what it meant to be a good modern Shi'i Muslim.[10]

Framed in this manner, asking permission from Mohammad authenticated Maryam's knowledge. In a way, this authentication enabled her to continue learning, working, and attempting to excel in her endeavors, including teaching about the rights of women in Islam, researching issues pertaining to family, and providing legal advice to those who requested it.

The idea of belonging seems to be of great value here. Belonging to a family, a *khanevadeh*, was in many ways a requisite to being a howzevi. Belonging in this sense was both biologically established and a sustained social labor. A good portion of admissions interview questions were designed around the theme of family belonging. Belonging to and knowing the proper way to belong to a khanevadeh were markers of someone who might also know the way to belong to a group of people ideally responsible for imparting Islamic knowledge to others. That is, they were not only concerned with what kind of family or moral fabric this person was socialized in. They were also interested in whether this person knew the way to properly appreciate and reciprocate, and when to accommodate or give way for others to benefit from a given set of experiences. They wanted to find out if the prospective student knew the importance of knowing when and when not to follow protocol, including the proper application of deference.

Though the howzevi context of deference in this instance is not only about veiling and sexuality, in some way the howzevi experience of deference aligns with the work of Abu-Lughod with the Awlad 'Ali in Egypt and Meneley with Zabidi women in Yemen. Abu-Lughod's explanation of deference among the Bedouin in Egypt describes that women's veiling, "avoidance and self-effacing gestures of various sorts," are some of the many expressions of voluntary deference toward the Awlad 'Ali elders in Egypt. She writes, "All of these vocabulary elements are gestures of deference to hierarchical superiors who more closely adhere to Awlad 'Ali honor-linked values." Women deny their sexuality as a way "to show respect for that social order and the people who represent it."[11] It also corresponds with Meneley's work on sociability and hierarchy among the women from Zabid, Yemen. An act of deference "extends beyond sexual comportment.... There are acts of deference between women of different status." Acts of deference take place "in the company of those more powerful than oneself."[12] For instance, young Zabidi men and women are expected to have deference to older men and women. In the howzevi context, forms of deference to those understood to be responsible for their well-being, who are their husbands and their families, were manifestations of knowing Islam.

The khanevadeh is personified through one symbol—the patriarch of her family, referred to as *agha*. The title is rooted in the Mongolian *aqa*, which, by implication, means "the elder in the family." Combined with the word *ini*, or younger brother, its meaning would change to "the entire family."[13] For Maryam, this *agha* was Mohammad, and sometimes her father in the absence of Mohammad. Women who were invited to an event often responded with, "Let me ask agha first, and I will let you know." By saying this, Maryam would reveal many things about herself to her colleagues and friends. First, it made her knowledge of Islamic practices around marriage legible to others. Second, no matter how challenging it could sometimes be, she abided by an order, a system, a convention of proper process of "doing family," which those before them, the Prophet and his family, had fought to defend and protect. Third, Maryam reminded others that her decisions came from a place of belonging, that she knew the way to value the khanevadeh that also valued her. She belonged to them, and they belonged to her. In many ways, it could serve as an advance notice—"Don't try me, I don't walk this path alone"—to those who might want to present her with difficulties. This value of and being valued by is expressed between family members through deference.

Above all else, Maryam's attempt to imitate the Prophet Mohammad and his household marked her as a woman who placed necessary attention to her work of khod shenasi. Though imperfect, her presence among her colleagues and her students registered her as committed to this process. Her father's and brothers' and Mohammad's gheyrat provided Maryam with a sense of familiarity. In particular, the visibility of Mohammad's gheyrat set the tone of "order" or "certainty" for her. Mohammad's assertiveness, which signified a guarantee of order ("I know where I stand in my relationship to you"), enabled Maryam to progress through her educative endeavors. In other words, both clarity of where she stood in relation to his position and Mohammad's gheyrat gave Maryam a feeling of home to which she could return in times of uncertainty. Through expressions of his sentiments, there was a certainty that she was loved and cared for by a man who was harnessing gheyrat in its proper form and in his social relations. It was meaningful to be assured that she had been chosen as the wife of someone who knew the worth of struggling in striking a fine balance between gheyrat and ta'asob. Simultaneously, as she tried to do right by a set of howzevi ethics, Maryam, by divine right, had the force to demand support from those around her, including revolutionaries and clerics, to continue providing and bettering access to her Islamic education. This exchange is never equal or unequal at any given moment. But it happens, and things are produced for women like Maryam when they do. So much so that out of seventy-two million Iranians, it became possible for her to make it to the supreme leader's exclusive circle of students.

Maryam's story is not one of a woman whose choices have been predetermined for her, nor is it one of a woman who uses her Islamic education to liberate herself from those around her. It is a story of an educated woman who did not consider herself the sole source of moral order and willingly stayed within the bounds of her obligations according to her Islamic teachings about marriage. Like Farideh and Zaynab, her work of khod shenasi was marked by struggles that she had overcome, but only for more to be expected. These were struggles that were seen as testing grounds for the previous work they had been doing for themselves to develop a spiritual nearness to God.

In this chapter, we learned that becoming a specific kind of woman in a marriage to a particular kind of man is a source of mobility. Those around her, her family and her social circles, valued her effort. Maryam and others will preserve and protect their right to be valued. This is vital in our understanding because the fact remains that there are thousands of women who continue, endure, and succeed in such contexts. This is one of the many human possibilities.

In a previous chapter, I noted that listening was a full-body experience, and the howzevi learn from their teachers the way to become worthy of being listened to. Through years of being observant of their Islamic practices, women like Maryam and the more senior howzevi had earned this worthiness. In the following final chapter of this book, I describe a gathering of women from various social circles who hold different religiopolitical outtakes. They have come together in Khanum-e Tabesh's home to do the work of listening and deliberating about their future against a common enemy: the United States and its allies.

NOTES

1. This chapter has been developed from a previously published article entitled "Towards the Ideal Revolutionary Shi'i Woman: The Howzevi (Seminarian), the Requisites of Marriage and Islamic Education in Iran," in *Hawwa: The Journal of Women of the Middle East and the Islamic World* in 2015.

2. For emancipatory and regulatory, see Najmabadi, "Crafting an Educated," 91-125.

3. Haeri, *Law of Desire*, 49–72.

4. Le Renard, *A Society of Young*, 100.

5. Meneley, *Tournaments of Value*, 156.

6. Tawasil, "Towards the Ideal," 99–126.

7. Bukhari, *Sahih Bukhari*, Book 62 (Chapter on Nikah), Chapter 30, Numbers 150–53.

8. Adelkhah, *Being Modern*, 40–42, 69.

9. Metcalf, *Moral Conduct and Authority*, 9–10.

10. Deeb, *An Enchanted*, 165-219.

11. Abu-Lughod, *Veiled Sentiments*, 165.

12. Meneley, *Tournaments of Value*, 92.

13. Encyclopedia Iranica, https://www.iranicaonline.org/articles/aqa-or-aca, Vol. II, Fasc. 2, 168.

EIGHT

—ɯɯ—

JANG-E NARM AND KHOD SHENASI

IN OCTOBER 2011, KHANUM-E ALIZADEH invited me to accompany her to the 2011 International Digital Media Fair and Festival in Mosalla, Tehran. We began preparing in their 520 square foot office a few days before, mulling over the tendency to delay preparation until the last minute. The office secretary, Khanum-e Hijazi, led a handful of volunteers in sorting, labeling, and boxing the posters, pamphlets, DVDs, and books Khanum-e Alizadeh and Khanum-e Tabesh had published and produced.

There were hundreds of booths at the fair, ranging from information on howzeh, software development companies, web bloggers, and cybersecurity, to educational materials on the Iran-Iraq War. Booths for families of martyrs to access their benefits online were also set up. Khanum-e Alizadeh's booth was right across from the Basij bloggers.[1] Their DVDs and CDs were laid out on the table, and a banner propped on the right-side wall read "Hijab, the charter of great awareness, fortress against offensive evil." The woman tending to the table expressed that I was very fortunate to have met Khanum-e Alizadeh and Khanum-e Tabesh. Khanum-e Alizadeh, she said, was "the best Basij who worked hard for Iran and its people." Her work was an expression of dedication to a Shi'i nation.

The section right behind Khanum-e Alizadeh and Tabesh's booth was devoted to the explanation of *Jang-e Narm*, entitled "Soft War in Digital Media: An exhibition of collection of all my enemies introducing to overthrow the institutions of the Islamic Republic." Thick, glossy placards hung from the ceiling with small chains just at eye level. Information about the Israel Project, USAID, Brookings, East West, Foreign Policy, American Enterprise, Center for Applied Nonviolent Action Strategies, German Marshall Fund, Freedom House, National

Endowment for Democracy, Albert Einstein, Hoover, Club Bilderberg, RAND Corporation, and Carnegie Endowment for International Peace were all part of this exhibit. Each poster provided an explanation about each think tank or research institute directly involved in the Soft War against Iran and the greater Middle East and, more specifically, the occupation of Palestine. Thousands of people attended the fair, which lasted for ten days. Attending this event gave me insight into the kinds of work the Iranian government and women like Khanum-e Alizadeh and Tabesh had been doing in recent decades in response to a war of social engineering, which they referred to as Jang-e Narm, the Soft War.

In this chapter, I provide a political backdrop for their work and describe what for them constitutes the Soft War. The women discovered there were anti-regime groups that were reframing the concept of khod shenasi to influence university students. This was evidence that too many Iranians were divorced from the remembrance of God, according to Khanum-e Tabesh and Alizadeh. The women saw it as their responsibility to teach and create programs against these groups. Though unseen in their efforts, howzevi women were at work in response. Khanum-e Tabesh and Alizadeh in particular attempted to normalize the discussions about khod shenasi among university students. I end the chapter by describing a gathering of women for Khanum-e Tabesh's annual birthday party for Fatimah, the Prophet's Mohammad's daughter. With the help of Khanum-e Alizadeh, she facilitated a discussion between women of different social circles about the way to fend off the impact of the Soft War. Examining this provides a glimpse of the way they saw themselves, their education, and the work of khod shenasi in this perpetually charged moment.

THE SOFT WAR AGAINST IRAN

Khanum-e Alizadeh and Tabesh expressed their dismay at the prevalence of young women leaving the practice of wearing the chador in exchange for wearing makeup and tight clothing and openly socializing with young men. They saw these as symptoms of oppressive conditions, as indications of something more troubling, the problem of khod shenasi. They spoke of something foreign tugging away at this generation of Iranian women, which placed women in a vulnerable position. Jang-e Narm, the Soft War, made this foreign presence possible.

By Soft War, Khanum-e Tabesh was referring to what she called "Western propaganda" through the internet, satellite television, and other digital technologies. By Western, they were referring to a social and political project that sought to universalize a specific version of personhood that could be easily exploited for the benefit of a few. In this project, the self is a worker self to accumulate wealth or promised wealth. This project was hegemonic, perpetual, and historically emerged out of the United States and European countries. Its objective in

Figure 8.1. Posters, which include Club Bilderberg, Rand Corporation, and the Carnegie Endowment for International Peace, as part of an exhibit on the think tanks behind the Soft War. Tehran, 2011. ©Amina Tawasil.

Iran was to get Iranians to eventually do the bidding for the United States and its allies without necessarily being conscious of doing so. This was to be achieved by way of digital technologies.

Khanum-e Tabesh and Alizadeh were convinced that the United States and its allies were tirelessly working to destroy what their generation of Iranians had built, to slowly undermine the internal social fabric of Iranian society. In other words, not only were Iranians forced to endure harsh economic sanctions, but they were also being subjected to the Soft War promulgated by the United States and its allies. But given that Iran called itself an Islamic Republic in a world dominated by the narrative that Islam was a threat to civilization, the women said they knew this Soft War was inevitable. It comes as no surprise that the women of this book saw themselves engaged in a war of social engineering.

THE POLITICAL CONTEXT

One way to understand the anxieties around the Soft War is to look briefly at the way freedom of expression is conceptualized between that of the Universal

Declaration of Human Rights and Iran's constitution, and the way the Iranian government attempted to co-opt the availability of satellite channels. According to Article 19 of the Universal Declaration of Human Rights, "Everyone has the right to freedom of opinion and expression; this right includes freedom to hold opinions without interference and to seek, receive and impart information and ideas through any media and regardless of frontiers." This, however, like many universalized provisions in the declaration, creates a problematic relationship with existing locally defined laws in many countries. In the context of Iran, Article 19 is in direct opposition to Article 175 of Iran's constitution, which states, "The freedom of expression and dissemination of thoughts in the Radio and Television of the Islamic Republic of Iran must be guaranteed in keeping with the Islamic criteria and the best interests of the country." Iranian media outlets were to serve as a medium for exchange of ideas within the bounds of Islamic rulings and practices.

Regardless of what Article 175 stated, satellite dishes that received foreign-based media outlets made their first appearance on the rooftops of the affluent in north Tehran in 1991. These media outlets mirrored Article 19's universalized declaration by positioning themselves as providers to the Iranian public of the basic right to entertainment, varying points of view, and up-to-date information via satellite technology. Over time, the Iranian government became wary as dish numbers increased, suspecting that satellite television would become a medium for Western cultural invasion. In following Article 175 of its constitution, the government officially banned satellite dishes in 1994, with key clauses detailing equipment confiscations by the police and Basij, and penalty fines for distributors and users. The Ministry of Culture and Islamic Guidance, in cooperation with the Ministry of Post and Telecommunications and like institutions, were named responsible for protecting Iran from this Western cultural invasion.

Despite the efforts to ban them, private use of satellite dishes increased under the Khatami administration. The administration's policies consented to the use of satellite dishes guided by strict government regulation and encouraged the exploration of satellite broadcasting for Islamic propagation. As a result, satellite dishes opened the door for a mishmash of state-run and foreign-based channels by 2008, thirty-seven of which were Persian-language channels, most in opposition to the Islamic Republic.[2] At some point, there were over 120 Persian-language satellite channels broadcasted by Iranians in exile into Iran.[3]

There are differences among programming on these networks. Some of these channels sought to erode the legitimacy of the Iranian clerical establishment, its political leaders, and its system of governance through various thematic programming like satire and comedy. Other networks routinely pushed to idealize American and European political systems through documentaries or roundtable discussions. The political leanings of various networks include pan-Iranism, monarchism, secularism, and reformism. Some have also attempted to mobilize people into political unrest inside Iran. Fardin Alikhani writes, "On television networks which oppose the Islamic Republic, the refrain is hard to miss: 'Isn't it a pity for us Iranians that the clergymen should be the rulers of our country?"[4] In 2011, the Iranian government considered satellite channels weapons to undermine the legitimacy of the Islamic Republic.

The way the women spoke of the Soft War as fact was similar to the way the Occupy Wall Street movement described corporate America as using the media to normalize unbridled consumption. Their speech also echoed the way the antiwar movement in the United States accused the major television networks of collaborating with those who benefit from war-making.[5] More recently, it is reminiscent of the way YouTube channels have fueled the COVID-19 anti-vaccine movement. The women's accusation is not unfounded. In Iran, the established links between two of the largest broadcasting networks and their governments' policies toward Iran support the concept of a Soft War. BBC Persian Service as part of BBC World Service has had a long history in Iran. Right before the 1979 revolution, the shah had accused BBC of helping to foment mass protests against the monarchy. In 2009, Ayatollah Khamenei launched the same accusation.[6] BBC Persian Service, which sees itself as providing public diplomacy inside Iran, as BBC World Service does in the greater Middle East, is one of the largest recipients of British government funding for advocating public diplomacy inside Iran.[7]

Voice of America Persian News Network (VOA-PNN) also claims to provide a means to the rights stated in Article 19. VOA-PNN, which broadcasts twenty-four hours a day via internet, radio, and television inside Iran, is officially linked to the US federal government.[8] When I returned from fieldwork in 2012, a friend who was working for a cyber think tank wanted to introduce me to a colleague working on cyber-influencing young Iranians to mobilize against the Iranian government on issues around the veil and freedom of expression. Though I declined the offer, I became aware firsthand, beyond hearsay and spy novels, that these well-funded initiatives existed closer to me than I had imagined.

In response to this, the government has since wielded counterstrategies via satellite, internet, and digital technologies. State-run television channels carry programming produced or approved by the government and the formation of a new Basij cyberspace network were put into effect in June 2011.

THE WOMEN'S WORK IN RESPONSE

Concerns about the impact of satellite programming relate to the women's determination never to return to the social, political, and economic conditions they had experienced during the rule of the shah. The thought of this happening elic-ited something like an allergic reaction. Ayatollah Khomeini said at a mass rally after the revolution, "We're not afraid of sanctions. We're not afraid of military in-vasion. What frightens us is invasion of western culture."[9] Khanum-e Tabesh and her friends echoed this concern, which they referred to as a project of Western cultural hegemony marked by people's inability to recognize their exploitation, thus the overwhelming presence of moral corruption. During a group conversa-tion with Dr. Sajjadpour and his students, he shared his memories about being a student activist in Mashhad at the time of the revolution. He and other activists perceived the United States, because of its support for the shah, as having only one objective in Iran: "to sow moral corruption." For Iranians like the howzevi, moral corruption took many forms such as allowing banks to engage in usury; neglecting the economically impoverished and weak, *bitavon*, in the face of the excessive accumulation of wealth by the elite few; and normalizing the public visibility of violations of Islamic law. Some examples were women unveiling, legalizing gambling, turning a blind eye to prostitution, public consumption of alcohol, and unabated drug economies.

These conditions were, for many if not all of the howzevi, signs that collectively there were too many people divorced from the remembrance of God, that the majority of people had forgotten their purpose of life, to return to the Original Self. Because of these indications of godlessness under the shah, women like Khanum-e Alizadeh were kept at home and did not have many educational op-portunities. The anxiety around the thought of an invasion of Western anything is really about experiencing this kind of exclusion during the time of the shah. Khomeini and other revolutionaries fought to overturn these conditions in 1979.

Therefore, while satellite television networks saw themselves as entertainment providers, Khanum-e Tabesh and Alizadeh saw the Soft War as pitting daughters against mothers and husbands against wives. One battleground was women's rights, which would inevitably impact Iranian families. Citing Ayatollah Khame-nei's book *Rayhane Afarine*, where he writes women are obligated to work for their rights, Khanum-e Tabesh and Khanum-e Alizadeh saw it as their duty to put their Islamic education to use in confronting this problem. They established an orga-nization to do just this and focused their energy on research and teaching under the supervision of Nahad-e Rahbari, the Organization of the Supreme Leader. In 2011, both women were heavily involved with its projects in addition to fulfilling other obligations from the positions they occupied, as I explained in chapter 3.

Nahad offered Khanum-e Tabesh a research project on the Persian 1 television network about the social impact of its programming. She would design a plan of action for university counselors with the goal of dampening its impact on stu-dents. The women's friends told them about one television show that caught their attention. It was about a husband who discovered his wife's love affair, which then led to her pregnancy. The husband eventually accepted the situation. They were saddened by the fact that television shows like this were being translated into Persian. While the plot encouraged the virtue of forgiveness, it also encouraged the Self's lesser tendencies to deceive others without consequence. This form of encouragement was a violation of the sanctity of the marriage contract. The opportunity to collectively discuss, debate, or contemplate "the right context" of human action in these television shows was nonexistent. Khanum-e Tabesh explained, "It is from our enemies, they want to destroy our society. . . . It is the Zionists and the U.S. . . . This is Jang-e Narm."[10]

At the time, they were also concerned when some of their university students began to follow the teachings of a New Age mystic named Osho, whose popularity increased after his death in 1990. Osho, also known as Rajneeshpuram, was from India and scandalized the public in the 1980s with his long chain of Rolls-Royces, his active sexual relationships with members of his commune in Oregon, and the poisoning of local officials, leading to his deportation from the United States. "Osho's books and teachings have reached our young people in the universities," Khanum-e Alizadeh explained. They were made aware that part of Osho's teachings included normalizing group sex among Iranian youth. They suspected his teachings have something to do with the sex parties in north Tehran and the villas near the Caspian Sea.

Osho's followers in Iran dubbed his teachings as khod shenasi. For the women, khod shenasi was being nefariously reframed as a pleasure-serving paradigm by way of the physical body. Khanum-e Alizadeh explained the way Osho preached khod shenasi was merely trying to "see" what was happening to the self in the present, here and now, and encouraging immediate gratification without consequence.

For Osho, there was no singular self, or ego, separate from the rest of being. There was only the real self or consciousness that is one with existence. In a book entitled *A Sudden Clash of Thunder*, he writes of the self, "It is a constant flow, a constant sharing. . . . Thus, the real self is both: no-self in the sense that it is not only yours, and it is the ultimate self also because it is the self of all. . . . You have no cage around your being and infinite power starts flowing through you. You become a vehicle—clear, with no obstructions. You become a flute and Krishna can sing through you. You become just a passage—empty, nothing of your own. This is what I call surrender."[11]

It is in this idea of a "you" becoming a passage through surrender that consciousness (can be "God") may be realized through sexual intercourse, including group sex. Though the claim differs from Osho, research has been done on the phenomenon of group sex in Iran after the revolution. Pardis Mahdavi writes that various forms of sexual behavior, including orgies, among Iranian youth are subversive action against the state, which she refers to as "uprising" and "revolution."[12] But for women like Khanum-e Alizadeh and Tabesh, who were invested in the Islamic Republic, these behaviors were a product of influence from another system of power that continuously sought to alienate human beings from God. In their view, teachings like Osho's turn people into exploited pods by desensitizing them through sexual gratification.

Osho's teachings were problematic for them in many ways. First, for Khanum-e Alizadeh, Tabesh, and others, the project of life is about conditioning the body and its desires to become free from attachment to the material world and to return to the Original Self that remembers God. The absence of such effort individually leads to collective oppression and tyranny caused by greed, envy, and anger. Osho's teachings also inevitably produce a society reminiscent of life under the shah, conjuring images of unhinged accumulation of wealth by the elites, abject poverty, and the sex shows the shah staged for his guests during the infamous 2,500th-year celebration of the Persian Empire in Takht-e Jamshid. Because of the circulation of Osho's teachings in universities, the very space the revolution had made safe for women like Khanum-e Tabesh, Alizadeh, and Shahriari was now at risk of becoming what it used to be at the time of the shah.

The idealization of sexual intercourse outside marriage as a way to become conscious of God placed Iranian women at a serious disadvantage, especially those who migrated to cities from the rural areas. Khanum-e Tabesh worried that men would have the unrestricted means to take advantage of young women sexually and emotionally. Following Osho's teaching was not a mistake that young Iranian women could afford to make, given that Iranian families placed enormous value on virginity before marriage and on the sanctity of a woman's reproductive system. They risked being disowned by their families in the aftermath.

Khanum-e Alizadeh and Tabesh were careful not to vilify the university women who were affected by the Soft War. The makeup phenomenon, tight-fitting clothes, and the resistance against wearing hijab were, to them, signs of riya', a desire to show off, to be the center of attention, a concept I detailed in a previous chapter. These were signs of a troubled self, of people forgetting their purpose in life. "The young people [women], they wear bad hijab and makeup, but they are not bad people. This problem is from *mahvareh* [satellite technology]," Khanum-e Tabesh explained. She saw young women as would-be victims who must be informed about their Islamic rights and encouraged to use them to protect themselves. The concept of a Soft War only showed that they had more work to do. It was a priority for them to educate women on the irreversible consequences of Osho's teachings and other such influences in the future. Khanum-e Tabesh explained that they needed to work harder to design better programs to educate women about Islamic philosophies on the concept of self, nafs, as a way to help protect themselves.

Toward Khod Shenasi

The work of Westernization was in the guise of feminism, which was in the guise of universal human rights. Khanum-e Tabesh thought that the problem began not with women's rights but with the concept of universal human rights, which had become popular among university students. Many of the students she had become acquainted with through her Islamic lectures at different universities consistently asked her questions about women's rights as part of the universal doctrine of human rights. As a howzevi in the 1990s, she became exposed to the idea of universality while studying the rights of women in Islamic law. The notion of universality seemed obviously flawed to her. She did not imagine back then that the concept would gain traction among university women. Yet, there she was in 2011, trying to figure out the best way to reason with students about the dangers of assuming universality, in this case universality of human rights, which was simply another way the United States and its allies were attempting to dominate the region.

"I think the work of human rights does not care about women," Khanum-e Tabesh said. She and Khanum-e Alizadeh were of the opinion that this Western project of women's rights was incomplete because its approach to womanhood placed women at a disadvantage. Most of the women I spent time with shared this concern. In her understanding of feminism, Khanum-e Yasseri pointed out that its focal or starting point was men. The standards are set around being a man or having what men have. She said, "Feminism comes from the rights of men . . . It will make more advantages for men again, but in a hidden way, under some beautiful cover that women don't understand at first." On this point, Khanum-e Tabesh and Alizadeh explained that it encouraged women to mimic the actions of men in order for women to be accepted as equals. This gave more power to men. For Khanum-e Tabesh and Alizadeh, this was also a form of oppression. It was this version of womanhood that was being imposed on the rest of the world through television, film, and other forms of media. Because this version disregarded what different women from different places like Iran valued, universalizing human rights was not about rights; it was a project to create Western women. In other words, Western propaganda was nothing but a project of exporting Western forms of oppression. The howzevi women I spent time with expressed a similar viewpoint, which also resonates with those of Iranian women like Zahra Rahnavard and Maryam Behruzi, who have argued that these rights may be arrived at through Islamic text.

Instead of accepting the push for universal human rights in her lectures to university women, Khanum-e Tabesh looked to Ayatollah Khomeini's teachings as a reference to define these rights. She wanted to motivate Iranian women toward khod shenasi on Islamic terms as an effort someone makes to become self-aware of their life's purpose. It's worth a pause to clarify what constitutes this awareness, in particular the idea of gender through the lens of self-knowing. I return to what Khanum-e Yasseri explained: "that the worth of people will depend on their spirit not their body, not their sex.... It is [already] equal for both men and women.... Though both are valued equally, they experience the material world differently because difference is ... the necessity of the material world."

Khanum-e Tabesh urged all her students to learn about their rights in Islamic law. "I am worried about [us] not paying attention to Islamic Laws about women. I am worried about not knowing about women as human beings, not knowing them in their real situation," she explained. Khanum-e Tabesh's solution to the problem of Western propaganda was Islamically educating women so they could protect themselves. Another way of putting it was that women would be subjecting themselves to one system of power, the Islamic sense of Self, in order to ward off another system of power, the Western model of womanhood. This, for her, was not inherently a bad thing, since Islamic teachings were supposed to guide believers away from becoming dependent and attached to the material world and into cultivating the Self that naturally worships God.

When we reunited in 2011, she explained, "I am worried about discrimination against women in Tehran and small towns and big cities. The women have to know themselves as human beings, and they have to know their laws according to what Imam Khomeini, our leader, said in his speeches. Women should know their important roles in society, family, and workplace because women play an important role ... and even a more important role in bringing up children, and we know children are important to the future of the society." Khanum-e Tabesh argued that women would be placed at a disadvantage without the kind of knowledge of Self that emphasizes knowing life's purpose. This knowing turns into action by nurturing relationships in society and with the family.

Khanum-e Tabesh held strong views about the significance of educating women on the many ways to value themselves for their character and intellect. In one of her lectures to an audience of over one hundred university women in western Tehran, Khanum-e Tabesh spoke of the importance of women expressing self-value during the period of courtship. She appealed to what she saw as positive social markers established by intellectual labor by encouraging the audience to "walk in society as if you are a doctor, or an accomplished person, high." She urged them to know their rights in Islam, to communicate and ask about these rights with others so men would not have free rein to take advantage of them. She added, "Khoshoo' [submissiveness] is good. But when you are speaking with a man do not have khoshoo. Speak proudly with a man." This advice reflects a paradox that comes with the attempt to turn knowledge into practice. Although "walking in society as if you are an accomplished person" was a sign of riya', being prideful, and contradicts the teaching of humility and sincerity, she turned it into a weapon for women so they would not be perceived as weak during the courtship period before marriage.

Much of the work involved in creating government-supported initiatives in response to the Soft War began with conversations, as I show in what follows. In the case of the howzevi, these conversations took place behind the scenes with their social circles. I look back to the notion of khod shenasi and the complex idea of a khod, self, which I discussed in the introductory chapter. This makes khod shenasi, the effort to become self-aware of life's purpose, open to interpretation. While Khanum-e Tabesh and Alizadeh focused on khod shenasi as a way for their students to strengthen themselves against the impact of the Soft War, it also forced women like themselves, responsible for the moral development of society, to foster a sense of commonality with those who were not religiously conservative. Thus, it compelled participants in these conversations to look beyond the Islam-and-other divide.

ON FATIMAH'S BIRTHDAY

Like many of the howzevi I met during my time in Iran, Khanum-e Tabesh brought together women who had been part of her social circle, influential women, in her home in Pirouzi to discuss social problems in Iran, in the hopes that these gatherings became catalysts for action. The discussions were often contentious, without a resolution in sight, and frequently took place during religious celebrations. Every year in the month of Khordad, Khanum-e Tabesh held a party for Fatimah's birthday, the daughter of the Prophet Mohammad and wife of Imam Ali. I attended two of these with Maryam, my first in 2008 and my second in 2011. The following story provides insight on the kind of work the women did in the context of the Soft War to create space for concerns that mattered to them and the many ways they addressed problems. Some women took more practical and immediate approaches while others took a more contemplative approach that demanded long-term engagement with Islamic philosophies. By bringing these women together, Khanum-e Tabesh created a space for assessing what khod shenasi might mean for women who held positions of influence over other women.

There were about fifty women of different ages in the room. Some of the women in attendance had been active participants during the revolution and

were daughters of scholars. Others were active Basij members, university professors, heads of Islamic education–related institutes, howzeh teachers, study group
leaders or khanum-e jaleseh, counselors, writers, researchers working under the
president or Nahad-e Rahbari, and wives of bazaris. Women and children accompanied some of them. All, in order to be a part of Khanum-e Tabesh's circle and
be heard in these gatherings, had socially established themselves as trustworthy
and credible by following Islamic practices. As with the previous party I attended,
the women entering Khanum-e Tabesh's living room first greeted two elderly
women who were mothers of shahid. One of them had lost both her husband and
her son in the Iran-Iraq War.

Khanum-e Alizadeh's six-year-old granddaughter, who was running back and
forth in the living room with other children, was dressed in a deep blue spaghetti-
strap sequined dress. Because she was not yet considered "mentally mature," or
'aql-res, she was not expected to wear hijab or dress like the women around her.
This will expectedly change on her ninth birthday, when girls are expected to begin carrying out their religious duties marked by a ritual called *Jashn-e Mas'uliyat*,
or Celebration of Responsibility.[13] Khanum-e Alizadeh spoke through the echo-
ing karaoke machine, which I had seen many instructors and ceremonial hosts
repurpose from the forbidden musical karaoke use to mournful elegies.

Khanum-e Alizadeh began describing the way Iranian families were being
negatively impacted by two factors: the presence of satellite channels and the
fixation on accumulation of wealth. She then spoke of the more nuanced impact
of these on failed marriages and alarming divorce rates. Part of the problem,
she said, had to do with prioritizing the wrong criteria when selecting a spouse.
She stated that in Islam, there were two criteria to consider: *iman* (faith) and
akhlaq (morals), "but sadly, money comes first in Iran." Meaning, Iranian families
tended to prioritize looking at the person's wealth or the potential to produce
wealth. She then recited a verse from a chapter in the Qur'an, Surah an-Noor,
about having faith in God's provisions for people who decide to marry. That,
concerning oneself too much with wealth as a precondition for marriage, was a
sign of being attached to the idea of wealth itself. She suggested that maybe the
lack of patience and poor communication skills between husbands and wives,
especially in the beginning of the marriage during the period of adjustment, was
also a contributing factor. "In our society, communication skills between men
and women are poor. It is not like what the Qur'an prescribed. Additionally, men
and women should be a cover for each other's weaknesses. Sadly, what is happening is that they both expose each other's weaknesses instead of covering them,"
she exclaimed.

Small children ran around the room chasing each other, sometimes tumbling,
sometimes diving chest first onto Khanum-e Tabesh's silk carpet. A woman asked

for silence in the audience, and another led the salavat, which are words of praise for the Prophet Mohammad and his successors, to be uttered in unison when people who are present are in solid agreement, or at the end of a gathering. She exclaimed, *"Allahuma salli ʿala Mohammad va ʿale Mohammad va ʿajjel farajahu!"* This is translated as, "May the praise and blessings of God be upon Mohammad and the progeny of Mohammad, and hasten the return [of Imam Mahdi]."

Khanum-e Tabesh's house helper began walking around the room slowly and quietly, offering the guests fruits from a tray. She, Maryam, and I were the only ones wearing the headscarf, as the rest of the women wore party outfits, some with shiny beads and tassels. Similar to the other parties I had attended, the house helpers often kept their headscarves on around the guests. Following Maryam's lead, I did not remove mine. Though she could have her headscarf on for various reasons, I assumed it was because we attended this party around the time Maryam was having difficulty balancing her studies and taking care of Fereshteh. When we received a phone call to attend the party this time around, she did not have time to dress for the occasion, as she had done in 2008. Fereshteh, Maryam's baby, who was sitting on the carpet, managed to pull one of the bowls with wrapped chocolate cubes to where we were sitting. She began opening each one without eating the chocolate, and Maryam struggled to distract her to play with the other children.

Khanum-e Alizadeh then opened the floor for discussion and passed the microphone around the room. She asked the women to suggest ways to make marriage successful. One woman said she thought avoiding jumping to conclusions and being patient were keys to a successful marriage. Communicating effectively with each other's family was another woman's suggestion.

Khanum-e Tabesh picked up the microphone at the other end of the room. She added that it was unfortunate many young, educated women were unsuccessful in their marriages. She thought it was common for them to react excessively because they were not fully aware of the way men behaved. Khanum-e Tabesh emphasized the importance of mothers developing a closer relationship with daughters to solve this problem, because mothers could then teach their daughters about men's behavior. The problem, for her, was that girls did not have a close relationship with their mothers and thus could not consult with their mothers about their problems. This was something she had shared in private with me as one of the negative repercussions of the Soft War.

Khanum-e Tabesh saw herself as someone who could help young women protect themselves from men. She explained her experience from counseling university women to those in the room, that they had a tendency to share everything about themselves with suitors because "girls behaved according to the virtue of truthfulness." She urged her guests to advise their students to be wiser and not

to divulge everything about themselves to a suitor from the start of the courtship because the information could be used against them in the future. Much of
her concern hinted at what she thought about men in general: they would take
advantage of anyone who appeared to be vulnerable, if they could.

Women like Khanum-e Tabesh had to confront issues of misogyny despite
remaining suspicious of projects that seemed Western. Not defining their efforts
as Western, feminist, or following a feminist model was a vital aspect of their
work. Deliberation was one of these methods. A voice in the crowd shouted, "Do
not forget some people here have boys!" The women laughed and made their own
side comments. They began talking with each other, saying that men needed to
do their part to address the spike in divorce rates, and mothers needed to educate
their sons to be good to women.

A birthday cake half the size of the coffee table was brought out and placed
slanted on the table. It read "Happy Birthday Hazrat Fatimah!" Women stood up
and took pictures of the cake. Everyone sang a birthday song, clapping their hands
as children danced in the middle. A little boy jumped at the sight of the cake and
put his hands together toward his chest. The discussion continued. Khanum-e
Tabesh then challenged the common practice among mazhabi families during the
namzadi, the marriage courtship and engagement period, which took an average
of three to four weeks, sometimes less. This period of engagement took place
before the 'aqd, the marriage contract ceremony, and consisted of shortened and
counted visitations between a man and a woman. She proposed to lengthen the
namzadi, the engagement, to two months in order to avoid misunderstandings
and over-expectations between a potential couple and their families. Both man
and woman would then assess their own and their family's compatibility by talking, traveling, and doing activities together. Normalizing this practice would
allow families to see if words corresponded with actions. "It will cause less pain
for the young woman later on if this approach is used," Khanum-e Tabesh said.

When Khanum-e Tabesh challenged the custom of namzadi, which many
women here agreed with, she was aware of the many ways Iranians observed the
period of engagement and that the two months was an arbitrary time frame. But
her suggestion was about more than time. It was, more importantly, a way to push
for families to acknowledge the value of giving young women the time to gain
awareness of themselves and to explore the compatibility of habits at the early
stages of courtship. Lengthening the namzadi period would give them time to
change their minds early on in the process. In other words, it would force Iranian
families who did not already make their daughters' futures matter to make them
matter. According to Khanum-e Tabesh, families must accept this. Her suggestion helped her circle of women see that the burden of a bad marriage could not
be placed only on a woman. Everyone around her must share the responsibility.

Reading Books as a Path toward Khod Shenasi

Khanum-e Azimi, a thin woman and one of the few without makeup, was sitting by the wall facing the window. She requested to have her turn on the microphone. She began by complicating the idea of divorce. While there were negative consequences of divorce, she pointed out that it was also a sign that their programs on educating women about their Islamic rights in marriage were effective. "In the old times, women tolerated, [*misookhtano misookhtan*, burn what is burning], the conditions. But now they understand. Women became more aware of their rights," she remarked.

For Khanum-e Azimi, reading was an important way to achieve khod shenasi. Literature offered a basis for discussing with others its relationship to one's life experiences. "We need good programs so that families should read more about social issues." Reading was once part of an intellectual tradition in Iran, she said, "our thoughts." In her opinion, if the interest in reading books was uncommon among a group of people, then good marriages should not be expected. When people read books, which she likened to light, people eventually became more aware, and social conditions improved. She reminded the guests that reading was the foundation for religious propagation such as giving speeches, filmmaking, and conference organizing.

She then explained the function of reading for families: "Those who read, those who think, will find their way. Those families who read, think, will solve problems." Here, self-awareness was not confined to the work of one individual but was work toward a greater whole, the family, which then worked together toward improving social conditions. Khod shenasi for Khanum-e Azimi was not the awareness of self on its own but the self-striving to reach a level of knowing one's place in the world around them and developing social connections with others. This was to be achieved through reading, by creating norms among families to read together as well as norms that would draw people of all ages to enjoy reading.

Before another lengthy explanation on the relationship between reading and the Soft War, Khanum-e Azimi said, "We should ask God to help us think, that we follow Lady Fatimah, that we become excited in creating these programs for reading. We think about [public] appearances, holding meetings, making *hayehoo* [noise]. Instead of these, we should give more time for reading." She asserted that reading could address more social problems besides marriage and repeated Khanum-e Tabesh's point: "Marriage is one aspect, but there is another problem—the communication between mothers and girls. Mothers cannot accept their girls, and girls cannot accept their mothers. We have a lot of social problems." With a firmness in her voice, she said, "The West has planned for this.

Eighty percent of the money in the world is in the hands of Zionists, and they had a plan for this. The West has planned for this, to have a *mobareze*, a battle. To fight against this plan, we should read our own intellectuals and philosophies to maintain our own awareness, and not be affected by this plan." Learning about the works of their intellectuals was, for her, a way to confront the Soft War. But in order for this learning to take place, books must be made available, and there must be some interest in reading. Khanum-e Azimi proposed that intellectual books be sold "in every corner of society."

She concluded that while the television fed images and ideas to the viewer, the act of reading a book gave the reader time to think and imagine a multitude of possibilities and questions, and to remake what was being read. She urged those in the room to create programs to encourage women to read and to target a specific group of women who enjoyed watching television more than reading.

Lists, Mentorship, Forgiveness, Morals

Khanum-e Alizadeh thanked Khanum-e Azimi but complicated her suggestion: "Reading is only one of the ways to address the problem of divorce. There are many women who do not have the desire or interest to read. What will we do then? Maybe another way to prevent the possibility of a failed marriage, especially for women who did not like to read, is to help create a list of skills they should have before marriage, during the engagement, and once the marriage contract is signed." Creating a list meant the woman took the time to become more self-aware.

She asked the women in the room again to share the ways to make a marriage work. The microphone was passed around once again, and the women contributed ideas about what constituted a successful marriage. These related to making space for either a spouse or a younger person through the act of mentorship, or emotions of tolerance like forgiveness, mercy, and patience. A woman wearing a white blouse and black pants suggested finding a way to teach young people to be patient, perhaps through mentorship, with older women sharing their experiences with younger women. "*Dast bezane!* [clap!]" Khanum-e Tabesh cheered. The women clapped in support of the idea.

Khanum-e Alizadeh's daughter took the microphone and elaborated on the notion of forgiveness. She encouraged the virtue of forgiveness between husbands and wives but also the importance of knowing the difference between forgiveness and accepting a bad situation. "To be patient and accept the situation is different from forgiving. Forgiving is better for the soul, but accepting the situation is something different." She then considered feelings of taking revenge and said, "But you feel much better when you forgive something instead of indulging in revenge."

A woman to my left asked for the microphone to say she thought women should prioritize morals over rights. She promoted the idea that couples be merciful and intimate with each other like partners in life, practicing self-restraint to avoid second-guessing each other. When it came to in-laws, she encouraged exercising effective communication. She was advocating for compromise in prioritizing morals over rights.

The Intellect and Expanding Boundaries as Self-Awareness

Khanum-e Abtahi, who was sitting to our left wearing a blue gown, guided the discussion beyond the interaction within the family. Something else must shift before people become willing to make space for others, to restrain themselves, to compromise or balance conflicting positions. Khod shenasi for Khanum-e Abtahi was about having a sense of accountability for problems in a society they had fought so hard to change in 1979 and challenging oneself to expand social boundaries by transforming the way one thinks of people who do not share their ideas of what constitutes a good life. She offered her rationale for how this could take place.

She dovetailed off of Khanum-e Azimi's proposal to increase awareness through reading.

"I agree that young people do not read. Unfortunately, people look through the internet and think this is reading, but it is not reading. The problem is we are not accepting the responsibility that this [social problems in Iran] is our fault. We say it is because of the West, but it is our fault. In the West, people read more, people read inside the metro, people read everywhere." When she was in England to visit her son, she was shocked to see a drunk man on the street reading a book: "He was drunk and he was reading! It shows the importance of reading in their culture."

Khanum-e Shahriari, wearing her eyeglasses, also one of the few without makeup, interrupted. "It's important to know what he was reading!" The other women laughed. Khanum-e Abtahi replied that what was being read was not of importance but rather that people in England placed greater value on the activity of reading during early childhood and into adulthood. She remarked, "Young people in Iran have a problem of what to read. Many of the references we introduce to young people to read are not acceptable in their point of view. Like news from the media, many people do not accept these." Khod shenasi here was about looking inward, the action or lack of action, in the face of resistance from a generation of Iranians who did not experience what life was like before the revolution.

The discussion began to get charged as the children continued to run around and play in the middle of the room. Khanum-e Abtahi increased the volume of her voice: "It is our fault that we do not teach our children to read. We do not dedicate time to answer our children's questions!" This was because Iranian parents were too focused on material gains. She began speaking in terms of khod shenasi and childrearing by first explaining the stages of child development and the kinds of questions children asked in each stage. Before the age of twelve, children's questions were *'aqli*, of the intellect. Meaning at this age, children commonly asked questions related to existence—questions like, who am I? Where did I come from? Where do things come from? Because of the hormonal changes that take place at around twelve years of age, children eventually lose interest in these existential questions. When parents do not know the phases of child development, they are unaware that "there are three potentials [capabilities] of human beings; *shahavat* [lust], *kazab* [deception], *'aql* [intellectual reasoning]. [When] We concentrate on the first two, and the *'aql* is neglected. When the *'aql* is weak, these two *qoveh* [forces] will over-take. If this happens, the child will behave guided by lust and deception. Because the child was raised to focus on these [immediate gratification of physical and emotional needs] rather than the intellect, the child will either behave immorally or become passive." For Khanum-e Abtahi, parents must indulge children in their existential questions so these may be continuously explored into adulthood.

Khanum-e Abtahi emphasized that it was critical for parents to engage their children in this kind of self-awareness at this stage. Early childhood was a window of opportunity for parents to foster khod shenasi early in their children's lives. But Iranian families tended to neglect this stage of childhood because, she said, "The direction of society right now is focused on business [making money]." She added that instead of engaging a child's existential questions before the age of twelve, parents focused on the child's physical appearance and emotions. Like an endless cycle, the more they provided for their children in this way, the more the need to do so increased. Then this required making more money. So, parents bypassed this critical stage without even knowing it.

Surface versus Depth

For Khanum-e Abtahi, parents' efforts would give children the necessary tools to compare the value of the material world, alam-e tabiat o madeh, to that of the spiritual world, alam-e bala tar. Khanum-e Abtahi advised the guests to influence those around them to direct children away from focusing on material possessions to focusing on reason, and to be the best role models for children in doing the same. She drew silence from the women. She had an overarching point to make: through this effort, the child would eventually come to realize that the appear-ance of difference among human beings was only on the surface. Instead, all human beings had one thing in common: the disposition for worship. This was the core of the work of khod shenasi, the outcome of which is ma'rifat en-nafs, a spirituality composed of a person's attempt to answer existential questions about themselves. For Khanum-e Abtahi, khod shenasi was about challenging oneself to recognize this commonality.

She then began to draw a distinction between the surface and the core of Islamic beliefs and practices. "Unfortunately, in society the moral economy is poor because we are in the surface of religion—we do not go deep. If we remain in the surface, they [the youth] react against it," she argued. By the surface of Islamic beliefs, she was referring to bodily practices. She continued to explain, "If we go deep behind it, it is different. . . . The core message of religious books, the rivayat, is [about] the direction or compass of the person's morality. It is not the surface of religion. The core of the religion is the direction of the person, reaching the core in its completeness." By core, she was referring to the contemplative aspects of these bodily practices and the philosophical significance of Islamic teachings about life and personhood in relation to God.

Khanum-e Abtahi insisted, "We should tell our children to be good people, to live correctly." She demonstrated what she meant by providing a personal example. She advised her son before attending university that he should consider people as human beings, not as a man or a woman. She explained to him that if he saw every person as a human being, his communication with boys and girls would be easier. Khod shenasi for Khanum-e Abtahi was also about expanding one's social boundaries, being more accepting of others who were different from them, the mazhabi. This was achieved through mindful childrearing and indulging the child in his or her existential questions.

These words became a turning point in the discussion. Many appeared to have been triggered by her suggestion not to distinguish people according to gender. Khanum-e Abtahi pushed this idea further: "If we tell young people to be careful because she is a girl, or you should beware of her, vice versa, they will encounter problems when they want to communicate with each other." For her, gender was one of many causes of division. She clarified, "We have many divisions, Islam, Judaism, Christianity, and we should reach unity from these and find something in common. We should clean the borders between Shi'i, Islami'ili, Ahmadiyeh. Clean these borders! Do not make religion hard for young people. Let them find unity with each other. Do not lie, tell them to live correctly, to not bother other people."

As Khanum-e Abtahi continued to talk, Khanum-e Azimi, who had urged the guests to make books more accessible, took the other microphone at the other end of the room and began speaking over Khanum-e Abtahi. She disagreed. A heated debate ensued. Khanum-e Abtahi persisted in asking for permission to finish. "Lotfan, ejaze bede! Ejaze bede!" (Please, give me permission [to continue]! Give me permission!). But Khanum-e Azimi, with the other microphone, repeated herself. "Cleaning the borders causes a problem with the other women! It's a problem. It's a problem."

Talking over each other, Khanum-e Abtahi recited in Arabic the first verse from the chapter an-Nisa in the Qur'an. "*Ya ayoha al nas, itako rabakom alathy khalakakom min nafsin wahida wakhalaka minha zawjah.*" The translation of this verse is, "O humanity! Be mindful of your Lord Who created you from a single soul, and from it He created its mate, and through both He spread countless men and women. And be mindful of Allah—in Whose Name you appeal to one another—and honor family ties. Surely Allah is ever Watchful over you."[14] She then advanced that Imam Ali was of the opinion that ma'rifati was the most important part of life, and more important than the surface of religion.

The women in the room began talking over each other all at once, enough so there were fewer children in the middle of the room playing. Khanum-e Tabesh stepped in to take the microphone to make an announcement and proceeded to give the *madda*, a woman who recites the ceremonial story, the floor. The madda began reciting a story of Lady Fatimah. Thirty minutes later, the food was served, and the large decorative cake was sliced and distributed to the guests.

During my time with the howzevi, there were very rare moments when they came to a resolution of a problem at the end of a discussion. The topics were often left hanging and became ongoing conversations elsewhere. There was a noticeable process involved. When I asked Maryam, for example, about the same topic at another time, she would provide a slightly different answer, explaining her uncertainty. The guests in gatherings like this valued these interactions as an opportunity to exchange ideas. They expected the discussion to be contentious and to reveal political tensions. As it should, the cake for Fatimah took the guests' attention away from the political tension, an invitation of sorts to think through the suggestions, the commonalities, and the differences among these, in order to continue the conversations until ideas became actionable.

By holding guided discussions in her home, Khanum-e Tabesh created a space for women of various circles of influence who held differing political outlooks and positions, for a movement of ideas and expressions, for the crossing of life paths, which they might not have been comfortable talking about in their offices. The birthday, the cake, the salavat, children playing, and the presence of mothers of the Iran-Iraq War martyrs validated the gathering as Islamic in purpose. The presentation of the cake with a birthday song to Fatimah reminded all in attendance that she was a woman whose character they emulated. Reciting the salavat served as a reminder that they had a guide, Mohammad, sent by God as a mercy to humankind. Children playing around them during the discussion would be their perpetual concern. Finally, the presence of the elderly mothers of Shahid was a reminder of the sacrifice people made to support their project of Islamizing Iran away from the exclusions experienced under the Westernizing project of the shah.

Figure 8.2. A birthday cake for Fatimah, daughter of the Prophet Mohammad. Tehran, 2008. ©Amina Tawasil.

Having a seat in Khanum-e Tabesh's gathering was earned. One needed to be a specific kind of woman to be invited. For this reason, Khanum-e Tabesh and Alizadeh did not need to lay out the basic foundation or guidelines of the discussion. Being a "specific kind of woman" meant being accustomed to a similar life script in which Islamic knowledge and all that it entailed served as the absolute guide to life above all other forms of knowledge.

The proposed solutions displayed a kind of logic that aligned with Islamic teachings about gender. The problem they described as an obsession with wealth was about having an attachment to having wealth, not about the logic of socioeconomic compatibility in choosing a spouse. The women acknowledged that having been separated from the opposite gender most of their lives, newly married couples have imagined expectations of each other. However, their solution to educating women about men's behavior was not to break down the practice of gender segregation but to strengthen the relationship between mothers and daughters. The suggestion to include men or boys in the solution seemed almost insignificant until Khanum-e Abtahi explained that she taught her son not to place gender at the forefront of identity.

Some suggested solutions to deal with the impact of the Soft War on Iranian families were pragmatic like forming reading groups, making lists of weaknesses, and making an effort to mentor young women. Some were more reflexive, asking others to take accountability for why many of the younger generation were not receptive to their concerns. Some addressed the importance of raising children in a way that was grounded in the Islamic teachings of khod shenasi and that khod shenasi was a collective responsibility. In her attempt to soften established notions through her suggestions about the courtship period, Khanum-e Tabesh first modeled for women of different backgrounds to push boundaries and to share different ideas. She showed, in her subtle approach, that young women mattered, and the responsibility of failed marriages must fall on everyone around the woman in the divorce.

In the women's participation, unintended outcomes emerged, inevitably recasting their work as a perpetually unfinished project. A close look at their active participation to resist the Soft War launched by their enemies revealed various ways khod shenasi was conceived of and used in the interactions. This mounts a challenge to normative ideas in contemporary discourse on resistance and women in Iran—a resistance commonly described as subversion of Islamic ideals as a necessary component for transformation. Guided by the objectives of the revolution to produce a Shi'i Islamic society, the howzevi defined and redefined khod shenasi on their own terms. They did so in the context of the work they participated in. In other words, to know oneself was to stand against the tests of time, and to stand against the tests of time together would allow for the continued work of the revolution.

NOTES

1. For more on basij pro-regime media producers, see Narjes Bajoghli, *Iran Reframed*, 1-112.
2. Alikhani, "The Politics of Satellite," 94.
3. A Small Media Report, "Satellite Jamming in Iran."
4. Alikhani, "The Politics of Satellite," 104.
5. Goodman, "2003 Charlie Rose Interview."
6. Sreberny and Torfeh, "The BBC Persian Service," 530–32.
7. Baumman et al., "Transcultural Journalism," 139–40. The BBC in the Middle East; Sreberny and Torfeh, "The BBC Persian Service," 515–35. Public diplomacy in Iran.
8. "Voice of America Charter"; US Agency for Global Media, "U.S. Government Agency Launches."
9. Richards, *The Man Who Changed the World*.
10. Khanum-e Tabesh, Tehran, August 16, 2011.
11. Rajneesh, *A Sudden Clash*, 58.
12. Mahdavi, *Passionate Uprisings*, 91–92, 180–82.
13. Torab, *Performing Islam*, 169.
14. Qur'an, Chapter 4:1.

CODA

I MADE IT A HABIT to take afternoon walks in Park-e Gheytarieh in north Tehran after coming home from fieldwork since moving from Pirouzi. I would sit on one of the wooden stumps lining the children's playground and pass time watching fathers talk to each other as their wives chatted while looking after their toddlers. It was rare to see anyone in chador or the full hijab in this playground. Women often wore light makeup and wraparound designer scarves while men had either shadow beards or none at all. Children wearing brand-name clothing were also noticeable. It was much easier for me to understand people here when they spoke Persian. In this park, visitors usually pronounced the words clearly and arranged the verbs in the same formal way we had learned in my Persian language class located in the most expensive neighborhood of Tehran, Elahiyeh. This was not the case in south Tehran, where people spoke Persian with accents from different regions of Iran.

Gheytarieh was an affluent neighborhood with high-rise condominiums. It was like Elahiyeh, where I lived in 2008, except Gheytarieh had wider streets. The cars parked along the street were usually larger in size, shiny and brand new, often Japanese or European made. The park had two large fountains near the community center, which was once the home of the Qajar Dynasty minister, Amir Kabir. Tall trees hovered over the paved walkways, and patches of grass on the side of the park were manicured with small rowing boats converted into a garden patch with different types of flowers. A noticeable number of East Asian expatriates visited the park as well. Men and women played badminton together in front of the library where high school students studied for their concour exams. Equally common were women in tight-fitting outfits jogging, teenage boys and girls walking together, or young couples walking and holding hands. I had watched two concerts at the park and shopped at the small bazaar every Thursday.

The community center held classes for those interested in playing Persian musical instruments and taking up voice lessons, alongside foreign language classes. The social and material features of the park, even the thickness of the metal used on the play sets for children, were different in comparison to the park where Maryam and I used to take Fereshteh in Pirouzi.

Maryam and Mohammad came to visit me for the first time in Gheytarieh in late 2011. Like my other howzevi friends from Pirouzi, they had been putting off this visit for a while. By early evening, we finally made it to the playground. I sat a few feet away from the three of them as I watched them play with Fereshteh on the slide. Mohammad's body language was not his usual; it was more cautious. He stayed near Maryam and Fereshteh but at a distance from other women. None of the men came near him.

Maryam stood next to the slide to hold Fereshteh's hand as she slid down. Maryam held one side of her chador close to her chest with her other hand. Fereshteh smiled from ear to ear by the time she made it to the bottom of the slide. Mohammad, finally smiling, stood and watched them. A woman with a toddler not much bigger than Fereshteh followed right behind them down the slide. The woman approached and talked to Maryam before Maryam could put Fereshteh back on the slide. Maryam turned and walked slowly toward me with Fereshteh in tow with one hand. Mohammad followed. I stood up and asked what happened. Maryam shrugged her shoulders. She smiled and said the woman told her there was a different place for them to play somewhere in the park. This was the woman's way of telling Maryam that she and Fereshteh could not play there. I remained silent, hoping they would ignore the woman. Mohammad tilted his head slightly lower to avoid having to look at me. He was upset but forcefully put on a half smile. As we walked away from the playground, I suggested we buy ice cream for Fereshteh. Maryam said they should go home to avoid traffic. Mohammad, usually making humorous comments whenever we traveled, remained silent for the rest of our walk back to his white Saipa.

Maryam's experience at Park-e Gheytarieh and others with similar experiences served as a reminder for the howzevi of what it was like before the revolution and for those too young to remember what life might have been like. The experience of marginalization in specific public spaces in north Tehran, as sampled in this vignette, was not unusual. Perhaps things have changed in north Tehran since then, however. A direct metro line from the south to the north of the city had just been completed when I left Iran, which could mean many things. But I tell this story to further encourage ethnographic research in Iran, in ways that could mend even for a brief moment the problem of dehumanization that takes place within and outside Iran about Iran. The dynamics between different factions informs the way Iran continues to be presented outside Iran, and regardless of what research is conducted, the polarization of the politics about Iran must be taken into serious consideration. Who decolonizes and how? There are bound to be those within a polity that are silenced. But it must be asked, each time on all sides, which polity has greater access to what and how we are to understand an Iran at any moment in time?

By being a neighbor to the howzevi, Tehran's complexity was brought back to life, out of readability from the distance and into the ambiguity of processes, into the obscurity of the everyday. I had the great opportunity to be with these women who spoke of the revolution as beneficial for them as they worked on themselves and on laws they saw as also benefiting women. There were those who disagreed with them, but for them, laws that benefited women benefited the rest of Iran. They worked on their roles as mothers, sisters, daughters, wives, and mentors to other women. I had the opportunity to see their colorful ways of being in the world as meaningful on their own terms.

In bearing witness to these women's interactions, this book has offered a closer look at the experiences of women who have been historically dismissed as insignificant or unfit to be part of a governing body. They are women who have chosen versions of womanhood that most likely differs from those made by the audience of this book. This helps us rethink the taken for granted notions of empowerment, personhood, and education. Drawing strength from tracking between small actions of daily life, educational aspirations, and institutional policy transformations, it also demonstrates a way to understand women's participation at the intersection of religion, education, and the state.

But there is more. There are plenty of unanswered questions that must be subject to further inquiry. This research was only about the howzevi women of Tehran, even though I traveled to Qom and Esfahan to meet individuals who informed this research. The cities of Esfahan, Mashhad, and Shiraz both have their own systems. I am certain there are howzevi who do not necessarily resist or undermine but distance themselves from the government all together. The howzeh in the city of Najaf Abad, for instance. Although they are not under the auspices of the centralized system in Qom, these kinds of howzeh are out there. There is very little known about these precisely because of the unstable situation in doing this type of research in Iran. It would also be of interest to know about the people behind the endowments that provide almost 100 percent of the funding for the howzeh elmiyeh for women. They have remained elusive.

In the summer of 2013, Maryam and a group of women were asked to draft a bill, grounded in Islamic text and scholarship, about allowing prostitutes infected with HIV/AIDS to have abortions. More drafts of bills followed. I continued to communicate with Maryam for some time. Fereshteh is now fourteen years old and is learning the Korean language. Her father, Mohammad, now has a doctorate degree. Maryam's entire household caught COVID, Maryam twice, the last one during her pregnancy with her second child. She gave birth to a healthy baby boy. Maryam and some of the other junior howzevi I barely mentioned here are now teaching at Madraseh Ali, the various Tehran howzeh, and Al-Zahra University. She and Sara recently co-published an article about Ayatollah Khomeini's teachings on women's mobility.

Khanum-e Refaei eventually became the deputy of education of a Region One women's howzeh in south Tehran, affecting the lives of many howzevi women. She oversees instructor hiring, admissions policies, course sequence development, and lecture programming and is responsible for approving requirements for degree completion. Zaynab is now married and completing her PhD in Islamic jurisprudence and Islamic law. Farideh continued to work odd jobs and eventually completed her PhD. She continues to do research on interpretations of Islamic law while the senior howzevi of this study experienced for the first time marrying their children off and becoming grandparents. Fatimah from Howzeh-ye Kowsar gave birth to a baby boy while her sister, Hoda, and many of the women from their class eventually married and started families of their own. A handful remained unmarried.

I end this book by returning my gaze to the difficult work of my other group of friends who are committed to bettering the conditions of women everywhere. They share a logic with public figures who have spent their lives working to improve women's conditions. "The news is the first crack at history." If women's participation in historical events do not make it into the news, they won't "make it into the books, the scholarship, and will disappear." [1] "What women must do is to refuse to be forgotten."[2] I documented my interactions with some of the howzevi women in Iran using my recorder, camera, and notebook as a testament to this, and I wrote about them here.

NOTES

1. Disney, Abigail. "Women Creating Change."
2. Afshar, *Islam and Feminisms*, 10.

APPENDIX A:
SAMPLE LIST OF BOOKS

Lum'e al Dameshqi by Shahid Avval

Sharh-e Lum'e by Shahid at-Thani

Usool-e Fiqh by Allameh Mohammad Reza Mozafar

Usool-e Estenbat by Allame Heydari

Mantegh by Allameh Mohammad Reza Mozafar

Eshkhas va Mahjoorian (Persons and Persons under Legal Incapacity) by Dr. Katuzian

Amval va Malekiat (Chattels and Possession) by Dr. Katuzian

Oxford Dictionary of Law

Shahe Ebne Aghil

Bedayat alhekmat by Allameh Tabatabaie

Elementary Law by Dr. Katuzian

Criminal Procedure by Dr. Ali Khaleghi

The Law of Negotiable Instruments by Dr. Koorosh Kavyani

The Labor Law by Dr. Araghi

Islamic Jurisprudence by Reza Islami

Derayatel Hadith

Muqaddamat—Arabic Grammar

Suyuti-Alfiyyat—learning grammar through poetry

Moghni—grammar with poems in the prophet's time

Itqan—Tafseer Qur'an

Uloom Belaghat—Arabic

Derayeh—Hadith—Shanechi

Tajrit—Baba Hadiash (*Tawhid of the Prophet*) by Mesbah Yazdi

Mab'dao Maad by Javadi Amoli

Tarikh Islam: Furughe Abdiyat by Ahlili

Uloom al Qur'an by Allameh Tabatabaei

Al-Makasib by Sheikh Morteza Ansari

Ar-Rasail by Sheikh Morteza Ansari

Kifayatol-Usool by Akhoonde Khorasani

Nahayatol-hikmah by Allameh Tabatabaie

Melal and Nehal by Shahrestany

Bedayath Nehaya

Shahr Manzoom by Sabsvari

Askar by Mulla Sadra

Akhlaq

Mi'raj Saada

Arbain Hadith by Khomeini

Ilm'e Hay'at—Astronomy

Ravon Shenasi by Dr. Qaami

Zamimi Tarbiyat

Almizan by Allameh Tabatabaei

Nemuneh by Makarameh Shiraz

Shavohedol Rububiyya by Mulla Sadra

Esharat—Ibn Sina (before)

Uloom al Rijal by Sobhane

Ilm al Hadith by Shanechi

APPENDIX B:
TABLE OF GENERAL FORMAT OF A HOWZEH ELMIYEH FOR WOMEN PROGRAM

Level	Equivalent	Content	Years to Complete
Maktab	High school	Narration-focused Reading the Arabic alphabet in the Qur'an, Memorization	-3 years -Madraseh Ali, 4 years
Sat'h 1 (Surface)	Level 1/ Associates/ Pre-university/ Kardani	Narration-focused Language, Poetry, Morals, Arabic Grammar, Syntax, Introduction to Aristotelian Logic	-1 year -Madraseh Ali, combined with high school
Sat'h 2	Level 2/ Undergraduate/ Lisans/Arshad Karshenasi	Disputation-focused Aristotelian logic applied in mobaheseh, basic books on the principles of Islamic jurisprudence (Usool), Islamic jurisprudence (Fiqh), Rights (Huquq), Islamic philosophy	-without a high school diploma, 7 years to finish -5 years -Madraseh Ali, 4 years
Sat'h 3	Level 3/ Master's/Fogeh Lisans	Disputation-focused Mastering specialized books on the principles of Islamic jurisprudence (Usool), Islamic jurisprudence (Fiqh), rights (Huquq), Islamic philosophy Students choose a topic of choice and write a research paper in their third year Students begin teaching	-3 years -Madraseh Ali, 3 years

(continued)

Level	Equivalent	Content	Years to Complete
Sat'h 4	Level 4/ Doctoral	Program development in progress (2011)	Program development in progress (2011) -Madraseh Ali, 3–5 years
Dars-e Kharij (A Lesson of the Outside, Beyond the Surface)	Postdoctoral	Disputation-focused. Training in ijtihad, students choose any class of interest offered Students do not use text in the classes and in their debates Information is drawn from memory Students publish from their own research	More than 15 years

GLOSSARY

Aaqed: the Overseer (the one who will marry the bride and the groom)

'Adil: in Arabic, is translated as the state of being "just," which assumes that one has earned a moral and legal credibility in society with virtues such as piety by ordaining the good in the Shari'a and forbidding what is illegal in the Shari'a

Agha/ye: gentleman/mister

Ahkam: Islamic rulings

Ahl-e Kitab: people of the book

'Ajr: a payment of consideration that must be clearly stated in the contract along with the duration of the temporary union

Akhlaq: morals

Alam-e bala tar: the divine world

Alam-e tabiat o madeh: the material world

Al-Imam al Muntazar: The Awaited Imam

Alimat: women Islamic scholars

'Amr: a will of power or command from God

Anjumans: semisecret societies of women

'Aqd: the marriage contract, the marriage contract ceremony

'Aql: intellect, reason

'Aql bashe: with sound awareness or intellect

'Aql res: mentally mature

'**Aqli:** of the intellect

Ashura: the day Imam Hossein was killed in the Battle of Karbala

Ayatollah: those who carry the title are experts in Islamic studies such as jurisprudence, ethics, and philosophy and usually teach in Islamic seminaries

Arzesh: value

B

Bahes: teaching-student dialectic

Ba housh: clever

Balegh bashe: mature in age

Banu: lady

Banuvan: women

Basij/Basij-e Mostaz'afin: Mobilization of the Oppressed, a volunteer paramilitary organization

Basij-e Daneshjooyi: University Basij

Bayt-e Rahbari: house/compound of the supreme leader

Bazari/s: individuals/families who own stalls or are wholesale distributors in the bazaar

C

Chador: an outer garment or open cloak worn by many Iranian women in public spaces

Chador-e arabi: a chador with sleeves

D

Dars-e Kharij: "Lessons of the Outside"; "External" level or the highest level of the howzeh system of education

Deen: religion/way of life

Diyeh: blood money

Doost pesar: boyfriend

E

Efrat: excess

Eftar: dinner, the breaking of fast, several times during the month

Emtehan: exam or assessment of progress

Engelobi: revolutionary

Ensan-e Kamel: the ideal person

Etaa'at: a wife's obedience to the husband specifically about where she takes her body

F

Falsafe-ye Islami: Islamic philosophy

Fiqh: Islamic jurisprudence

Fisabilillah: for the sake of God

Fitrah: the original disposition of the self to worship God

Fogeh Lisans: equivalent to a master's degree

G

Galyon: hookah

Gardesh: an excursion

Gheyrat: a protective kind of jealous-responsible emotion, not jealousy or anger

Ghira: in both Persian and Arabic languages, connotes some kind of honorable attachment to something; commonly used in the context of choosing a spouse as well as in commentaries on marital or familial responsibilities

Gonah: sin

H

Hadith: narrations from the Prophet or about the Prophet Mohammad about his lifeways

Hajj: pilgrimage to Mecca

Haqiqat: a truth

Haraka jawhariyya: essential motion

Haram: forbidden action

Hay'at: religious gathering

Hayehoo: noise

Hazrat: a title used to honor a person, comparable to "her holiness"

Hijab: "to cover, to veil, to shelter"; in popular use, hijab means "head cover and modest dress for women" among Muslims, which most Islamic legal systems define as covering everything except the face, feet, and hands in public.

Hosseiniyeh: halls where religious mourning ceremonies take place and where religious study groups meet

Howzeh: in Arabic, means "to hold or grasp something firmly"; in Persian, means "a side of, a part of, or middle of a kingdom"; in this book, short for howzeh elmiyeh

Howzeh elmiyeh: Islamic seminaries of Iran; a place of knowledge or a circle of knowledge

Howzevi: seminarian

Huquq: Islamic rights

I

Ihtiram: admiration

Ijaza: certificate of transmission of Islamic knowledge

Ijtihad: the process of making a legal decision through independent interpretation of the Qur'an

Ikhlaas: sincerity

Imam: Islamic leadership position; in Shi'i Islam, the honorific used for divinely chosen leaders of the community to be perfect examples and lead all humanity in all aspects of life; this figure is central to Twelver and Ismaili Shi'i belief

Iman: faith

Isnad: the chain of transmission of knowledge

Ittisaliyah: the need or desire for personal "connection" across generations with the time and personages of Islamic origins

J

Jahadi Basij: or Jahad Sazandegi, Reconstruction Corps

Jalbe tavajo kardan: to be the center of attention

Jaleseh: religious study group or meeting

Jang-e Narm: Soft War

Jashn-e Mas'uliyat: Celebration of Responsibility, takes place on a girl's ninth birthday

Javanmardi: a man known for his chivalry, courage, open-handedness, and generosity

Jilbab: a long coat over another layer of clothing

K

Kalam: fundamentals of Islamic thought

Kashf hejab: the decree of unveiling in 1936

Kazab: mendacity, deception

Khanevadeh: family

Khanum/e: lady

Khastegari: courtship

Khob bashe: good

Khod: self

Khod-e Asil: the original form of the self; the Self fully immersed in its fitrah, the natural disposition to worship God

Khod Shenasi: self-work; the lifelong work of self-knowing, self-examination, self-awareness, and self-scrutiny to recuperate and protect the Original Self, a self that is godly

Khoshoo': humbleness (specific to context), submissiveness

Khums tax: One-fifth of a person's income given to the leading mujtahid; half of that is given to Imam Mahdi, who is in occultation

Kibr: arrogance

Kuku: frittata made of green vegetables

L

Lisans: equivalent to an undergraduate degree, also known as karshenasi arshad

M

Madda: a woman who recites the ceremonial story

Maadar: mother

Madrak: certificate of program completion

Madraseh: a place where learning/teaching is done

Maghnae: slip-on headscarf sewn below the chin area

Mahjoub: a purposeful act to be unseen

Mahram: spouse or close kin with whom one cannot marry and before whom the woman needs to veil

Mahvareh: satellite technology

Majlis: Iranian parliament, Islamic Consultative Assembly

Majlis-e khobregan-e rahbari: the Assembly of Experts

Makam-e mahv: maho in Arabic; mahv doshtan, a station in Islamic mysticism; station of obliteration of the ego

Maktab: an informal form of schooling before the howzeh

Makruh: disapproved action

Mal-e mani: you are mine

Mantaqe: region

Manto: a blouse type of coat that reaches the knees

Marifat en nafs: existential essence, spiritual essence, divine essence

Marja'e Taqlid: Grand Ayatollah, Source of Emulation

Maydoon: fruit and vegetable section of the Tehran bazar

Mazhab: practice

Mazhabi: religious conservative, ultra-religious conservative

Mazhabi motavaset: average religiously conservative

Mehriye: bride price; the money or gold coins the groom agrees to pay to the bride in the case of divorce or separation

Mithaq: al-Mithaq, an event called the Covenant, when all souls were gathered to bear witness to God's Lordship

Mobaheseh: Disputation circle

Mobareze: battle

Modir: manager/manageress

Mohabbat: love, kindness

Moharram: a month in the Islamic calendar

Mokhtar bashe: has the power/authority to decide

Moqademati: novice level

Mubariz: militant

Muhadith: a women transmitter of the narrations of the Prophet Mohammad

Mujtahid: a man who does ijtihad, the process of making a legal decision through independent interpretation of the Qur'an and Sunnah

Mujtahideh: a woman who does ijtihad, the process of making a legal decision through independent interpretation of the Qur'an and Sunnah

Murshidat: a woman religious preacher

Musalman: Muslim

N

Nafaqeh: a husband's responsibility toward the wife of financial maintenance throughout the marriage

Nafs: self

Nahad-e Rahbari: Organization of the supreme leader

Namzadi: the marriage engagement period

O

Ojratol Mesl: during divorce, a woman's right to financial compensation for work she carried out in the duration of the marriage for duties beyond sexual intercourse and asking permission from her husband

P

Parti bazi: insider networking to get ahead

Payan-e nameh: research paper

Peshkel mochalag: a pregnant female donkey's dried manure

Posht: a network of followers and allies

Q

Qalb: the spiritual heart

Qavi: powerful

Qoveh: forces

Querencia: where the bull begins to make his home in the course of the bullfight

R

Rangi: colorful chador

Rivayat: narrations from the Prophet or his family

Riya': the desire for recognition and praise

Ro migire: pulling the chador three-quarters over the face

Rowzeh: rowzeh-khani; a religious meeting, a reading of an elegy, a mourning session

Rowzeh-khan: the person leading the elegy reading or mourning session

Ruh: soul or spirit

Rusari: a square cloth folded into a triangle and pinned at the chin

S

Sajdah: prostration

Salavat: words of praise for the Prophet Mohammad

Sat'h: the levels before Kharij level; means superficies and refers to reading directly from books and learning from them

Shahadat-e: martyrdom of

Shahavat: lust

Shahid: martyr for the sake of God

Shari'a: Islamic law

Shawl: a rectangular cloth used to wrap around the head

Shi'i Islam: a sect of Islam that believes that Ali, the Prophet's cousin, is the rightful successor after the Prophet's death; in Shi'a Islam, the imam is the successor of the Prophet Muhammad and acts as the preserver and interpreter of Islam and its laws

Shirini: literally, a confection; a positive feeling from the labor of overpowering the temptation to abandon personal effort

Shohardari: married

Shol: a rectangular cloth used to wrap around the head

Sighe: a temporary marriage or the formula of the marriage contract

Sofreh: tablecloth

Sofreh-ye Nazr: a women's religious gathering that involves feeding guests as a votive offering to God

Sonnati-ye howzeh: a trademark practice in the seminary

Surah: chapter in the Qur'an

T

Ta'abbudi: immutable

Ta'adod-e Zawjat: the number of wives

Ta'asob: extreme, intolerable temperament

Tafsir: the study of established interpretation of the verses of the Qur'an

Talabeh: a woman student of Islamic sciences; could be used to refer to a student in the howzeh

Talabeh azad: "free" or roaming students

Talaq: divorce

Taqdir: appreciation

Taqiyya: denial of religious belief in the face of persecution

Taqlid: imitation, observed in the details of religion, of the "how to" worship, but not in the fundamentals of the faith, the "what to" believe in

Taqrirat: an exposition where a student provides an explanation of the previous lecture

Tasu'a: ninth day of the month of Muharram

Tawadhu': humility; recognition that God is the source of all

Tawhid: belief in the oneness of God

V

Vaqf: endowment

Vasati: a game similar to dodgeball

Vilayat bar nikah: consent for marriage from the father as the guardian

Vilayat-e faqih: guardianship of the Islamic jurist

Z

Zaghred: high-pitched sound made by women to celebrate an event

Zerang: clever

Zuhd: freedom from material attachments

WORKS CITED

Abrahamian, Ervand. *A History of Modern Iran*. New York: Cambridge University Press, 2008.

Abtahi, Mir Sayyed Hojjat Mohaved. *Risheho va Jeloho-ye Teshia va Houzeh Elmieh-e Esfahan*. Qom: Daftar Tablighat Al-Mahdi, 1997.

Abu-Lughod, Lila. *Veiled Sentiments: Honor and Poetry in a Bedouin Society*. Cairo: American University in Cairo Press, 1986.

———. "Writing against Culture." In *Recapturing Anthropology: Working in the Present*, 466–79. Santa Fe, NM: School of American Research Press, 1991.

Abu Talib, Ali ibn (Imam Ali). *Peak of Eloquence: Nahjul Balagha*. Edited by Y. Al-Jibouri. New York: Tahrike Tarsile Qur'an, 2009.

Adelkhah, Fariba. *Being Modern in Iran*. New York: Columbia University Press, 2000.

Afary, Janet. "On the Origins of Feminism in Early 20th-Century Iran." *Journal of Women's History* 1, no. 2 (Fall 1989): 65–87.

———. "Portraits of Two Islamist Women: Escape from Freedom or from Tradition?" *Critique* 19 (Fall 2001): 47–77.

———. *Sexual Politics in Modern Iran*. Cambridge, UK: Cambridge University Press, 2009.

———. "Steering between Scylla and Charybdis: Shifting Gender Roles in Twentieth Century Iran." *NWSA Journal* 8, no. 1, Global Perspectives (Spring 1996): 28–49.

Afshar, Haleh. *Islam and Feminisms: An Iranian Case Study*. New York: St. Martin's, 1998.

Ahmed, Leila. *Women and Gender in Islam: Historical Roots of a Modern Debate*. New Haven, CT: Yale University Press, 1992.

Alikhani, Fardin. "The Politics of Satellite Television in Iran." In *Media, Culture and Society in Iran: Living with Globalization and the Islamic State*, edited by Mehdi Semati, 94–110. New York: Routledge, 2008.

Alinejad, Masih. *The Wind in My Hair: My Fight for Freedom in Modern Iran.* New York: Little Brown and Company/Hachette, 2018.

Anderson, Brenda, and Franz Greifanhagen. "Covering Up on the Prairies: Perceptions of Muslim Identity, Multiculturalism and Security in Canada." In *Islamic Fashion and Anti-fashion: New Perspectives from Europe and North America,* edited by Emma Tarlo and Annelies Moors, 55–72. New York: Bloomsbury, 2013.

A Small Media Report. "Satellite Jamming in Iran: A War Over Airwaves." A Small Media Report Executive Summary. November 2012. https://www-tc.pbs.org/wgbh/pages/frontline/tehranbureau/SatelliteJammingInIranSmallMedia.pdf.

Bahramitash, Roksana. "Saving Iranian Women: Orientalist Feminism and the Axis of Evil." In *Security Disarmed: Critical Perspectives on Gender, Race, and Militarization,* 101–10. New Brunswick, NJ: Rutgers University Press, 2008.

———. "The War on Terror, Feminist Orientalism and Orientalist Feminism: Case Studies of Two North American Bestsellers." *Critique: Critical Middle Eastern Studies,* 14:2 (2005): 221–235.

Bajoghli, Narjes. *Iran Reframed: Anxieties of Power in the Islamic Republic.* Stanford, CA: Stanford University Press, 2019.

Bakhshayishi, Aqiqi. *Ten Decades of Ulama's Struggle.* Translated by Alaedin Pazargadi. Tehran, Islamic Republic of Iran. Tehran, Iran: Islamic Propagation Organization, 1985.

Basso, Keith. "Stalking with Stories: Names, Places, and Moral Narratives among the Western Apache." In *Text, Play, and Story: The Construction and Reconstruction of Self and Society,* edited by E. M. Bruner, 19–55. Prospect Heights, IL: Waveland, 1984.

———. *Wisdom Sits in Places: Landscape and Language among the Western Apache.* Albuquerque: University of New Mexico, 1996.

Bateson, Gregory. *Mind and Nature: A Necessary Unity.* New York: E. P. Dutton, 1979.

———. *Steps to an Ecology of Mind: Collected Essays in Anthropology, Psychiatry, Evolution, and Epistemology.* Northvale, NJ: Jason Aronson Inc., 1972.

Baumann, Gerd, Marie Gillespie, and Annabelle Sreberny. "Transcultural Journalism and the Politics of Translation: Interrogating the BBC World Service." *Journalism* 12, no. 2 (2011): 135–42.

Berkey, Jonathan. *Formation of Islam: Religion and Society in the Near East, 600–1800.* Cambridge, UK: Cambridge University Press, 2003.

Betteridge, Anne. "Muslim Women and Shrines in Shiraz." In *Everyday Life in the Muslim Middle East,* edited by Donna Lee Bowen and Evelyn A. Early, 276–89. Bloomington: Indiana University Press, 2002.

Biehl, João, and Peter Locke. *Unfinished: The Anthropology of Becoming.* Edited by J. Biehl and P. Locke. Durham, NC: Duke University Press, 2017.

Bignall, Simone. *Postcolonial Agency: Critique and Constructivism.* Edinburgh, Scotland: Edinburgh University Press, 2010.

"Bomb Threat against University of Chicago Is Latest in Campaign to Silence and Divide Iranian Americans." *NIAC Action,* October 19, 2022. https://www

.niacouncil.org/press-releases/bomb-threat-against-university-of-chicago-is
-latest-threat-to-silence-and-divide-iranian-americans/?locale=en.

Boyarin, Daniel. "Placing Reading: Ancient Israel and Medieval Europe." In *The Ethnography of Reading*, edited by Daniel Boyarin, 10–39. Berkeley, CA: UC Press, 1993.

Buccar, Elizabeth. "Dianomy: Understanding Religious Women's Moral Agency as Creative Conformity." *Journal of the American Academy of Religion* 78, no. 3 (2010): 662–86.

Bukhari, Muḥammad ibn Ismaill. *Sahih Bukhari*. Lahaur, Pakistan: Maktabah-yi Quddusiyyah, 2004.

Casey, Edward. "How to Get from Space to Place in a Fairly Short Stretch of Time: Phenomenological Prolegomena." In *Senses of Place*, edited by Steven Feld and Keith H. Basso, 13–52. Santa Fe, NM: School of American Research Press, 1996.

Christiansen, Connie. "Miss Headscarf: Islamic Fashion and the Danish Media." In *Islamic Fashion and Anti-Fashion: New Perspectives from Europe and North America*, edited by Emma Tarlo and Annelies Moors, 225–40. London: Bloomsbury, 2013.

Clifford, James. "Spatial Practices: Fieldwork, Travel, and the Disciplining of Anthropology." In *Anthropological Locations: Boundaries and Grounds of a Field Science*, edited by Akhil Gupta and James Ferguson, 185–222. Berkeley, CA: UC Press, 1997.

Cronin-Furman, Kate, Nimmi Gowrinathan, and Rafia Zakaria. "Emmissaries of Empowerment." New York: Colin Powell School for Civic and Public Leadership, The City College of New York, 2017. Accessed August 25, 2023. https://www.ccny .cuny.edu/colinpowellschool/emissaries-empowerment.

De Certeau, Michel. "Practices of Space." In *On Signs*, edited by Marshall Blonsky, 123–45. Baltimore, MD: Johns Hopkins University, 1985.

———. *The Practice of Everyday Life*. Translated by Steven Rendall. Berkeley: University of California Press, 1984.

Deeb, Lara. *An Enchanted Modern: Gender and Public Piety in Shi'i Lebanon*. Princeton, NJ: Princeton University Press, 2006.

Disney, Abigail. "Women Creating Change." Center for the Study of Social Difference, Columbia University, New York, February 25, 2013. YouTube video, 1:05:53. https://www.youtube.com/watch?v=5ClQfh4phtI.

Douglas, Mary. *Natural Symbols: Explorations in Cosmology*. New York: Routledge, 1996.

El Guindi, Fadwa. *Veil: Modesty, Privacy and Resistance*. London: Bloomsbury Academic, 1999.

El Haitami, Meriam. "Restructuring Female Religious Authority: State-Sponsored Women Religious Guides (Murshidat) and Scholars ('Alimat) in Contemporary Morocco." *Mediterranean Studies*, 20, no. 2 (2012): 228–40.

Fayyaz, Sam, and Roozbeh Shirazi. "Good Iranian, Bad Iranian: Representations of Iran and Iranians in Time and Newsweek (1998–2009)." *Iranian Studies*, 46, no. 1 (January 1, 2013): 53–72.

Fazaeli, Roja. *Islamic Feminisms: Rights and Interpretations Across Generations in Iran.* New York: Routledge, 2017.

Fischer, Michael J. *Iran: From Religious Dispute to Revolution.* Madison: University of Wisconsin Press, 1980.

———. "The Rhythmic Beat of the Revolution in Iran." *Cultural Anthropology,* 25, no. 3 (2010): 497–543.

Fiske, John. *Understanding Popular Culture.* New York: Routledge, 1989.

Foucault, Michel. *Discipline and Punish: The Birth of the Prison.* New York: Vintage, 1975.

———. "What Is Enlightenment?" In *The Foucault Reader,* edited by Paul Rabinow, 32–50. New York: Pantheon, 1984.

Freire, Paulo. *Pedagogy of the Oppressed.* London: Continuum, 2000.

Friedl, Erika. "The Dynamics of Women's Spheres of Action in Rural Iran." In *Women in Middle Eastern History: Shifting Boundaries in Sex and Gender,* 195–214. New Haven, CT: Yale University Press, 1991.

Gee, James. *An Introduction to Discourse Analysis: Theory and Method.* New York: Routledge, 1999.

Geertz, Clifford. "Common Sense as a Cultural System." *The Antioch Review,* 33, no. 1 (Spring 1975): 5–26.

Gheiby, Bijan, James R. Russell, and Hamid Algar. "Cador (2)." In *Encyclopedia Iranica* Vol. IV, Fasc. 6 (1990): 609–11. December 15, 1990. https://www.iranica online.org/articles/cador-a-loose-female-garment-covering-the-body-sometimes -also-the-face.

Goodwin, Charles. "Audience Diversity, Participation and Interpretation." *Text* 6, no. 3 (1986): 284–316.

Graham, William. "Traditionalism in Islam: An Essay in Interpretation." *Journal of Interdisciplinary History* 23, no. 3, Religion and History (1993): 495–522.

Gutas, Dimitri. *Greek Thought, Arabic Culture: The Graeco-Arabic Translation Movement in Baghdad and Early ʿAbbāsid Society (2nd–4th/8th–10th Centuries).* New York: Routledge, 1998.

Haeri, Shahla. *Law of Desire: Temporary Marriage in Shiʾi Iran.* Syracuse, NY: Syracuse University Press, 1989.

Hamayon, Roberte. *Why We Play: An Anthropological Study.* Chicago, IL: HAU, 2016.

Harding, Susan. "Representing Fundamentalism: The Problem of the Repugnant Cultural Other." *Social Research* 52, no. 2 (Summer 1991): 373–93.

Hassan, Mona. "Women at the Intersection of Turkish Politics, Religion, and Education: The Unexpected Path to Becoming a State-Sponsored Female Preacher." *Comparative Islamic Studies* 5, no. 1 (August 2011): 112–30.

Hatam, Nassim. "Why Iranian Women Are Wearing White on Wednesdays." *BBC News,* June 14, 2017. https://www.bbc.com/news/world-middle-east-40218711.

Hegland, Mary. "Political Roles of Aliabad Women: The Public-Private Dichotomy Transcended." In *Women in Middle Eastern History: Shifting Boundaries in Sex and Gender,* 215–32. New Haven, CT: Yale University Press, 1991.

Heidegger, Martin. "Being-in-the-World as Being-With and Being-One's-Self. The They." In *Being and Time*, translated by J. Macquarrie and E. Robinson, 149–68. London: Harper Row, 1962.

Hemingway, Ernest. *Death in the Afternoon*. New York: Scribner, 1960.

Ingold, Tim. *Lines: A Brief History*. New York: Taylor & Francis, 2007.

———. *The Perception of the Environment: Essays on Livelihood, Dwelling and Skill*. London: Routledge, 2000.

"Iran: Authorities Defiant on Rights Record Executions Soar, Activists and Dissidents Systematically Suppressed." *Human Rights Watch*. Accessed May 20, 2022. https://www.hrw.org/news/2012/01/22/iran-authorities-defiant-rights-record.

Jaiswal, Nikhil, and Emma Janssen. "IOP Staff Sent Home Following Bomb Threat." *The Chicago Maroon*. October 18, 2022. https://chicagomaroon.com/36976/news /breaking-critics-of-iop-panelist-send-bomb-threat-staff-sent-home.

Jambet, Christian. *The Act of Being: The Philosophy of Revelation in Mulla Sadra*. Translated by Jeff Fort. Boston, MA: MIT Press, 2006.

Jeffrey, Patricia. *Frogs in a Well: Indian Women in Purdah*. London: Zed, 1979.

Kamalkhani, Zahra. *Women's Islam: Religious Practice among Women in Today's Iran*. London: Kegan Paul International, 1998.

Keddie, Nikki. *Modern Iran: Roots and Results of Revolution*. New Haven, CT: Yale University Press, 2003.

Kian-Thiébaut, Azadeh. "From Islamization to the Individualization of Women in Post-Revolutionary Iran." In *Women, Religion and Culture in Iran*, edited by S. Anzari and V. Martin, 127–42. Richmond, VA: Curzon in association with the Royal Asiatic Society of Great Britian and Ireland, 2002.

Künkler, Mirjam, and Roja Fazaeli. "The Life of Two Mujtahidahs: Female Religious Authority in Twentieth-Century Iran." In *Women, Leadership and Mosques: Changes in Contemporary Islamic Authority*, edited by Masooda Bano and Hilary Kalmbach, 127–60. Boston, MA: Brill, 2012.

Lave, Jean. *Cognition in Practice: Mind, Mathematics and Culture in Everyday Life*. Cambridge, UK: Cambridge University Press, 1988.

Lave, Jean, and Etienne Wenger. *Situated Learning: Legitimate Peripheral Participation*. Cambridge, UK: Cambridge University Press, 1991.

Le Renard, Amélie. *A Society of Young Women: Opportunities of Place, Power, and Reform in Saudi Arabia*. Stanford, CA: Stanford University Press, 2014.

Mahdavi, Pardis. *Passionate Uprisings: Iran's Sexual Revolution*. Stanford, CA: Stanford University Press, 2007.

Mahmood, Saba. "Feminist Theory, Embodiment, and the Docile Agent: Some Reflections on the Egyptian Islamic Revival." *Cultural Anthropology* 6, no. 2 (2001): 202–36.

———. *Politics of Piety: The Islamic Revival and the Feminist Subject*. Princeton, NJ: Princeton University Press, 2005.

Majid, Anouar. "The Politics of Feminism in Islam." *Signs: Journal of Women in Culture and Society* 23, no. 2 (1998): 321–361.

Malpas, Jeffrey. "Rethinking Dwelling: Heidegger and the Question of Place." *Environmental and Architectural Phenomenology* 25, no. 1 (2014): 15–23.

Mauss, Marcel. "'Techniques of the Body [1936].'" Translated by Ben Brewster. *Economy and Society* 2 (1973): 70–88.

Mbembe. Achille. "Provincializing France?" Translated by Janet Roitman. *Public Culture* 23, no. 1 (2011): 85–119.

McKinnon, Susan. "On Kinship and Marriage: A Critique of the Genetic and Gender Calculus of Evolutionary Psychology." In *Complexities: Beyond Nature and Nurture*, edited by Susan McKinnon and Sydel Silverman, 106–31. Chicago, IL: University of Chicago Press, 2005.

Mehran, Golnar. "Iran: A Shi'ite Curriculum to Serve the Islamic State." In *Teaching Islam: Textbooks and Religion in the Middle East*, edited by G. Starrett and E. A. Doumato, 53–70. Boulder, CO: Lynne Rienner, 2007.

Meillassoux, Claude. *Maidens, Meal and Money: Capitalism and the Domestic Community*. Cambridge. UK: Cambridge University Press, 1981.

Menashri, David. *Education and the Making of Modern Iran*. Ithaca, NY: Cornell University Press, 1992.

Meneley, Anne. *Tournaments of Value: Sociability and Hierarchy in a Yemeni Town*. Toronto, Canada: University of Toronto Press, 1996.

Metcalf, Barbara. *Moral Conduct and Authority: The Place of Adab in South Asian Islam*. Edited by Barbara Daly Metcalf. Berkeley: University of California Press, 1984.

Minganti, Pia K. "Burqinis, Bikinis and Bodies: Encounters in Public Pools in Italy and Sweden." In *Islamic Fashion and Anti-Fashion: New Perspectives from Europe and North America*, edited by Emma Tarlo and Annelies Moors, 33–54. New York: Bloomsbury, 2013.

Mir-Hosseini, Ziba. *Islam and Gender: The Religious Debate in Contemporary Iran*. Princeton, NJ: Princeton University Press, 1999.

———. "Women and Politics in Post-Khomeini Iran: Divorce, Veiling and Emerging Feminist Voices." In *Women and Politics in the Third World*, edited by Haleh Afshar, 145–1733. New York: Routledge, 1996.

Moghissi, Haideh. *Populism and Feminism in Iran: Women's Struggle in a Male-Defined Revolutionary Movement*. New York: St. Martin's, 1994.

Momen, Moojan. *Introduction to Shi'i Islam: The History and Doctrines of Twelver Shi'ism*. New Haven, CT: Yale University Press, 1985.

Motahhari, Morteza. *The Principle of Ijtihad in Islam*, Vol. X, No. 1. Al-Islam.org. Accessed August 25, 2023. https://www.al-islam.org/al-serat/ijtihad.htm.

Motamedi, Maziar. "Iran's 'Morality Police' Return as Authorities Enforce Hijab Rule." *Al Jazeera*, July 16, 2023.

Naeeni, Nahleh. *Shi'ah Women Transmitters of Hadith: A Collection of Biographies of the Women Who Have Transmitted Traditions*. Qom, Iran: Ansariyan, 2011.

Nafisi, Azar. "Tales of Subversion: Women Challenging Fundamentalism in the Islamic Republic of Iran." In *Religious Fundamentalisms and the Human Rights of Women*, edited by Courtney Howland, 257–70. New York: Palgrave, 1999.

Najmabadi, Afsaneh. "Crafting an Educated Housewife in Iran." In *Remaking Women: Feminism and Modernity in the Middle East,* edited by L. Abu-Lughod, 91–135. Princeton, NJ: Princeton University Press, 1998.

———. "(Un)veiling Feminism." In *Secularisms,* edited by Janet Jakobsen and Ann Pellegrini, 39–57. Durham, NC: Duke University Press, 2008.

Nasr, Hossein. "Part I: Religious, Intellectual, and Cultural Context." In *History of Islamic Philosophy Part I,* edited by Seyyed Hossein Nasr and Oliver Leaman, 21–39. Qom, Iran: Ansariyan, 2001.

———. "Self-Awareness and Ultimate Selfhood." *Religious Studies* 13 (1977): 319–25.

Okin, Susan. *Justice, Gender and the Family* (New York: Basic Books, 1989).

———. "Is Multiculturalism Bad for Women?" In *Is Multiculturalism Bad for Women?,* edited by Joshua Cohen, Matthew Howard, and Martha Nussbaum, 9–24. Princeton, NJ: Princeton University Press, 1999.

Ortega y Gasset, Jose. "The Difficulty of Reading." *Diogenes* 28 (1959): 1–17.

Osanloo, Arzoo. *The Politics of Women's Rights in Iran.* Princeton, NJ: Princeton University Press, 2009.

Pacifica Radio. "2003 Charlie Rose Interview with Amy Goodman about Iraq War Protests." March 12, 2003. Online video, 17:05. http://www.democracynow.org /blog/2013/3/19/video_2003_charlie_rose_interview_with_amy_goodman _about_iraq_war_protests.

Paidar, Parvin. *Women and the Political Process in Twentieth-Century Iran.* Cambridge, UK: Cambridge University Press, 1995.

Papanek, Hanna. "Purdah: Separate Worlds and Symbolic Shelter." *Comparative Studies in Society and History* 15, no. 3 (June 1973): 289–325.

Partridge, Damani. *Hypersexuality and Headscarves: Race, Sex, and Citizenship in the New Germany.* Bloomington: Indiana University Press, 2012.

Piela, Anna. "Wearing the Niqab in the UK: Exploring the Embodied 'Shape a Moral Action One Can Take.'" *Journal of the American Academy of Religion* 87, no. 2 (June 2019): 512–42.

Poya, Maryam. *Women, Work, and Islamism: Ideology and Resistance in Iran.* New York: Zed, 1999.

Rajavi, Maryam. *Women, Voice of the Oppressed.* Accessed February 14, 2024. https://www.maryam-rajavi.com/en/women-voice-of-the-oppressed-earlscourt -london/.

Rajneesh, Bhagwan Shree. *A Sudden Clash of Thunder.* Poona, India: Rajneesh Foundation, 1977.

Richards, Dai, dir. "The Man Who Changed the World." BBC Two: Iran and the West. July 4, 2009. *BBC Documentary,* 1 hour. https://www.bbc.co.uk/programmes /boohmrvt.

Saeidi, Shirin. *Women and the Islamic Republic: How Gendered Citizenship Conditions the Iranian State.* Cambridge, UK: Cambridge University Press, 2021.

Said, Edward. *Covering Islam.* New York: Pantheon, 1981.

Sakurai, Keiko. "Shi'ite Women's Seminaries (howzeh-ey 'elmiyyeh-ye khahran) in Iran: Possibilities and Limitations." *International Society for Iranian Studies* 45, no. 6 (2012): 727–44.

———. "Women's Empowerment and Iranian-Style Seminaries in Iran and Pakistan." In *The Moral Economy of the Madrasa: Islam and Education Today*, edited by Keiko Sakurai and Fariba Adelkhah, 32–58. London and New York: Routledge, 2011.

Salime, Zakia. *Between Feminism and Islam: Human Rights and Sharia Law in Morocco*. St. Paul: University of Minnesota Press, 2011.

Sanasarian, Eliz. *The Women's Rights Movement in Iran: Mutiny, Appeasement, and Repression from 1900 to Khomeini*. New York: Praeger, 1982.

Sciolino, Elain. "The Chanel under the Chador" *New York Times*, May 4, 1997. https://www.nytimes.com/1997/05/04/magazine/the-chanel-under-the-chador.html.

Sedghi, Hamideh. *Women and Politics in Iran: Veiling, Unveiling, and Reveiling*. Cambridge, UK: Cambridge University Press, 2007.

Sener, Kayra. "NES Chair Ghamari-Tabirizi Responds after Tory Panelist Alleged Links to Iranian Regime." *Daily Princetonian,* December 20, 2022. https://www.dailyprincetonian.com/article/2022/12/princeton-professor-iran-regime-support-allegations.

Shahrokni, Nazanin. *Women in Place: The Politics of Gender Segregation in Iran*. Oakland: University of California Press, 2020.

Shimamoto, Takamitsu. "The Question of 'Self Knowledge' in Islam: Mortaza Motahhari's Theory of the Perfect Man." *Journal of the Interdisciplinary Study of Monotheistic Religions* 4 (2008): 25–44.

Shomali, Mohammad. *Self-Knowledge*. Qom, Iran: Mahdiyar, 2006.

Siavoshi, Sussan. "Islamist Women Activists: Allies or Enemies?" In *Iran: Between Tradition and Modernity*, edited by Ramin Jahanbegloo, 169–82. Oxford, England: Lexington, 2004.

Sreberny, Annabelle, and Massoumeh Torfeh. "The BBC Persian Service 1941–1979." *Historical Journal of Film, Radio and Television* 28, no. 4 (2010): 515–35.

Street, Brian. *Literacy in Theory in Practice*. Cambridge, UK: Cambridge University Press, 1984.

Sullivan, Zohreh. "Eluding the Feminist, Overthrowing the Modern? Transformations in Twentieth-Century Iran." In *Remaking Women: Feminism and Modernity in the Middle East*, edited by Lila Abu-Lughod, 215–42. Princeton, NJ: Princeton University Press, 1998.

Tawasil, Amina. "Reading as Practice: The Howzevi (Seminarian) Women in Iran and Clair de Lune." *Anthropology and Education Quarterly* 50, no. 1 (2019): 66–83.

———. "Towards the Ideal Revolutionary Shi'i Woman: The Howzevi (Seminarian), the Requisites of Marriage and Islamic Education in Iran." *HAWWA: Journal of Women of the Middle East and the Islamic World* 13 (2015): 99–126.

Tohidi, Nayereh. "Beyond Islamic Feminism: Women and Representation in Iran's Democracy Movement." *Islamic Feminism and Beyond: The New Frontier* (Fall 2010): 18–22. https://www.wilsoncenter.org/publication/islamic-feminism-and-beyond-the-new-frontier-fall-2010.

Torab, Azam. *Performing Islam: Gender and Ritual in Iran*. Boston, MA: Brill, 2007.

"U.S. Government Agency Launches News Network Targeting Persian Speakers." *US Agency for Global Media*. February 7, 2019. https://www.usagm.gov/2019/02/07/u-s-government-agency-launches-news-network-targeting-persian-speakers.

Varenne, Hervé. "The Social Facting of Education: Durkheim's Legacy." *Journal of Curriculum Studies* 27 (1995): 373–89.

Wellman, Rose. *Feeding Iran: Shi'i Families and the Making of the Islamic Republic*. Berkeley, CA: UC Press, 2021.

Zaman, Muhammad. "Competing Conceptions of Religious Education." In *Schooling Islam: The Culture and Politics of Modern Education*, edited by Robert W. Hefner and Muhammad Qasim Zaman, 242–68. Princeton, NJ: Princeton University Press, 2007.

INDEX

1979 Revolution, xi, xvi; chador, 143; bazaar merchants, 107; BBC, 259; bringing outside Iran, 120; checking oneself, 135; development of women's howzeh elmiyeh, 58, 63, 193; Islamist women, 12; women giving credit to 1–3; women's Islamic scholarship, 34, 39

Abu Bakr, Asma bint, 244
Abu-Lughod, Lila, xvii, xviii, 4, 28, 237, 251
Adelkhah, Fariba, 100
'adil, 104, 121, 122, 123–124, 193
administration, 3, 67, 83, 198, 258; governance, 2, 15, 65, 258
Afary, Janet, 12, 28n29, 28n32, 56n25–26, 57n53–55, 83n12, 83n23
Sharifi (Agha-ye), 59, 76, 77–80, 83, 131, 138, 148, 163–168
agency, 9, 11, 17, 28, 147, 151, 276, 296, 297, 303. *See also* mobility
ahkam (arbitration), 90
Ahmadi (Khanum-e), 79, 168, 181–182, 255, 273
Ahmadinejad, Mahmoud, xii, xiii, 3, 33
Alizadeh (Khanum-e), 91, 141, 178, 181, 243; basij work, 255–257; educational background, 96–108; Jami'at Zaynab, 102–103, 185; practices of khod shenasi, 131–134, 141; talabeh azad, 96–99; Soft War, 135, 255–276; work with university women, 260–267, 270–275

Alikhani, Fardin, 259
Alosvand (Khanum-e), 26; becoming mujtahideh, 92–94, 98, 101, 109; howzeh and the revolution, 39–43, 50; women's center, 35–36; women's scholarship, 54; women's work, 61–62, 64–65, 68
Al-Mahdi, 160
Al-Muzaffar (ayatollah), 161
Amin, Banu, 38; Maktab-e Fatimah, 39, 52–54, 86, 99
Amini, Mahsa, 3
anjumans, 46, 285. *See also* schooling
anonymity, 26, 167; avoidance of praise, 93, 130, 135; catch attention, 21, 91, 133, 146, 166; downplaying achievements, 93, 134, 158; lack of visibility, 92–93; limitations, 106; mobility via, 133–135; not always, 158–159; resolve via unseen, 135; unseen, 2, 4, 92–93, 116, 127; unseen/hidden, 128–129; unseen as obstacle, 133–134; validation via unseen, 159; visibility, 233; work, unseen, 128, 256
Anderson, Brenda, 117
Ansari, Sheikh Morteza, 89
aql, 23, 161; aql bashe, 172, 285; aql-res, 266; of the intellect, 272
Articles, Article 23, 88–89; Article 19, 258–259; Article 175, 258
Aristotelian logic, 160–161, 171. *See also* mantiq
assessment: quantifying, 66; changes in, 70, 98; experience of, 105, 109; ijtihad-related,

AMINA TAWASIL is a faculty lecturer in the Programs in Anthropology, Teachers College, Columbia University.

For Indiana University Press

Lesley Bolton, Project Manager/Editor
Anna Garnai, Editorial Assistant
Sophia Hebert, Assistant Acquisitions Editor
Samantha Heffner, Marketing and Publicity Manager
Brenna Hosman, Production Coordinator
Katie Huggins, Production Manager
Bethany Mowry, Acquisitions Editor
Dan Pyle, Online Publishing Manager
Jennifer Witzke, Senior Artist and Book Designer